Georgia State Politics

The Constitutional Foundation

Sixth Edition

Lee M. Allen

Valdosta State University

with Marc G. Pufong and Jason S. Kassel

Kendall Hunt
publishing company

Dedication

The authors would like to dedicate this edition to our families: to Joyce. D. Allen and Su-Zan Harper; to Irene K. Pufong, and the boys Eloui-Jospin and Kelog-Pier Pufong; and to Elizabeth Kassel and Stephen and Dina Kassel. Without their help this book could not have been published. We would also like to thank Ms. Amanda Smith and Ms. Katie Wendler at Kendall Hunt for their help and advice.

Kendall Hunt
publishing company

www.kendallhunt.com
Send all inquiries to:
4050 Westmark Drive
Dubuque, IA 52004-1840

Contents

1 Introduction to Georgia Politics   1

2 Civil Rights and Civil Liberties   15

3 Political Participation in Georgia 39

4 The Legislative Branch 55

5 The Plural Executive of Georgia 77

6 Administration and Agencies   99

7 The Georgia Judiciary   117

11 The State Constitution   207

List of Photos and Figures

List of Cartoons

List of Tables

Preface

Many of the more future oriented of the American Founding Fathers, patriots like Thomas Jefferson and Benjamin Franklin, articulated the primary importance of education to a secure democracy. Since then every state, including Georgia has made laws establishing public support for primary and secondary schools, and also for public colleges and universities. These institutions are specifically designed to provide their students with a basic education about the practice and theory of the state governments in our federal system.

To help students understand their responsibilities to maintain the freedoms purchased for them by their forebears, often at heavy prices, academicians must take care to provide suitable textbooks, and make them available to those who will protect the continued growth of our 'Tree of Liberty.' The State of Georgia has had several such textbooks in the past, often supplemented by publications of documents and pamphlets on issues of the day, published by groups like the League of Women Voters. Today we enjoy having several such textbooks. *Georgia State Politics: The Constitutional Foundation* is written and illustrated to be brief enough to remain interesting, while being long enough and current enough to build a solid understanding of Georgia State Government. It is also designed to stand alone or to be compatible with joint State/American Government courses or comparative studies of American States. In sum, the book's brevity and comprehensiveness sets it apart from most text on Georgia State Government and/or comparative state politics.

Our theoretical approach is Constitutional, yet framed within the State's traditional, individualistic, and moralistic political culture. This approach traces and assesses the development of the various Constitutions of Georgia, linking the current Constitution to the existing institutions of government, and showing how recent amendments to the Constitution may or may not maintain some of the more traditional elements of Georgia's complex culture and politics. Understanding the necessary give and take of democratic politics and American Government can be a difficult project, but we believe that using this book will make it easier. Several features were designed to increase interest and readability, but the present authors are primarily dedicated to tracing the continuing threads of political continuity and modern change wherever possible among Georgia's many communities, local governments, and enduring state institutions.

The Organization of the 6th Edition

This 6th edition of *Georgia State Politics: The Constitutional Foundation* retains the same structure, order and number of chapters, and appendices as those preceding it although material has been condensed and updated throughout. As in the past, Chapter 1 continues to serve as a compass that points to what we propose to do, the *objectives* we hope to reach, and more specifically, it sets into perspective the theoretical foundation of the book. It introduces Georgia politics and the basic political concepts underlying the government and its people. The only changes are statistical updates of population increases. The introduction is designed to invite discussions of the constitutional basis of State Government as well as to present a general outline of the latest version of Georgia's State Constitution.

Chapter 2 presents the Civil Rights and Liberties of the citizens of the State of Georgia. Updated by Marc G. Pufong, it includes modification from previous editions that account for recent amendments to the Georgia Constitution such as the definition of marriage and the prohibition of same sex marriages. While maintaining the past structure, the updates and modifications also include the historical background of Georgia's Bill of Rights which traces its origins from the first Constitution of 1777 through the full and comprehensive treatment in 1861 to subsequent versions, including the Constitution of 1983.

Chapter 3 focuses on all kinds of political participation in the State of Georgia and has been updated in the 6th edition by Jason S. Kassel. Divided into three broad sections, updates have been made to some parts and new charts provided to include political linkages and participation. Specifically, citizen's linkages to the two political parties and interest groups demonstrate their ability to influence Georgia state and local politics.

In Chapter 4, Jason S. Kassel also presented needed updates of the Georgia Legislature and the legislative process. Presented in three parts, the updates made cover the discussions of (a) the legal process governed by constitutional and statutory mandates such as the requirements that appropriations and tax measures originate in the lower House, etc; (b) the parliamentary process, and rules and procedures that specify how legislation is considered in each House; and lastly (c) the political process where legislators and non-legislators (including the Governor) compete for power and advantages that shapes lawmaking in the Georgia Assembly.

Chapter 5 is also an update by Lee M. Allen from the previous edition on Georgia's "plural executive." The plural executive structure means that a variety of separately elected officials, each supported by independent bureaus, act in concert with the Governor and an additional large variety of appointed administrators, to collectively execute public policies in the State of Georgia. While basically that structure remains unchanged, Professor Allen provides recent updates in this to demonstrate how evolving changes affect the powers of the various entities that make up the pluralistic administrative structure as set forth by the State Constitution of 1983. From a few political perspectives, this hampers unified political control, and so may be referred to as a 'bureaucratic' constitution.

Chapter 6 on the administrative apparatus of state government has also been updated for this edition of the book by Professor Allen. As in the past editions, the original focus of the chapter has been retained while showing how it allows modern modifications, thus demonstrating the flexibility inherent in Article IV of the Georgia Constitution which provides for an administrative branch of government. In light of these evolving changes in government operations, much diligence has been devoted to reassessing the functions, duties, and responsibilities of Georgia's administrative State to include changes in some of the major administrative organs, and especially how they fit into the overall governing system.

Chapter 7 on the Georgia Judiciary has been modified significantly for this 6th edition by Marc G. Pufong. It presents an overview of the Georgia Court System with discussions that situate the role of Georgia courts as they act within the broader Georgia traditionalistic political culture. A careful overview of the courts, their jurisdictions, procedures, and functions are presented with new illustrations of Georgia's judicial institutions to ease understanding of this limited and yet intriguing branch of government.

Chapter 8 has also been modified by Lee M. Allen and is by far the most significantly updated chapter in this 6th edition. This section focuses on Georgia's budgeting process during a single year, to show how unrealized expectations can lead to the need for corrections in the anticipatory budgets. Given the changing nature of politics and budgeting, especially during the 'Great Recession,' such an update was very necessary. Budgetary politics often involve a fierce struggle over who really gets what, and who pays . . . as provided by law in Georgia. Thus, the people of Georgia provide in their Constitution a complex array of checks and balances designed to ensure that the powers of the State are used effectively only to benefit the health and well-being of all of its citizens, especially in times of fiscal crisis. A detail overview of these and other assessments that include numerous tables and figures are included in this new update.

Chapter 9 on Educational Policy includes significant updates by Marc G. Pufong and Mandi B. Bailey. They both reviewed and updated major educational policies, institutions and structures, their goals and policies, and more importantly: their finances. They also examined the state of education within the current financial constraints in light of serious overall cuts in budgets in the last few years. This is especially so in light of the fact that Georgia continues to devote almost half of its entire budget each year to primary, secondary, and higher education.

Chapter 10 on Local Government has been updated by Lee M. Allen. While the overall posture of the chapter has been maintained, some substantive changes have been made in the chapter to keep up with changes in local governance in the State, especially in the City of Atlanta, in light of their immediate and primary responsibility to the people. Consistent with the current financial crisis since the 'Great Recession' of 2008, many cities are significantly affected and therefore scaling down and tightening existing services, while opposing plans for new services.

Chapter 11 on the State Constitution has been updated thanks to the scholarly legal research service of Kendra A Hinton to include the changes incorporated from recent amendments to the Georgia State Constitution. As in past editions, this chapter continues to provide details of the Georgia Constitution and does so with the focus that explains how the Georgia system of government reflects the will of the people to help modernize the State of Georgia. Alternatively prescriptive and descriptive in presentation, it reflects on the varied desires and policy preferences of many different groups of people, illustrating how multiple wills and desires, along with different ideas, can be incorporated into one government and one Constitution.

Overall, the new 6th edition in our view represents continuity rather than a break away from the past and previous editions. New in this edition, we have provided a list of key words and essay questions at the end of each chapter to help stimulate learning and classroom discussions. This also includes a significantly modified multiple choice question bank provided at the end of the book for each chapter for student examinations. A new and completely redone test bank and answers is available on-line from the publisher to instructors who adopt this edition of the book. It is our utmost hope that this book's new format will open new landscape to readers who like to better their understanding of Georgia and state politics.

Acknowledgments

We are indebted to our many disciplinary colleagues over the years for their advice, suggestions, and occasional contributions to *Georgia State Politics: The Constitutional Foundation*. These include our own teachers and professors, from many institutions, but all sharing the same commitment to promote democracy and a republican form of government. We especially thank colleagues who worked on this or previous editions of this book. We particularly thank Professor Richard T. Saeger for his past contributions and Dr. Mandy B. Bailey and legal scholar Kendra A. Hinton for their invaluable input in this edition along with comments and suggestions from many colleagues here and around the State. We also must acknowledge the support and assistance offered by the staff and administration of Valdosta State University, and we are grateful to many of our students for their perspectives and continued frank comments over the years. Lastly, we express our deepest gratitude to the staff of Kendall Hunt Publishing Company, to Hal Hawkins in conception, and especially Katie Wendler and Amanda Smith for their invaluable stylistic and organizational suggestions for this edition. Most of all we thank our families, who have encouraged our educational endeavors.

Of course, we accept all the blame for any errors of omission and commission which may appear herein. There are a few differences on matters of fact and interpretation which may have been compromised, or left vague so that the readers can supply their own interpretations. We believe we have written a useful book for a variety of audiences, both in Georgia and in other States, and welcome your comments.

Lee M. Allen
with Marc G. Pufong
and Jason S. Kassel
Valdosta, April 6, 2011

Figure 1.1 Monument to Governor James Oglethorpe.

Introduction to Georgia Politics

Introduction to Georgia Politics

Georgia is the largest state east of the Mississippi River. It contains 58,977 square miles of land area, which ranges from the Appalachian Mountains of the northwest region to the rolling hills and plains of the Piedmont and its great pine forests, and down to the fertile river deltas and the Savannahs, the coastal beaches and the lush off-shore islands. This area is drained by two watersheds, one leading to the Mississippi River and then to the Gulf of Mexico; the other leading south and east, ending in the Atlantic Ocean. Georgia was founded in 1733 by one hundred and fourteen European colonists, led by James Oglethorpe, who came on the good ship Anne (Duncan). Today the modern state of Georgia is inhabited by nearly nine million people, both rural and urban dwellers of diverse backgrounds.

Economically, raw materials and food are produced by an active population of farmers, ranchers, and lumbermen; and the people in the Atlanta metroplex staff a world-class center of trade, commerce, and information. Several years ago, it was predicted that the population of the state would grow from over eight and a half million people to about twelve million people by the year 2030 (Macon Telegraph.com 04-21-05). Apparently we are well on our way there. The state population, as of 2010, is estimated at 9,685,744 people (NYTWABF, p. 584). We are growing, and soon expect that the 2010 census will show we are entitled to another seat in Congress. Politically, the people of Georgia have created a dynamic and flexible system of public and private sector organizations to help them achieve their goals and aspirations. Until recently, Georgia was dominated as a one-party state, the Democratic party; now it is the Republican Party which dominates. But it has consistently had a plural executive and a weak but sometimes influential governor. There are over one thousand government entities in Georgia (Hepburn, 138). Chief among these organizations is the State Government of the State of Georgia, and its agencies.

The Importance of State Government

The late U.S. Senator Everett McKinley Dirksen of Illinois used to complain that the way things were going, pretty soon the only people who would care about state boundaries would be Rand-McNally (the mapmakers). What Senator Dirksen was lamenting was the transfer of power from the states to the national (federal) government in Washington, D.C. The Senator's complaint was that states were losing their very reason for existing as they allowed or encouraged the national government to become involved in more and more areas of public policy. And, to be sure, the states have given up a great deal of their power to the national government.

Since the 1930s, the relationship between the national government and the states has become much more cooperative, replacing the competitive federalism (the relationship between the national government and the states is known as federalism) that existed before President Roosevelt's New Deal (the name for the programs that F.D.R. proposed to get the nation out of the Great Depression). This cooperation frequently takes the form of the national government's identifying a problem, passing legislation to address that problem, and providing carrots (inducements often in the form of money) or sticks (threats to withhold money if the states don't comply) to tackle the problem. Normally, the states do not have the option of choosing to do nothing. Cooperation, then, really becomes coerced cooperation.

To draw the conclusion that this transfer of power to Washington has left the states powerless would be to go far beyond what the facts warrant. In fact, this is an error of thinking which assumes that there is a finite amount of power, and that if one side gains power, then the other side must lose power. This is a zero sum fallacy. In fact, the power of all governments to regulate their citizens, and to control nature and improve living conditions, has grown tremendously over the years. The states are hardly powerless; they just don't have the same kinds of power they used to have in relation to the national government. The national government started off small but has grown very large in recent years, in our complex federal system. Many people believe that the federal government has become *too* large, and much of its power should devolve to the states. The watchword of the Republican "revolution" that captured control of the 104th Congress in 1994 was, in fact, "devolution."

Also, other levels of government operate in the United States and Georgia, such as international treaties and organizations, multistate agencies, and sub-local neighborhood compacts, which work together well. The unity of federalism has been highlighted by studies which stress the increasing vertical bureaucratization of programs in the United States, created by the lobbying of special interest groups

(Beer). In fact, every policy and program exists at every level, administratively integrated, with costs shared by all three levels.

State government entities may no longer officially discriminate on the basis of race; they may, however, enact affirmative action guidelines that exceed federal guidelines. States cannot pollute the environment; they may, however, pass environmental protection laws that exceed the national pollution standards. States have lots of powers. What they lack is the power to deprive their citizens of the equal protection of the laws, or to subject them to unreasonable dangers. In other words, the states' power to do evil is curtailed; their power to do good is limitless.

We look to state governments to provide us with education, with transportation, with police protection, with health care and sanitation, with jobs and economic development, with recreation, and with justice. The national government cooperates with the states in all of these areas. States, however, bear most of the responsibility. States then, are not merely important; in the areas that affect us most directly, states are the most important tier of our governments. And their strength is a protection against factions and special interest groups that dominate the nation (Madison).

The Constitutional Basis of State Government
Because some state governments existed prior to the writing of the Constitution of the United States, the national Constitution could not be said to have created the states. Nor did the states create the national government; rather, the people created both levels of government. And although each level of government has its own powers, ultimately some political authority has to decide which level has which powers. Article VI of the U.S. Constitution contains the "Supremacy Clause" which states that "This Constitution . . . the laws . . . and all treaties . . . of the United States, shall be the supreme law of the land." Therefore, any state constitution or state law (states can make treaties or compacts only with congressional approval) that contravenes the U.S. Constitution, federal law, or a U.S. Treaty is unconstitutional on the face of it.

If Georgia wanted a state constitutional provision or a law establishing a state church, the state could not do so because it would violate the federal laws, particularly the Establishment Clause of the First Amendment of the U.S. Constitution. If Georgia wanted to reestablish slavery, the Thirteenth Amendment to the U.S. Constitution would preclude the state from doing so. And if Georgia wanted a law prohibiting interracial marriage (in fact, such a law existed until fairly recently), provisions of the U.S. Constitution and federal law would invalidate such a blatant violation of personal freedom. In short, states are free to exceed federal constitutional protections; they are not free, however, to supersede those protections. They are not free to deny, disparage, or abuse peoples' rights. Thus states sometimes offer greater protections to its citizens than does the federal government to the national population.

Sometimes government agencies or overzealous bureaucrats, both state and federal, do "ride roughshod" over rights and must be ordered to stop. Frequently, it is a state's Attorney General who offers the opinion that an action, law, or constitutional provision is legally unenforceable. Occasionally, it is the state courts which rule that a law violates the state constitution or that a state law or the state constitution violates federal law or the U.S. Constitution. On even rarer occasions, it is a federal appellate court, exercising the power of judicial review (determining whether a law is consonant with the Constitution) that holds some state law or constitutional provision to be in violation of federal laws and the U.S. Constitution. Regardless of which legal authority reviews it, they all agree that the hierarchy of law in the United States is in the following order: 1) the U.S. Constitution; 2) Federal laws; 3) Treaties of the United States; 4) State constitutions; 5) State laws; 6) Local (City and County) Ordinances. Each must be consistent with all the laws above it.

Relationships among the various levels of government in the United States are not always about power or high principles. Sometimes mundane business matters and strategies of economic growth at the local government level take center stage. In the Five Points Neighborhood in the City of Atlanta, the federal government proposed to operate a new office complex, the Atlanta Federal Center, and to relocate about 8,000 workers to that facility (land and building would be owned by the city). The consolidation would allow federal employees to work together with associated savings in amenities such as a cafeteria, day-care center, and a clinic. One impact study estimated that the entire project would add $68.6 million to the local economy (Salter, C7). While the merchants in the area were optimistic about the proposed project, other merchants and politicians worried that the relocations and changes in work habits and transportation would injure existing businesses (Parker, C7).

In a democracy such as ours, politicians are always in the market for new ideas to impress the voters and to inspire other politicians to close ranks and pursue a mutually beneficial program. Such was the necessity facing Governor Zell Miller at the beginning of the 1994 legislative session. Although his previous legislative agenda, *Georgia Rebound,* could be considered a success (the economy did improve afterward), every program has its critics and naysayers. Yet, at least theoretically, new programs have one outstanding advantage: they lack a track record to be attacked by opponents during the heat of an election campaign. Usually the flag, mom, and apple pie are good old standbys, but in Georgia, the issues of the flag (confederate symbol or historical tradition?) and mom (affected by the gay rights problem) were tarnished; and apple pie is not a top priority in the Peach State. Governor Miller had been burned pretty badly during the flag controversy, so he needed some new issue.

Ah, how about anti-crime and educational issues? So suddenly there was a new agenda for the 1994 legislative session, a package the people purportedly wanted and needed, and that Miller could tie into the traditional conservative values of the state, and so he and his fellow democrats could face the strengthening Republican party candidates in the following fall election with a politically popular platform. In fact, this strategy worked so well that Miller would continue to employ it throughout the rest of his second term. Roy Barnes, his successor, followed much the same strategy, but without the same level of success; and, in fact, his stances on the old standby issues became so unpopular that on November 5, 2002, he lost his own bid for a second term, when the electorate elected "Sonny" Purdue in a historically significant change of party loyalty. Sonny Purdue became the first republican elected as Governor of the State of Georgia since the Reconstruction Era of the 1870s.

State Constitutions

Although the theory of constitutional government has a long history, real constitutions were first created by colonists in North America. In addition to the national constitution, every one of the fifty states has a constitution. To a significant extent all are modeled on American revolutionary ideas and reflect a common pattern. They all reflect a belief in popular sovereignty and democracy, they all contain preambles, which state the basic purposes of the state government. They all have bills of rights, which largely mimic the original Virginia Bill of Rights written by Thomas Jefferson, although most expand on it. They all have articles outlining the organization, powers, and selection procedures for the three branches of government: legislative, executive, and judicial. They all spell out the methods of selection for these branches.

But beyond these similarities there are also significant differences. One such difference is length. The U.S. Constitution is short, containing only about 8,700 words. State constitutions tend to be much longer (averaging 26,000 words), although the newer ones are much shorter than the older ones. One reason why they are longer is because they usually have articles pertaining to the specific duties of the state government. For example, they contain articles on taxation, boards and commissions, education, the environment, licensing, transportation, etc. Another reason why they are longer is that they tend to be amended more often. The U.S. Constitution has only twenty-seven amendments. Alabama's has had over seven hundred.

Even though Georgia modernized its constitution in 1983, it has been amended scores of times since then. The last chapter details these more recent changes. Since voters can only ratify state amendments in statewide elections, and since Georgia does not have statewide elections in odd-numbered years, a new crop of potential amendments may be ratified in 2008.

Georgia's Constitution

The Constitution of the State of Georgia, unlike the national constitution, begins with a Bill of Rights. Georgia's Bill of Rights emphasizes the power of the people to alter or reform government, and it is often used. In fact, Georgia is second only to Louisiana in terms of the number of constitutions enacted. Louisiana has had eleven since 1812; Georgia has had ten since 1777. Nineteen states still operate with their original constitution, much amended. And one state, Massachusetts, still uses its colonial charter. In Georgia, the political tradition has been more dynamic, calling for periodic revisions to meet the needs of a changing society.

Georgia's ten constitutions reflect this alert response. Political changes at the national level justified new constitutions in 1777 and 1789. Popular dissatisfaction led to a new constitution in 1798, and the turmoil of the Civil War produced several controversial new constitutions; the Secession in 1861, the Lincoln Plan in 1865, the Reconstruction Era in 1868, and the Bourbon Coup or Restoration Constitution of 1877. More recently, the pressures of modern life led to Executive Reform in 1945, an Interim Constitution in 1976, and the contemporary Bureaucratic Constitution which went into effect on July 1, 1983.

In comparison, the federal Constitution has been amended (but not revised) over a dozen times during the same period, substantially altering the federal relationship and the tax structure between 1965 and the present. In another decade or two, new problems will probably result in a call for another modernization of the Constitution of the State of Georgia. Some critics say the people are apathetic and powerless. In Georgia, the people are like a slumbering giant; when they are jolted awake by scandals or hard times, the political system takes notice. Our state's people shape the constitution to their needs. In Georgia, the people rule.

The 1983 Constitution reflects the modern trend in state constitutions: it is short (only 25,000 words); it is less specific and its language is much less legalistic. The Georgia Constitution consists of a preamble and eleven articles. The preamble is similar to that of the U.S. Constitution except that Georgia's invokes divine protection and guidance, a common feature of preambles to state constitutions. As noted above, over sixty-six (66) amendments have been added to the present Constitution as of 2006.

Figure 1.2   The Voice of the People

The people of the State of Georgia enjoy the protection of a Bill of Rights which is in many ways more libertarian than that of the federal document. The Georgia Bill of Rights is in Article One, Section One of the State Constitution, and included within it are several provisions which provide protections beyond those of the federal government. Paragraph VI expressly allows us to assert *'truth'* as a defense against charges of libel; Paragraph XII is the right to prosecute or defend lawsuits in person (although lawyers are recommended); and in Paragraph XIV we find the right to an attorney whenever charged with a criminal offense. The Georgia Bill of Rights also, in Paragraph XXVI protects the separate property of spouses, a modern note of gender sensitivity. And finally, the Constitution of Georgia, like that of the United States, has a reserve clause which protects the inherent rights of the people even if those rights have not been articulated, like the penumbral right of privacy. The Georgia Bill of Rights is more extensive than the federal provisions.

While few persons will deny or protest that the civil liberties movement (limiting government encroachment on all citizens' lives) is alive and growing in Georgia, the area of Civil Rights (whether different people have the same rights) continues to be contentious and provocative. Should minors be allowed to drink alcohol, or ex-convicts be allowed to vote, or homosexuals be allowed to marry? Among these groups, the National Gay and Lesbian Task Force is one of the most active in attempting to change political and cultural beliefs and customs. On the other side of the issue are political entities like conservative Cobb County, which passed legislation saying *"homosexuality is incompatible with community standards"* (Watson, 3A). The issue was highlighted as both sides moved in a series of demonstrations and marches to take advantage of the spotlights thrown on Georgia when the national media converged on the state for the 1996 Olympic Games.

Article II continues the theme of popular sovereignty, by providing for voting and elections and detailing procedures for suspension and removal of public officials. This section also provides for secret ballots, first used in Australia. Article III is the legislative article, its position in the constitution reflects the legislative primacy established after the Revolutionary War. This illustrates the importance of the representatives of the people in framing the laws of the state. The Third Article describes the composition of the legislature, called, in Georgia, the General Assembly; it also identifies the officers of the General Assembly, and outlines its organization, procedures, and its powers.

Georgia does not have a unitary chief executive like the presidency of the federal government. Instead, it has a complex array of independent agencies and a plural executive. Indeed, the increasing complexities of modern life have led to a strengthening of bureaucratic structures. This is reflected in the Fourth Article, dealing with constitutional boards and commissions, some of which are elected by the people, one of which (the State Transportation Board) is elected by the members of the General Assembly, and some of which are appointed by the Governor, subject to confirmation by the State Senate. The relationship between the Governor and the state bureaucracy is often subtle, held together as much by personal charisma and by politics as by formal Constitutional provisions.

Article V describes the executive branch per se; the administrative agencies (or the *bureaucracy,* as it is called by those who don't like it). Unlike Article II of the U.S. Constitution, which is the federal executive article, and which describes the methods of election (the Electoral College) and the powers of the Chief Executive officers (the President and Vice-President), Georgia's Constitution addresses the election and powers of Georgia's various separately elected executive officers. Most states have more than two popularly elected executive officers. Georgia has eight, which places it in the middle range of states in terms of the number of independently elected executives required. These executive officers in Georgia include the Governor, the Lieutenant Governor, the Secretary of State, the Attorney General, State School Superintendent, Commissioner of Insurance, Commissioner of Agriculture, and Commissioner of Labor. All these independently elected constitutional officers are known as a plural executive.

Article VI completes the establishment of the major officials of the state, by outlining the judicial branch of government. It also identifies the types of courts, their jurisdiction, and the procedures for selection of judges, their compensation, and discipline. The article creates a network of specialized courts to deal with the complex problems presented to a modern society. It also includes district attorneys, who are major players in the legal system. And as foreshadowed in Article I of the Constitution, the state courts are specifically given the authority of judicial review over legislative acts.

Just as the creation of a national income tax required a separate federal Constitutional Amendment (the 16th Amendment), Georgia also deals with taxation policy at the constitutional level. Article VII is the taxation article, granting the power to tax, the power to exempt from taxation, and discusses the purposes for which debt may be incurred. Since education is the most important function of state government, it has its own article in the State Constitution. Thus Article VIII is the public education article, providing for the governance, bureaucratic structure and for the financial support of education at the elementary, secondary, and college levels.

Local city governments do not merit mention in the national Constitution; these governments lack sovereignty and are creatures of the states. Because counties and cities derive their powers from the state, a separate article is necessary to address the legal status and duties of substate governments. Article IX of the Georgia Constitution describes the structure, powers, and governance of city and county governments. It also concerns the many special districts, and relations among these and between the state and its substate governments.

Article X is the amending article. It allows amendments to the Constitution to be proposed either by the General Assembly or by a constitutional convention. It is based on the Madisonian idea that frequent elections to facilitate change is superior to suppressing dissent and risking violent change. It provides for amendments to be submitted to the voters, with a majority of those voting necessary for ratification. Finally, Article XI is the implementing article. That is, it provides for the effectuation of the Constitution, concluding in Paragraph VI: "this Constitution shall become effective on July 1, 1983; and except as otherwise provided in this Constitution, all previous Constitutions and all amendments thereto shall thereupon stand repealed."

Georgia's Politics

Georgia's government is based on its Constitution which delegates and limits powers. Understand that Constitution is a necessary condition for understanding the Peach State's government. But it is not a sufficient condition. To truly understand its government, one must examine Georgia politics. To understand the political system, that is the operation of political parties, belief systems, and patterns of political participation, we must understand the political culture of the state. Of course, the complex economic system and the variety of ethnic and racial groups in Georgia means that there are lots of different perspectives in the state. But there is a pattern, a political culture defined as the general collection of political beliefs, practices, and behaviors of a people.

The dominant political culture in Georgia can be described as traditionalistic. Political scientist Daniel Elazar has identified three major patterns of political culture in the United States. These are the traditionalistic, individualistic, and the moralistic cultures. He describes Georgia's political culture as a blend of traditionalistic and individualistic, with a trace of the moralistic political culture in the mountains of north Georgia. The individualistic and traditionalistic political cultures are alike in that persons active in politics are expected to benefit personally from their activity, although not necessarily by direct pecuniary gain (Elazar, 1984, at 118–119).

> The traditionalistic political culture accepts government as an actor with a positive role in the community, but it tries to limit that role to securing the continued maintenance of the existing social order. To do so, it functions to confine real political power to a relatively small and self-perpetuating group drawn from an established elite who often inherit their right to govern through family ties or social position. . . .
>
> The individualistic political culture emphasizes the conception of the democratic order as a marketplace. In this view, government is instituted for strictly utilitarian reasons, to handle those functions demanded by the people it is created to serve. A government need not have any direct concern with questions of the good society, except insofar as it may be used to advance some common conception of the good society. . . .
>
> The moralistic political culture emphasizes the commonwealth conception as the basis for democratic government. Politics, to the moralistic political culture, is considered one of the great activities of humanity in its search for the good society . . . Good government . . . is measured by the degree to which it promotes the public good and in terms of the honesty, selflessness, and commitment to the public welfare of those who govern (Elazar, 1984, 115–119).

An understanding of Georgia's political culture as being traditionalistic helps us to understand why Georgia for so long had a one-party system, why voter turnout in Georgia is among the lowest in the nation, and also why Georgia has had so many Constitutions in her history. It also helps to explain Georgia's political conservatism. That conservatism is also explained, in part, by ethnicity, which is tied closely to political culture. Indeed, as political scientist Thomas R. Dye writes:

> The location of . . . political subcultures throughout the American states is largely determined by the migration patterns of different

ethnic and religious groups . . . it appears that the *moralistic* subculture is a product of northern European, English, and German liberal Protestantism; the *individualistic* subculture is a product of southern and eastern European and Irish Catholicism; and the *traditionalist* subculture is a product of fundamentalist white Protestantism in potential conflict with large black populations (Dye, 1997, 10).

The Constitution of 1983

Georgia is governed constitutionally. Although common today, constitutional government is a recent innovation in human civilization. It grew out of British social contract theory, which asserts that government rests on the consent of the governed, evolving to cope with the conflicts and tensions that arose among the various ethnic groups and political factions within those small but energetic island nations. The theory of a government of laws, instead of a government of autocratic monarchy, took root in the British colonies, and has become a venerable tradition in the area now known as the State of Georgia. In the new American nation, the older idea of Parliamentary supremacy became the normal standard instead of deviation from monarchical rule, and legislative government came into its own. In the new world, Constitutional government is limited government, a restraint on politicians, bureaucrats, and special interest groups.

Modern Georgia began as a tiny colony of the United Kingdom on the southwestern fringes of the British Empire seagoing trade; near rival Spanish Florida. The new arrivals brought a highly productive food production system, and the literary heritage of the old world. Because their crops, livestock, and technology was geographically suited to the new temperate conditions, the European colonists prospered (Diamond). The new land of Georgia, and its sister colonies, eventually grew industrially, socially, and politically, far beyond the wildest dreams of its founders, due in large part not only to their technology, but also to the flexibility and fairness of constitutional government, part of the heritage of western civilization. This limited government framework still governs Georgia today.

By convention, the original operating British charters are not thought of as constitutional *per se*, but they served the same purpose: a fundamental outline of official powers and official limits. Thus the 1732 Charter of the Colony of Georgia, a Grant of George II, was the first legal organic act of the new colony. Scholars differ on whether Georgia and the other colonies became independent nations after the Revolutionary War. But by the simple language of the Articles of Confederation, succeeding states claimed themselves to be sovereign, and Georgia's first Constitution was, from that perspective, a national one. However, after Georgia joined the Union in 1788, with its broadened constitutional system, claims of sovereignty became muted for awhile, and finally almost ceased entirely a hundred years later, but only after violent conflict. While the people of the United States as a whole have adopted only two constitutions since the Revolutionary War, the people of the State of Georgia have adopted ten. These ten constitutions can be divided into three groups: the founding era, the federalizing era, and the modern era; these are displayed in Table 1.1 below.

In the founding era, legislative primacy was the rule of the day, and constitutions adopted in that period reflected the common revolutionary bias against the excesses of monarchical or executive rule. At both the national and state level, constitutions exalted the representative legislature. During the federalizing era, regional and ethnic strife mingled with bitter debate over the extent and legitimacy of states' rights, and the great amount of constitutional revision of that time period shows the stresses and strains of the Civil War era.

Going into modern times, the executive branch has seen a revival of its historic strength, but the most modern trend endangers the chief executive system itself, with the burgeoning growth of modern bureaucracy eclipsing it. According to some scholars, the world is experiencing an emerging bureaucratic government (Nachmias, 14). Georgia goes with this general trend. In 1945, Georgia Governor Ellis Arnall sponsored constitutional reform, including a new Article Three insulating the Public Utilities Commission from interference by political hacks (Pound & Saye, 55–56).

Table 1.1   Georgia Constitutional Systems

Founding Era

Legislative Primacy Constitution (1777)
Union Constitution (1789)
Reform Constitution (1798)

Federalizing Era

Confederal Constitution (1861)
Reconciliation Constitution (1865)
Reconstruction Constitution (1868)
Restoration Constitution (1877)

Modern Era

Executive Reform Constitution (1945)
Interim Constitution (1976)
Bureaucratic Constitution (1983)

Source: Compiled by authors.

The latest Georgia Constitution, adopted in 1983, continued to follow the emerging global pattern, and created a large number of independent commissions, agency boards, and local authorities that largely operate outside of the formal control of the chief executive. A notable feature was the independence of educational institutions. In Georgia, the modern trend toward bureaucratic government has blended nicely into the state's traditionalistic and individualistic culture. The feudal plantation systems of the past have evolved into the functional fiefdoms of the present. The result is a continuation of a venerable way of life, localistic and decentralized.

Key Terms

Competitive Federalism
Cooperative Federalism
Devolution
Evolution
Individualistic Political Subculture
Moralistic Political Subculture
Political Culture
Daniel Elazar
Thomas R. Dye
Traditionalistic Political Subculture
The Constitution of 1983
The Founding Era
The Federalizing Era
The Modern Era

Essay Questions

1. Arguably the national government has become more powerful leaving the states powerless. What is the reasoning behind this argument? Is the argument true?
2. Explain the basis for various state constitutions in the United States Constitution.
3. State constitutions may vary considerably. In what ways are state constitutions similar? How does the Georgia State Constitution compare to constitutions adopted in other states?
4. Why is the United States Constitution more concise (brief) than the Georgia State Constitution (as well as other state constitutions)?
5. How does the latest Georgia State Constitution follow the emerging global pattern?
6. List and carefully discuss the three groups that defines the various Constitutions of the State of Georgia.

Figure 2.1 Martin Luther King Jr.
Library of Congress

Civil Rights and Civil Liberties

This chapter discusses Civil Rights and Civil Liberties in the State of Georgia. First, it presents the historical background of Georgia's Bill of Rights. It does so by tracing its origins from the first Constitution in 1777 to its full and comprehensive treatment provided in the Constitution of 1861 and through subsequent versions, and onto the last Constitution in 1983. Second, we frame the focus of the Bill of Rights into three major parts, namely, the Rights of Persons with primary focuses on the Civil Rights and Liberties of citizens and persons of the State of Georgia, the origin and structure of Government of the State of Georgia, and lastly, other provisions of the Constitution and general law.

Historical Background

The Georgia Bill of Rights was ratified, along with the Constitution of the State of Georgia in 1861, soon after the State of Georgia seceded from the Union on January 18, 1861. The reasons for the emergence of a Bill of Rights at this point in history of the State has been the object of much debate, but it is important to observe that between the enactment of the first Georgia Constitution in 1777 and 1861 while Georgians lived under four constitutions, these constitutions did not contain a comprehensive bill of rights. To be sure, these constitutions did protect a few individual liberties; these included the freedom of religion and the press, the right to trial by jury, and the all-important *writ of habeas corpus*. All of these liberties are still protected by the Georgia Constitution's Bill of Rights today. One common justification provided for their inclusion during this period seemed to be because the British were the most likely to violate these rights, a factor that had also led to the initial Revolutionary War in 1775–1783 (Bratcher 2005).

Written by Thomas R. R. Cobb in 1861, the Georgia Bill of Rights, as commonly known today, was known as the "Declaration of Fundamental Principles." These "principles" added many rights to the

Georgia State Constitution, which included all of the rights then provided for by the Constitution of the United States, as well as some original provisions. In addition to the rights enumerated, the Constitution of 1861 explicitly provided for judicial review and forcefully stated that "the enumeration of those rights shall not be construed to deny other inherent rights of citizens." In subsequent versions (such as the Georgia Constitution of 1865) the prohibition against servitude was added to the Bill of Rights. This was at the end of the American Civil War, which saw the abolition of slavery with the passage and inclusion of the 13th Amendment of the U.S. Constitution.

The Georgia Constitution of 1868, adopted during Reconstruction (1867–76), included Georgia's version of the federally mandated Equal Protection Clause and added several protections, including the prohibition of whipping as the punishment for a crime. Also added to the Bill of Rights in the old Georgia Constitution of 1877 was the prohibition against banishment of criminals. In 1945 a few notable changes were also made to the Georgia Constitution. In 1976 two provisions were added. First, certain properties were exempted from levy and sale, and second, in recognition of the progress of women's rights, a provision protecting separate spousal property was included in that constitution. All of these historical developments were brought forth into the 1983 Georgia Bill of Rights. While most of the enumerated rights in that version have their origins in the Constitution of 1861, some can be traced as far back as the first Georgia Constitution of 1777. Some have been lost. Alas, banishment has also practically been re-established in Georgia, and even people of minor crimes can be instructed not to return to their home counties.

There is consensus among scholars that the 1861 liberties have proven remarkably stable. So far since 1861, Georgia has adopted six new constitutions, all basically with the same listed rights brought forth into each new version of the constitution, in essentially the same form, but with a few modifications to keep up with contemporary usage and understandings. In our modern world of developing new technologies, constitutions have to be living documents to allow society to adapt. We should expect that the Georgia Bill of Rights will continue to provide these historical protections, while remaining adaptable to the recognition of new liberties and rights when demanded by new social circumstances (Katz 1986, Beasley 1985). From a constitutional point of view, some facets of Civil Rights and Liberties have always been a steady feature of the Constitution of the State of Georgia. But whether those rights have in fact been similarly enjoyed by its citizens is an entirely different question, and the actual implementation of the law for everyone is harder to assert.

Civil Rights and Civil Liberties

Our Civil Rights and Civil Liberties are two of the most fundamental features of Georgia's State Constitution. After all, the original purpose of the new Georgia colony was to provide a haven for people in debt and for the unemployed poor, although in fact the majority of the actual settlers were ordinary working people. Our Civil Rights and Civil Liberties include such important political values as our religious liberty, the popular rights of free speech, free press, freedom of assembly, and the freedom from imprisonment for debt (except for child support). Both the 18th Century founder and proprietor James Edward Oglethorpe and the 20th Century Civil Rights leader Martin Luther King Jr. worked to support these efforts.

A common understanding is that Civil Rights are positive acts because it obligates the government to protect persons against arbitrary or discriminatory treatment by the government or by other people. Similarly, civil liberties may be viewed as negative rights because they impose constraints by refraining government from abridging liberties such as the freedom of speech, press, and the related rights of assembly and association, and the exercise of religion. So, for example, Paragraph V of the Georgia Constitution which guarantees the freedom of speech and of the press states that "No law shall be passed to curtail or restrain the freedom of speech or of the press . . . ." Negatively phrased rights also include the right to bear arms, the freedom from violent crime, and from involuntary servitude (except for conviction of crimes).

Many other rights and privileges are part of the traditional political culture of the state, rooted in a historical tradition that dates back over two hundred and fifty years. This makes Georgia one of the leading developers of democracy at a time when monarchy and elite privilege was the rule in most of the world. While this chapter focuses on describing the scope and extent of the Georgia's Bill of Rights per se, the various Civil Liberties and Civil Rights enjoyed by the citizens of the State of Georgia student readers are advised to read the exact wording of the Constitution after they have read this chapter.

A Bill of Rights enumerates certain individual liberties and protects those liberties from governmental intrusion, unless there is a sufficiently compelling justification for government action (Bratcher 2005). All of the rights protected by the U.S. Constitution are also protected under the Georgia Bill of Rights. The first article of the Georgia State Constitution, sometimes referred to as the Georgia Bill of Rights, has three parts. These are the Rights of Persons, the Origin and Structure of Government, and other General Provisions. The first part, focusing on the rights of persons, describes and enshrines some of our most basic Civil Liberties and Civil Rights. As noted above, Civil Liberties and Civil Rights are two different concepts.

This first part on the Rights of Persons, lists twenty-eight paragraphs of individual rights. Many of these rights are similar to the rights listed in the United States Bill of Rights. Yet, there are some big differences. For instance, the Georgia Bill of Rights lists among its freedoms the Freedom of Conscience, which is the *"natural and inalienable right to worship God, each according to the dictates of that person's own conscience"* without interference, and adds the right to religious opinion along with freedom of religion. The second part explains the primary conception of the origins and purposes of popular government. In so doing it describes the "origin and foundation of government," the "object of government," the separation of powers, and the superiority of civil authority over military authority. Also, this section explicitly describes the separation of church and state. Lastly, the third part which the general principle set forth other general provisions as well which control the structure and operation of the state and its political institutions. These provisions include those that impose limitations on official powers, the basic patterns of intergovernmental relationships among state institutions, and protection for private property rights.

Courts and the Bill of Rights

Within Georgia, the courts play the role of final arbiter as to the meaning of the Georgia Constitution. As a result, some provisions of the Georgia Bill of Rights, as interpreted by the state courts, are more protective of individual liberty than textually similar provisions of the Constitution of the United States. It should be observed that as a general rule, state constitutions can and should provide more, not less, protection to individual liberty than the Constitution of the United States. Thus, as stated above, the Georgia Constitution also includes some liberties that are simply not mentioned by the federal Constitution. For example, the Georgia Constitution protects "freedom of Conscience," that is the natural and inalienable right to worship God; the right not to be abused during arrest or imprisonment, and it forbids whipping as punishment for crimes.

However, pending the United States Supreme Courts ruling on these matters, some states through their constitutions or amendments can and do deny its courts the power to decide cases in some areas of Civil Rights even if such prohibition may be presumptively unconstitutional under the United States Constitution. The State of Georgia for example recently made one such an amendment to its Constitution. Thus, Article I Section IV, Paragraph I (a) of the Georgia Constitution states that "Marriages between persons of the same sex are prohibited in this state" and in furtherance to that prohibition in paragraph I (b) of the same Section also states that "No union between persons of the same sex shall be recognized by this state as entitled to the benefits of marriage." This state, the Section IV paragraph states further, "shall not give effect to any public act, record, or judicial proceeding of any other state or jurisdiction respecting a relationship between persons of the same sex that is treated as a marriage under the laws of such other state or jurisdiction." Lastly, Paragraph I (b) directing commands to the courts of the State of Georgia states that *"the courts of this state shall have "no jurisdiction" to grant a divorce or separate maintenance with respect to any such relationship or otherwise to consider or rule on any of the parties' respective rights arising as a result of or in connection with such relationship."* The concept of jurisdiction here simply restates the fact that courts do have only so much power as the attentive people of the state are willing to give them.

Civil Liberties

Section One of Article One of the Georgia Constitution contains twenty-eight different paragraphs, of which the great majority concentrates on protection of our liberty. Civil liberties issues focus on the question of the general degree and limits of freedom allowed by society, and whether or not some types of activities will be forbidden to everyone. Twenty-one of the paragraphs, as described below, detail the liberties enjoyed by the people of the State of Georgia. Another four paragraphs discuss libertarian topics as well as Civil Rights issues. In Civil Liberty issues the concern is over the limits on liberty and the boundaries between our freedom and the power of government.

The first paragraph of Article One guarantees that no Georgian shall be deprived of three of the most important possessions of a free citizen: life, liberty, or property; unless a government agency deliberately (and properly) acts to deprive a person of these things. These freedoms are also explicitly provided for in the national constitution. But if the government perceives a need to act in such a fashion, it must move carefully, by an official and formal proceeding marked by all of the requirements of due process of law. Due process of law usually requires that a person be notified in advance of the intended action, that an official public hearing shall be held, and that the person shall have an opportunity to dispute the state's action, including calling witnesses and having the benefit of legal counsel during the process.

Another Civil Liberty is found in the third paragraph, which provides for freedom of conscience and guaranteeing that each person has the natural and inalienable right to worship God in her own way, and that no human authority should control or interfere with anyone's right of conscience. Similarly, the next paragraph guarantees that we all shall enjoy freedom of speech and of the press. So in Georgia, every person may speak, write, and publish sentiments on all subjects. But of course everyone shall be responsible for the abuse of that liberty, such as inciting to riot or falsely shouting "fire" and thus threatening the lives and safety of other citizens.

Another new problem in modern Georgia concerns the rapidly evolving technologies of electronic computing, data collection and storing of information about citizens, and censorship and regulation of public access to various Web sites. Government at all levels in the world today has, of course, an interest in electronic monitoring of communications lines. Both the national government and the state governments are properly concerned with the vast communication network and its influence with the War on Terror; the state and local governments are interested in taxation of sales taxes across state lines; and of course parents are often interested in limiting their children's access to depictions of pornography and violence. In addition, the new interactive capabilities of cable TV allow commercial cable firms and their sponsors to monitor the programs and frequency of television in our daily viewing. In Georgia, where the Bible Belt brand of morality is exceptionally strong, questions are being raised about the extent to which these doubtful channels and Web sites can be censored by families.

We are living in a world that has shrunk to a global village owing to the advent of rapid connectivity technology. Social networking sites have paved the way of getting people's messages across to their own kind; thus mankind's motivation to take action against some hegemonic tyrannies has been enhanced. This is a factor not only increasing the will and power of the people who fuelled the regime change protests in Tunisia and Egypt, but also protestors in the United States and Georgia. This empowerment has made citizens of all countries better able to speak up and declare their desire to claim freedom as their birth right. The "Shot Heard 'Round the World" continues to reverberate in the new Global Era.

A number of people say that the Internet is like traveling. They say each trip is like a new journey and they never know where they are going to be taken to. But a new problem is that some spend so much time on the Internet that they withdraw from regular society. They escape reality into a realm with no real boundaries or existence. While lost in the cyber world for long periods of time, they are neglecting other important activities such as: time with the family, socializing, work, and health concerns. Internet addiction has been cited as a contributing factor in the disintegration of marriages and families, and the collapse of promising careers. And the loss of personal interaction has led to a great increase in incivility generally, and particularly in the realm of political compromise.

In the 2011 uprisings in Tunisia and Egypt, new social media such as Facebook and Twitter helped dissidents rise up against the government. When Tunisian protestors took to the street and toppled the government of Zine El Abidine Ben Ali, social media tools like Facebook and Twitter helped organize the protests. When the government realized this, officials began to covertly and slyly attack the Facebook users. So while the new techno community arguably makes it possible for people to communicate despite the power of repressive governments and its leaders, new counterstrategies are also evolving. Humans are defined by their ability to use complex language to communicate, and thereby to establish a community. Nevertheless, when communication is suppressed for the majority of the people of a

Figure 2.2   The Internet: A New Social Problem

nation, the pattern of revolution is ultimately inevitable. Facebook, Twitter, and other social networking are the latest form of technology facilitating confrontation over serious issues across traditional lines of authority.

What if you call someone a thief, and that person says you are lying? Well, Paragraph VI covers that situation, under the provision governing libel lawsuits. In all civil or criminal actions for libel, the defendant may offer evidence that the matter is true, and if a trial determines that the matter charged as libelous is in fact true, then the defendant shall be discharged. Of course citizens are well-advised to be soft-spoken, and not to "shoot off their mouths" unless they are prepared to back up everything they say with hard evidence.

One of the most controversial liberties possessed by all Americans is the right to keep and bear weapons, including firearms. Currently it is disputed whether this right belongs to each individual citizen or only to organized and approved militia companies. It is clear that this right originated as a result of the successful American Revolution against the tyrannical British government. These revolutionaries in Georgia and the other twelve colonies insisted on their right to use weapons to protect themselves. But nowadays some political action groups think that times have changed, and that since the problem of controlling violent criminals is greater than problems of abusive government, the liberty should be re-interpreted and severely restricted. Currently, the right of the people to keep and bear arms remains intact, subject to the power of the General Assembly to proscribe the manner in which arms may be bought and sold, carried, and used. Today firearms of all types are closely regulated.

The ninth and tenth paragraphs describe some relatively non-controversial liberties. These include the rights of people to assemble in groups, and to circulate petitions calling for redress of their public grievances. The people have the right to assemble peaceably for their common good or pleasure, and to sign petitions to send to officials of their government so that their problems can be attended to. Sometimes laws do not attract attention simply because they are good laws and are working well. Examples of this are found in the next paragraph, which prevents several of the most favorite abuses by bad governments. These include: bills of attainder (legislative targeting of individuals) and ex post facto laws (punishing someone for something he or she did which was legal at the time), also known as retroactive laws. This section also prohibits any laws impairing the obligation of contract, or voluntarily surrendering or recanting any of their special privileges or immunities.

The Jury System

Paragraph XI focuses on the important matter of citizen juries. It is a prime tenet of our culture that when the government accuses people of crimes they should be tried by a jury of their citizen peers, and not by a government official. It specifies that the right to trial by jury shall remain inviolate, except perhaps where a jury is not demanded in writing by either party. But in all criminal cases, defendants are guaranteed the right to a public and speedy trial by an impartial jury; and the jury shall be the judges of the law and the facts. While in extremely rare cases a judge may set aside a jury verdict, the system of review by higher courts and public opinion ensures that this possibility is not abused.

Usually a trial jury will consist of 12 persons, especially in important felony cases. However, to save time and money the General Assembly may prescribe any number, not less than six, to constitute a trial jury in the smaller courts of limited jurisdiction and in the state superior courts in misdemeanor cases. The General Assembly regulates by law for the selection and compensation to persons to serve as grand jurors and trial jurors. The monetary compensation for jury duty is not very high; the major reward for citizens comes in the satisfaction of knowing that they have helped to maintain our rights and liberties.

Paragraph XII of the Georgia Constitution makes sure that all Georgians have full and unrestricted rights of access to the state courts. More specifically, it provides that no person shall be deprived of the right to prosecute or defend his or her legal causes, either in person or by representation by an attorney. It would be unfair if a person was not allowed to defend himself if charged with a crime. Our continued liberty depends on being able to defend ourselves in such circumstances. This concern is also the subject of the next constitutional paragraph, which limits the government's use of searches, seizures, and warrants. The people have a right to be secure in their persons, houses, papers, and effects against unreasonable searches and seizures. Generally a state judge or magistrate will issue a search warrant only if witnesses make an oath or affirmation asserting that there is probable cause to suspect criminal activity, and if the warrant particularly describes the place or places to be searched by the official officers, and if it also specifies the persons or things to be seized.

Paragraph XIV outlines the rights and liberties that people have if they are charged with an offense against society, a crime or other risk to their freedom such as imprisonment for contempt of court. These include having the benefit of a defense lawyer, which is almost essential if a person is to be able to defend herself in a modern court of law. Other elements of this section include being furnished with a copy of the accusation or indictment and, on demand, with a list of witnesses on whose testimony such charge is founded. Accused persons also have the right to use compulsory process (the power to subpoena) to obtain the testimony of their own witnesses; and the right to be confronted with the witnesses testifying against such person.

In our modern society, two new issues have arisen which have caused considerable debate over our cherished right to be confronted by our accusers. First, society's mounting concern over child abuse cases and the sensitivity of underage witnesses to intimidation have raised questions of the right of confrontation in those kinds of cases. Prosecutors will sometimes demand that a child's testimony be pre-recorded, and that cross-examination will not be conducted in open court. Also, sometimes an agency will leak accusations against persons to the mass media, and in effect conduct a trial that leaves persons unable to defend themselves against supposition, rumors, and innuendo. Under these conditions, innocent people may be fired from their jobs, turned out by their families, and sometimes hounded by their neighbors.

In modern Georgia, few if any people have been secretly thrown in jail without a public trial, but that used to be a real problem in historical times. The remedy for this abuse of government power was for someone to go to a regular judge and seek a writ of *habeas corpus,* which is an order to the jailer to produce the prisoner and to show proof that the person was being lawful detained. This protection is provided in Paragraph XV of the first Article of the Georgia Constitution. It is still used often today, however, as a procedure where a defendant can claim that there was some serious defect in his original trial, and to request an appeals court to let him have another chance to demonstrate his innocence. The Constitution provides that this *writ of habeas corpus* shall not be suspended unless the public safety may require it, as in the extremely unlikely event of rebellion or invasion. Of course, rebellion is unlikely in our democratic society where people are free and realize the fact. It is only when people are severely mistreated by their government and their leaders that they begin to think about using force and violence to secure their liberty. Ever since the days of Spartacus in ancient Rome, even tyrants learned not to push people too far.

The next two paragraphs in Article I, Section I provide further Protections for persons accused of crimes. Because we disapprove of torture, and because we know that persons can sometimes be forced to confess to crimes that they did not commit, the Georgia Bill of

Rights ensures that no person shall be compelled to give testimony tending in any manner to be self-incriminating. Furthermore, the Constitution provides that excessive bail shall not be required, nor excessive fines imposed, nor cruel or any unusual punishments inflicted; nor shall any person be abused in being arrested, while under arrest, or in prison. While there are occasional reports of such abuses occurring, the criminal justice system is closely watched, and proven incidents of beating of inmates will result in the punishment of the guards and officials involved.

Paragraph XVIII ensures that no persons shall be put in jeopardy of life or liberty more than once for the same offense. There are exceptions however, such as when a new trial has been granted after conviction, or in case of mistrial. Because of the overcrowding of our prison systems in Georgia, it has become common for prosecutors to charge defendants with every possible offense arising from a criminal activity. Thus someone who hits a victim several times might be charged with several counts of battery. Faced with the prospect of several trials and several possible convictions, many criminals may plea bargain; plead guilty to one charge in return for less time in jail. In some states, prosecutors may even have the right to appeal a jury verdict of not guilty, and try a defendant again for the very same crime!

The next section, Paragraph XIX, concerns the rare problem of someone accused of treason against the State of Georgia. Treason against the State of Georgia is defined as insurrection against the State, adhering to the state's enemies, or giving them aid and comfort. No person shall be convicted of treason except on the testimony of two witnesses to the same overt act or confession in open court. Many government officials and state agency employees are required to take a loyalty oath asserting their allegiance to the State of Georgia.

The consequences of being convicted of a crime in Georgia are described in the next few paragraphs, limiting the kinds and effects of punishment. Number twenty guarantees that no conviction shall work corruption of blood (punishing a criminal's relatives as well as the criminal); or allowing the courts to engage in forfeiture of a criminal's estate (although stolen property, or property used for criminal activity, or purchased with tainted funds can and will be confiscated). Paragraph XXI forbids using banishment and whipping as punishment for crime. The next paragraph provides that there shall be no involuntary servitude within the State of Georgia, except as a punishment, except for crime after legal conviction thereof or for contempt of court. This outlaws slavery within the State of Georgia. Similarly, number twenty-three prohibited imprisonment for debt but federal law and interstate compacts regarding parents who fail to pay their child support obligations can be jailed until they pay up. And

Paragraph XXI, the last of the sections dealing with Civil Liberties per se, guarantees that no person shall be compelled to pay costs in any criminal case except after conviction on final trial.

Georgia thus has a long list of guarantees for persons which prevent many of the old abusive actions that historically were used to limit the liberties of the people. However, there are some civil liberties which exist in some states, but not in Georgia. Of these, perhaps the significance is whether citizens have the right to initiate new laws and policies without the approval of the state government? In some states, such as California, the people have the liberty to circulate petitions for new laws which, if signed by a sufficient number of voting citizens, puts the proposed new laws directed on the ballot for popular approval, completely bypassing the ordinary legislative role in enacting new laws. While the Georgia Constitution does permit ballot initiatives in some local government matters, it is not as liberal as California. Civil liberties, protections against overzealous government officials, are traditionally important and protected elements of our state constitutional system.

Civil Rights

Civil Rights are a closely related, but still a different, concept. Civil Rights focus on egalitarian issues. In other words the question is whether or not all people are treated equally by the government. Interest and participation in the full extent and scope of civil rights is arguably among the most controversial issues in any democratic society, including Georgia. The major questions sparking our lively debates include asking about the distribution of rights of equality and privilege among the people. Should all citizens have exactly the same rights and opportunities under government and its agencies? Does discrimination exist and when should the powers of government be used to ensure that no one has unfair advantages under the policies and the operations of state government? Arguably, the Civil Rights Movement in the American South, and definitely including Georgia, was one of the most significant and successful social movements that helped to bring about some modern changes (Stephen Tuck 2009).

Black Georgians accordingly formed part of this southern movement for full Civil Rights and the wider national struggle for racial equality. What followed is that all ethnic groups are now guaranteed equal opportunity, the right to vote, and both genders are also provided with equal treatment in educational and occupational settings. The Georgia Constitution addressed these important Civil Rights matters.

The political culture of Georgia has often supported advances in Civil Rights. Perhaps the most significant inequality in human history has been the different treatment of men and women. Perhaps in early history primitive conditions made it advisable for society to channel women into domestic servant roles, with low status. But the modern technological revolution, and its requirements for a highly trained intelligent work force, does not allow us to exclude fifty percent of our human resources from full access to skilled employment opportunities. Georgia has been a leader in women's rights. For example, in 1802 the Georgian Sarah P. Hillhouse became the first woman to own and edit a newspaper. And Wesleyan College in Macon, in 1836, became the first college in the world to be chartered to confer degrees to women. Similarly, in 1866 Georgia became the first to allow women to have full property rights, and in 1922 Georgia chose Rebecca Felton as the first elected United States Senator.

Civil Rights and equal opportunity is as important to Georgians as making sure that government does not infringe on our liberties.

The second paragraph of Article I provides protection to persons and their property by guaranteeing equal protection under the law. It proclaims that protection to persons and property is the paramount duty of government, and that the state government shall be impartial in its administration of the laws. In Georgia no person shall be denied equal protection of the laws. No individual or group can be denied rights which are granted to other citizens. Similarly, Paragraph IV specifically orders that no inhabitant of this state shall be molested in person or property or be prohibited from holding any public office or trust on account of religious opinions. However, it takes the precaution of ensuring that the right of freedom of religion shall not be constructed as to excuse acts of licentiousness or justify practices inconsistent with the peace and safety of the state.

Echoing the national constitution, the Constitution of the State of Georgia in Paragraph VII proclaims that all citizens of the United States, resident in this state, are hereby declared citizens of this state; and that it shall be the affirmative duty of the General Assembly to enact such laws as will protect them in the full enjoyment of the rights, privileges, and immunities due to such citizenship. And Paragraph XXIV was inserted to make sure that the social status of any citizen shall never be the subject of legislation. This reflected the national Constitution, which prohibits the federal government from proclaiming any elite individuals being granted any title of nobility.

Thus Georgia cannot declare that anyone is either a peasant or an aristocrat. And, in line with modern practice to guarantee that women are treated equally, the State Constitution prohibits the practice of putting wives and their property under the control of their husbands. Paragraph XXVII says that the separate property of each spouse shall remain the separate property of that spouse, except as may otherwise be provided by the laws of the State, such as prenuptial agreements, contracts, and divorce decrees.

One major reason for the adoption of the present Georgia Constitution was disenchantment with the antebellum treatment of the issue of Civil Rights, particularly freed slaves, in many states following reconstruction. Civil Rights are always the subject of debate and controversy, partly because of prejudice and partly because social progress creates new inventions and customs which raise or revive questions of claims for privilege for the elite few. During the turmoil of the 1960s' Civil Rights Movement in Georgia, great pressure grew to modernize the constitutional wording to reflect the new social and political conditions of the 20th Century. During the political struggles that ensued, the Reverend Martin Luther King, Jr. became the leader of the Civil Rights Movement in the 1960s.

Case Study: Martin Luther King Jr.

Individuals participate in politics or seek political careers for many reasons, and sometimes they may become great leaders who effect great changes in politics and society. One such individual was the Reverend Martin Luther King Jr. Probably nothing makes people more active and politicized than being subjected to bias and discrimination, especially when it interferes with their rights and opportunities, or results in being treated as second class citizens. Following the Second World War, an increased sensitivity to equality and equal rights resulted in the great Civil Rights Movement that culminated in an end to official racial segregation and Congressional passage of important Civil Rights acts. Martin Luther King grew up in Atlanta, Georgia, and became the leader of the Civil Rights Movement in the 1960s. His dedication and sacrifice to that cause has earned him recognition as one of the most important and progressive American figures of the Twentieth Century. His "I have a dream" speech will long be remembered as one of the most eloquent statements of human Civil Rights.

Both Liberty and Rights

Some of the sections of the Georgia Bill of Rights concern issues which touch on both Civil Rights and on Civil Liberties. For example, Paragraph XI deals with operation of the state's jury system. The provisions here are oriented to making sure that Civil Liberties and Civil Rights are not just handled by government officials, who may have institutional agendas, but rather by ordinary citizens chosen at random. This is designed to make sure that people have their cases decided by a jury of their peers. Felony trials always require a jury of twelve persons. And further protections against arbitrary government specifies that grand jurors, who issue complaints charging people with crimes and the trial jurors who decide guilt, will operate separately. Still, a report released by the Georgia State Board of Pardons and Paroles (GSBPP) indicated that one out of every ten Georgians will likely serve time in a state jail or prison; and studies showed that the odds were worse for black males (Associated Press, 2-23-99).

Paragraph XXVI has a homestead exemption. The basic idea is that an elderly person's home should not be taken away just because she owes a lot of money and cannot repay it in a timely fashion. A homestead exemption was set at not less than $1,600.00; and it also gives the General Assembly the authority to define when or if any additional exemptions shall be allowed and to specify the amount of such exemptions. The State Assembly is also required to provide for the manner of exempting such property and for the sale, alienation, and encumbrance thereof; and it should be noted that the law actually provides for the waiver of the homestead exemptions by a debtor. So if people want to waive their homestead exemptions, to obtain a mortgage loan for example, they can do so, if they want to take the risk. Today, unfortunately, the "Great Recession of 2008" and its attendant revenue shortfalls for the state coffers, has led the legislature to almost eliminate the homestead exemption in many local cases.

Finally, the last part of Section I of Article I, Paragraph number XXVIII, has a reserve clause for Civil Liberties and Civil Rights. It provides that the enumeration of the rights described above shall not be interpreted as meaning that there is an automatic denial of other rights. The enumeration of rights herein contained as a part of this Constitution shall not be construed to deny to the people any inherent rights which he may have hitherto enjoyed. To use a somewhat silly example, suppose that our legislature imposed a tax on the air we need to breathe. Under the reserve clause, a citizen could go to the courts for a ruling that the new tax violated our inherent right to use the atmosphere.

Automatic Restoration of Rights

In the State of Georgia, one loses their Civil Rights if they are convicted of a "felony involving moral turpitude" or if they have been judicially determined to be mentally incompetent. This is provided under the Georgia Constitution, Article II, Section 1, III items (a) and (b). However, the rights to vote, for example, are restored automatically upon completion of an imposed sentence. So, for example, a convicted person may not hold public office "unless their civil rights have been restored and at least ten years have lapsed from the date of the completion of the sentence as long as there is no subsequent conviction for another crime that involves moral turpitude." According to a Georgia Attorney General opinion on this matter, to regain the right to sit on a jury, either a pardon or the restoration of one's civil rights is necessary (Georgia Opinion of the Attorney General #69, No. 83-33, 1983). In particular cases, an official Opinion of Attorney Generals in the State of Georgia may be very important in clarifying some points of Georgia law before a particular court may ever get to decide that law in an actual case or controversy.

Other opinions have involved state constitutional prohibitions against felony offenders holding an appointment of honor or trust, such as the position of deputy sheriff, a peace officer, except where they have been pardoned. However, one Attorney General took the position that because those appointments are precisely to positions of honor and trust, it does not prevent the state General Assembly from acting to increase the onus of these offenses, and making convictions an absolute prohibition to the qualification for those positions. As opined by that Attorney General's opinion, this is the case because the General Assembly is authorized by law to provide even a much higher qualification for the officers under Georgia law [see Georgia Code Annotated Section 92A-2108(d)].

Discretionary Restoration of Rights

In the State of Georgia, as in many other states, the power to pardon and to remove disabilities from prior conviction is vested on a State Board of Pardons and Paroles. However, the board may be prohibited from issuing a pardon and its powers may be superseded by the legislature; as in the cases involving recidivists and persons serving life sentences (see Georgia Constitution Article IV, Section 2, Paragraph II). Although the Governor appoints the members of the State Board of Pardons and Paroles the law prohibits the Governor from exercising power or any authority whatsoever over Pardon and Paroles administration and processes (see Georgia Code Annotated Section 42-9-56). In addition to issuing pardons and sentence commutations, the Board may issue "Restoration of Civil and Political Rights" to felony offenders including those from out-of-state and federal convictions (See Board instructions, at *http://www.pap.state.ga.us/other_forms_clemency.html*).

For the restoration of Civil Rights more specifically, a petitioner must have completed his or her sentence including the payment of fine with no impending charges, if applicable, and lastly, two years must have lapsed without any criminal activity (after the completion of the initial conviction). For a full pardon, however, the petitioner must have completed a five-year waiting period after the completion of the sentence without any criminal activity. However, waivers can be extended to those petitioners who can show that the five years waiting period would be detrimental to their livelihood. For example, if a petitioner can show that the five years waiting period would impact upon their qualification for employment in their chosen profession they might be extended a waiver. Finally, Georgia law also extends and makes the restoration of rights to federal and out-of-state offenders living in the state of Georgia.

In the end, it is important to understand that the restoration of rights only affect people's Basic Civil Rights, i.e., the right to jury and access to public office, because even a full pardon does not always imply complete innocence. For example, a pardon does not restore a convicted felony offender to a public office he or she was forced to relinquish as a result of a conviction (see *Morris v. Hartsfield*, 197 S.E. 251 (Ga. 1938)). What a pardon is and what it really does is that it relieves the burden of civil and political disabilities imposed by a conviction (see Georgia Code Annotated Section 42-9-54 and Georgia compilation of the Rules and Regulations (475–3)).

Article I–Section II:
Origin and Structure of Government

The second section of Article One concerning the origin, foundations, and structure of government, focuses on the basic political concepts underlying our state government. Paragraph I proclaims our fundamental belief that all government, of right, originates with the people, is founded upon their will only, and is instituted solely for the good of the whole. Public officers are considered to be the trustees and servants of the people and must at all times be answerable to them. The second paragraph concerns the object of government. It reflects our value system, asserting that the people of this state have the inherent right of regulating their internal government. Government is instituted for the protection, security, and benefit of the people; and at all times they have the right to alter or reform the same whenever the public good may require it.

Paragraph III concerns the separation of legislative, judicial, and executive powers. The legislative, judicial, and executive powers are intended to forever remain separate and distinct; and no person discharging the duties of one shall at the same time exercise the function of either of the others except as herein provided. As we see in following paragraphs, the Constitution puts particular limits on the powers of the government institutions by what can be called a check and balance system. In Paragraph IV, the power of the courts to punish for contempt shall be limited by legislative acts. As detailed in Paragraph V, if the General Assembly enacts legislation in violation of this Constitution or the Constitution of the United States, the judiciary branch shall be required to declare them void. And Paragraph VI declares that the civil authority shall be superior to the military.

The next two paragraphs deal with narrower topics. Paragraph seven prevents the government from trying to favor the establishment of a religion. It definitely asserts that no money shall ever be taken from the public treasury, directly or indirectly, in aid of any church, sect, cult, or religious denomination or of any sectarian institution. And Paragraph VIII deals with gambling and lotteries, contains amendments to the Constitution, and supersedes the previous ban on gambling. Prior to 1991, all gambling and lotteries were prohibited in Georgia. But due to budgeting problems, the State Constitution was amended to permit gambling and lotteries as long as the proceeds were used for the purposes of education, e.g., funding public kindergartens and Hope Scholarships. Certainly, what the legislature giveth, it could also take away, and the Georgia Lottery could be abolished by a subsequent constitutional amendment. But after more than a decade, the lottery remains a popular institution with many Georgians. Thus, the likelihood that it would be abolished is slim, and the fact that its originally publicized purpose, to support education, is ensconced in the Constitution makes it doubly secure.

Under the old British system of monarchy, the King could do no wrong, and therefore people could not sue the King for any misdeeds; there was sovereign immunity. But in our democracy, it is understood that state government may sometimes inadvertently injure someone, and that person should be able to sue for compensation. Lawsuits filed to get repayment for injuries are called tort actions, and we believe that everyone should have the right to sue anyone who injures them. Accordingly, Paragraph IX provides that the General Assembly may waive the state's sovereign immunity from suit, and that the General Assembly may provide by law for procedures for the making, handling, and disposition of actions or claims against the state and its departments, agencies, offices, and employees.

There are other limitations designed to protect the state treasury. The General Assembly is allowed to provide by law for the processing and disposition of claims against the state which does not exceed certain maximum amounts. And the state's traditional defense of sovereign immunity is also generally waived for the breach of any valid written contract entered into by the state or its departments and agencies. So for example, state agencies are required to honor their contracts with citizens and businesses. Thus, unless otherwise stated or provided for by law by the General Assembly, all officers and employees of the state or its departments and agencies may be subject to suit and may be liable for injuries and damages caused by their negligent performance of, or even of a negligent failure to perform, their official functions.

And state employees may be personally liable for injuries and damages if they act with actual malice or with actual intent to cause injury to persons during the performance of their official functions. But otherwise, with some exceptions, officers and employees of the state or its departments and agencies are not subject to suit or liability, and no judgment shall be entered against them, merely because someone is injured or doesn't like the approved actions or duties of these government officials. The provisions are further strengthened by other parts of the State Constitution, which students are advised to read in their entirety.

Article I—Section III:
General Provision and Operations

In our capitalist society, the lure of wealth and the acquisition of private property is used to encourage people to work hard to create new inventions and to improve the general economy. But sometimes the public good requires that the state take or damage property, as for example, for building roads or bridges. The last section of Article One sets out some basic rules controlling such state action. Generally, the state is allowed to appropriate property, but it is required to pay people for their property. The first paragraph of this section sets out some fairly complicated and detailed language on this complicated area of private property rights.

When a government body asserts its right to take property, the legal term used may be *eminent domain* or condemnation. The first paragraph says that: (a) except as otherwise provided, private property shall not be taken or damaged for public purposes without just and adequate compensation being first paid. However, part (b) says that when private property is taken or damaged by the state (or by counties or municipalities), for public road or street purposes, or for public transportation purposes, or for any other public purpose as determined by the General Assembly, that just and adequate compensation therefore need not be paid until the same has been finally fixed and determined as provided by law; but such just and adequate compensation shall then be paid in preference to all other obligations except bonded indebtedness.

This means that people whose property is taken get paid first, even before people who lent money to the public body. Of course, the fiscal system in the State of Georgia is very well-administered, and the chance that Georgia might fail to repay any of its debts is extremely remote. Other parts of this paragraph specify that: (c) the General Assembly may by law require the condemner (such as a local government) to make prepayment against adequate compensation as a condition precedent to the exercise of the right of eminent domain. This is to make sure that all parties with claims to the property are protected. And in part (d) the Constitution provides that the General Assembly may provide by law for the payment by the condemnor of reasonable expenses, including attorney's fees, incurred by the property owner in determining just and adequate compensation.

The framers of the Constitution of the State of Georgia were also concerned about other problems that might happen to people whose property has to be taken for the public good, under the power of eminent domain. So in part (e), the law provides that notwithstanding any other provision of the Constitution, the General Assembly may provide by law for relocation assistance and payments to persons displaced through the exercise of the powers of the government and that tax money may be spent for that purpose. But this provided insufficient protection against an alarming trend of allowing wealthy developers to persuade local officials to condemn small properties for forced consolidation, new economic development, and thus a larger tax base. In 2006, Georgia voters overwhelmingly voted (by 83.4%) to place restrictions on the power of eminent domain by Constitution amendment. Local governments cannot now easily allow private developers to condemn other's private property for their own, or ostensibly for public use. The U.S. Supreme Court had determined that this practice passed federal constitutional muster, and Georgians, as did citizens in several other states, reacted angrily by amending their State Constitution so as to shout: "not here."

In a related but different problem, government is sometimes called upon to settle disputes between two private landowners, most particularly if one person's property is surrounded by another person's property. If a court or other government agency determines that someone should have a right to go across someone else's private property, then Paragraph II of this last section of Article One provides that in case of necessity, private ways may be granted, but only if just and adequate compensation is first paid by the applicant.

Finally, because the State of Georgia borders on the Atlantic Ocean, there have been disputes about the ownership of beachfront property. Throughout history there have been a lot of different laws about the ownership of waterfront property. In some countries, private citizens are forbidden to own any property near the ocean. In America, citizens are allowed to own such property, and sometimes even to build houses right next to the water. But on oceanfront property, the tides move in and out, and the land between high tide and low tide may be considerable. State laws vary on the subject. In California, property can only be owned to the high tide level, and ordinary citizens are allowed to walk on the low areas left above the water line. But in Texas, property may be privately owned down to the low tide mark. In Georgia, the last paragraph in this section follows the latter example, and provides that the Act of the General Assembly approved back in December 16, 1902, extending the title of ownership of lands abutting on tidal water to the low water mark, is ratified and confirmed by the Constitution of Georgia. So in our state a property owner has a right to prevent citizens from walking along the beach at low tide and beachcombing for shells and driftwood.

Conclusion

In summary, this chapter focuses primarily on Article I of the Constitution of the State of Georgia which provides for the Bill of Rights. Civil Liberties, as outlined in the Bill of Rights of the State of Georgia and the U.S. Constitution, guarantees the protection of persons, expressions, and property from the arbitrary interference of government officials. There are no special classes of citizens with superior rights. Civil Rights issues pertain to positive acts of government which may be designed to subject citizens to arbitrary or discriminatory treatment by government or individuals; these are prohibited by the Constitution. The modern Georgia State Constitution emphasizes the importance of Civil Rights and Civil Liberties, as should be expected given the state's history and traditions. Our civil rights focus on our belief that people should be treated equally whenever possible, and our Civil Liberties reflect our determination that government should not be abusive or tyrannical.

The modern effectuations of our traditional beliefs have made Georgia one of the leading developers of democracy, starting over two hundred years ago when monarchy and elite privilege dominated government in the world. Generally, in order to ensure that our liberties and our rights are protected, both general democratic institutions and governmental bodies have to be designed to protect these values. Perhaps the most important of these institutions are the many different organized economic and cultural interest groups in Georgia. These interest groups, competing for power and influence, promote their agendas in our free speech, our free press, and through the elections of leaders of the political parties. Thus the average citizen has many avenues to participate in political activities, which are further described in Chapters three and four below.

Key Terms

Bill of Attainder
Civil Liberties
Civil Rights
Ex post facto laws
General Provisions
Homestead Exemption
Social media and evolving technologies
Eminent Domain
Sovereign Immunity
Twelve-person jury system

Essay Questions

1. What is the difference between civil rights and civil liberties?

2. What are the constitutional safeguards provided by the Georgia Constitution to protect someone who is accused from the trial and sentencing phase of a criminal proceeding?

3. In what ways has the political culture in Georgia supported advances in civil rights?

4. List and discuss in the correct order the hierarchy of law from top to bottom as provided in Chapter Two.

5. Explain why the authors of this text in Chapter Two assert almost emphatically that while the constitution is a necessary condition for understanding the Peach State government, it is not a sufficient condition.

Figure 3.1   Historical Legislative Photo

Source: Courtesy of Georgia State Department of Archives and History

Political Participation in Georgia

This Chapter is divided into three broad sections focusing on the major political linkages between the participation of the citizens, the two political parties, and a wide variety of interest groups.

Citizen Participation

In 2008, over 61% of Georgia voters turned out and participated in the presidential election. Normally turnout in presidential elections is much higher than turnout in other elections where a presidential nominee does not head the ticket. The 2010 election, however, somewhat defied that trend when 57% of eligible voters turned out.

But even these numbers are not as good as they should be. What does it say about our system when 4 out of 10 people choose to not participate? There are certainly structural barriers to voting such as voter registration, which necessarily precedes the act of voting. While other states allow residents to register as late as the day of the election, Georgia requires voters to register at least 30 days prior to the election. Once registered, voters are able to vote by mail, through absentee ballot, or at the ballot box. However, while voter registration requirements are an effective barrier, once Georgians are registered they are more immune than residents in most states to losing their registration because the state has "permanent" rather than "periodic" registration. With permanent registration, once one is properly registered and votes at regular intervals, his or her name remains inscribed on the rolls. In contrast, periodic registration means that rolls are regularly purged after a certain time whether the voter votes or not. Because of this, registration is less of a barrier in Georgia than in many other states and it may actually help increase voter participation.

This is not to suggest that voting barriers don't exist. The most controversial barrier is known as the 'no match, no vote,' identification restrictions. In the 2005 session of the General Assembly, the new Republican majority was able to pass legislation requiring voters to produce photo identification card and proof of citizenship in order to vote. Democrats argued that this was aimed at reducing minority voter participation, which tends to be democratic. Republicans claimed that they were not trying to discourage minorities from voting, instead they were concerned about voter fraud.

A federal district court judge subsequently held that the photo I.D. law was tantamount to a poll tax, prohibited by the 24th Amendment to the U.S. Constitution, and struck it down. The court's argument was that forcing citizens to obtain a photo I.D. is akin to forcing them to pay for the privilege of voting. In response to this ruling, the General Assembly introduced another bill that would still require a photo I.D., but now the required state issued I.D. would be paid for by the state, not the voter.

Both federal and state courts challenged the constitutionality of Georgia's law and its implementation was stayed for 2006 primary and general elections. Republicans, however, continued to bring the issue to the floor, and the courts dealt with the issue through 2010. In May 2009 officials from the U.S. Department of Justice blocked two new Georgia voter verification requirements, telling state Attorney General Thurbert Baker that the state's scheme discriminated against black, Hispanic, and Asian voters. In what it said was an effort to deter voter fraud, Georgia set two "no match, no vote" requirements. One would reject a voter's registration application if driver's license or Social Security information failed to match official databases. The second was a check on citizenship status in the driver database.

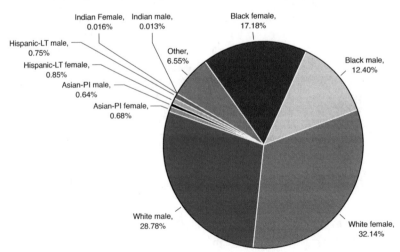

Total Registered Voters by Race and Sex, Statewide (March 1, 2011)

Figure 3.2   Georgia Registered Voters 2011

Graphic taken from Georgia Secretary of State Website

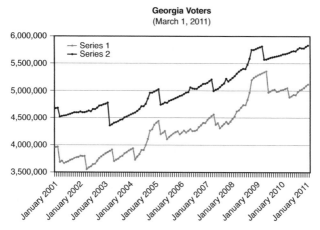

Figure 3.3   Increase in Georgia Registered Voters across Time
Graphic taken from Georgia Secretary of State Website

At the time, the Justice Department said Georgia's records were so flawed that thousands of eligible voters were wrongly flagged, and that a disproportionate share were minorities. An error as simple as transposing a single number from a driver's license could produce a "no-match," and the citizenship check incorrectly flagged thousands of people, many born in the U.S. In 2010, Georgia's top court considered the legality of the state law. The state court's ruling, however, was superseded in August 2010 by the U.S. Department of Justice which announced that the Georgia law was legal and fulfilled the requirements of the Voting Rights Act of 1965. Prior to this, the voter identification system had been tied up in federal courts since 2008 and the Justice Department repeatedly refused to approve the process by which the state checks voter registration information against driver's license and Social Security databases. The sitting Georgia Secretary of State, Brian Kemp, had sued the Justice Department in federal court in search of approval. The Justice Department in 2008, under Republican President George W. Bush, first questioned the system and said federal law required the state to verify a voter's identity, but not his or her citizenship. The matter was settled in March 2011 when the Georgia Supreme Court ruled that the no-match requirement was constitutional.

Apart from registration, another reason why people don't participate is because they lack faith in the political system, or feel that it is too complex for them to understand. Ignorance of candidates, parties, or issues serves as a barrier to participation. Thus, turnout in states with low levels of political education is usually quite low. Georgia is, unfortunately, such a state, ranking at or near the bottom of the list of states in terms of educational attainment. The result for Georgians is

high dropout rates, poor scores on standardized tests, poor performance on the Armed Forces Literacy Test, low percentages of students
pursuing higher educational opportunities, and low voter turnout.

Several other factors positively associated with political participation include a high degree of urbanization, high median family
incomes, and small percentages of disadvantaged minority groups. As
a whole, Georgia strikes out on all three counts. Georgia is largely a
rural state (some people count Atlanta as a separate state) still fairly
poor in terms of income, especially outside the Atlanta metropolitan
area, and has very high numbers of minority group members who
have not been incorporated into the middle class. The largest minority group, blacks or African-Americans, constitute about 28 percent of
the total population, and historically have not been able to achieve
the economic or educational levels of other ethnic groups. The effect
of these demographic factors is obvious. However, well-educated,
well-to-do urban minorities actually participate more than do whites
from poor rural areas.

Georgia's Political Parties

There are many reasons why any state has the party system it does. The
history of a state or region often reveals the significant factors, and in
this context the Civil War continues to have an influence on Georgia's
political parties. With regard to political party affiliations, states tend
to "vote as they shot." Along the eastern Atlantic seaboard, both the
northern states and the more southern states established their prevailing political patterns more than a hundred years ago. Until
recently, all of the states of the southern Confederacy, except Florida,
had either one-party democratic dominance or modified one-party
democratic systems. Historically, Georgia could have been described
as the most democratic, or perhaps as the least republican, of all of
them. But the historical links between southern democrats and northern democrats, established by President Franklin D. Roosevelt's New
Deal coalition, started to fray with the passage of the Civil Rights Act
by President Johnson, and the conservative coalition on the right,
established by President Ronald Reagan, completed the transition to a
republican sweep in 2010.

In the United States, there really is not a unified national democratic party system, no real national democratic party. What appears to
be a national party system is really a collection of state party systems,
and in turn what appears to be a state party system is actually little
more than an amalgam of local (mostly county) party systems. For
most democratic, politics is local. In fact, the repeated use of the word
"system" by the authors may be misleading. American party politics is

a lot less than systematic. Similarly, there is really not a unified national Republican party system, no real national Republican Party. What appears to be a national party system is in large part a fiction, a public relations campaign funded in large part by national industrial and financial interest groups and supported by a broad coalition of disparate religious groups. While Sarah Palin's influence in Georgia has been muted by the new republican reality, the existence of the emerging Tea Party and its challenge to relatively liberal spending republicans has revealed the gapping cracks in the supposed republican monolith.

Different authors use different typologies for classifying state party systems, but virtually all of them considered Georgia's party system as one-party dominant or as modified one-party democratic, even in the late 1990s. However, most of those assessments were seriously dated, even in those general State and Local Government texts published as late as 1998. The gains that republicans have made in Georgia since 1994 are nothing short of phenomenal, culminating in the election of a republican Governor for the first time since Reconstruction in the 2002 election. Owing to the defection of three democratic senators following that election, the Georgia State Senate also fell under republican control for the first time since Reconstruction, and the GOP even managed to defeat the venerable Speaker of the House, Tom Murphy, in 2002. In 2004 the State House of Representatives followed the State Senate into the republican dominated ranks. By 2010 all of the leaders of state government were republican. Accordingly, Georgia is once again a one-party state.

Figure 3.4   Leading the Campaign

To help guide candidates to achieve victories of this sort, both parties have state executive committees that meet periodically and recommend policies and procedures for their respective parties. Members of these committees are chosen in local caucuses by their fellow partisans for long terms. The duties of these committees include fund-raising, policy-making, and approving choices for membership in the Electoral College (a reward for faithful service). Each of the state organizations elects officers, including a chairperson, a vice-chairperson, and an executive board. Each of the state party committees has a paid staff headed by an executive director who coordinates the day-to-day activities of the state party. Given the increasing candidate-centeredness of political campaigns, the state executive committees have relatively little to do with directing campaigns. Moreover, while fund-raising may be numbered among the committee's duties, they never seen to collect enough, and the resulting dearth of funds to distribute forces candidates to rely on their own devices to raise money.

If one were to think that the state executive committees were answerable to the democratic and/or republican national committees, one would be making a natural mistake, but a mistake nonetheless. Samuel J. Eldersveld described our party system as "stratarchical" not hierarchical, so as to emphasize that each stratum—federal, state, and local, is largely independent of the others (Eldersveld, Chapter 5). Thus the national committees do not dictate to the state committees, and the state committees do not (although they may try) dictate to the various county committees. Insofar as there is any action in the party organization, the county organization is where the action is.

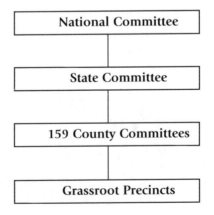

Figure 3.5   Political Party Organization
Source: Compiled by authors.

Perhaps the main reason for the locally based party system is the fact that the vast majority of elected officials in the United States are locally based, paid, and organized. Although it varies somewhat from county to county in Georgia (and with 159 counties that is a lot of room for variation), Georgians elect the following officials to county offices: county commissioners and county sheriffs; judges of state and superior courts, probate courts, juvenile courts; magistrates and district attorneys; various clerks of the courts; school board members and school superintendents. While some of these—particularly the judges—are elected on nominally nonpartisan ballots, parties still play a role in endorsing them for office.

Each of the county committee members is elected in the primary elections, and each appoints a chairperson and such other officers as are called for in their party charters. The electoral base of all of this activity is the precinct. In a state-by-state ranking of the strength of local party organizations (basically the county committees), Georgia's republican committees were the weakest of all fifty states, and the democrats were not far behind; their rank was 46th in the nation (Gibson, 154–155). It would appear, therefore, that local "party organization" in Georgia may be a bit of an oxymoron, a contradiction in terms; there is precious little organization in either of the two political parties. However, that too may be changing. While the Democratic Party organization appears to be somewhat demoralized and moribund after the midterm congressional and state elections of 2010, anecdotal evidence suggests that the republican organization is optimistic and invigorated, suggesting that majority party status has now been achieved and in their minds must be protected against internal Tea Partiers.

Owing to its long existing one-party tradition, Georgia requires candidates for public office to win a majority of the votes cast in a primary election. If a candidate does not do so, a run-off election between the top two vote-getters is provided for. Legislation passed by the Georgia General Assembly in 1998, however, required only a forty-five percent plurality to win general elections. The democratically controlled legislature at that time calculated that the Libertarian Party was more likely to take votes away from republicans than from democrats, because of the similarity of republican and libertarian ideology, and that democrats could easily win 45%, since libertarians seldom got more than two or three percent of the votes in a general election. When republicans captured control of the General Assembly, they repealed the 45% law.

In 2010, this turned out to significantly impact the republican's choice for Governor in the primary elections when Karen Handel won about 33 percent of the vote, Deal 23 percent, Eric Johnson 20 percent, and John Oxendine 17 percent, leading to a contentious run-off between Handel and Deal. Both candidates boasted high-profile endorsements and argued over which was more influential. Handel held a rally on Monday with former Alaska Gov. Sarah Palin, the 2008 GOP nominee for vice president, while former Arkansas Gov. Mike Huckabee, who won the state's 2008 Republican presidential primary, stumped for Deal in Gainesville on Sunday. Handel called herself the outsider, fighting the "good old boy network," while Deal had the support of the vast majority of republican lawmakers in Atlanta and Washington.

By the end of the primary, Handel took a particularly aggressive tone, calling Deal, a former congressman, "a corrupt relic of Washington" and repeatedly pointing out a congressional ethics report that said he likely violated federal ethics rules. Deal at first refused to respond in kind, but in the final week or so lashed out at Handel for, among other things, having hedged on whether she once supported a gay rights organization. A primary election runoff was held on May 10, and the results gave a black eye to Palin's image. The difference between Handel and Deal was roughly 2,400 votes, but Handel quickly conceded and threw her support behind Deal. Figure 3.6 reveals the electorate of the Georgia Tea Party. Handel had dominated the Atlanta urban and sub-

Figure 3.6   Results of Republican Primary Run-Off
Nathan Deal (R) 50.2%; Karen Handel (R) 49.8%

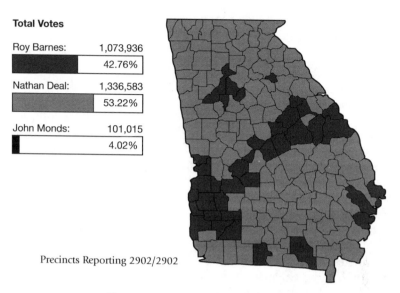

Total Votes

| Roy Barnes: | 1,073,936 |
| | 42.76% |

| Nathan Deal: | 1,336,583 |
| | 53.22% |

| John Monds: | 101,015 |
| | 4.02% |

Precincts Reporting 2902/2902

Figure 3.7 2010 Election Results

From *The Atlanta Journal-Constitution*, 11/3/2010 issue, © 2010 *The Atlanta Journal-Constitution*. All rights reserved. Used by permission and protected by the Copyright Laws of the United States. The printing, copying, redistribution, or retransmission of this Content without express written permission is prohibited.

urban region, where the Republican electorate is both white and generally upper-middle-class, thus very keen on the low taxes message.

This set up the general election battle between Republican Nathan Deal and democratic candidate Roy Barnes. As can be seen from Figure 3.7, when Gov. Deal won the 2010 election he did so by carrying nearly every county in the state, apart from the urban areas surrounding Atlanta. In all, Deal won 120 of Georgia's 159 counties, while Democrat Roy Barnes won 39, including Clayton, DeKalb, Fulton, and Rockdale. Deal also captured most of the counties below the so-called "gnat line" that separates metro Atlanta and north Georgia from middle and south Georgia. Both Barnes and Deal focused intently on that region, which falls below a line roughly from Columbus to Macon to Augusta.

Georgia's Interest Groups

Power abhors a vacuum. In states where political parties are weak, as in Georgia, political interest groups are strong (Froman, 956–94). Variously called interest groups, special interest groups, or pressure groups, political interest groups are organized associations created to affect or effectuate public policy. They differ from political parties in that their members do not seek public office as such, but rather desire to influence policy outcomes and outputs. The more and varied the regions, industries, peoples and purposes that a state government encompasses, the more and varied the interest groups will be. Georgia has a lot of such varied interests, and hence, a lot of interest groups.

In fact, reflecting its large size and diverse economy, Georgia has an awful lot of interest groups. They cannot all be described here, because even identifying the basic groupings would be a long list. Interest groups can be business associations and labor unions, farmers and fishermen, sportsmen, professional and trades groups; that is, they are often organized around the various occupational or economic groups found in Georgia. On the other hand, they can be established on the basis of achieved religious preferences such as the National Council of Churches (NCC); or ascribed racial groupings, such as the National Association for the Advancement of Colored People (NAACP).

Interest groups may be built up from shared experiences leading to a desire to participate in policymaking. The League of Women Voters (LWV) and the American Legion (AL) are examples of such groups. Furthermore, ideological interest groups may organize to shape general policies; the liberal Americans for Democratic Action (ADA) or the conservative Eagle Forum (AF) are two such groups. Many interest groups represent recipients (or hopeful recipients) of government services, such as welfare, student loans, and business subsidies. Curiously, because of the complexities of the nearly 1,270 governments in the state of Georgia alone, the actual governments themselves, and their agencies and officials, often find it necessary or expedient to try to lobby each other to influence the course of public policy in Georgia and in adjoining states, and across the nation. Groups of government entities band together for such purposes, such as the nationally based State Municipal Association, the National Association of Counties, and the National Association of Chiefs of Police (Dye, 107).

To determine which interest groups were the most powerful in Georgia politics, Professors Ronald J. Hrebenar and Clive S. Thomas asked knowledgeable persons both within and without the state to put together two lists of interest groups: the first identifying those which were consistently influential, and the second to list those which were either rising or falling in power, or which were only occasionally active (Gray and Jacob). On the second list were the Board of Regents of the University System, The Georgia Municipal Association, the Association of County Commissioners, and the Georgia Trial Lawyers Association. Influential Georgia organizations of the first rank are depicted in Table 3.1 on the following page.

In Georgia, and in much of the United States, business organizations certainly do dominate. They have both the means and the deter-

Table 3.1   Government Entities in Georgia

Government Units	Number
State Government	1
Counties	159
School Districts	180
Special Districts	620
Municipalities	529
Total:	1,489

Sources: Compiled by authors, including Hepburn, Lawrence R. "Politics and Government" in *Contemporary Georgia* (Athens, Georgia: University of Georgia, 1987), and "Georgia County Snapshots," (Atlanta: Department of Community Affairs, 2006).

Table 3.2   Georgia Interest Groups

Nation's Bank	Medical Assoc. of Georgia
Suntrust Bank	Georgia Assoc. of Educators
Wachovia Bank	St. Dept. of Transportation
Coca-Cola	Business Council of Georgia
Delta Airlines	

Assembled by the authors from various sources including Dye, Thomas R. *Politics in States and Communities,* 9th Ed. (Englewood Cliffs, N.J.: Prentice-Hall, 1997), and Gray, et al., *Politics in the American States: A Comparative Analysis,* 5th Ed. (Washington, D.C.: CQ Press, 1996).

mination to influence policy to their advantage, or at least not to the disadvantage, of their interests. But the Georgia Association of Educators is also a force to reckon with. It represents a significant number of well-educated, well-informed professionals located in every state House and Senate District, who vote and who are largely united in their goals, objectives, and concerns. And that description is a formula for political success.

A number of factors affect the ability of an interest group to influence public policy. Former Georgia Southern University President Nicholas Henry, a political scientist, identifies seven such factors (Henry, 65–68). These factors include not only the size of the membership and their financial wealth, but also intangibles such as leadership qualities and the effectiveness of their organization. The various factors are listed in Table 3.3 on the following page.

Based on results alone, The Georgia Association of Educators (GAE) appears to score highly on each of these factors. These factors, along with the importance of education for economic competitiveness, probably goes far to explain why the proportion of Georgia's state budget spent on education (over 50%) is as high as it is. Another highly rated group is the Medical Association of Georgia (MAG),

Table 3.3   Factors of Influence

1. The size of the group
2. The group's cohesiveness
3. Its geographical spread
4. Member's social status
5. Its leadership and organization
6. The features of its program
7. The political environment

which scores highly enough on these factors to cause its success rate to exceed its failure rate in its policy initiatives. In other words, what the MAG lacks in size it makes up for in other areas, particularly in money. And money, once described by Jesse Unruh, former speaker of the California House of Representatives as "the mother's milk of politics," can be influential indeed. Money alone is no substitute for all of the other factors, but in conjunction with the other factors it tends to give great power to those influential groups which have plenty of it to spare. In contrast, the organization calling itself Queer Nation/Atlanta ranks low on all of these factors and has correspondingly little influence in the State of Georgia.

Interest groups have two major political functions: lobbying and campaign financing. The term "lobbying" derives from the practice of interested parties contacting Members of the British Parliament (who had no individual offices) in the lobby of the Parliament Building (Westminster). The image evoked by the term is one of a petitioner sidling up to the very buttonholes of legislators to solicit support. While a bit simplistic today, the fundamental relationship described is still accurate.

The variety of techniques interest groups use to influence government almost matches their variety of interests. Often, they conduct public relations campaigns to persuade the public to their points of view. In our representative system, if they can get the public on their side, the legislator will soon follow. In addition, they encourage, campaign for, and fund the campaigns of, elected executive officials. They also pressure appointed bureaucrats, seeking special rules, regulations, and strict or lax enforcement of standards. Interest group lawyers threaten litigation in the courts, seeking and obtaining injunctions, mediation, settlements, decisions, and appeals. But most obvious of all, hundreds of their representatives, known as lobbyists, can be seen during each session of the General Assembly, and in smaller numbers at county commissions and city council meetings. They attempt to "buttonhole" legislative policymakers in the halls of government, and wine and dine our elected representatives in fancy restaurants and plush hospitality suites set up in hotels and at sporting arenas.

The reputation of lobbyists for bribing legislators is based partly on historical fact, the Yazoo Land Fraud, but it is not a particularly common practice in the modern era. For a number of reasons, attempts at bribery are chilled by fears of detection and the consequences of disclosure, leading to the lobbyist's loss of effectiveness and loss of office for the legislator. Indeed, legislators who pride themselves on their integrity are prone to "blow the whistle" on lobbyists who attempt to buy their votes.

What lobbyists really want is *access* to decision-makers, and today that access is "bought" with information, not with money. Faced with a dizzying array of issues, most beyond the comprehension of a single legislator, our representatives cry out for information about problems: what are the real goals of a bill, what effect will it have on the legislator's constituents, and how will it affect their own districts? The legislative committee system, the state bureaucracy and the limited research facilities of the General Assembly all welcome lobbyists who have thoroughly studied a bill and who are in a position to explain it. Of course, the information provided by some may be biased, but it is a place to start, and by weighing it against other sources of information, often from opposing lobbyists, the legislators can make a more informed and better decision.

Sometimes it seems as if everyone is lobbying everyone else, especially during the annual sessions of the General Assembly. Actually, lobbying was illegal in Georgia before 1992. Under this quaint fiction, an ancient law made lobbying akin to bribery and a misdemeanor. Indeed, lobbyists were called "registered agents" in the State of Georgia and had to pay a $5.00 fee to the Secretary of State at the start of each legislative session. They were then free to go about their "registered agent" business, unhampered by any additional laws, rules, or regulations.

Prior to passage of the 1992 ethics legislation by the General Assembly, lobbyists in Georgia did not have to declare publicly which bills they were working to pass or defeat; nor did they have to report the amounts they were spending on their efforts. Nor did they have to report any meals, drinks, gifts, or entertainments they provided to their legislative friends, except for their formal monetary campaign contributions. The Secretary of State's Office received $5.00 from each of 1,229 individual registered agents for the 1990 legislative session, almost five for each legislator (Pettys, 2).

The 1992 ethics law was perhaps the most hotly debated issue at that session of the Georgia General Assembly. In its final form it made lobbying legal, but it actually regulated it much more closely than it had been before. Instead of a nominal one-time fee, lobbyists were required to pay an annual $200.00 registration fee to the State Ethics Commission plus an additional $15.00 for supplemental registration and a lobbyist identification tag. However, the fees were rescinded in 1994, although registration with the Ethics Commission is still required by law. All lobbying expenditures must be reported, along with the names of the legislators whom the lobbyists were trying to influence. The law sets a maximum of $1,000.00 that an interest group can give in campaign contributions for local offices and for the General Assembly seats, and, over a four-year election cycle $5,000 per primary, $5,000 per general election, and $3,000 per runoff to candidates for statewide office. However, lobbyist money can be given to politicians in other ways. For example, questions were raised in 2010 when House Speaker David Ralston took his family and staff members to an all expense paid $17,000.00 trip to Germany at Thanksgiving, supposedly to study magnetic levitation, when he could have studied the same technology in Power Springs at an esti-mated cost of only $74.00 (Yarbrough, 02-19-11).

Perhaps the main reason why lobbyists don't have to illegally bribe legislators is that there are two perfectly legal ways to transfer money directly. In Georgia, legislators are allowed to engage in busi-ness ventures with lobbyists. However, the real return here is long-term future benefit. The other technique is quick up-front money, and is called a campaign contribution. The transfer is usually handled by specially created groups called political action committees (PACs). While these PACs are limited in the amount they can contribute to any one candidate (Pettys, 2), there is no limit on the number of can-didates they may contribute to, and more importantly there is no limit to the number of PACs that can be formed by any one interest group. As a result, PACs are becoming increasing influential, espe-cially as the costs of political campaigning escalate. With this complex system, a particular PAC will be unable to "buy" a legislator, but it can certainly get a legislator to return its telephone calls whenever it deems necessary. That's access. That's influence. That's power.

What about those who are not members of organized interest groups? Do they have access? Certainly they can write or call their legislators. They can attend the periodic town meetings and pre-legislative forums that some legislators hold. But unless they organize, their interests and concerns are unlikely to be heeded. People who lack the factors of political influence, and who are unable to create effective organizations to pursue their goals in the political system, have little or no influence (Parenti). Increasing the share of the state's budget, gathering more political influence, and changing the law and the state's Constitution are most effectively done by organized special interest groups. Georgia ranks tenth in the nation in terms of the number of interest groups it has. It also ranks as a dominant/complementary state in terms of the overall impact that interest groups have. That means that political interest groups are more powerful than political parties in the state, but the interest groups are not so powerful that they eclipse or subordinate the parties (Gray and Jacob, 1996). Considering the fact that in 1987 the Georgia General Assembly was ranked second in the nation in terms of its accountability to interest groups, or forty-ninth in its accountability to the unorganized public, the Peach State seems to be becoming more democratic (the ideology) as it becomes less democratic (the Party). That is, as party competition increases, interest group dominance decreases.

Key Terms

Access
Factors influencing group formation
Interest Group
Lobby (Lobbying)
One-Party state political system
Party system in Georgia
Party Organization
Political Action Committee
Political Participation
Political Party
Registration requirement
Run-off election
Voting Rights Act of 1965

Essay Questions

1. How does the Georgia State Constitution address removing public officials?
2. Why has Georgia historically been characterized as a noncompetitive one-party democratic state? Does this characterization still apply? Why/why not?
3. Who is responsible for recommending policies and procedures for their respective political parties in Georgia and how are they selected?
4. How do interest groups differ from political parties?
5. What factors influence interest groups' ability to impact public policy in Georgia?

Figure 4.1 Georgia State Capitol Building

The Legislative Branch

The most important function of the General Assembly is to pass the state's operating budget each year. In fact, approximately half of the hours spent in session are related to the budget. This includes establishing spending priorities and setting tax rates. Additionally, lawmakers must enact other laws on a broad array of topics from education to roads and transportation. Another task of the General Assembly is to consider all proposed amendments to the Georgia Constitution. A two-thirds vote in both Houses is the primary means for approving resolutions to place proposed constitutional changes on the ballot. Voters will then decide if the Constitution is to be amended.

The legislative process in Georgia has three components. First, it is a legal process governed by constitutional and statutory provisions (such as the requirement that appropriations and tax measures must originate in the House) as interpreted by state and federal court decisions. It is also a parliamentary process governed by a host of special rules of procedure that specify how legislation will be considered in each House. Finally, and perhaps most importantly, it is a political process whereby both legislators and non-legislators (particularly the Governor) compete for power and advantage.

The 151st General Assembly

The 2010 election was particularly painful for the Democratic Party (Sheinin, AJC 11/2/10). As the smoke cleared, the Democratic Party controlled only 85 of 236 seats in the House and Senate. For the first time since Reconstruction the state would have no statewide-elected democrats.

Democratic candidates lost all races above the county level, from Congress to the state's executive and legislative branches. Democrats unseated exactly one republican (State Rep. Jill Chambers of DeKalb County). A glaring statistic is that the highest vote total for any democrat (Ken Hodges in the attorney general's race) was the party's lowest *since 1998*, when the state had 1.9 million *fewer voters*. It was as if

55

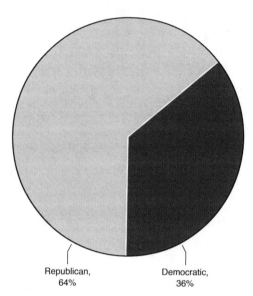

Figure 4.2   Republican Control of Assembly
Republican (64%); Democratic (36%)

every new voter in Georgia over the past 12 years had decided to vote republican. While democrats had dominated Georgia politics through one-party rule, by 2010 a noticeable decline in split-ticket voting glaringly revealed the party's weakened state.

And the democrats' problems continued to pile on (JGalloway, AJC, 12/21/11). On the day of its first meeting the republican caucus in the House grew to 109 members—its most ever—when Rep. Alan Powell, of Hartwell, switched sides. The very next day, two long-time South Georgia democratic lawmakers made the switch. Less than two weeks later, two more democrats moved to the republican side. Then, joining this parade, Sen. Tim Golden of Valdosta moved over to the republican side. Adding insult to injury, and in a move that was particularly embarrassing, Representative Doug McKillip, who had just been elected by the democratic members as Caucus Chair (the party's second highest position in the House) defected to the Republican Party. Two weeks later, Rep. Mike Cheokas of Americus joined the crowd. By the time the dust had settled, the republican caucus had grown to 114.

The problems weren't limited to democrats, as newly reelected Republican Lieutenant Governor Casey Cagle quickly discovered that ideology trumped partisanship (JGalloway, AJC, 11/6/2010). In what was billed as a "power-sharing" agreement the Senate Republican Caucus voted to strip him of his power to appoint committee chairmen, the key to his influence. Others saw this move as more of a "palace coup" by republican leaders in response to Cagle's support for a hospital tax during the prior session. Within days of the election, the caucus announced that they were going to significantly alter the power relationship between themselves and Cagle through three rules changes. These removed his power to appoint committee chairmen, the core component of the Lt. Governor's power; stripped him of his ability to determine the make-up of Senate committees; and stifled his ability to direct legislation to committees by forcing these decisions to be confirmed by the entire Senate. The real clout in the Senate devolved to an eight-member committee composed of President pro tem Tommie Williams, five GOP caucus officers, and two Senate appointees by Cagle. Cagle was expressly prohibited from membership on the committee.

All of these election results, and institutional changes, will be particularly painful throughout the decade. Apart from the general ways in which party control matters for legislative output, the 151st General Assembly is especially important due to its role in drawing new boundaries for national Representatives in the aftermath of the 2010 census. In a sign of the political nature of this task, republican leaders in the House and Senate created a new joint office to handle the process of redrawing legislative district maps, ending an established pattern of using University of Georgia researchers for the work (Sheinin, AJC, 2/4/2011). If the process continues to move away from independent non-partisan sources, and into the hands of partisans, the democrats are sure to suffer increasingly poor results in congressional elections throughout the decade.

Constitutional Construction of the General Assembly

The Georgia Constitution created a bicameral legislative branch, known as the General Assembly, composed of the Georgia House of Representatives and the Georgia Senate. Unlike the national legislative branch, however, members of both the House and Senate serve two-year terms and the entire General Assembly is up for reelection each term. The Senate is a smaller body, consisting of 56 Senators, each of whom is from a single member district. The House of Representatives has 180 Representatives, who are also elected from single-member districts.

At the beginning of each term, on the second Monday in January, the legislative session begins. Opening day is almost, literally, a circus. Owing to the differences in the legislators' geographical districts, their religious, racial, and ethnic diversity, and their differences in

Figure 4.3   The Clowns Together

occupations and their preoccupations, observing the opening day is a studied contrast in representation. The image can be amusing, as shown in Figure 4.3 and in Barber's legislative types.

As a part-time legislature, the General Assembly usually continues in session for a period of 40 working days; the 1992 session set a modern record by meeting from January 13th until March 31st. By concurrent resolution, the General Assembly may adjourn during any regular session to later dates at its own convenience, but neither House may adjourn during a regular session for more than three days or meet in any place other than the state capitol without the consent of the other House.

During special sessions, neither House may adjourn more than twice, or for more than seven days at a time. If after thirty days of a session one House adjourns without similar action by the other House, the governor may adjourn both Houses for up to ten days. However, if an impeachment trial is pending at the end of any session, the House can adjourn while the Senate remains in session until the trial is completed.

The Constitution Gives and Takes Powers

Among the specific powers granted to the legislature by the Constitution are: (1) to restrict land use in order to protect and preserve the state's natural resources and environment; (2) to maintain and regulate a state militia in cooperation with the Governor as Commander in Chief; (3) to tax, spend money, zone and condemn property to comply with federal law and grant-in-aid requirements; (4) to ensure the continuity of state and local governments in periods of emergency resulting from disasters caused by enemy attack; (5) to act in concert with any county, municipality, nonprofit organization, or any combination thereof for promoting tourism; and (6) to tax, spend money, and regulate outdoor advertising near federal highways.

On the other hand, various specific limitations are placed on the lawmaking power. Some of these are geared to economic activities. For example, the General Assembly does not have the power to grant incorporation to private persons except by formal enactment with standardized procedures, and modification of corporate charters and debts are specifically restricted. And it lacks the power to authorize any contract or agreement which may have the effect of defeating or lessening competition, or encouraging a monopoly. In addition, monopolies are declared to be unlawful and void in the State of Georgia. The General Assembly does not have the power to regulate the fees or charges of public utilities owned or operated by counties or municipalities except as authorized by the Constitution.

The drafters of the Georgia Constitution were careful to include checks and balances to ensure that state government officials would remain accountable to the people. So, on occasion, the legislature may act to remove other officials from office via the impeachment process. The process starts in the House of Representatives, which has the sole power to vote impeachment charges against any executive or judicial officer of the state or any member of the General Assembly.

The Senate has the sole power to try impeachments. When sitting as a court during impeachments the Senate is presided over by the Chief Justice of the Supreme Court. But no official can be impeached, or removed from office, unless convicted by two-thirds of the full membership. Upon such conviction, the defendant is removed from office and disqualified to hold and enjoy any office of honor, trust, or profit within the state or to receive a pension, but no other penalties are attached. However, impeachment does not relieve any party from any other criminal or civil liability.

The interesting case of the *Yazoo Land Grant Fraud* resulted in specific prohibitions against corrupt practices. Prior to ceding its territorial claims to the lands reaching to the Mississippi River, successive Georgia legislatures made and then canceled millions of acres of land grants to the Yazoo Land Company (Current, 211). When the 1796 legislature attempted to void the land grant, the United States Supreme Court used the case of *Fletcher v. Peck (1810)* to void the state law, on grounds of "no impairment of contracts" (Current, 271). Since then, except as specifically permitted, the General Assembly may not grant any donation or gratuity or forgive any debt or obligation owing to the public, and it cannot grant or authorize extra compensation to any public officer, agent, or contractor after the contract has been formalized or performed. Similarly, Article III of the Constitution specifically vests the power to issue insurance licenses to the Commissioner of Insurance instead of to the legislature perse.

Constitutional Requirements for Members of the General Assembly

At the time of their election, the members of the Senate must be citizens of the United States, at least 25 years of age, citizens of Georgia for two years, and residents within their districts for at least one year. The members of the House of Representatives must meet similar requirements, except that they need to be only 21 years old when elected to office. Each Senator and Representative, before taking his or her legislative seat, must take an oath or affirmation as required by law. But some people who meet these qualifications are still not eligible for office, such as persons recently convicted of felonies; or persons holding civil offices under the United States, or who are on active duty with any branch of the armed forces of the United States. The latter provision is to avoid conflicts of interest and competing loyalties.

During their terms of office, legislators may not hold another state office. Except for a few leadership posts, they cannot be elected by the General Assembly or appointed by the Governor to any office or appointment having any "emolument annexed thereto" (salary or stipend), unless they resign their seat. And they may not be appointed to any civil office created during their term of office. Each House is the sole judge of the elections of their members. When a vacancy occurs, it is filled by the Governor as provided by the Constitution and by statute.

Paying Members of the General Assembly

The pay of the members of the General Assembly is set by the legislature itself, but no increases in salary can take effect until the next session. Currently, legislators receive their $17,342 annual salary and they may receive up to $6,900 for expenses during the annual legislative session. The expenses are known as per diem accounts and a mini-scandal arose in 2010 because of them.

One of the perks of being a member of the General Assembly is the per diem that pays some lawmakers more than $20,000 per year for travel and expenses while performing government duties (Sheinin, AJC, 4/13/10). This money is granted with little oversight, minimal auditing, and few questions asked. A 2010 analysis found that lawmakers had billed the state for travel and expenses on more than one out of every four days while the General Assembly was out of session in 2008, 2009, and the first few months of 2010. Overall, their study found, members of the General Assembly billed the state for nearly $3.6 million in so-called per diem payments from January 1, 2008, through March 19, 2010.

The per diem payment system is justified in a state where the 180 members of the House and 56 members of the Senate are part-time legislators who meet for 40 days in an annual legislative session that can stretch for four months or more. But their obligations don't end when the gavel falls on *sine die,* marking the end of the session. And the demands are greater on top leadership and the heads of key committees. In the so-called offseason, many serve on special committees charged with studying a particular policy area or in regular committees, like Transportation, which often meets throughout the year in search of the elusive fix to the state's traffic woes. Constituent needs, too, don't end when the session ends. The per diem system is designed to compensate lawmakers when they must take time off from work and travel, in some cases, hundreds of miles to Atlanta for off-session work. Most legislators, too, have taken furlough days to help cut costs.

The system, however, is largely self-policed. Say it's July and a lawmaker needs to drive from his home district to the Capitol for a meeting. If the legislator is a rank-and-file member, he is supposed to first ask his committee chairman to approve the per diem payment. But every lawmaker can get per diem payments for up to seven days a year with no questions asked. Those days are known as a "committee of one days." If the lawmaker's committee chair signs off on the expense, the lawmaker comes to Atlanta and does his business. He then signs a voucher saying he worked that particular day and lists how many miles he drove. The voucher gets submitted to the Legislative Fiscal Office, and the lawmaker gets paid. Committee chairmen said the requests are largely on the "honor" system, although it is a crime to claim unearned expenses.

Lawmakers don't have to submit receipts to justify the $173 expense or keep a mileage log or even document the mileage driven. But once a month, the Fiscal Office produces a report detailing how much each lawmaker was paid in travel and expenses. In the House, the report goes to the chairman of the Committee on Information and Audits. In the Senate, it goes to chairman of the Rules Committee.

Most members of the General Assembly are in a difficult position. They are expected to be at the Capitol for 40 days of session, but even that is misleading. For example, the House and Senate may meet only on Monday, Tuesday, and Wednesday but there are also committee meetings on Thursday, even though Thursday doesn't count against the 40-day countdown. In the offseason, too, there are constituent concerns or occasions when local community groups make pilgrimages to the Capitol. They often expect their local lawmaker to show them around. As one member said, "Some people, they'll do it for nothing. They just won't get paid that day. I've got a job. I've got a business to run."

Public Attitudes Toward the General Assembly

Students of legislative politics are fond of quoting Nelson Polsby's statement that, "we hate Congress while we love our own congressmen." This is because our representative is a statesman; theirs is a politician. Ours is an astute fiscal manager; theirs is a spendthrift. Ours tends to the people's business; theirs plays around. The legislative circus would be really sound and reasonable, except for the fact that this odd collection of other peoples' representatives controls the state's purse strings, the taxing, and spending policies.

However, quite apart from this national finding, Georgians tend to show indifference toward the General Assembly rather than anger or contempt. A 2002 online questionnaire administered by the Marketing Workshop for the Atlanta Journal-Constitution revealed that respondents found the General Assembly to be largely irrelevant to their daily lives and that these respondents were paying little or no attention to what the legislature was doing (AJC, 1/14/02). Less than a third were paying a lot or some attention, and only sixteen percent found the decisions made by the legislature to be very or somewhat relevant to their daily lives.

The General Assembly's Leadership

The General Assembly is composed of both party leaders and positions created by the Georgia Constitution which created three major legislative officials in each chamber. The Senate is governed by President of the Senate (who is also the Lt. Governor); a President Pro Tempore, to preside when the Lt. Governor is absent and to act as President in case of the temporary or permanent disability of that official; and a Secretary of the Senate is also selected to maintain its official records. The primary officers of the House of Representatives are the Speaker of the House of Representatives; a Speaker Pro Tempore, elected to preside when the Speaker is absent; and a Clerk of the House who is chosen to oversee the maintenance of the records of that chamber.

General Assembly Responsibilities

The duties of the General Assembly include not only legislation but responsibility for the general welfare of the people of the state. Because of the obligation of each branch to maintain separation of powers, the Constitution requires the legislature to protect its prerogatives. The General Assembly cannot abridge its own powers, nor can any law enacted by the General Assembly be construed by the courts as acting to limit its powers.

Two major tasks of the General Assembly are to consider legislation and to enact law. Legislative proposals for new laws (bills) must go through a complex process before becoming law. Many bills never make it. The majority of bills are sponsored and introduced in the House, but the General Assembly may provide by law for the joint sponsorship of bills and resolutions.

First, in order to transact official business a quorum is necessary, which must consist of a majority of the members of each chamber. However, a smaller number may adjourn from day to day and compel the presence of its absent members. Each house determines its own rules of procedure and regulates its own employees.

General Assembly and Committees

Because legislation is so complex in modern society, the real work of the legislature is done in interim committees instead of on the floor of one or the other legislative chamber. Legislators can then specialize in areas which interest their constituents. By creating committees, each house in the General Assembly divides their membership into

Figure 4.4 General Assembly Leadership

House of Representatives		Senate	
Majority	Minority	Majority	Minority
Speaker of the House David Ralston	Minority Leader Stacey Abrams	President Casey Cagle, Lt. Gov	Minority Leader Robert Brown
Speaker Pro-Tempore Jan Jones	Minority Whip Carolyn Hugley	President Pro Tempore Tommie Williams	Minority Caucus Chair Tim Golden
Majority Leader Larry O'Neal	Minority Caucus Chairman Brian Thomas	Majority Leader Chip Rogers	Minority Whip Vacant
Majority Whip Edward Lindsey	Minority Caucus Vice Chairman Rashad Taylor	Majority Caucus Chair Bill Cowsert	
Majority Caucus Chairman Donna Sheldon	Minority Caucus Secretary Stephanie Stuckey Benfield	Majority Whip John Wiles	
Majority Caucus Vice Chairman Matt Ramsey			

Source: Information taken from Georgia General Assembly Website numerous small groups that specialize in one broad policy topic. This allows for members of the Assembly to position themselves within areas that are of special concern to their constituents and for the opportunity to more closely study bills than would be possible solely during a debate on the floor. Committees can be thought of as the legislative arenas in which the preliminary arena in which the committee will hear from the legislator who introduced the bill, other legislators who either favor or oppose the bill. Committees also go outside the General Assembly to learn the opinion of interests or persons concerned with a policy position. Committees are provided with very strong powers and can subpoena witnesses and records.

The General Assembly has four types of committees. The first is the standing committee. Standing committees are established by the Senate and the House of Representatives for the management of their business. They are established by authority of rules separately adopted by the Senate and by the House. The appointment of committee members, chairs, and vice-chairs occurs at the beginning of each new term. The committee then has the responsibility of vetting the legislation. Each committee considers legislation within its field of expertise.

The second type of committee is study committees. These are committees that have been appointed or selected to perform a specific task or study a specific issue and meet year-round. As they examine these issues, reports are released which include any findings, recommendations, or legislative proposals a committee deems appropriate. Legislative study committees have become a forum for leaders concerned about public policy to stay active. While moving legislation to a study committee in the Georgia General Assembly was often the political equivalent of being banished to Siberia, study committees are increasingly at work in public where they gather facts and provide forums for lively debate and public input.

The third type of committee is conference committees. Conference committees are a response to the constitutional requirement that, to become an Act, it must be passed by both Houses in precisely the same words and figures. In the case of significant bills, with substantial differences, the shortcut of a conference committee likely will be taken almost immediately. The use of conference committees reflects an ability to reconcile differences between the two chambers and suggests a give-and-take process because if the conference would be stalemated, the bill could fail. Each conference committee is composed of three members from the Senate and three members from the House of Representatives, chosen by the Standing Committee responsible for the bill. As a separate committee, they vote separately, not only on the final product but on any subsidiary questions put to a vote. A majority of the committee prevails.

Once a conference committee votes, it issues a "Conference Committee Report." These are presented to both the Senate and House and they must either accept or reject the Report in its entirety without amendments. While Reports will occasionally be rejected, causing it to be sent back to conference, they are generally submitted in the final hours of a session when the shortness of time might mean the bill would be lost or the General Assembly called into an extended or special session. Because of their strategic capability, conference committees can be used by party leaders to pressure their memberships.

The fourth type of committees are joint committees, standing or special, which are composed of both House and Senate members. They usually address current controversial topics of interest for many interest groups. If they last over several session, they are standing, if they last just one session, they are special. Actually, every conference committee is a unique joint committee.

The General Assembly and "The Art of the Possible"

Politics is often called the *"Art of the Possible."* Very often well-intentioned but naive people ask the state legislature to pass a law that is realistically impossible, politically unfeasible, or simply stupid. Since legislators cannot tell their constituents that they are unwise or unintelligent, they have devised ways to *"kill"* a bill without triggering a confrontation with the voters. Two time-honored ways of doing this are to bury it in a committee, or to send it to some other group for study and evaluation. Each session of the Georgia legislature creates dozens of these so-called study commissions or task forces whose real job is to bury the new ideas. Sometimes they will issue reports, but often the proposed material simply vanishes without a trace, and the legislators are off the hook.

Legislative bills can be enacted only if they are approved by a majority vote of all the members of both Houses. In either House, when ordered by the presiding officer or at the desire of one-fifth of the members present, a roll-call vote on any question must be taken and officially recorded in the journal. For appropriation bills, or on any issue requiring a two-thirds vote, each separate yea and nay vote is recorded. After a general bill has cleared the committee process, and reached the floor for debate, its title must be read three times and on three separate days in each House before it can be voted on; and the third reading of such bill and resolution must be in the entirety when ordered by the presiding officer or by a majority of the members voting on the bill.

Once a bill has been passed by both Houses it must be signed by both the President of the Senate and the Speaker of the House of Representatives before being sent to the Governor. No bill can become law unless the Governor signs it or fails to act upon it within six days from its transmission to the Governor, except where it is passed over the Governor's veto. Sometimes the General Assembly adjourns *sine die* or adjourns for more than 40 days prior to the expiration of the six day period. In such cases, the bill becomes law if approved or not vetoed by the Governor within 40 days from the date of any such adjournment. Unlike the U.S. Constitution, the Georgia Constitution does not provide for an executive pocket veto.

If the Governor does veto a bill and if the legislature is still in session, the bill must be returned within three days, along with the reasons for the veto, to the presiding officer of the House where it originated. But if the General Assembly had adjourned *sine die,* or adjourned for more than 40 days, the Governor has 60 days to return it. However, in modern times the legislature has never lasted that long.

During legislative sessions, any vetoed bill or resolution may upon receipt be immediately considered by the originating House for the purpose of overriding the veto. If two-thirds of the membership votes to override the veto, and the other House does the same, it becomes law despite the Governor's opposition. In the rare cases where bills and resolutions are vetoed during the last three days of the session and not reconsidered for overriding, the General Assembly can consider the issue at its next yearly session.

The General Assembly and Open Government

Georgia is especially sensitive to the desires of the citizens for open government. The State Constitution requires that sessions of the General Assembly and all standing committee meetings shall be open to the public, except where reasons of public policy justify. Each House has power to punish members for disorderly behavior or misconduct. This punishment can include censure or monetary fines, and in extreme cases even imprisonment or expulsion. However, no member can be expelled except by a vote of two-thirds of their fellow members. Just prior to the opening of the 1998 session of the General Assembly State Senator Ralph David Abernathy III, the son of the Civil Rights leader whose name he shares, was arrested for attempting to smuggle a small amount of marijuana into the country through Hartsfield Airport in Atlanta. The Customs Service confiscated the substance and imposed a small fine on the Senator, which reports indicated was a routine punishment for a first and minor infraction.

However, the Senate moved to censure the Senator, and Republicans, particularly in the House, moved to impeach Abernathy, arguing that he had brought disrespect to the entire General Assembly. By the end of the session nothing had come of the impeachment attempt.

The General Assembly and Home Rule

As might be expected according to the individualistic side of its culture, Georgia has a strong commitment to home rule, which is defined as giving primary power to local authorities. While the General Assembly can enact laws overriding local legislation these bills not only require the usual reading requirements, the rules also stipulate that no such bill or resolution can be voted upon prior to the second day following the day of introduction, and the General Assembly must advertise a notice of intention to introduce specific local bills. This reflects Georgia's localistic traditions.

Laws of a general nature always have uniform operation throughout the state, and preempt the enactment of local and special laws, except that the General Assembly may by general law authorize local governments to use their powers of local ordinance or resolution to exercise police powers, as long as they do not conflict with the general laws. This encourages flexibility.

No personal or population bills can be passed. Partly because of fears of rural versus city politics, and partly out of fears of favoritism, the State Constitution prohibits any bill using classification by size of population as a means of determining the applicability of any bill or law to any political subdivision, or as a means of using size to amend or repeal the general law. Similarly, no special law relating to the rights or status of particular private persons can be enacted.

The General Assembly and the 2000 Census

Few things so engage the attention of a legislator as the necessity for redrawing electoral district boundaries after a national census. Because Georgia's population is increasing, it qualified after the 1990 Census for a new 11th Congressional District. Many people are concerned about redistricting changes, and the state lawmakers are not often given a free hand. Georgia is one of fifteen states whose proposed election law changes are reviewed by the U.S. Justice Department.

In January of 1992, Georgia lawmakers were shocked when the U.S. Justice Department rejected the proposed redistricting maps for

Figure 4.5   Process by Which a Bill Moves Through the General Assembly

Senate	House
IDEA Conceived by Legislator, Legislative Committees, citizens, groups of citizens or copied from another state. **DRAFTING** Bills are drafted by Legislative Counsel and entered into legislative management system. **INTRODUCTION AND FIRST READING** Filed by a Senator with Secretary of the Senate who assigns it a number and prints. On next legislative day, read first time and referred to Committee by President of the Senate. Bills are routinely assigned by subject matter; discretion lies with President. **COMMITTEE ACTION** Committee considers and studies Bill, receives expert testimony and hears from all interested parties. Committee alternatives are to: (1) Recommend Bill or Resolution Do Pass; (2) Recommend Do NOT Pass; (3) Recommend Do Pass with changes (amendments or substitutes); (4) Hold Bill. Final Committee action reported to the Senate in a written report. **SECOND READING** Bill read second time on legislative day following Committee report. **THIRD READING AND PASSAGE** The following legislative day, third reading and debate; amendments and substitutes adopted; final vote taken by roll call and recorded on passage of all General Bills. **TRANSMITTAL TO HOUSE** Bill then Engrossed, signed by the Secretary of the Senate and transmitted to the House of Representatives.	**FIRST READING** Bill read first time and referred to Committee by Speaker of the House. **SECOND READING** On next legislative day, read second time. **COMMITTEE ACTION** Committee considers and studies Bill, receives expert testimony and hears from all interested parties. Committee alternatives are: (1) Recommend Bill or Resolution Do Pass; (2) Recommend Do NOT Pass; (3) Recommend Do Pass with changes (amendments or substitutes); (4) Report without recommendation; (5) Hold Bill. Final Committee action reported to the House in a written report. **THIRD READING AND PASSAGE** The following legislative day, third reading and debate; amendments and substitutes adopted and final vote taken. **TRANSMITTAL BACK TO SENATE** Bill signed by the Clerk of the House of Representatives and transmitted back to the Senate. If House makes changes, Senate must agree or disagree to changes. If the two Houses fail to reach agreement on a measure, a Conference Committee may be established with three members from each House appointed by the Presiding Officer. To complete passage, both Houses must agree to report of Conference Committee.

Source: Information taken from Georgia General Assembly Website

Georgia, which had been drawn up nearly seven months earlier. The rejection letter, signed by Assistant Attorney General John R. Dunne, said that the state's pattern of "racially polarized voting . . . appears to be exacerbated" by the proposed plans (Cook, A1). As a result of this federal bureaucratic decision, State House and Senate district maps, as well as U.S. Congressional district maps, were thrown back on the drawing board.

There were two reasons for the rejection: that they worked to benefit incumbents and that the proposed districts minimized black voting strength. The problem areas involved southern rural Baldwin, Dougherty, Houston, and Peach Counties; and growing minority areas in suburban Atlanta Counties such as Clayton, Cobb, and Fayette. Overall, the Justice Department found fault with the legislative plans for almost all of Georgia south of Interstate 20. Since the Georgia Legislature was in session, the House and Senate reapportionment committees immediately scheduled action on the matter. One prominent politician agreed that some white incumbents had benefitted from the legislatively crafted districts (Cook, A1).

While State Rep. Tyrone Brooks (D-Atlanta) a critic of the proposed redistricting proposal, said voters should be angry with the legislators, not the Justice Department, another legislator took a different view. State Sen. Gene Walker (D-DeKalb), chairman of the Senate Reapportionment Committee, said "I'm disappointed in the kind of tone they used. I'm black, and I'm not a racist." The Lt. Governor, Pierre Howard, also was disappointed at the federal bureaucratic ruling, saying that the legislature had tried to follow the federal Voting Rights Act (Walston, A8).

One state legislator took the high moral ground. State Sen. Don Johnson, announced candidate for the proposed new 10th Congressional District seat, said he would ask Lt. Governor Pierre Howard to take him off the map-drawing reapportionment committee to avoid potential conflicts of interest. He also chaired the Senate Appropriations Committee (Staff, A5). The authors are forced to conclude that charges of gerrymandering are perhaps an inescapable part of Georgia politics. The constitutionality of gerrymandering the new 11th Congressional District was challenged in 1994. The case was brought for a decision to a federal panel of three judges and alleged that this majority black district, stretching from Stone Mountain to Savannah (approximately two hundred and sixty miles) was neither compact nor contiguous as the high court had required. In 1996, the U.S. Supreme Court in *Miller v. Johnson* held that the 11th District, which had been drawn with racial politics in mind, was unconstitutional, and its boundaries must be redrawn.

With the *Miller v. Johnson* decision very much on their minds, the members of the Georgia General Assembly had to revisit the reapportionment "political thicket" following the 2000 Census. Since the U.S. Supreme Court had stated that race could not be the sole criterion for drawing or redrawing district boundaries, the question on the minds of the legislators was the degree to which race *could* count. Democrats, who controlled both Houses, assumed that race would count for a whole lot less than it had previously, and that reapportionment maps that did not move large numbers of African-Americans into a few districts, as they had after the 1990 Census, would pass constitutional muster. Republicans argued that districts that did not guarantee black victories discriminated on the basis of race, meaning that fewer overwhelmingly black districts meant fewer republican districts. Besides, a new Bush Administration controlled the Department of Justice in Washington to which the maps, it was assumed, would have to go for "preclearance" (see Chapter Three) under the Voting Rights Act.

But the democrats had an unexpected ace up their sleeves. Rather than submitting their reapportionment maps to the Civil Rights Division of the Department of Justice, they bypassed the bureaucracy and took the new district plans to the Federal District Court for the District of Columbia, an option always available but seldom exercised. Republicans cried foul and asked that four Georgia voters, represented by republican lawyers, be allowed to testify in the trial before the Federal District Court for D.C. That was permitted, but had little bearing on the outcome. The maps for thirteen new congressional districts—Georgia gained two additional districts in the 2000 Census—and all 180 state House districts were approved by the Court. An issue was raised regarding the map for the state Senate districts, contending that their construction diluted black voting strength in Savannah, Albany, and Macon, and the Federal Court ordered the Georgia General Assembly to respond. It quickly did so, redrawing the lines in compliance with the Court's order, and the matter was resolved (*http://www.ajc.com*, 1/31/02). The upshot of this reapportionment fracas is that democrats expected to win a majority of congressional seats in the 2002 election, and continue to control both Houses of the General Assembly. Neither expectation came true. They lost control of the House, and while the number of seats they controlled did increase to five, the number of seats controlled by the Republicans stayed at eight.

The General Assembly and Appropriations and Budgets

Another issue raises almost as much smoke and fire—the appropriation and budgeting process. Funding for education, the biggest single expenditure of Georgia State Government, also engages the avid attention of dutiful legislators. The complex funding formulas are a ripe area for legislative debate.

Since the British barons forced King John to sign the Magna Carta, it has been truly said that the power of the legislature is the power of the purse. As is traditional in former British colonies, all bills for raising revenue, or appropriating money, originate in the most representative body of the legislature; in Georgia this is the House of Representatives. More is presented on this topic in Chapter Eight: Budgeting and Finance.

However, the power of the purse is somewhat restricted in Georgia, which gives some strong budgetary powers to the Chief Executive. An important feature of the Georgia Constitution is that it requires the Governor to play a major legislative role. Within five days after the legislature convenes, the Governor must submit a budget message and a budget report, accompanied by a draft of a general appropriations bill. This bill must provide for the appropriation of the funds necessary to operate all the various state departments and agencies, and to meet the current expenses of the state for the next fiscal year.

In addition, the Constitution strictly prohibits riders on appropriation bills. Every bill must have a descriptive title, and no bill which refers to more than one subject matter can pass. Furthermore, no law or section of the State Code can be amended or repealed by mere reference to its title or to its number. The Constitution places precise restrictions on the way the legislature handles the finances of state government. The most important provision is that no money can be drawn from the treasury except by appropriation made by law.

Ultimately, the General Assembly is responsible for annual appropriation of state funds necessary to operate the state government. In addition, the state budget must include federal funds as well. To the extent that federal funds received by the state for various programs and projects exceed the amount appropriated in the general appropriations Act, these federal funds are appropriated by the state according to federal rules. The fiscal year of the state begins on the first day of July of each year and terminates on the thirtieth day of June in the following year. The budget for State Fiscal Year 2007 is well over $18 billion dollars.

The scope of the general appropriations bill is strictly defined by Constitutional provision. Revenues appropriated by this bill can include only: (1) materials fixed by previous laws; (2) the ordinary expenses of the executive, legislative, and judicial branches and bureaucratic departments; (3) payment of the public debt and interest thereon; and (4) support of the public institutions and educational interests of the state. All other appropriations must be made by separate bills, and each such bill can only embrace one subject.

Each annual general appropriations Act can continue in effect for only one fiscal year after adoption, after which it expires and a new one must be enacted. There is no perpetual funding in Georgia. In brief, the State of Georgia is required to balance its operational budget. The General Assembly cannot appropriate funds for any given fiscal year which exceed anticipated revenues and on-hand surpluses, as estimated in the Governor's Budget Report. Supplementary appropriations, if any, also cannot exceed these limits unless based on a tax base and collections, and these appropriations expire along with the annual appropriations. Neither House can pass a supplementary appropriation bill until the general appropriations Act has been finally adopted by both Houses and approved by the Governor.

All such appropriations must be made for specific sums, and no appropriation can allocate to any object the proceeds of any particular tax or fund unless the Constitution permits an exception. One major exception is money derived from gasoline and motor fuel taxes, which are set aside for providing and maintaining an adequate system of public roads and bridges in the state. Of course, in times of emergency, these rules are relaxed. In the event of invasion of the state by enemies, or in case of a major catastrophe, including even the economic disaster of the great Recession of 2008, state funds may be utilized for defense or relief purposes according to the Governor's Executive Orders.

Other exceptions to the annual appropriations bill include the creation and administration of a trust fund for workers' compensation injuries and disabilities. And in any case in which any court imposes a fine or orders the forfeiture of any bond, the proceeds may be allocated for the specific purpose of providing training to law enforcement officers and to prosecuting officials. Another exception allows the General Assembly, by a three-fifths' vote of both houses, to designate any part or all of the proceeds of any state tax on alcoholic beverages to be used for prevention, education, and treatment relating to alcohol and drug abuse.

Public funds may be expended for the purpose of paying benefits and costs of retirement and pension systems for public officers and employees and their beneficiaries; and to establish or modify local retirement systems covering employees of county boards of education. The General Assembly may pass appropriations bills for the purpose of paying for a firemen's pension system. In these cases, the legislature must define funding standards which will assure the actuarial soundness of these retirement or pension systems.

In addition to the power of drafting the initial general appropriations bill, the Governor of Georgia has an item veto over appropriations bills passed by the General Assembly. The Governor may approve any appropriation and veto any other appropriation in the same bill, and any appropriation vetoed is eliminated unless the General Assembly overrides the item veto. Despite the powers of the Governor, the General Assembly remains very powerful.

Conclusion

At the beginning of every year, the old experienced hands and the newly elected freshmen converge on the Gold Dome in the sprawling city of Atlanta. They assemble with fire in their eyes, missions in their hearts, and IOU's in their pockets. As a group, they represent diverse economic and geographical interests. When one considers the vast differences in the legislator's occupational backgrounds, and their religious, racial, and ethnic diversity, it is a wonder that they can get together on anything. But when they do act, exercising the power of the purse, they are a potent force in Georgia's state politics.

Key Terms

Appropriations
Home Rule
Joint Committee
Multi-Member District
Sine Die
Single-Member District
Standing Committee
Miller v. Johnson

Essay Questions

1. In spite of the fact that the Republican Party has recently dominated the Georgia legislature, there is demographic diversity among legislators. Discuss this diversity and address how it relates to Georgians' perception of their legislature.
2. In what way(s) does the committee structure within the Georgia General Assembly impact or facilitate the passage of bills?
3. How does a bill become a law in the state of Georgia?
4. In what way(s) has the federal system in the United States impacted legislative reapportionment in the state of Georgia? How does this relate to the U.S. Supreme Court case, *Miller v. Johnson?*
5. How does the Governor of Georgia impact legislative appropriations?

Figure 5.1 The Governor's Mansion

The Plural Executive of Georgia

The Governor of Georgia

The Governor of the State of Georgia, Nathan Deal, is the heir to not only Governor Perdue, but also to untold generations of native tribal chieftains. Creek and Cherokee peoples were living in the region prior to the European discovery of the lands of the western hemisphere (W. Almanac, 2010, p. 584); after which the lands and territories of what was to become Georgia came under the doubtful assertions of control and dominion by several royal Spanish Viceroys. While earlier leaders of the area now known as Georgia would have based their personal power on might of arms or sycophancy, modern Georgia chief executives owe their positions to popular elections. The modern governor is the ultimate successor to James Oglethorpe, Proprietor and Trustee of the British colony of Georgia, and after him to the three Proprietary Presidents, three Royal British governors, and to seventeen post-colonial and pre-federal state governors. Many of the political traditions of our pre-historic and colonial peoples still influence the state in the modern era.

In addition, the Georgia Governor is the inheritor of the legacies of twenty-five pre-civil war governors, five wartime governors, and thirty-seven governors since the Civil War. In short, the modern chief executive is the latest of a long and distinguished line of Georgia governors, and presides over the most prosperous, largest population that the state of Georgia has ever had. This is not a history book, but a political science textbook, so it focuses on how political affairs function in the State of Georgia in the present day. Unlike many predecessors, and unlike the federal President, the Governor of the State of Georgia is not an all-powerful unitary chief executive. Instead of presiding over a responsive bureaucracy directed by their personal appointees, Georgia Governors must contend with a pluralistic structure directed by a variety of separately elected officials and a variety of appointed administrators. Thus, instead of a simple pyramidal power

77

structure, culminating in one person, the apex of the Georgia State Government structure resembles an oval crown with many points and no center of gravity. The other elected officials often contest the power of the governor. Many of these other officials are topical experts who control their own separate administrative agencies. This complex structure is a main reason for declaring that the present Constitution of Georgia has created a bureaucratic governmental system. How can the Governor effectively initiate policy in this system?

These other elected executives include the Lieutenant Governor, who presides over the Senate; the Secretary of State, who has widely ranging administrative duties; the Attorney General who presides over the Department of Law; the State School Superintendent; and the Commissioners of Agriculture, Insurance and Labor, each presiding over their own departments. These officials are separately elected by the people and do not have to belong to the same party or share the same political philosophy as the Governor. The result is often a lack of coordination, administrative headaches, and political conflict. Today, even though the Republican Party has in fact swept the polls to dominate the legislative and executive branches of government, much in-fighting and policy maneuvering still occur. How will our newly elected Governor cope with the challenges facing the state today?

To make things more complex, in addition to the individual elected officials, there are various constitutional boards and commissions which run their own specialized agencies. These include the state's Public Service Commission, the State Transportation Board, the State Board of Pardons and Paroles, the State Personnel Board, the Veterans Service Board and the Board of Natural Resources. Generally, the boards function as committees with administrative powers defined in the Constitution and therefore largely independently of the Governor's formal control. Each board has its own chairman, who presides over meetings and who has the power to break tying votes. Some of these boards are separately elected by the people of Georgia in general elections, some are elected by legislators, and some are appointed by the Governor with the advice and confirmation of the Senate. Governor Deal needs to try to coordinate these many different administrative actors if he hopes to address the economic problems that face the state today. How will he cope with our aging infrastructure, the growing water shortage problem, immigration pressures, and the many other issues confronting him?

The Powers of the Governor

With such a wide variety of executive officers sharing power, it may be surprising that the Governor of Georgia has been ranked among the more influential governors in the U.S.A. But although the formal powers are only moderate (Gray and Jacob, 202), the Governor of Georgia has informal power based on that fact that the office enjoys high prestige (Hepburn, 147). There are two reasons for this ranking. In one classical analysis of power, an Italian scholar suggested that when a ruler can rely on strong formal powers and resources to solve problems, those powers should be used vigorously. But when the formal powers of the ruler are insufficient, a wise ruler must use guile to achieve goals. In short, a prince must sometimes act like a lion, and sometimes like a fox (Machiavelli, 91). The key to the success of a Georgia Governor is how well he can balance these two sources of power.

In Georgia, with its history of suspicion of strong chief executives, its oppressive historical experiences, and many reform constitutions restricting the Governor's formal powers, guile became a necessary qualification for the job. But there was an additional pillar of support for a wily Governor: Georgia's strong element of consensus politics in its long-time one-party system. The prestige of the Governor, both as titular head of government and as chief of the dominant political party, enabled the incumbent to influence events even when the formal powers might have been inadequate. This is as true today, with a newly resurgent republican dominance, as it has been for the Democratic Party which recently lost the loyalty of voters.

The Constitution of the State of Georgia specifies that the chief executive powers shall be vested in the Governor. These formal powers enable the Governor to exploit several avenues of power and influence. The power and influence of governors depends on their facility in playing various political roles. Perhaps most important of all these roles is his visibility as a mythical and symbolic leader, linked with the expectations of the general public. In this capacity, the Governor interacts with other state leaders and agencies, with cities and other states, and with the federal government, and sometimes foreign powers. In fulfilling these roles, the Governor is acting as an intergovernmental middleman, a fulcrum of power, and a center of political gravity.

In our federal system of government, the middleman role is complex. In the beginning, the system could be described as dual federalism, with separate spheres of responsibilities for state governments and the federal government, a sort of *layer cake* model. Until the Civil War, there was little overlap. But in time, as the states agreed to amend the Constitution of the United States, a more complex cooperative federalism developed, with commingling spheres, like a *marble cake* (Wilson, 67). This is especially true regarding economic powers, and with the exercise of our civil rights and liberties.

This cooperative federalism is characterized by a vertical bureaucratization of programs in the United States (Beer). In fact, every public policy with implementing programs is manifested at every level of government, and they are all functionally integrated, with costs shared by all three levels: federal, state, and local. One author suggested a *picket fence* model, in which the three "rails" of local, state, and federal government are crossed by a wide variety of policy arena "slats" (Nice, 10). However, this model does not help to explain how the "middleman" concept glues the components of the system together.

The authors suggest an *apple pie* or perhaps *peach cobbler* model of government, emphasizing the sticky unity of our federal system. In this model, we start with a heavy foundation of dough, filled with nuts and fruits and sweets, crisscrossed on top with more intersecting lines of doughy influence, some horizontal to reflect the various levels of government, and some vertical to reflect the varied organized interest groups and policy concerns seeking favorable acceptance by decision makers. This complex mixture is put under tremendous heat and pressure (see the *melting pot*), and the result is government like *apple pie*. In this cooperative model, the governor is the only state official with the power and visibility to influence the mixture, soften the impact of the nuts, and suggest the amount of dough to be used, to determine the consistency of the final product, and when to apply the heat to bring it to political completion.

The Chief Executive of a state has various roles to play. To be an effective governor, Nathan Deal will have to function as formal head of state (FHS), chief executive officer (CEO), chief financial officer (CFO), chief legislator, the commander of our state police and national guard forces, chief diplomat, and chief representative of the people. But he will not be the only legislator, he shares that role with the Lieutenant Governor, Casey Cagle. Nor is he the top lawyer, that elected position is the Attorney General, Samuel S. Olens. Similarly, the person who oversees educational functions in the state, which comprise the largest part of the state's overall operating budget, is yet another official, State School Superintendent, John D. Barge. The Governor has to be a wily fox to get his way, because these other officials do not simply take orders from the Governor of Georgia.

The Chief Executive of a state has various roles to play, and one of the most important of these is Head of State, ceremonial and ritual leader, serving as the focus of identification of all the people of the state. To some, it came as a bit of a surprise when Governor Miller attacked the state flag during his State of the State speech to the 1993 legislative session. In Georgia the flag issue has varying symbolic importance to different groups. Miller argued that the flag was

Figure 5.2   Choosing Today's Role
Source: Adapted by Authors

There are many other popular and separately elected officials, which are discussed later in this chapter. Nonetheless, the governor is the vital linchpin, and he can pick and choose the roles he plays to maximize his effectiveness.

adopted in 1956 to include the Confederate battle cross in opposition to court rulings for school desegregation (Winder, 5). This raised a storm of controversy: does the flag exist for internal purposes of uniting and representing people within the state, for representing the complex history and traditions of the state, or for the external purpose of representing the state to the outside world to maximize tourism, trade, and economic growth?

Miller's proposal to change the flag to reduce the prominence of the Confederate Stars and Bars was introduced into the Georgia State Senate, which wisely decided that so potent an issue should be referred directly to the voters, and passed Senate Bill 71 calling for a public referendum on the issue. But with an increasing level of anxiety, the House Speaker at the time, Thomas Murphy, and other leaders could not support the measure. Especially troubling to many powerful state politicians was the decision by various local government bodies, some controlled by African-American representatives, to refuse to fly the state flag, the first being the Atlanta-Fulton County Recreation Authority, which voted to remove the flag from the Atlanta-Fulton County Stadium, then the home of the Atlanta Braves baseball team (Salzer, D1). Finally Governor Miller requested that the House take no action on the matter, citing constitutional issues and costs. He summarized the issue by declaring: *"I made the fight and I lost the fight"* (Winder, 8). Politically, it had become a "no-win" situation, and the Governor would never bring it up again.

But while Governor Miller would never touch the flag issue again, his successor, Governor Barnes, was not so reluctant. Early on in the 2001 legislative session, Barnes announced to a somewhat stunned General Assembly that he was bringing up the flag issue again and, just a week after it was introduced, Barnes called for a vote. Both democrats and republicans were caught off balance. Most democrats followed the lead of the Governor. Most republicans did not. On January 31, 2001, Barnes signed H.B. 16, adopting a new compromise flag that reduced the stars and bars flag to a little banner, among other flags, at the bottom of a flag with the state seal in a blue field and with three broad stripes. To look at these flags, go to *http://www.sos.ga.gov/ museum/html/georgia_flag_history.html.*

Some democrats who voted against the Governor and some who did not vote at all complained that the flag issue should have been decided in a referendum, which the Governor claimed was unconstitutional. Most republicans, except for a number from the metro Atlanta area, agreed that a referendum was the proper way to go. Prompting the opposition to changing the flag were the public opinion polls indicating an even split between Georgians over changing the state flag. However, on closer inspection, the evenness of the issue broke down. While only 37 percent of Georgia's majority white population approved of the change, 78 percent of African-American Georgians supported it. Governor Barnes figured that if the issue was not resolved immediately, it would have poisoned the legislative well for the remainder of the session. Although his haste, and the heavy-handed manner in which he would exercise it, would further contribute to his reputation as "King Roy," Governor Barnes had managed to boost the reputation of the state externally as the progressive "Empire State of the South" without, he thought, doing great damage to his political career. In fact, it was argued that since the republicans had to tone down their support for leaving the old flag alone, for fear of being labeled racist and mean-spirited, the Governor had really won a major victory on all fronts.

But the matter did not end there. Many would contend that the new Georgia flag was ugly and meaningless, with its inclusion of previous state flags and the U.S. flag so small as to be virtually unnoticeable at the bottom of a yellow banner in a blue background. But flags are not usually judged for their aesthetic appearance. It is their symbolism that makes them important to the people over whom they fly.

And, while after the September 11, 2001, terrorist attacks on Washington D.C. and New York City, Barnes could say: "There is only one flag, and it's the flag of the United States of America." "That's our flag." (ajc.com, 1/31/02), not everyone was willing to disregard Georgia's traditional symbols. One might ask who would want to argue with that sentiment, but if Barnes assumed that no one would, he was quite wrong. The flag became one of the main sleeper issues in the 2002 campaign for governor.

Barnes defended his action; but many republicans, outside the metro Atlanta area and in the business communities, condemned it. Sonny Perdue, who became the GOP nominee, made it a centerpiece of his campaign, promising that, when elected, he would submit the decision on what flag to have flying over Georgia to the voters in a referendum. The issue turned out to be a crucial one. Although Perdue stated on the day following his election that the flag issue was not a high priority with him, his supporters seem to feel differently. An analysis of the 2002 Georgia election reveals that heavy voter turnout

---

State Flag

Georgia's current official flag was adopted on May 8, 2003. It became official when the new Governor, Sonny Perdue signed H.B. 380. The Governor then took the added step of holding a referendum giving voters a choice between it and Barnes' compromise flag, based in part on the Confederate flag, which was a painful reminder of slavery to many people. The new flag is more abstract, and more acceptable. So now the flag has a deep blue field with the state seal in the center, surrounded by 13 white stars (that symbolize the original 13 colonies). The state seal pictures three pillars (symbolizing the three branches of government in the USA: the Legislative, the Executive, and the Judicial) under an arch (symbolizing the Constitution).

Figure 5.3   The State Flag
Courtesy Georgia Secretary of State.

was primarily responsible for the republicans' gains statewide, the beginning of the end for Democratic Party rule. As a disappointed Roy Barnes quipped on leaving an Atlanta hotel ballroom following his concession to Perdue, "The flag brought out a white rural vote," and that voter sentiment was overwhelmingly republican. Perdue promised that he would resolve the flag issue once and for all by submitting it to the voters in a referendum, which he did in 2004. However, the choice confronting the voters did not include any flag with the confederate battle emblem, except the then-current Barnes compromise flag. As a result, Perdue succeeded in getting the electorate to approve his suggestion. Of course, in our overheated apple pie form of democracy, there are still lingering controversies. Did the voters really approve a new flag, or really an old version of another flag? After all, the thirteen stars could refer either to the early United States flag, or to the Confederate flag! So many of Perdue's new supporters, the ones known as the "flaggers" cried foul, claiming betrayal by Perdue. But the issue was practically resolved. Thanks to Sonny Perdue, Georgia now had its third flag in as many years, but this one is likely to hang around, ah, wave proudly for many years to come.

Besides Head of State, the Governor has several other important roles. Since the State of Georgia existed before it joined the United States, the Governor has traditionally exercised some of the prerogatives of a nation state leader. While these include the role of commander of the military and law enforcement arms of the state, the State Patrol and the National Guard, these are not a major concern of most governors today. More important are the political roles of the governor as the chief legislator: setting the agenda, initiating the budget, and signing or vetoing legislative bills. There are two major parts to this latter role, the first with regard to legislation itself, especially the preparation of the annual budget proposal, and the second involving the convening of the legislature and the filling of vacancies in it. A good state governor analyzes situations and figures out which roles would maximize his or her political influence and power.

As we saw in Chapter Four, the Governor's lawmaking role is significant. The Governor can convene special sessions, and his planning and budgeting staff always writes the annual appropriation bill. The Governor can set the agenda of each session by giving the opening speech: the State of the State Address. Governor Zell Miller used this forum to give the General Assembly information on current problems of the state and to recommend legislative measures. Governor Miller had a notable record of prior public service, as a citizen, and as a college professor and finally as a Lieutenant Governor. In 1992, the *Georgia Rebound Program* Miller offered demonstrated his grasp of the legislative options. In addition, the Governor used his appointment powers and political power over his party and over public opinion to influence the members of the General Assembly to support his policies. But as the flag controversy showed, he also knew when to back off from a controversial issue. More routinely, most governors review each proposed bill or resolution and decide whether to approve and sign it, or to veto it. The governor can use the veto power as a tool to reward or punish members of the General Assembly for their support of or opposition to his legislative agenda.

Following the 1997 legislative session, Miller used his item veto to veto several legislators' pet projects ("infamous pork barrel") for which appropriations had been voted as a way of "paying back" legislators who had opposed several of his favorite projects. Members were not happy with this turn of events, but they realized that, although a "lame duck" governor, Miller was still in control, and with an approval rating of over 70%, could and would make good on his threats. However, having made his point, Miller relented, and most of the money was ultimately restored. More recently, Governor Barnes had demonstrated a superb grasp on power, but he overreached, and his stance on the flag issue lost his re-election bid. His successor, Governor Perdue, adroitly handled not only the flag issue, but also the budget crisis caused by deregulating Wall Street, and the "Great Recession" that opened in 2008. Perhaps the most important issue that Governor Perdue failed to resolve was the water issue, turning to prayers for rain instead of addressing the need for building an extensive system of water reservoirs. Unfortunately, water issues are not exciting, and they are controversial and very, very expensive. Our new Governor is going to confront this issue, the state has lost court cases claiming rights to water from the Tennessee River and the reservoirs shared with other states. There are whispers that the north Georgians and the Atlanta metropolis are planning to raid the water resources of the south Georgia plains. Governor Deal will have his hands full with these issues, as the "Great Recession" still grips the state, depressing its revenues.

The Plural Executive of Georgia

Parallel powers exist vis-à-vis the administrative apparatus of the state. The appointment of individuals to vacant positions is a significant tool in the administration of state government. When constitutional public offices such as the Attorney General become vacant, the Governor usually fills the vacancy. In most cases the appointment will be for the remainder of the unexpired term unless otherwise provided for by the Constitution. However, many appointments are conditional upon the confirmation of the State Senate.

The Governor is the top bureaucrat in the state system, and has the power to require information in writing from the other constitutional officers, as well as from all other officers and employees of the executive branch. The Governor may inquire into any subject relating to their duties. Along the same lines, the chief executive is charged with the responsibility to take care that the laws are faithfully executed, and he is the conservator of the peace throughout the state. The Governor must take an oath or affirmation to fulfill these duties as prescribed by law.

The terms of office, compensation and allowances of Constitutional Officers are set by the current Georgia Constitution. Elections for Governor are held once every four years, beginning in 1986, on Tuesdays after the first Monday in November. The elections occur in the same way as for the state legislators, and by the same voters. The Governor-elect is installed in office at the next session of the General Assembly, and serves a four-year term with the possibility of one succession.

If Georgia Governors want a third term, they have to wait four years after their second term before they can run again. In order to qualify for the office of Governor, a person must have been a citizen of the United States for at least 15 years and a legal resident of the state for at least six years preceding the election, and must be at least 30 years old when assuming office. These requirements ensure that the Governor is familiar with the state, and can make informed decisions and appointments. But in America, state governors should be able to do more than make decisions, they should be able to provide their people with a vision of a better future.

Vision and Policy Initiative

Georgia has had lots of leaders with vision. Jimmy Carter's adroit ability to gauge the public mood led him all the way to the White House. Martin Luther King's "I have a dream" speech was an example of a leader's vision and ability to motivate followers. In the early 1990s the depressed state of the American economy cracked even Georgia's well-run economy. Beset by rising unemployment, reduced growth, and economic shortfalls, Governor Zell Miller, in 1992, created the *Georgia Rebound* proposal as the centerpiece of his budgetary and policy recommendations. The basic program goals were to anticipate and spur economic recovery and competitiveness in the state of Georgia. The plan balanced expenditures primarily with a slight increase in user fees, usually in areas where the fees were not sufficiently self-sustaining. The total estimated cost of his annual budget proposal was over 8.3 billion dollars.

In his first term, Miller's four-point expenditure program focused on economic development, educational improvements, environmental planning, and public safety. By increasing support for capital improvements and teacher salaries, the state workforce was better able to exploit economic opportunities such as new environmental technologies. At the conclusion of the 1992 legislative session, Governor Miller proclaimed the legislative session a success, with most of the *Georgia Rebound* approved and funded (LoMonte, B1). But, in politics, a Governor can only rarely afford to rest on his laurels, and stiff competition in his campaign for a second term in office led to his offering of a new vision, and a new message for the people and a new agenda for the legislature.

Whereas in his first term his plan had relied heavily on public construction projects such as transportation facilities, waterways, and airways development, his new plan focused on education. Georgia had been a southern leader in educational progress, but had in recent years slipped back and lost ground. Governor Miller's new vision centered on building hope for better schools. Awakening to the financial problems of schools and students alike, the *Hope Scholarship Program* linked the idea of government scholarships and educational appropriations to a risky new revenue source: a state-sponsored lottery which promised to bring millions of new dollars into state coffers. The *Hope Scholarship* program basically pays the college tuition of any Georgia student who maintains a "B" or better grade point average. It all came together: a politician's vision, a legislative agenda, a constitutional amendment, and in 2007 the legislature was able to draw eight hundred forty-one million dollars ($841,000,000.00) for education.

Today, this program still supports several different educational grant and loan programs, all expected to expand as lottery revenues increase, designed to foster better pre-schools, grade schools, and ensure that every college student can pursue their educational dreams and help Georgia be better able to compete in the emerging global marketplace. Unfortunately, due again to the recession, lottery money is proving to be unable to meet projected needs, and so Governor Deal has already suggested cutting back on Hope Scholarships, restricting full funding grants to students with 9.7 GPA's. This subject will be developed in more detail in the chapter on education.

One would expect that a Governor with vision, who proposes bold new programs and initiatives, would be rewarded with reelection by the Georgia people who appreciate that Governor's energy and work ethic. But, according to columnist Bill Shipp, just the opposite is true. Shipp argues that activist Governors in Georgia are likely either

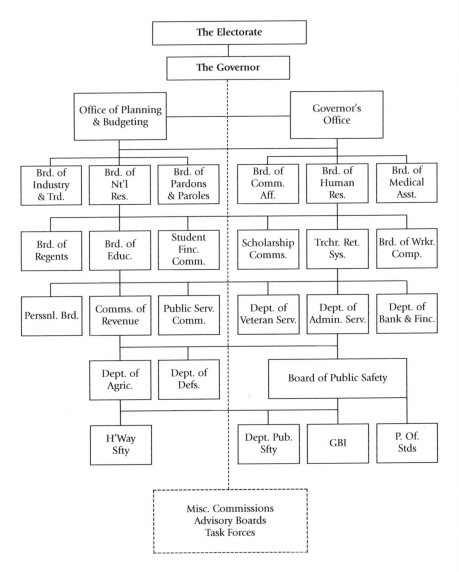

Figure 5.4   Selected Governor's Appointments
Source: Compiled by authors.

to just "squeak by" into a second term, or are defeated. Miller just squeaked by; Barnes was defeated. George Busbee and Joe Frank Harris were governors who did relatively little, and won reelection handily. Shipp believes that Sonny Perdue has modeled his Administration after Busbee's and Harris's (see VDT, "Of Fuzzy Images and Perdue," October 13, 2005, p. 6A). The fact that Perdue won reelection overwhelmingly in 2006, despite a record of little accomplishment and some complaints of ethical violations, suggests that Shipp's thesis has some merit. And of course we need to remember that in the modern world no one person can do it all.

A good governor must have a good management team, and be able to appoint strong and active managers who share a common vision onto all of the boards and commissions over which a Governor has appointive authority or political influence. However, in Georgia, the Constitution provides for the direct election of several other major state officials.

The Lieutenant Governor

Like most states, Georgia elects a Lieutenant Governor. This is a relatively new position in Georgia, created for the first time in the 1945 Constitution (Pound & Saye, 60). Governor Perdue's first Lieutenant Governor, Mark Taylor, was elected at the same time, for the same term, and in the same manner as the Governor. However, they were unable to work together or share a governing philosophy. In fact, Perdue and Taylor came from different parties, and were known to dislike each other, owing to the fact that Taylor insulted then-senator Perdue when he switched parties in 1998. While the Lieutenant Governor's job is basically to replace the Governor if necessary, he also serves as the President of the Senate. This can be a powerful position in its own right, almost as powerful as the Speaker of the House of Representatives. Custom and tradition gave the Lt. Governor power to appoint members to committees, and to assign bills to committees.

But when republicans captured control of the Senate in 2002, they stripped the democratic Lieutenant Governor of much of his power as payback for payback. The new Lieutenant Governor, Casey Cagle, indicated a desire to have the traditional power returned to the

Office of Lieutenant Governor. Given the fact that he was a republican, close to Governor Perdue, and that republicans control both houses of the General Assembly, no one was surprised when Republican Senators did just that on the first day of the 2007 session. After all, one reason for republican success was that they had promised that they would be more efficient than the democratic-controlled legislature. But when Cagle supported Perdue initiatives over those of ranking republicans in the Senate, they conducted a "palace coup" and stripped him of those legislative powers (Yarbrough, p. 6A). Still, Lieutenant Governors have various other executive duties as may be prescribed by the Governor or by law. Primarily, in case of the temporary disability of the Governor, the Lieutenant Governor exercises the powers and duties of the Governor, until such time as the disability ends. But in case of the death, resignation, or permanent disability of the Governor, the Lieutenant Governor becomes the new Governor until a successor is elected at the next general election.

But if such death, resignation, or permanent disability occurs within 30 days of the next general election, or if the term expires 90 days after the next general election, the Lieutenant Governor becomes Governor for the remainder of the unexpired term. When that happens, the office of Lieutenant Governor remains vacant, since the Georgia Constitution does not provide for a new Lieutenant Governor to be appointed. On those rare occasions where both the Governorship and the Lieutenant Governorship are vacant, the Speaker of the House of Representatives exercises the powers and duties of the Governor until a special election can be held within 90 days.

Attorney General

Another important Constitutional Official in Georgia is the Attorney General. Samuel Olens was elected in 2010 in the historical republican sweep of state government. The Attorney General acts as the legal advisor of the Department of Law, and represents the state in the State Supreme Court for all capital felonies, and performs such other legal duties as may be required by the Governor or by law. One of the most important of these is authoring legal opinions on problems of interpretation of law for other state officials and agencies. No person can be Attorney General unless he or she has been an active-status member of the State Bar of Georgia for seven years. The Attorney General is a vital link between the executive branch and the judicial branch of government.

Just as the Governor and the Lieutenant Governor may be at odds with each other, so, too, the Governor and the Attorney General may have difficulty getting along. Disputes over redistricting and other political matters pitted Governor Perdue against Attorney General Thurbert Baker, a democrat. Perdue insisted that he was the legal voice of Georgia; Baker said that he was. The courts resolved the dispute in the Attorney General's favor, but the two did not resolve their differences. Now Georgia has a new Governor, and a new republican Attorney General, Samuel S. Olens, and many people are watching to see how closely they will work together.

Educational Executives

There are two major education agencies serving in the State of Georgia and responsible for spending the bulk of taxpayer money. The first is the State Board of Education, dealing with primary and secondary education. The second is the Board of Regents. John D. Barge is the State School Superintendent and is the elected chief executive officer of the State Board of Education, so unlike local school superintendents he is not appointed by the Board of Education. The Constitution specifies that the Superintendent shall be elected at the same time and in the same manner and for the same terms as that of the Governor. Only sixteen states elect their School Superintendent. In the other thirty-four states s/he is either appointed by the Governor or by the Board of Education itself. Some consideration has been given to having the Georgia Superintendent appointed and incumbent Superintendents have endorsed that suggestion. However, Georgia citizens like to elect as many of their public officials as possible, and once a position is elective it is hard to change; the General Assembly has not yet made the change to an appointive state Superintendent. And as long as the General Assembly and the Office of School Superintendent are controlled by republicans, a move toward appointment is not likely to happen.

Unfortunately, the examples of Governors fighting with their Lieutenant Governors and Attorneys General have been repeated with School Superintendents. Both Miller and Barnes had issues with republican superintendent Linda Schrenko. In fact, Schrenko gave up the office in 2002 to run for the GOP nomination for Governor, so that she could take on Barnes. But she was defeated by Perdue in the primary election. As a footnote, she was subsequently indicted and convicted for stealing over $600,000 in federal education funds, some of which went to defraying campaign expenses for her abortive gubernatorial race. As of the writing of this textbook, she was serving a prison sentence in a federal penitentiary in Florida.

Ms. Schrenko was succeeded in the Superintendent's Office by Kathy Cox, another republican office holder. Her tenure was marred by a couple of controversial issues. One of those was her political surrender to the anti-science movement, the new luddites of our time. Specifically, she attempted to strike all references to the teaching of "evolution" in favor of the term "biological changes over time" as favored by some right wing conservatives. In fact, evolution is a term that has tremendous importance in science, applying to subjects in astronomy and physics as well as botany and biology. Georgia cannot expect new companies to move here if its educational environment is hostile to a good scientific education for company employees.

The global market is too competitive for the state to pander to modern luddites. She later said that she learned from the public outcry that accompanied her ill-advised effort, and learned that classroom standards represented something very important to the larger public, and to the larger entity of the nation; and that that was a great lesson for her (Galloway, 07-06-10). The other controversial issue was that after winning a multimillion dollar prize on a national game show, and announcing that she was going to give the money to three schools for the handicapped in Georgia, she declared bankruptcy instead. She then resigned from her position, moved to Washington D.C. to work as the C.E.O. of a new non-profit institute, and created a cloud of confusion about her motives and her values. When the voters elect someone to represent their interests, they expect the official to fulfill her obligations, and not cut and run after the fast bucks.

As stated, there are two separate educational entities in the State of Georgia. The entity responsible for colleges and universities is the Georgia State Board of Regents, whose regular members, like the Board of Education, are appointed by the Governor of Georgia and confirmed by the Senate. However, in addition to representatives chosen from the congressional districts, there are also five more regents who are chosen at large; all Regents serve seven-year terms. Among state agencies, the Board of Regents is unique in the sense that its budget is not line-itemed. To insulate the University System from politics, the General Assembly appropriates monies to the Board of Regents in a lump sum, and the Constitution instructs the regents to allocate these monies as the Board sees fit. This seemingly peculiar insulation of the Board of Regents was initiated during the reform administration of Governor Arnall in the 1940s as part of a strategy to secure educational re-accreditation for the university system, whose professional accreditation had been lost.

The withdrawal of professional accreditation originally occurred when the previous Governor, Eugene Talmadge, had tried to manipulate and intimidate the Board and the entire university system for partisan purposes. This had been a typical problem in many states when corrupt party machines had used school systems to give jobs to party loyalists, regardless of any professional qualifications. In an attempt to prevent similar problems in the future, Governor Arnall and the legislature placed the system for micro-financing and micro-managing of higher education out of the budgetary reach of both the executive and the legislative branches. We will see more of the clash between reformist and partisan party organizations when discussing the "Three Governors Controversy" a little further in this chapter.

Other Elected Executives

The Secretary of State is another vitally important official but is dealt with primarily in another chapter. Some other major constitutionally elected officials include the Commissioner of Insurance, the Commissioner of Agriculture, and the Commissioner of Labor. These officials are elected in the same manner as the members of the General Assembly, and hold their offices for the same term as the Governor, although, unlike the Governor, they are indefinitely eligible for reelection. That is, they may serve as many terms as the voters will reelect them to serve. In 2010, the retirement of the long-serving Tommy Irving, a democrat, finally provided the republican candidate Gary Black a chance to be elected, thus completing the historic republican sweep of state-wide offices for the first time since Reconstruction.

Together with the other officials discussed above, these officials have another power in addition to their departmental duties. Any four of these elected constitutional officers can petition the Supreme Court of Georgia to declare that another elected constitutional executive

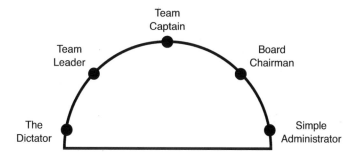

Figure 5.5   Team Management Style
Source: Compiled by authors and inspired by James D. Barber.

officer (including the Governor) is unable to perform the duties of his or her office. When the grounds are properly based on physical or mental disability, the Supreme Court will provide a speedy and public hearing on the matter. This is a formal process that includes notice of the nature and cause of the accusation, process for obtaining witnesses, and assistance of counsel. Evidence at such hearings must include testimony from at least three qualified physicians in private practice, one of whom must be a psychiatrist. If, after hearing the evidence on disability, the Supreme Court determines that there is a disability and that it is permanent, the office will be declared vacant and a successor to that office will be chosen according to the Constitution and the laws of Georgia. But if the disability is not permanent, the Supreme Court must later determine when the disability has ended and when the officer can resume the exercise of powers of office. During the period of temporary disability, the powers of such office will be exercised according to law, usually by an assistant administrator, selected by the management team. The figure on page 93 shows a spectrum of executive team management styles, ranging from unilateral one person rule to an administrative pluralism where the nominal executive head is merely one of the management team players.

As was stated earlier, modern government is too large and complex to be administered by any one person. The Chief Executive Officer may be called a governor, or a president or a director, but they can only function effectively if they have assistants with delegated power and authority. In Georgia, the Governor's departmental assistants are the other constitutional officers. But while there has to be a team, there are several different ways the Governor can interact with the other team members. For example, Thomas H. Ruger, the military governor of Georgia from January 13, 1868, to July 4, 1868, can be seen as a dictatorial manager imposing his will by fiat on other state leaders. He acted as a forceful lion in controlling people and events around him.

Governor Roy Barnes on the other hand, Governor from 1999 to 2003, was more of a leader type of manager. As our review of the flag issue demonstrated, operating in the same general environment as his predecessor Miller, and with generally the same people in government, he was able to lead them in adopting a new flag for the state. When his popularity waned, and the democrats were replaced by a new management team, the republicans, the new team was able to reverse Barnes' policy. Perhaps the best example of a Governor who was really a team player was Joseph E. Brown, whose tenure ran from 1857 to 1865. Although not really a member of the elite plantation class, he helped put together a new secessionist management team, while acting the role of the star player, and captain of the team.

As a general rule, charismatic politicians are the most likely type of persons to win a governorship and shine in the office, their success due to their ability to exercise a dictatorial, leadership, or team captain style of management. But sometimes less political types get into the office, people who are more comfortable with just being members of the management team. In the year 1946 this happened when the popular Governor-elect, Eugene Talmadge, died before taking office. The new 1945 State Constitution did not specify who would assume the governorship in such a situation. At that point the incumbent Governor Arnall claimed a stewardship role, but the Lieutenant Governor-elect Thompson also claimed the post, as did the son of the deceased candidate, Herman Talmadge. In the period known as "the Three Governors Controversy" the Talmadge forces persuaded the legislature to "elect" him; but the Supreme Court ruled against Talmadge and designated Thompson as the true winner. But Melvin Thompson lacked the charisma for the job, and although he did preside over the state until the next general election (losing to Talmadge) he really functioned more as a simple administrator caretaker, just part of the state's management team. Governor Thompson was never again elected to state office, and retired to Valdosta as a businessman and private citizen (Paulk, 02/27/11).

Governor James E. Carter

A generation or two ago, one Georgia Governor, James Earl Carter, succeeded in applying his understanding of the role of the chief executive to the Presidency of the United States. After serving in the United States Navy as a nuclear engineering officer, Jimmy Carter returned home to manage the family's peanut farm business, and to engage in public service. After serving in the State Senate, he became Governor in 1971; and then established a reputation as an honest political reformer in the wake of the national Watergate scandal. He built a national political organization from scratch and became elected as President of the United States in January, 1977.

He made his mark on the federal government by establishing two new cabinet departments, Energy and Education, and in passing the Civil Service Reform Act of 1978 (Allen). His training in science, engineering, and in the military had made him an administrator par excellence, presiding as the active chairman of the complex federal government. But even though he received the 2002 Nobel Prize for Peace due to his role brokering peace for a besieged Israel, he is perhaps best known for his failure to respond militarily to the Iranian Revolution, the hostage crisis and the rise of the Shiite Theocracy. These issues, plus the intractable energy crisis, marred any chance of his being remembered as a great president.

Conclusion

How is a Governor to cope with such a complex and decentralized system of government and administration? How can a Governor be evaluated? Some researchers suggest that a good governor can identify the needs of the people of the state, develop intergovernmental strategies to meet these needs, and persuade at least half the people (or their legislative representatives) to adopt his proposals. And then of course the implemented proposals must be acknowledged as having solved the problem. The Governor must be foxy enough to understand the problems, aggressive enough to act on the information, and, sometimes, just be plain lucky.

Key Terms

Apple Pie model of government
Attorney General
Educational Executive
Governor
Georgia Rebound Program
Head of State
James (Jimmy) E. Carter
King Roy
Layer Cake Federalism
Marble Cake Federalism
Old Elected Executive
Plural Executive
State Flag
Roy Barnes and the Georgia Flag

Essay Questions

1. In spite of the fact that Georgia has a plural executive, the Governor of Georgia is considered one of the more powerful Governors in the United States. Why?
2. In what ways may the Governor of Georgia set the legislative agenda and impact policy?
3. How is the Georgia Governor capable of impacting the bureaucracy? How does the plural executive model affect this ability?
4. What are the constitutional responsibilities of the office of Lieutenant Governor of Georgia?
5. In Georgia, State School Superintendent is an elected office. What are the arguments for and against electing this member of the state's executive branch?
6. Describe the formal and informal powers of the Governor of the State of Georgia.

Figure 6.1 Department of Transportation

Administration and Agencies

The Georgia State Administration

What do a female tourist, a group of senior citizens, and a county commissioner have in common? They have all had negative experiences with modern bureaucracy. When the government machinery runs well, we call it an administration; when it runs badly, we call it a bureaucracy. In today's mass society, composed largely of alienated strangers, bureaucracy can be a nightmare. Administration can be defined as a complex rationally designed system of organization that relies on training, specialization, division of labor, record keeping, and hierarchical control to meet the needs of a technological mass society. Its evil twin brother, bureaucracy, can be defined simply as a nightmare of either personal but biased treatment, or an impersonal and perhaps even negligent government. This chapter describes some of the major administrative organizations and how they fit into the governmental system of the State of Georgia, and how they affect the lives of our citizens.

In what is becoming an increasingly common phenomenon among our corporate common carriers, who seem more concerned with maximizing their cash profits and less about simply providing a reasonable service for a reasonable fee, one tourist, a 300-pound woman returning from a bus trip to Ft. Lauderdale, was arrested in Macon, Georgia, for disturbing the peace when she objected to being kicked off the bus because the bus company driver was attempting to squeeze in a maximum number of passengers (Associated Press, 3-29-92). She had a right to complain, because once you have a ticket, the common carrier has traditionally had a duty to get you to your destination and not leave you stranded and alone in a strange place. In another case, a few resident senior citizens were playing their usual private game of bingo at McDonalds in Lavonia, Georgia, when the Georgia Bureau of Investigation closed the games down because they were not properly run by a non-profit, tax-exempt organization with a bingo license (Associated Press, 4-2-92).

In reaction, one elected official, Jimmy Helms, Chairman of the Paulding County Board of Commissioners, announced that he wanted to hire a professional manager to cope with the demands of modern population growth, because amateurs such as he could not adequately run the county bureaucracy as efficiently as a professional public administrator (Associated Press, 2-23-92). Indeed, the existence of professional county managers, city managers, and school superintendents who are trained to moderate the conflicting demands of ordinary citizens, special interest groups, and corporations, and mindless bureaucrats running rampant is a major reason our complex government works as well as it does, most of the time.

Article IV of the Georgia Constitution establishes an administrative branch of government. Just as the principle of legislative primacy has yielded to executive dominance, so in turn the executive model is being replaced by an administrative model of government organization and policymaking. Most of the administrative machinery of the State of Georgia is run by various constitutional boards and elected and appointed officials whose names are largely unknown to the average citizen. Generally, these officials are not formally subordinate to the Governor, except for reporting obligations, as we saw in the last chapter.

Public Administrators

Administrators are basically people. State government is one of the largest employers in Georgia. Including higher education personnel, over 114,000 people work for the State of Georgia (Fleischmann, 146). They are headquartered in buildings in Atlanta and their basic job is implementing the state's laws and policies. Together, since the beginning of the state's history, the numbers of state employees have increased every time new programs and policies were created to cope with the increasing complexity of everyday life. But the real reason for administrative growth is an ever-increasing size of the population. A town with hundreds of people needs little bureaucracy, a city with millions needs a large administrative apparatus.

The growth of population has led to modern mass organization and an increasingly complex interdependent society. Few people really like the system, preferring the more individualistic lifestyles of the past, but rational organization is necessary today. When the invention of the railroad created jobs for conductors and engineers, it also required a Railroad Commission (the forerunner of the Public Service Commission); and the invention of the airplane created a need for both pilots and the employees of the Atlanta Airport. In fact, in every major policy area, such as education, law enforcement, health care, welfare, and economic regulation, a new bureaucracy has had to be created to ensure that the general public good will be protected. In addition, bureaucratic proliferation occurs in five technical areas of bureaucratic activity: information, service, regulation, licensing, and promoting. The result is an expanding administrative structure which in its size, complexity, and impersonality sometimes takes on a bureaucratic aspect in the minds of some citizens.

The stages by which modern societies have come to rely on mechanical bureaucracies can be traced. In the beginning, individuals and families took care of their own needs. But as society progressed, people learned that specialization and division of labor in a free market were more productive. Slowly, private organizations evolved which better satisfied peoples' needs. Except for taxation to support charities for the poor and disabled, monarchical governments encouraged these organizations with a minimum of interference, a laissez-faire approach. But as private organizations increased in power, adapting bureaucratic structures to profit-making enterprises, some became too self-serving and a few created destructive monopolies. Entering the industrial revolution, western democratic societies attempted to retain their sense of community by curbing monopolies and by creating welfare agencies.

As populations grew, the western societies created ever larger bureaucratic institutions to deal with large masses of people: armies, schools, social work agencies, and even prisons. But these facilities are very expensive to operate. Reforms and modification of the institutional society led to attempts to directly subsidize individuals. Poorhouses were closed, mental institutions were emptied, and individuals were given government pensions and welfare checks to take care of themselves, but bureaucracies continued to grow. Even recent suggestions to cut costs and bureaucracy by passing regulations requiring families to provide child support and for employers to provide family and health care, envision new enforcement bureaucracies. Truly, we live in a bureaucratic age.

In just one year the various agencies of the Georgia State Government made millions of phone calls, processed over a million driver's licenses, almost two million vehicle titles, almost two and a half million income tax returns, close to six million vehicle registrations, and handled fifty million criminal justice inquiries (Christenberry, 19). Electronic media have added even more hundreds or thousands, if not millions, of more e-mails, faxes, and duplicative reporting requirements. Over one hundred thousand state employees carried on a bewildering array of activities. They administered the largest self-insurance program in the state, maintained real estate leases in almost two hundred cities, provided services for many thousands of telephones, cell phones, and other new engineering

Figure 6.2   Bureaucratic Empire Building

marvels, and managed over six hundred thousand procurements transactions (Ibid). The state's personnel workforce is big business.

Constitutional Administration

Decades ago, Leonard White, a political scientist, predicted an eventual shift from legislative-based government to bureaucratic-based government (Nachmias, viii). In fact there is a long history of such predictions; most of the serious scholars who have contemplated the issue have agreed that a new locus of bureaucratic power is developing. This is reasonable, because bureaucratic government has several advantages over legislative and executive government. Some of the major ones are rational planning, specialization and division of labor, record keeping, and a career orientation (Weber, 1958, 196–199). Perhaps the major one is that it avoids what Max Weber called the "succession crisis." Max Weber identified a typology of historical change in government organization. According to that typology, new charismatic governments created by gifted individuals would experience a crisis when the leader died; much energy and effort would be diverted to solidify gains and create traditional governments based on the leader's ideas. But these governments too often hardened into rigid forms; and western political systems developed legalistic means of choosing new leaders and new policies. These legalistic procedures are the fundamental basis of bureaucratic organization (Weber, 1913, at 112).

Of course, researchers have found some instances of this system of bureaucracy to be dysfunctional. It has been suggested that the Reagan Administration, which succeeded the Carter Administration, acted on assumptions that regulatory agencies and commissions were often harmful to society. In one well-known assertion, he said that government was not the solution to the problem, that government WAS the problem. These assumptions are that such organizations create contradictory policies with heavy compliance costs, perceive regulations as ends in themselves, and tend to devote resources to advance their own interests (Friedman, 24).

Perhaps the most influential of the anti-regulatory studies was the one conducted by Murray Weidenbaum, who calculated that the total economic impact of federal regulations was more than $100 billion dollars (Cooper, 253). This report was cited in Congress, and charged regulatory agencies with being staffed by overly zealous and impractical officials. However, analysis of the Weidenbaum report by Mark Green showed that it was seriously flawed, that it was largely "puffing" for partisanship purposes, and that it exaggerated the costs of regulation and completely neglected the economic benefits of regulatory activity (Cooper, 254–45). The reason that bureaucratic techniques and regulations are so pervasive is that they are superior to other forms of mass organization.

The old mold of traditionalistic monarchical government was broken in the new world. In America, new states and new governments were created by charismatic individuals with the vision and energy to implement their ideas. Colonial Georgia's Oglethorpe is a good example of a charismatic visionary. The creation of constitutional government, influenced by John Locke and Jean Rousseau, traditionalized many of Oglethorpe's principles for a new social order, and the American Revolution solidified them. Georgia's political evolution has largely been a continuation of the legalistic and bureaucratic transformations identified and articulated by Max Weber.

The student should note the similarities and differences between the structure of the federal government and the government of Georgia. The State of Georgia has a plural executive, not a unitary one. The powers of the chief executive must be shared with a number of other elected and appointed executive officers working in a number of agencies and departments.

In Georgia, the relationship between these officials is complex, requiring skill in intergovernmental relations. The Governor must be a lion and a fox, able and willing to assume a variety of roles with

Table 6.1   Administrative Subdivisions

Executive Departments	33
Executive Agencies	48
Statutory Advisory Boards	37
Decreed Advisory Boards	20
Authorities and Corporations	30
Interstate Agencies	8
Judicial Agencies	24
Legislative Agencies	12
Inactive Agencies	12
Total:	**224**

Source: After Jackson and Stokes, Handbook of Georgia State Agencies, Univ. of Georgia. (Note: This is not an exhaustive list.)

facility. With such an able Governor in charge, state government can be as sweet as an apple pie, or in this case, as sweet as a peach cobbler. In Georgia, under an effective leadership the various units of government can work together harmoniously, with joint policymaking and mutual accommodation.

While the Constitution of the State of Georgia specifies that the chief executive powers shall be vested in the Governor, sometimes the administrative agencies function as a separate branch of government. This is especially true in Georgia, where the enactment of Article IV of the Constitution created an emphasis on independent administrative government. The primary thrust of this bureaucratic approach is due to a growing recognition of the need for expertise in governing and coordinating today's complex society. This tendency is reflected not only by the features of the plural executive described in the last chapter, but also by a wide variety of autonomous and independent departments, regulatory agencies, commissions, and authorities, described in Table 6.1 above.

Administrative Leaders
The Attorney General is probably, except for the Governor in the executive branch, and possibly the Lt. Governor and the Speaker in the legislative branch, the single most powerful individual official in Georgia's State Government. As the state's chief lawyer, the Attorney General issues opinions on state law which serve to guide much of the state's and local government's administrative apparatus. By exercising this power, the Attorney General can (1) interpret vaguely worded laws and regulations, (2) influence enforcement of laws and regulations, (3) advise legislators on probable constitutionality of pending

bills, and (4) determine the scope of agency jurisdiction, and thus (5) can significantly determine public policy across the entire state. The Attorney General is also the state's chief administrative link with the courts and the legal profession.

The Secretary of State is another extremely important constitutionally elected official. The Secretary of State, along with the Board of Elections, oversees the elections process, and tracks electoral changes in the State Constitution. Other duties include (1) recording financial statements from politicians, (2) granting charters to corporate entities, (3) issuing permits to do business, (4) maintaining registers of public officials, and (5) oversight of a myriad of occupational boards.

Workers in many trades and professions must be licensed before they can practice in the State of Georgia. Dozens of commissions and boards administer occupation admission standards and licensing procedures, regulate their particular areas of employment, and deal with complaints by consumers. Except for attorneys, oversight of these examining, certification and regulatory boards and commissions is usually the responsibility of the Secretary of State, acting through the Office of the Joint-Secretary of the State Examining Boards. Some of the Examining Boards are listed below. The first table shows the major health professional boards, the second depicts a variety of other occupational groups that are closely regulated.

Executive Commissions

Article IV of the Georgia Constitution creates several powerful executive Boards and Commissions. These boards and commissions include the Public Service Commission; the State Board of Pardons and Paroles; the State Personnel Board; the State Transportation Board; the Veterans Service Board; and the Board of Natural Resources. In each case, the qualifications, salaries, powers, and duties of their members are controlled by the Constitution and not by the Governor. The presiding chairmen of these boards are selected by a variety of complicated two-step processes, some of which are described in the paragraphs below.

The Public Service Commission
The Public Service Commission is created for the purpose of regulating utilities such as electrical power. It is composed of five members who are elected directly by the people for six-year terms. The chairman is selected by the members of the commission from among themselves. The exact jurisdiction, powers, and duties of the Commission are provided for by statutes enacted by the legislature and by regulations promulgated by the Commission.

The members of the Public Service Commission regulate the railroads, issue licenses, and set rates for power companies, telephone companies, and other public utilities. There is a great deal of controversy over the scope of powers of the Public Service Commission. As Georgia becomes increasingly urbanized and modernized, there are cries for an increase in regulatory efforts and for reform. Some of the areas of concern involve consumer complaints over the cost of electrical power; manufacturing interest in the adequacy of the transportation systems; general distress over the quality of water; and preservation of the state's unique environmental resources.

The State Transportation Board
In contrast, the members of the State Transportation Board, who serve five-year terms, are chosen by designated members of the General Assembly. There are as many members of this Board as there are congressional districts in the state. The member of the board from each congressional district is elected by a special caucus meeting of members of both Houses whose respective districts are embraced or partly embraced within each congressional district. A majority vote of these legislators chooses the members of the board, who in turn pick their chief executive officer from among their ranks. This commission is responsible for building and maintaining the roads and highways of the state of Georgia, and such other duties as provided by the legislature.

The patronage and politics involved in this area can be very considerable. For example, one businessman who had tried unsuccess-

---

Administrative Case Study

Former state Insurance Commissioner John Oxendine is an example of an administrative chieftain who served as a student assistant to a Georgia Governor (Joe F. Harris) who then appointed him as Chairman of the State Personnel Board and was then elected to four terms of office before relinquishing his political position in 2010. Lawyer, businessman, and right wing politician, he was a colorful individual who was fond of using his emergency lights to bypass traffic jams. But he turned more heads when, upon leaving office he awarded himself several insurance licenses without taking any of the usually required tests. In reaction, a bill has been introduced into the assembly to prevent a repetition of the stunt (WALB News, 02-22-11).

Figure 6.3

Table 6.2   Examining and Licensing Boards

Selected Health Professions

Composite State Board of Medical Examiners
Georgia Board of Dentistry
Georgia Board of Nursing
Board of Examiners of Licensed Practical Nurses
Georgia State Board of Nursing Home Administrators
Georgia State Board of Pharmacy

State Board of Dispensing Opticians
State Board of Examiners in Optometry
Board of Examiners for Speech Pathology and Audiology
Board of Hearing Aid Dealers and Dispensers

Georgia State Board of Physical Therapy
State Board of Podiatry Examiners
State Board of Examiners of Psychologists
Georgia Board of Chiropractic Examiners
Georgia Board of Occupational Therapy

State Board of Examiners for Certified Waters and Wastewater
    Treatment Plant
Operators and Laboratory Analysts
Water Well Standards Advisory Council
Board of Veterinary Medicine
State Board of Examiners for Registered Professional Sanitarians

Source: Compiled by authors from materials in Jackson and Stakes, *Handbook of Georgia State Agencies,* Univ. of Georgia.

fully for years to persuade the State Department of Transportation (DOT) to pave the road to his sod farm finally gave up and tried an alternative approach. He began donating money to political candidates. He was impartial, giving money to candidates of both parties. Soon, he was appointed to a special commission to ferret out waste in state government. As a result, the next time the businessman called DOT about his road he received prompt and friendly service (AJAC, 2-21-92). Not all citizens end up as happy as this individual.

Table 6.3   Other Examining Boards

Office of the Joint-Secretary of State
Examining Boards
Asbestos Licensing Board
State Board of Accountancy
State Board for Certification of Librarians

Georgia Real Estate Commission
State Board of Georgia Architects
Georgia State Board of Landscape Architects
State Board of Registration for Professional Engineers and Land
   Surveyors
State Board of Registration for Professional Geologists
State Board of Registration for Foresters
Georgia Construction Industry Licensing Board
State Structural Pest Control Commission

State Board of Barbers
Georgia State Boards of Cosmetology
Board of Recreation Examiners
Georgia Board of Athletic Trainers

Board of Polygraph Examiners
Georgia Board of Private Detectives and Private Security Agencies
State Board of Registration of Used Car Dealers

Georgia Auctioneers Commission
Georgia Athletic Agent Regulatory Commission
Georgia State Board of Funeral Service

Source: Compiled by authors from materials in Jackson and Stakes, *Handbook of Georgia State Agencies,* Univ. of Georgia.

Commissioner of Insurance
Insurance regulation is required by Article III, Section VIII of the State
Constitution. That provision calls for the General Assembly to provide
for statutory regulation of the insurance business, under the direction
of a Commissioner of Insurance. The Commissioner of Insurance regulates the state's multimillion dollar insurance industry. The
Commissioner sets criteria for licensing, sets standards for performance, and, within the framework of the law, sets rates for insurance

policies for automobile drivers and homeowners and for fire, theft, and casualty losses. The present commissioner Ralph Hudgens replaced John Oxendine in 2010.

The State Board of Pardons and Paroles

Historically, The British King had power to intervene in criminal cases to provide justice or to settle political and military disputes by exercising the pardon power. Although presidents and governors usually have similar powers, in Georgia the fear of abuse, corruption, and a desire to avoid hassle led to a delegation of that power to a five-person commission. The members of the State Board of Pardons and Paroles are appointed by the Governor, subject to confirmation by the Senate. The Chairman of the Board of Pardons and Paroles, or any member designated by the board, may suspend the execution of a sentence of death; until the full board has an opportunity to hear the application of the convicted person for relief. The State Board of Pardons and Paroles also has the authority to pardon any person convicted of a crime who is later found to be innocent of that crime.

Thus the board, and not the Governor, is vested with the power of executive clemency, including the powers to grant reprieves, pardons, and paroles; to commute penalties; to remove disabilities imposed by law; and to remit any part of a sentence for any offense against the state after conviction. However, the Constitution does not give the Board a completely free hand. In a further division of power, the General Assembly of Georgia has a lot of direct control over pardons and paroles under the Constitution. Under some circumstances the legislature may prohibit the board from granting a pardon or parole to habitual felons or notorious criminals, and may even prescribe the terms and conditions for the board's granting of a pardon or parole to such persons. These conditions pertain to any person incarcerated for a second time for any offense for which he or she could have been sentenced to life imprisonment; and to any person who has received consecutive life sentences as the result of multiple offenses occurring during the same series of acts.

And the ever-popular anti-crime movement has resulted in some recent amendments to the Constitution which allow the General Assembly to set mandatory sentencing guidelines, and in addition a "two-strikes" amendment means that a two-time loser is likely to face living in prison for a life term! When a sentence of death is commuted to life imprisonment, the board does not have the authority to grant a pardon to the convicted person until the person has served at least 25 years in the penitentiary. Georgia is not a good place for anyone to commit a crime and get caught.

The State Personnel Board

A strong governor usually has the power to directly hire and fire members of the administrative apparatus of the state, and thus to control the bureaucracy. With a weak executive, employees are more likely to respond to their immediate superiors instead of to the Governor. In Georgia, power over state employees is given to a State Personnel Board, consisting of five members nominated by the Governor and appointed after confirmation by the Senate. Their terms of office are five years, and they select their own chairman. This board sets policy for the State Merit System of Personnel Administration, and is further vested with such additional responsibilities and powers as provided by law. One critique may be in order here. While merit systems may indeed increase competency, it is sometimes at the cost of loyalty and adherence to executive policy. To further complicate matters, much of the sphere of authority of this Board overlaps with another one: the Board of Veterans Service, which is described below.

The Veterans Service Board

Article IV of the State Constitution creates a State Department of Veterans Service and its oversight body, the Veterans Service Board which consists of seven members appointed by the Governor, subject to confirmation by the Senate. The terms of its members are for seven years, and the members themselves appoint a commissioner who becomes the executive officer of the department. All members of the board and the department must be veterans of some war or armed conflict in which the United States has engaged. Exact duties and responsibilities of the board are described in statutes enacted by the General Assembly.

Any armed forces veteran who has been honorably discharged is given veterans preference in any civil service program established in state government. Wounded or disabled veterans are provided at least ten points if they have a 10 percent service connected disability, and all other veterans are entitled to at least five points. For, example if a passing grade on a test is required to get a job, the preference points are added to their scores. If tests are so easy that everyone gets high marks, veterans will get the jobs.

The Board of Natural Resources

The State of Georgia has traditionally relied heavily on its natural resources for trade and commerce. As environmental problems have developed, Georgia has acted to protect its fragile ecosystems by creating a Board of Natural Resources. Like the State Transportation Board, the size of the Board of Natural Resources is determined by according a member for each congressional district, with an additional five members to represent the state at large. And because of the geographical distribution of resources, at least one of the members must be from one of several counties specifically named in the Constitution. And the members of the board are supposed to be representative of all areas and functions encompassed within the Department of Natural Resources. All members are appointed by the Governor for seven years, subject to confirmation by the Senate. As usual, more powers and duties can be provided by legislative statute.

Intergovernmental Interactions

How do all of these agencies interact? The Legislature acts by committees. The executive branch per se operates by fiat and decree through the bureaucratic hierarchy. The judicial are trained in legal reasoning and hierarchy. How do the various agencies, representing a wide variety of perspectives and responsive to different interests, interact with each other to accomplish anything? Actually, there are four common patterns of agency interaction.

Usually, agencies are rational actors capable of identifying common interests and acting jointly to make and implement public policy. Sometimes one agency, perhaps enjoying sufficient funding levels, will take the initiative on a problem and other agencies will help out. This is called mutual accommodation. Sometimes, rival agencies will engage in friendly competition to see which can accomplish its goals first. This is called constructive rivalry. But unfortunately, there is yet another pattern. On rare occasions, two agencies will be controlled by opposing special interest groups, or will succumb to professional jealousy, and the result adversely affects the agencies and the public good. This pattern is called destructive conflict. Joint policymaking and mutual accommodation, formalized in contracts and memoranda of agreements, are the most routine patterns of bureaucratic interaction.

Federalism is a type of political system in which many disparate units and levels of government are coordinated by a central unit. In this apple pie mixture, the government of Georgia is part of the larger federal system. But that is not all, Georgia belongs to a variety of other coordinating units, such as the National Governor's Association. In addition, several interstate agencies exist, sometimes operating under binding compacts, such as the Southeastern Interstate Forest Fire Protection Compact Advisory Committee; other examples include the Southern States Energy Board and the Southern Growth Policies Board (Jackson, 341). The Fisheries Commission, the Radioactive Waste Management Commission, and the Historic Chattahoochee Commission are other examples. Of course, most of the daily grind of bureaucratic activity is determined by functional problems, such as conservation.

Conservation of the Environment

The conservation of environmental standards and resources is a problem of increasing significance. Georgia's farmers have long understood the necessity to replenish the land to support their agricultural crops. Taking care of topsoil, planting the right crops, and fertilizing the "back forty" is second nature to good farmers. For many citizens of the state it is a simple step from soil conservation to environmental preservation. But for other Georgians, concerned perhaps with post-war modernization, or focused on short-term self-interest, or simply unmindful of the necessities of long-range planning, environmental preservation has been a low priority. However, with our water tables polluted by industrial and agricultural waste and pesticides, with the virgin timber almost gone, and many wildlife species already extinct, the consequences of reckless destruction today commands our attention.

Georgia ranks near the bottom of the list of states in terms of state-owned park and wilderness land. The Board of Natural Resources is charged with increasing land holdings and protection of the environment. The duties of the department include maintenance and acquisition of land, regulation and conservation of fish and game, management of fisheries, and the enforcement of state hunting and fishing laws. Unfortunately, some of the goals of the board, as in the society at large, are often contradictory and irreconcilable.

Other Regulatory Areas

The promotion of economic development and trade and commerce is a major concern of Georgia State Government. As the traditional local forestry and agricultural economy of Georgia yields to manufacturing, commerce, and recreation, several agencies have been created to coordinate the efforts of private companies and public agencies to foster economic and industrial growth. In today's global marketplace, the attraction, location, and encouragement of business enterprises and economic opportunities are legitimate, indeed essential, concerns of state government.

Special Authorities

There are some economic and functional policy areas that require narrow expertise, technical administrative competency, and unique management skills. Sometimes these policy areas involve geographical considerations that cannot be easily handled by local government, or dealt with in a cost-effective fashion by generic state laws or state agencies. Two obvious examples are the metropolitan airport in Atlanta, and the international seaport in Savannah, but there are many more. In fact, there are 391 different special districts in the State of Georgia, some of the 1,271 different governmental entities in the state.

Their interactions often depend upon the functional issues but may center on the resolution of intergovernmental conflicts; the need to facilitate development, or to provide flexibility for quasi-commercial enterprises. Often the driving force behind the creation of a special authority is the desire to finance an enterprise without exceeding the debt limitations of a parent governmental entity; or to quiet a taxpayer revolt by financing operations with specific user fees instead of with general revenues or property taxes.

However, the proliferation of special authorities has led to increasing concerns about waste and mismanagement. In 1972 the General Assembly enacted a reorganization plan designed to deal with the problem. This plan created a centralized State Financing and Investment Commission. The State Financing and Investment Commission might be called a super commission. It is composed of the major state political leadership: the Governor, the Lt. Governor, the Speaker of the House of Representatives, the Attorney General, the Commissioner of Agriculture, the State Auditor, and the Director of the Fiscal Division. Together, this collective body of political power can coordinate a powerful response to any problem. The goal is to ensure that Special Authorities contribute to efficient government.

In 1996, Article IX, Section IV was amended to allow the creation of "regional facilities." These regional facilities mean industrial parks, business parks, conference centers, convention centers, airports, athletic facilities, recreation facilities, jails or correctional facilities, or other similar or related economic development facilities. Counties and municipalities are authorized to enter into contracts with contiguous counties for the purpose of allocating the proceeds of ad valorem taxes assessed and collected on real property for development purposes, and unless otherwise provided by law, the regional facilities can qualify for any income tax credits, regardless of where the business is located. Many people don't like bureaucracy. Although the pressures of modern society require the modification of government toward increasingly bureaucratic models, the creeping snails' pace and heartless impersonal nature of bureaucracy engenders hostility and anger. Nevertheless, the growth of bureaucracy is inevitable. One ironic effect is that the oversight powers of the legislature and the Governor have dwindled as the size and scope of bureaucracy has grown.

Table 6.4 Types of Authorities

Agricultural Authorities
Building Authorities
Development Authorities
Educational Authorities
Foundations
Highway Authorities
Municipal Authorities
Park Authorities
Port Authorities
Power Authorities
Residential Finance Authorities
State Tollway Authority
Stone Mountain Memorial Association
World Congress Center Authority

Source: Compiled by authors.

Conclusion

The administrative machinery grinds slowly, but it usually grinds well. The charges against the lady tourist arrested on the bus were dropped and she initiated a lawsuit against the bus company. The senior citizens who couldn't play bingo have received a sympathetic ear from their state representative who initiated a provision to exempt their organization from criminal categorization. And now, of course, non-profit organizations can run all sorts of raffles. And the county commission chairman who decided that a professionally-trained manager was necessary is simply falling in line with the trends, based on the requirements of the citizens of the State of Georgia.

The present Constitution of the State of Georgia, reflecting these pressures, has created the most administratively-oriented government in the history of the state. Unfortunately, once created, administrative organizations may turn into bureaucratic organizations, learning how to protect their funds, their resources and personnel staffing levels, and even their autonomy. It is the task of the other branches of government to ensure that the bureaucracy remains responsive to the general public, and not just to their particular clients and special interest group supporters.

Key Terms

Administration
Bureaucracy
Charismatic Government
Constructive Rivalry
Destructive Conflict
Executive Model vs. the Administrative Model
A "Lion" and a "fox"
Max Weber
Typology of Historical Change
Mutual Accommodation
Plural Executive
Peach cobbler
Public Administrators
Succession Crises
Traditional Government

Essay Questions

1. Why is the Attorney General arguably the most influential member of Georgia's Executive branch?
2. Compare and contrast the membership and responsibilities of the Public Service Commission and the State Transportation Board in Georgia.
3. How might the various administrative agencies within the state of Georgia work together in order to better benefit Georgians?
4. List and describe at least five constitutional executive boards or commissions, including their functions and tasks that they perform and how the members are appointed or elected.
5. What are the notable differences between the structure of the federal government and the government of Georgia? Explain how the Governor is able to be an "effective leader in such a context."
6. Discuss the advantages that a bureaucratic government has over a legislative and executive government.

Figure 7.1 Local Courthouse

7
The Georgia Judiciary

The Vested Judicial Power

Georgia's State Motto: "Wisdom, Justice and Moderation," not only reflects our traditional and individualistic cultural values, but also the rich heritage of the judiciary. The power of the courts is the power of the pen (reasonable explanations of decisions). Like the executive power, the judicial power is decentralized, but not as decentralized, because the judiciary is based on definite principles and has clear lines of authority running to a pinnacle of power, the state (and ultimately the national) Supreme Court. The judicial power of the state of Georgia is vested "exclusively" in seven classes of constitutional courts. Article VI, Paragraph II provides that all courts of the State shall comprise a unified judicial system.

Generally, the judicial branch of government enjoys a higher respect in the minds of the public than that of the other branches. As a result, the courts often resolve disputes between the other branches of government. For example, during the sorry political jockeying of the so-called three-governor fiasco, arising from the premature death of Governor-elect Eugene Talmadge on December 21, 1946, the State Supreme Court had to resolve a bitter controversy. Three people claimed the Governorship: Ellis Arnall, the sitting Governor attempted to stay on; political boss Herman Talmadge was elected by the legislature; and the newly elected Lt. Governor, M. E. Thompson claimed to be acting Governor (Wolfe). The Supreme Court decided in favor of Thompson and the issue was resolved.

Authorized by the Georgia Constitution in 1835, it was not until 1845 that the legislature formally established the Supreme Court of Georgia. Its first session was held at Talbotton, Georgia, on January 26, 1846, amidst uncertainty and skepticism. At issue was whether the court's very existence would endure since it was assumed that "within ten years the Court would decide all questions of law and thus [other branches] would no longer be necessary" (www.gasupreme.us/history/#history). Today, the Georgia Supreme Court stands at the top

117

of the legal ladder in the state judicial system. Starting at the bottom, in ascending hierarchal order, the seven constitutional courts provided under the 1983 Constitution are: magistrate courts, probate courts, juvenile courts, state courts, superior courts, the Court of Appeals, and the Supreme Court. Our current Constitution provides that the *judicial power* of the state is vested in the listed classes of courts. The concept of judicial powers has to do with the power of the courts to interpret and apply the law's generalities to particular cases. This also applies to the courts' *review powers* as well. Through judicial review, courts can determine whether or not earlier proceedings of a state court, executive acts and state legislative acts are valid (Gifis, 1975, p. 138).

In Georgia, the last three courts, namely, the superior courts, the Court of Appeals, and the Supreme Court, have high status because they have appellate powers and they are courts of unlimited (or general) jurisdiction, which can and do handle all types of legal cases, civil and criminal. By unlimited or general jurisdiction we mean that all three courts can and do handle all types of legal cases, civil and criminal. The general concept of jurisdiction speaks to "the range of legal authority (of the court) to hear and determine a case" or more specifically, the authority to enforce laws or pronounce legal judgments (Gifis, 2003). A descriptive overview of the various types of courts and their respective jurisdictions—unlimited and limited jurisdictions—is presented in the following pages.

Courts of Unlimited Jurisdiction

Moving up the hierarchical ladder, the first type of court with unlimited jurisdiction in the State of Georgia is the superior court. In practice superior courts are courts of both exclusive and unlimited (general) jurisdiction that are charged with the power to hear cases that involve state law. As provided by the 1983 Constitution, superior courts hear civil and criminal cases as well as felonies in the forty-eight superior court circuits in the State of Georgia. Unlike the Court of Appeals and the Supreme Court with appellate jurisdictional powers (charged with the authority to hear but not try cases), superior courts are primarily courts of first instance.

The Georgia Court of Appeals is the second court of unlimited jurisdiction which functions primarily as a court of first appellate review for many civil and criminal cases moving up from the superior courts in Georgia. For the most part the Court of Appeals hears cases that have already been tried by the state trial and superior courts, if the Supreme Court has no exclusive appellate jurisdiction over the subject matter. The purpose of such a review (whether performed by the

Court of Appeals or the State Supreme Court) is to look for, and if found, correct any legal errors or errors of law made at the trial level; it is not supposed to alter jury verdicts or the outcome of bench trials. The Georgia Court of Appeals was established by a constitutional amendment of 1906. Under the 1983 Constitution it became a court of review which exercises appellate and certiorari jurisdictions in all cases not reserved to the Supreme Court.

The third court of unlimited jurisdiction is the Supreme Court, which also is the state's highest court and the court of last resort. It functions as an appellate court as well as a review court. More importantly, its jurisdictional authority is unlimited (see Tables 7.1 and 7.2 on page 130). The 1983 State Constitution provides that the Supreme Court shall be a court of review and shall exercise exclusive appellate jurisdiction specified cases. Thus, it exercises exclusive appellate jurisdiction in (a) all cases involving the construction of a treaty or of the Constitution of the State of Georgia or of the United States, and all cases in which the constitutionality of a law, ordinance or constitutional provision has been drawn in question; and also (b) all cases of election contest. And (c) the Supreme Court also has general appellate jurisdiction over decisions made in civil and criminal cases by a trial court or by the Court of Appeals.

The Supreme Court of Georgia also exercises general appellate jurisdiction on cases involving title to land, equity, involving wills, habeas corpus, extraordinary remedies, divorce and alimony cases, certifications to it by the Court of Appeals, and all cases in which a sentence of death has been imposed or could be imposed. Additionally, the Supreme Court may answer any question of law from any state or federal appellate court and may review by certiorari cases in the Court of Appeals which are of gravity or great public importance. Lastly, the Supreme Court has the power to make such orders as are necessary in the aid of its jurisdiction or to protect or effectuate its judgments. Ordinarily, trials are not held at the appellate level nor are parties to such cases invited to appear or testify before either the Court of Appeals or the Supreme Court. In the rare event that attorneys are invited to present oral arguments, such arguments are heard by a full court.

Courts of Limited Jurisdiction

In contrast to the courts of unlimited jurisdictions, the following four types of lower courts—the magistrate, probate, juvenile, and the state courts—are courts of limited jurisdiction. Their powers are prescribed by law for the kind of cases they are called upon to hear and render judgment. Some of the courts are created and their jurisdictional powers conferred by the State Constitution and others are said to be established by statutes (that is, laws made by the legislature or the General Assembly) and municipal and county ordinances. However, the lower courts are similar in the sense that their range of legal authority to hear and determine cases is limited to the very specialized types of cases they called upon to determine. A descriptive overview of the scope and powers of the various courts of limited jurisdiction is presented below.

First, magistrate courts in the state of Georgia are created by county governments and therefore are primarily county courts. Under the 1983 Constitution, formerly justice of the peace courts, small claims courts, and county courts were unified to a new name, namely, the magistrate courts. They are primarily courts of first resort quite distinct from municipal courts which are creations of city or municipal governments. These courts have uniform jurisdiction as provided by law. Both types of courts have uniform jurisdiction and for the most part are courts of limited jurisdiction with primary authority to handle county and municipal ordinances violations and preliminary hearings for certain kinds of criminal cases.

Specific to magistrate courts, their jurisdictions include minor civil and criminal offenses in violations of county ordinance where civil claims accepted for resolution within their civil jurisdictions must not exceed $15,000. For the most part, cases typically handled by county magistrate courts include the issuance of arrest warrants, preliminary hearings that often include sitting as court of inquiry (binding an accused over to a higher court or ordering a discharge), the administration of oaths, affidavits, performing marriages, or issuing bail for defendants. In civil cases, the jurisdiction of magistrate courts extend to contract cases, property damage, injury or conversion cases, landlord-tenant disputes, and deposit account fraud (bad checks). In Georgia, magistrate courts do not offer jury trials, and even where a proper request for a jury trial is made, the case will be transferred (not appealed) to a superior or state court.

A second category of lower court is the juvenile court. There are 159 juvenile courts in the 159 counties in the State of Georgia. As specialized courts, they have exclusive and original jurisdiction over minor juvenile matters. However, jurisdiction over those juveniles who commit very serious or otherwise violent capital offense resides instead in the superior courts. Additionally, while there is one juvenile court each per county, in some counties juvenile courts have concurrent jurisdiction with superior courts in child custody and child support matters arising from divorces cases, as well as in proceedings to terminate parental rights. In Georgia, juvenile courts handle cases involving deprived and neglected children under 18 years of age; delinquent and unruly offenses committed by children under 17 years of age; and traffic violations committed by juveniles. They also hear cases involving consent to marriage for minors, enlistment of minors in the military, and procedures for return of a runaway child resident who is taken into custody in another state.

The probate court, formerly courts of ordinary, is a third type of court of limited jurisdiction in the State of Georgia. Probate courts have both original and exclusive jurisdictions in the probate of wills and inheritance, the administration of decedents' estates, appointment of guardians, issuance of lunacy commissions, and the issuance of marriage licenses. Probate judges are also authorized to order involuntary hospitalization of an incapacitated adult or other individual and to appoint a legal guardian to handle the affairs of certain specified individuals. Probate courts also supervise the printing of election ballots and the counting of votes, and in some counties they have jurisdiction over traffic and issues of compulsory school attendance laws.

The fourth category of court of limited jurisdiction in Georgia is the state court. As a class of courts they exercise limited jurisdiction within a county. State courts are established by local legislation introduced in the Georgia General Assembly to handle minor criminal and civil cases in the larger urban counties and thus in that sense serve as a "back up" for the superior courts since they handle almost identical type of cases. So for example, state courts would hear misdemeanor cases to include traffic violations, issue search and arrest warrants, hold preliminary hearings in criminal cases and try civil matters so long as they are not committed exclusively to the jurisdiction of the superior courts. There are 87 state courts in Georgia, with roughly 118 state court judges in the entire state. They are elected to four-year terms in county-wide nonpartisan elections. However, ordinal vacancies on state courts are filled by an appointment made by the Governor and when this happens, the appointed judges would then sit in competitive nonpartisan elections when the initial appointment lapses.

In summary, the judicial branch of state of Georgia consists of seven constitutional courts of limited and unlimited jurisdictions. Their jurisdictional powers range and vary from exclusive to general powers. Among these powers are the appellate and exclusive powers conferred to these constitutional courts especially to the Court of Appeals and the Supreme Court of Georgia.

Other Quasi–Judicial Institutions

In addition the courts noted above, the General Assembly may authorize the establishment of municipal courts and allow some administrative agencies to exercise quasi-judicial powers. When municipal courts are created, they are courts of limited jurisdiction in that they have jurisdiction only over violations of city laws, or ordinances, and such other jurisdiction as provided by law. For example, the City Court of Atlanta has unique status in the Georgia judicial system in that it blends municipal court powers, magistrate court powers, and civil court powers. Whenever such courts are created, they are said to be endowed with "original jurisdiction." This means that a person can begin the resolution of their legal issue by first going to that court for resolution of the problem. Often the scope of powers of these minor courts overlap with existing constitutional courts which often have the same original jurisdiction, thus allowing parties to go to convenient forums with their litigation. However, if a party is unhappy with the decision of the lower court, that person may appeal to a higher court, which will have the power of "appellate jurisdiction" and the authority to reverse the lower court's decision. Lower courts cannot reverse the decision of appellate courts.

Also, there are special units within some agencies that look like courts and function like courts, but are not really judicial courts at all. These are "quasi-judicial" units or administrative courts created by legislature and the authority to hold hearings into alleged violations of administrative laws (rules and regulations made by bureaucracies). These units usually have an officer called an administrative law judge (ALJ) who specializes in administrative law; functioning independently of the unified legal system, except of course for appellate courts' judicial review. As the trend toward an administrative state continues, such functional quasi-judicial units will become more common.

It should be noted that the powers of juries, judges, and courts are likely to be diminished when legislators push to establish a system of mandatory sentencing guidelines, because it takes sentencing discretion away from these institutions. For example, under a constitutional amendment enacted in 1996, the General Assembly may now enact legislation, which if approved by two-thirds of the members in each house would provide for the imposition of sentences of life without parole both for persons convicted of murder, and for those convicted for a second offense involving murder, armed robbery, kidnapping, rape, aggravated child molestation, aggravated sodomy, or aggravated sexual battery.

Figure 7.2   We Have the Final Decision

Another recent constitutional amendment provides authorization for the creation of special pilot projects for courts. These may serve as venues for experiments in social policy. In some jurisdictions, they might for example be used to minimalize incarceration for non-violent drug offenses, which can clog up the prisons while violent criminals may avoid prison terms or be let out early because of budget constraints. The General Assembly may enact legislation providing for, as pilot programs of limited duration, courts which are not uniform within their classes in jurisdiction, powers, rules of practice and procedure. Similarly the standards for selection, qualifications, terms, and discipline of judges for such pilot courts and other matters can now be enacted by the General Assembly. Although the constitutional amendment specifies that the new pilot courts created by the Georgia General Assembly shall not deny equal protection of the laws to any person, any kind of special treatment of particular kinds of accused persons should always be subjected to careful scrutiny.

Historically, a wide variety of other courts have existed under Georgia's prior constitutions. These include *Justice of the Peace Courts, small claims courts, county recorder's courts,* and *civil courts.* However, either these varied courts generally ceased to exist on June 30, 1983 (the date the new Constitution went into effect) unless they were incorporated into the present system. While the presiding officers of these courts had a variety of titles, the old and honorable title of "judge" is used to include magistrates, judges, senior judges, and even Justices of the Supreme Court. It is usually a good idea to address them as "Your Honor," and to address Supreme Court members as "Justice."

The power of judges is strictly limited by the Constitution. Judges can only react to existing cases and controversies properly brought before them. However, judges are mobile within the court system, and often substitute in other courts, if they are requested to do so, and if they have permission from the judges of their own court. In general, each court in the system may exercise only those powers necessary for it to perform its constitutional or statutory duty. However, in Georgia excluding the lower courts (i.e., the magistrate, probate, juvenile, and state courts), only the superior and appellate courts have the power to issue any of the following historical writs; notably, *mandamus, prohibition, specific performance, quo warranto*, habeas corpus, *and injunction*.

As a relic of early English common law, a writ is a formal written order issued by an administrative or judicial body (a court) enjoining the person to whom it is issued to do some specified act (Gifis, 1975, p. 226)." Some writs are positive and some are negative. For example, the writ of mandamus is a positive order directed to state officials to do their duty; when duly issued, specific perfor-mance enforces private contracts; and prohibitions and injunctions prevent specified actions from being committed or performed. In the end, each superior court, state court, and other courts of record in the State of Georgia may grant a new trial on any legal ground they may deem proper and necessary.

The Unified Judicial System

All courts of the state comprise a unified judicial system, according to Article VI, Paragraph II of Georgia Constitution which provides that all courts of the state shall comprise a unified judicial system. Georgia's courts can be roughly divided into three different categories. As discussed above the *courts of limited jurisdiction* are the first category of courts most Georgians encounter. They only hear certain specific types of cases and are local to their city or county. Courts in this category include: magistrate courts, juvenile courts, probate courts; state courts; and municipal courts. The second category of courts is the *superior courts* which hear serious crimes and larger civil cases in dollar amount. In Georgia, therefore, certain types of cases must go to superior courts; and others may go to superior courts.

The third category of courts is the *Court of Appeals* which review, and sometimes change, the rulings of the lower courts if an appeal is filed. An appeal would go first to the Court of Appeals of Georgia and from there, either party can ask for further review from the supreme court of Georgia, which is the highest court in Georgia. In addition, there are approximately 370 municipal courts with 350 judges actively operating locally. As observed above there are two appellate-level courts: the Supreme Court and Court of Appeals. Except otherwise provided in any recently amended Constitution, the courts of each class must have uniform jurisdiction, powers, rules of practice and procedure, and selection, qualifications, terms, and discipline of judges. However, probate courts are exempt from adhering to the uniform organizational or procedural standards.

The counties in Georgia are geographically divided into 46 *judicial circuits,* each of which has at least one judge. That is, each county has at least one superior court, magistrate court, a probate court, and where needed, a state court and a juvenile court. Some circuits are single county circuits and others are comprised of two or more counties. Sessions of court must be held in each county at least twice a year. The total number of superior court judges is 205. The number of judges per circuit ranges from one to fifteen. In rural areas with small case loads, the General Assembly may allow the judge of the probate court to serve as the judge of the magistrate court, but in the absence of a state court or a juvenile court, the superior court would exercise all of these jurisdictions. Superior courts have jurisdiction over title to land (see Figure 7.1).

The Lower Courts

Centuries of experience have shown that cases should be handled locally where the issues and persons are well-known. Forum shopping for judges who favor a particular point of view is generally prohibited. On some occasions, however, when a case is brought to the wrong court, that court will transfer it to the appropriate court in the state having proper jurisdiction or venue.

Divorce cases are usually tried in the county where the defendant resides, but if the defendant is not a resident of the state, then it will usually be tried in the county in which the plaintiff resides. Special rules apply to military personnel or their dependents residing on any United States army post or military station. The specific exemption in the rules allows military personnel to file for divorce in any adjacent county to their current resident.

Have you ever signed a loan for a car, or cashed a check written by a bank? If you have, and a legal problem develops, where can you be sued? Suits against the makers and endorser of promissory notes, or the drawers and acceptors of bills of exchange or like instruments, will be tried in the county where the maker or acceptor resides. Special problems develop when there are multiple parties on one side of a lawsuit. Determining the proper venue (court with jurisdiction) is often a problem in multiple party cases.

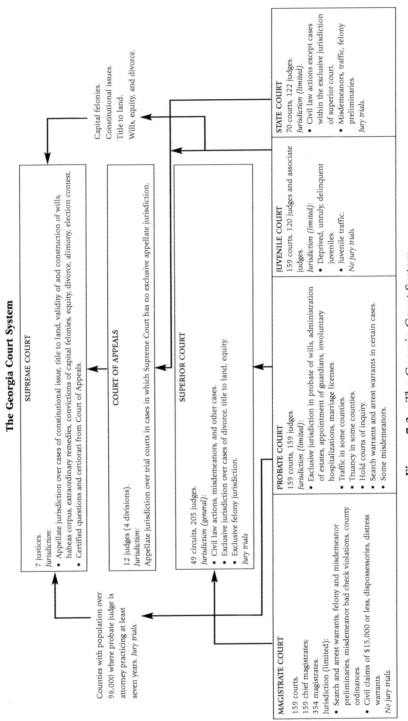

Figure 7.3   The Georgia Court System

Source: Profile Supreme Court of Georgia, reformulated with layout from Administrative Office of the Courts, *www.georgiacourts.org,* by authors, 2011.

Multiple parties may be joint obligors (owing child support), joint tort-feasors (two fraternity brothers hazing freshmen), joint cosigners or co-partners of a loan. Multiple party defendants may be tried either in their county of residence or in the county where the alleged offense occurred. All other civil cases, except juvenile court cases, are tried in the county where the defendant resides. Equity cases, such as injunctions in domestic disputes, are tried in the county where the defendant resides.

All criminal cases are tried where the crime was committed, except cases filed in the superior court where the judge is satisfied that an impartial jury cannot be obtained in that county. Superior courts have very broad jurisdictional powers. For example, except certain juvenile cases which are not within its jurisdiction, superior courts have exclusive jurisdiction over trials in all felony cases and in all cases with respect to titles to land, in divorce cases, and in equity cases. In addition, superior courts have appellate jurisdiction from municipal, magistrate, and probate courts—that is, a reviewing power to correct any legal mistakes that might have been made by the lower courts of limited jurisdiction.

Every week in Georgia, many hundreds of people are sent to prison. They are convicted of serious felonies such as murder, kidnapping, assault, robbery, and auto theft. A major reason for the Governor's emphasis on increasing the number of prison beds is that with over 53,000 inmates currently in the state prison system, there are numerous others sitting in county jails waiting to be transferred (www.ganet.org/corrections/population.html).

Prison Overcrowding

A popular approach throughout the nation to address the perception of out-of-control criminal activities is the so-called "three strikes and you're out" policy that was championed by former President Clinton in the 1990s. Under a three strikes plan, an offender sentenced for a third felony, regardless of the gravity of that crime, automatically receives a life sentence. Georgia has taken this one step behind; it has enacted the "two strikes and you're out" legislation. The result has been a significant increase to the size of the current prison population in Georgia (which already is one of the highest in the nation) to even greater proportions and to a league of its own. The math is a simple one. More prisoners need more prison beds, which leads to much more prison construction. But can the state keep up with the influx? The answer is worrisome. Despite a decrease in the crime rate in Georgia and elsewhere in the country, as a consequent of "two strikes you are out," Georgia keeps sending more and more people to prison.

With increasing budget problems, this is becoming increasingly problematic.

With approximately 14,100 staff the Georgia Department of Corrections currently operates 40 state prisons, 24 county work camps, transitional centers, prisoner boot camps, or pre-transitional centers, 17 diversion centers, 13 detention centers, and two probation boot camps. Throughout Georgia's 159 counties there are 162 jail facilities with a combined rated capacity of 40,000 inmates. In the past ten years, the inmate population in Georgia has doubled, giving the state the dubious distinction of having the country's eighth largest number of adults residing in prison. According to U.S. Dept. of Justice Bureau of Justice Statistics, in 2008, the crime rate in Georgia was about 16% higher than the national average of incarcerated adults per 100,000.

Also, property crimes accounted for around 89.3% of the crime rate in Georgia which was 20% higher than the national rate. The remaining 13.1% were violent crimes about 5% higher than other states. In 2009 Georgia had a probationers' rate 66% higher than the national average number of 100,000 people. What, no non-victimless crimes? While taxpayers paid 39% lower than the other states per inmate in 2008 Georgia still came ahead of most states in case ration rate (Bureau of Justice Statistics, U.S. Dept. of Justice 2008–2010).

Critics of this approach argue that "locking up" more people when the rate of crime is actually declining is certainly punitive but has little or no effect on the overall rate of crime. Moreover, it is quite costly for the following reasons: 1) prison beds are expensive and must come at the expense of something else, probably higher education, if the experience of California is instructive; 2) prisoners who are not released early grow old in prison, and while in their middle and late age they pose little threat to society, they are likely to be in poor health and in need of expensive medical treatment, and; 3) prisoners with no hope for parole require much more scrutiny and control by prison personnel and tend to be more violent than prisoners who know that "good behavior" may get them released.

Discretionary Venue

People are not the only civil and criminal defendants. Legally, corporations can also be classified as persons, and can be regulated, sued, and punished for violations. Where for example, should a case involving a large company be tried? Is it where the company has its multi-million dollar headquarters or where its truck, for example, ran over a pedestrian on a rural road? In Georgia, the Constitution provides that questions of venue will be determined by the state legislature by

statute. Nevertheless, the power to change the venue in civil and criminal cases is vested in superior courts. That is, such a power is reserved
by law to the expert discretion of the presiding judge in a case.

The Higher Courts

The Court of Appeals consists of nine judges who, like many of the
administrative commissions discussed in the previous chapter, elect
from among themselves a presiding officer, here called the Chief
Judge. Members of the Court of Appeals may sit in panels of not less
than three judges as prescribed by law or and by its rules.

Students should be mindful that the court of appeals is a court of
review, it exercises appellate and certiorari jurisdiction. Unlike appeals
that are styled as a matter of right of the petitioner, the writ certiorari
is a discretionary review. Georgia Courts of Appeals, therefore, exercises appellate and certiorari review in all cases not committed to the
supreme court or conferred on other courts by law. The decisions of
the court of appeals set precedents that bind all courts except the
Supreme Court. In Georgia, the Court of Appeals may also certify a
question to the supreme court for clarification of a point of law, to
which it will then be bound. Lastly, in the event of an equal division
of the judges when sitting as a body, the case will be immediately
transmitted to the Georgia Supreme Court.

The Supreme Court is composed of seven Justices, who elect their
own Chief Justice. That, however, had not always been the case. The
first three judges to the Georgia Supreme Court was chosen by the
General Assembly in 1846. The Constitution was amended in 1896 to
provide for the addition of three Justices to the Court and to provide
that Justices and the Chief Justice would be elected by the people. In
1945, one hundred years after the creation of the Court, a seventh justice was added as required by the Constitution of 1945 and since that
time the composition of the Court has remained the same. The Chief
Justice of the Supreme Court acts as the chief presiding and administrative officer of the court. In other words, the Chief Justice has
approximately the same role with regard to the court system that the
Governor has with the bureaucracy.

The Justices also elect a Presiding Justice to serve if the Chief
Justice is absent, disqualified, or otherwise is recused from a case. A
majority vote is necessary to hear and decide cases. If a Justice is disqualified or recused from any case, a substitute judge from the superior court may be designated by the remaining Justices to serve. The
Georgia Supreme Court is primarily a court of review, but relative to
other state courts, it exercises exclusive jurisdiction in the following
cases:

Table 7.1 Supreme Court's Exclusive Jurisdiction

1. In the construction of a state treaty,
2. The construction of the State Constitution,
3. In construction of the United States Constitution,
4. Determining the constitutionality of a law,
5. The constitutionality of an ordinance,
6. Interpretation of a constitutional provision,
7. All cases of election contest, and
8. Answer questions of law from other jurisdictions.

Source: Compiled by authors.

Unless otherwise provided by law, the Georgia Supreme Court also has appellate jurisdiction in the following classes of cases:

Table 7.2 Appellate Jurisdiction

1. Cases involving title to land;
2. In all equity cases;
3. All cases involving wills;
4. Any habeas corpus cases;
5. Cases involving extraordinary remedies;
6. All divorce and alimony cases;
7. Cases certified by the Court of Appeals; and
8. Cases in which a sentence of death was imposed or could be imposed.

Source: Compiled by authors.

In addition to the classes of cases described above, the Supreme Court of Georgia may review by certiorari cases from the Court of Appeals which are of gravity or great public importance. The decisions of the Supreme Court bind all other courts as precedents. The Supreme Court is required, with the advice and consent of the council of the affected class or classes of trial courts, to issue orders adopting and publishing uniform court rules and record keeping rules which shall provide for the speedy, efficient, and inexpensive resolution of disputes and prosecutions. Each council shall be comprised of all of the judges of the courts of that class. The Supreme Court and the Court of Appeals must dispose of every case at the term for which it is entered on the court's docket for hearing or at the next term.

There are also many judicial bureaucratic agencies, most of which operate under the oversight of the Supreme Court's administrative function. They supervise the state's practicing attorneys, create

Table 7.3 Georgia Judicial Agencies

State Bar of Georgia
Board of Bar Examiners
District Attorney's Offices
Judicial Administrative District Councils
Judicial Council and Administrative Office of the Courts

Judicial Qualifications Commission
Judicial Nominating Commission for the State of Georgia
Council of Juvenile Court Judges
Council of Magistrate Court Judges
The Council of Probate Court Judges of Georgia
Executive Probate Judges Council of Georgia
Advisory Council for Probation
Prosecuting Attorneys' Council of the State of Georgia
The Council of State Court Judges of Georgia
Superior Court Clerks Training Council
The Council of Superior Court Judges of Georgia
Superior Courts Sentence Review Panel

The Institute of Continuing Judicial Education of Georgia Board
     of Court Reporting of the Judicial Council

Georgia Indigent Defense Council

Source: After Jackson, E. L., *The Handbook of Georgia State Agencies.* (Athens, Georgia:
Institute of Government, Univ. of Georgia, 1975.)

Administrative District Councils, issue rules of court, and set standards in a wide variety of contexts. Twenty-four agencies are listed in The Handbook of Georgia State Agencies. Excluding the court entities discussed previously, these are listed on Table 7.3.

Controlling Judicial Personnel

Because of the neutral nonpartisan orientation of the courts, and the special training of judicial personnel, the selection, terms of office, compensation, and discipline of judges creates special problems. Superior court and state court judges are elected on a nonpartisan basis for a term of four years. The Judges of the Court of Appeals and the Justices of the Supreme Court are elected on a nonpartisan basis for a term of six years. In addition to age and residency requirements set by the state legislature, appellate, superior, and state court judges must have been admitted to practice law for seven years. Lesser experience is required for juvenile court judges who only need to have practiced law for five years. The level of experience for probate and magistrate judges is not set in the Constitution, but rather by the General Assembly. Probate and magistrate judges are not required to have formal legal training. In fact, it is not uncommon in rural areas for these judges to lack any formal education beyond high school.

In the higher courts, legal training, a license to practice law, and extensive experience in the courts is expected. When Justice George T. Smith lost his legal challenge to the mandatory retirement age, Governor Miller appointed an experienced replacement. The newest Georgia Supreme Court Justice was a 36-year-old African-American woman whose appointment was deemed "a dream come true" (Associated Press, 1-18-92, A3). Judge Leah Sears-Collins (later Leah Ward Sears), was at the time of her appointment in 1992 a trial court judge in Atlanta who became the first woman and the youngest justice to sit on the Supreme Court of Georgia.

Her appointment was followed by the appointment by Governor Miller of yet a second woman, Carol W. Hunstein that year. These two women, along with Justices Benham and Melton, both African-American males, gave the Georgia Supreme Court a truly representative composition in 1992: two women, one an African-American and another white woman, two African-American males, and three white males. Thirteen years later, in 2005, Justice Sears was elected by her fellow Justices to be Chief Justice of the Supreme Court of Georgia, thus becoming the first African-American woman to serve as Chief Justice of any State Supreme Court in the United States.

During her tenure, Chief Justice Sears earned a reputation as a justice committed to upholding both an independent judiciary and the rule of law. Chief Justice Sears served in that capacity until her retirement in 2009. She was succeeded by Carol W. Hunstein, the second female Justice who also became the Chief Justice to the Supreme Court of Georgia in 2009.

The unique training required to qualify as a judge sometimes makes it difficult to select candidates who are ideally representative of all of the various identity and interest groups in the State of Georgia.

The approximately two hundred and two (numbers vary with vacancies) superior court and appellate court judges receive compensation and allowances as provided by law, and may also receive county supplements. County governing authorities have authority to supplement salaries under the current Constitution. Over eight hundred judges who serve in the lower courts are paid by their respective entities. An incumbent's salary, allowance, or supplement cannot be decreased during the incumbent's term of office. Additionally, all

Figure 7.4   Beneath the Robes

judges must reside in the geographical area in which they are selected to serve. The age of 75 years is the mandatory retirement for all judges. The Georgia judicial structure is depicted on Figure 7.3. In a nutshell, the Georgia court system consists of courts of limited, general, and appellate jurisdictions. It has five classes of trial-level courts: the magistrate, probate, juvenile, state, and superior courts. All of these also include the approximately 350 municipal courts operating locally within the state of Georgia.

Judicial Vacancies and Removals

Article Six, Section VII, Paragraph III of the Georgia Constitution specifies that routine judicial vacancies will be filled by appointment by the Governor (except as otherwise provided by law). Generally, an appointee to an elective office serves until a successor is duly selected and qualified, following the next general election which is more than six months after such person's appointment. In Georgia, the Governor does not have the power to suspend or remove a judge for misconduct. Instead, the power to discipline, remove, and cause involuntary retirement of judges is vested in the Judicial Qualifications Commission.

The Judicial Qualifications Commission consists of seven members. Two are judges selected by the Supreme Court; three are members of the State Bar elected by the Board of Governors of the State Bar; and two are non-lawyer citizens appointed by the Governor. Any judge may be removed, suspended, or otherwise disciplined for willful misconduct in office, or for willful and persistent failure to perform the duties of office, or for habitual intemperance, or for conviction of a crime involving moral turpitude, or for conduct prejudicial to the administration of justice which brings the judicial office into disrepute.

In the unusual circumstance that a judge is indicted for a felony by a grand jury of the state or of the United States, the Attorney General or district attorney will inform the Judicial Qualifications Commission. The commission then reviews the indictment, and determines whether the indictment adversely affects the administration of the office or the rights and interests of the public. If so, the commission will suspend the judge immediately, pending the final disposition of the case or until the expiration of the judge's term of office, whichever occurs first.

It should be noted that indictments are not convictions, and sometimes are motivated by political considerations. If an indicted judge who is suspended from office is not immediately tried at the next regular or special court term, the suspension will be terminated and the judge will be reinstated to office. If the indictment is not prosecuted, or if the judge is acquitted, or if the conviction is later directly overturned, the judge shall be immediately reinstated to the office.

When a judge is suspended, he or she will continue to receive a salary. Furthermore, the commission does not review the indictment for a period of 14 days from the day the indictment is received. During this period of time, the indictment may be quashed, or the judge may resign or authorize the commission to suspend him from office. Any such voluntary suspension is subject to the same conditions for reinstatement, or declaration of vacancy as for a non-voluntary suspension. After any suspension is imposed, the suspended judge may petition the commission for a review. Then, if the commission determines that the judge should no longer be suspended, it may reinstate the office.

Of course, immediately upon initial conviction for any felony, the Constitution requires that the judicial official must be immediately suspended from office, and may not receive any more salary, allowance, or compensation. But if the conviction is later overturned and the judge is reinstated to the office, then he is entitled to receive any back pay. For the duration of any suspension, the Governor will appoint a replacement judge. And upon a final conviction with no appeal or review pending, the office shall be declared vacant and a successor to that office will be appointed by the Governor as described above.

It is interesting to note that the sunshine law does not apply to the Judicial Qualifications Commission. The findings and records of the commission, and even whether the judge has or has not been suspended, is not open to the public; nor is it admissible in evidence in any court for any purpose. Accordingly, no action shall be taken against a judge except after hearing and in accordance with due process of law. Also, no removal or involuntary retirement shall occur except upon order of the Supreme Court after review. However, any judge may be retired for disability which constitutes a serious and likely permanent interference with the performance of the duties of office. Because there is no perfect political or judicial system, and yet our society needs to inculcate a general trust in these systems, problems are downplayed and an internal peer review method is used to prevent widespread abuse of judicial misconduct.

The State Attorney General

As briefly mentioned in Chapter Five of this textbook, the Georgia Constitution provides for the office of the Attorney General, who is elected at-large to serve as the head of the department of law for the State of Georgia. As observed in Chapter Five, the Attorney General is a vital link between the executive branch and the judicial branch of government. The Attorney General or Georgia's chief legal officer is one of six popularly elected executive officers provided in the Georgia Constitution. Unlike the federal Constitution, our State Constitution does not vest most of the executive power in one office. Just as the state existed before the federal government existed, there was an office of the Attorney General long before there was a Supreme Court in the State of Georgia. Put differently, the history of that office determined its reputation, because it is traceable to legal actions and interventions in the colony that became our state.

The office was first opened in 1754 when King George II appointed William Clifton, an English lawyer, as the first Attorney General of the State of Georgia. Thereafter, there were three general requirements for those seeking the position of GA in Georgia, namely: residency and citizenship, a minimum age, and bar membership. First, it is a constitutional requirement that those seeking to serve the position of Attorney General must have been a resident of Georgia for four years and a U.S. citizen for ten. Second, the age requirement warrants that those seeking that office must also be at least twenty years of age, and must have been an active member of the State Bar of Georgia for at least seven years.

The Attorney General is the chief law enforcement officer of the state, but the duties of that office are carefully circumscribed by law. So, for example, the law prohibits whoever occupies the office from providing legal advice or assistance to the private citizens of Georgia. However, the Georgia Constitution and the Official Code of Georgia gives the Attorney General the authority to "offer opinions regarding various legal issues that concern the State of Georgia or its agencies." The Attorney General also has the authority to represent the State of Georgia in capital felony appeals before the Supreme Court of Georgia and in civil cases before any court of the state.

Similarly that office is also charged with the powers to prosecute the public corruption cases regarding criminal charges that were filed against any person or business involved in illegal activity with the State of Georgia. It may also conduct any investigation regarding questionable activity concerning any state agency, department, person, or business that has engaged in business with the State of Georgia. Finally, among its other duties are the power to initiate (or not) any civil or criminal action in accordance with the expressed request of the Governor of the state of Georgia, prepare all contracts and agreements for matters that involve the State of Georgia, and lastly, serve as a legal advisor for state agencies, departments, authorities, and the Governor of the State of Georgia.

The complexity of the multi-headed executive branch in Georgia, and the role of the Supreme Court as a political actor, is shown by a dispute that arose in 2003 between the republican Governor Sonny Perdue and the then-occupier of the office of the Attorney General of the State of Georgia, democrat Thurbert Baker. In the unsettled conditions prevailing as conservative republican partisans began to rise to prominence, Mr. Baker was perhaps the most powerful of the old guard democratic officeholders. He was initially appointed to office in 1997, and then was elected and re-elected in state-wide elections in 1998, 2002, and 2006. Mr. Baker received a Bachelor of Arts degree from the University of North Carolina at Chapel Hill in 1975 and a law degree from Emory University's School of Law in 1979. In addition to being an active member of his community, Mr. Baker also served as a lawyer for the U.S. Environmental Protection Agency and had managed his own firm prior to his appointment and subsequent election as the Attorney General of the State of Georgia. But when Sonny Perdue was elected governor and tried to order Mr. Baker to drop a legal appeal involving a democratically drawn legislative redistricting map, the Attorney General dug in his heels and refused to do so, citing his constitutional independence from the Governor. The Supreme Court sided with Baker, affirming the separation between the two offices (Perdue v. Baker). In 2010, Mr. Baker mounted a campaign for the governorship, but was defeated in the primary by the former Governor, Roy Barnes. The newest Attorney General in Georgia, the successor to Mr. Baker, is Mr. Sam Olens, who is the 53rd person to hold that title in Georgia. It is too early in his tenure to predict whether he will also uphold the independence of his office, or will yield to the political party leadership of the new Governor, Mr. Nathan Deal.

District Attorneys

Another significant official in the state's legal system is the district attorney. The Constitution mandates a district attorney for each judicial circuit, who is elected circuit-wide for a term of four years. More specifically, the Constitution required that all successors of present and subsequent incumbents are elected by the electors of their respective circuits at the general election held immediately preceding the expiration of their respective terms. It also requires that vacancies are filled by appointment of the Governor. The qualifications include having been an active-status member of the State Bar of Georgia for three years immediately preceding such person's election. The district attorneys receive such compensation and allowances as provided by law and like some judges may also receive local supplements to their compensation and allowances.

It is the duty of the district attorney to represent the state in all criminal cases in their superior court and in all cases appealed from the superior court or the juvenile courts and to perform such other duties as shall be required by law. District attorneys enjoy immunity from private suit for actions arising from the performance of their duties. Any district attorney may be disciplined, removed, or involuntarily retired as provided by general law (see Article VI, Section VIII).

Transitional Notes

The City Court system of Atlanta survived the constitutional revisions of 1983. In addition, the municipal courts, county recorders' courts, and Civil Courts of Richmond and Bibb counties, and several of the administrative agencies having quasi-judicial powers, also continued with the same jurisdiction as these courts and agencies had when the 1983 Constitution went into effect. On the other hand, justice of the peace courts, small claims courts, and magistrate courts operating on the effective date of the new Constitution and the County Court of Echols County became magistrate courts. The County Court of Baldwin County and the County Court of Putnam County became state courts, with the same jurisdiction and powers as other state courts. Reshaping of court systems and jurisdictions, along with the redistricting of legislative seats, and the redefinition and existence of municipalities and special purpose authorities, is part and parcel of the ferociously and ever-changing face of American federalism.

Conclusion

The structure and functioning of the state judiciary in Georgia is unique. It is perhaps the most traditionalistic of the branches of government. The power of the judiciary, and indeed the courts are seemingly dispersed among many agencies and jurisdictions. Judges, as members of the legal profession, are immersed in centuries of legal lore and tradition pre-dating democratic government itself. To a great extent, the profession attempts to embody what Daniel Elazar calls the basic traditionalistic ethic: a political actor attempting to carry out a positive role in the community, but limited to securing the continued maintenance of the existing order. However, unlike the historical monarchies and aristocracies that created judicial function, the members of the modern American judiciary are not expected to benefit personally from their activities.

Similarly, over time, the professional members of the regular public services, the career administrators and bureaucrats, may be expected to develop a similar high level of status and acceptance. However, the British judiciary existed for hundreds of years in a dependent relation with the British crown, before judges achieved constitutional independence in the Americas. If a similar amount of time is necessary for the various public administrators to achieve equal status in their own fields, it is no wonder that bureaucrats have a long way to go to match the esteem currently given to the judicial branch of government in the State of Georgia.

Key Terms

Administrative Law Judge
Appeal
Appellate Jurisdiction
Certiorari
Court of Appeal
Department of Law
Discretionary Venue
Exclusive Jurisdiction
Immunity

Judicial Circuit
Jurisdiction
Judicial Qualification Commission
Limited Jurisdiction
Magistrate Court
Original Jurisdiction
Sunshine Law
Superior Court
Supreme Court
Unlimited Jurisdiction
Vested Powers

Essay Questions

1. Discuss the hierarchical order of the seven constitutional courts in Georgia.
2. In what way does the City Court of Atlanta have a unique status in the Georgia legal system?
3. Explain the state of Georgia's "two strikes and you're out" policy. How is it related to prison overcrowding?
4. Explain the structure of the Georgia Supreme Court and address each court's jurisdiction. You should also detail each court and their respective numbers.
5. Compare and contrast the appointment of judges/justices and the nonpartisan election of judges/justices.
6. Who are the members of the Judicial Qualifications Commission in Georgia? How does the Judicial Qualifications Commission impact the removal of judges/justices in the state?
7. What is the role of the Department of Law and the Attorney General within the Georgia State Government? What is the relationship, if any, between the Department of Law and the Supreme Court of the State of Georgia?

Figure 8.1 Georgia Department of Revenue

Budgeting and Finance

Billions and Billions in Budgets

As Governor Deal took office in a blinding snowstorm, he faced a looming fiscal disaster as well. To study the problem, this chapter focuses on the year 2009, the last year of full budget information as this textbook goes to print. Students should also go to a current Internet site like *http://www.usdebtclock.org* and then click on State Debt Clocks, its links to the states, especially the State of Georgia. The complexity of the rapidly changing number flows is quite incredible. It shows the State of Georgia, like most of the other states in the union and like the federal government, to be close to a financial crisis as a result of the "Great Recession" initiated by the stock market crash in 2008. As a result of the stock market collapse and economic slowdown, for several years now revenues have failed to keep pace with the increasing costs of providing programs and services for our people. And in Georgia general revenues have really been seriously declining over the last couple of years, due not only to national economic crisis, but also due to an untimely combination of tax cuts, all while experiencing growth in services and expenses. The latter was further exacerbated by the Great Recession, as many normally working people became unemployed and needed help.

Then the real crunch began, when the hard times forced the Georgia Assembly to reduce its state spending and to try to cut back on services to the people. Many state employees were terminated, laid off, or furloughed to save more money. In 2011 our new governor, Nathan Deal, warned us that further reductions seemed to be necessary. How serious is the situation, and how will it affect the people of Georgia? To fully understand the magnitude of the problem, we need to look at the financial position of the state. How wealthy is Georgia and its people, and what are the finances, property assets, and debts of our state government? And of course we need to know its income and expenses. We are talking about large sums of money. The state government owns billions of dollars in assets ($17,687,608,810), but

Table 8.1   Selected Georgia Fiscal Statistics

Current Georgia GDP	$ 400,000,000,000
Value of State-Owned Assets	$ 17,687,608,810
Value of State Obligations	$ 14,616,131,557
2009 Operating Revenues (est):	$ 21,165,882,516
2009 Operating Expenditures (est):	$ 21,165,882,516
Tax Supported Indebtedness:	$ 9,689,903,540
Per Capita taxes/fees	$ 2,167
Per Capita debt:	$ 984

Source: Compiled by authors from 1) The Budget in Brief FY 2010/AFY 2009; 2) the 2011 Statistical Abstract: State Rankings; *Forbes.com*, 01-20-10 @ 8:00 pm, EST; and other sources.

it also owes billions of dollars ($14,616,131,557) to its many creditors and bond holders. Table 8.1 displays some selected sum totals and/or estimates of the assets, debts, and operational budgets and expenditures for the State of Georgia in 2009.

Table 8.1 also shows us 21,165,882,516 was the estimated budget appropriations, for fiscal year 2009. In fact, actual figures may vary. The twenty-one billion dollar figure is the same for both the billions of dollars in revenues and the billions of dollars appropriated for operations because the Constitution requires a balanced budget every year. It should be noted that the tax supported indebtedness is about one-half of annual revenues. Residents of Georgia have an on-going debt burden that amounts to approximately half of the amount they pay in taxes in any one year. In fiscal year 2009, the total appropriations slightly overran revenues, so then-Governor Perdue vetoed about $14 million of pending outlays to make it balance. When all is said and done, the State Government certainly needs to tighten its belt, but thanks to constitutional prohibitions and some sound decisions, in general the State of Georgia has low taxes and a sound fiscal structure.

Although some people think that large organizations, governments, and corporations should be budgeted just like families balance their budgets, that is not actually true. One good way to study any budgeting subject is to analyze its patterns and cycles, so the trends can be extrapolated and the future can be predicted and prepared for. Ordinary people have certain predictable realities. For example, when people are born they are supported by their parents. But when they grow up, they often have to borrow money to go to school, to buy a car, and eventually get married and buy a house and raise children of their own. This averages out to something like twenty years to study, followed by about forty or so years of working for a living. In short, each person has a definite time to learn, earn, borrow, and spend money and have it all balanced out in one lifetime. After a certain age, people may find it hard to borrow money, because creditors know that the borrower may not be able to pay it back. The human life cycle determines patterns and economic activity.

Unlike people, large organizations, like governments, churches, and corporations have longer life spans. In fact, they tend to exist for centuries. And so they can afford to take a much longer time to pay their debts. This is good, because such artificial entities build huge projects that people can't, like buildings, dams, roads, and bridges. These take decades to build, maintain, and pay for. Organizational life spans are far longer than are those of individual human beings. So corporations and governments play by different budget rules than those applied to ordinary people. And governments own vast amounts of land, resources, and real estate. The care and preservation of these kinds of properties takes years of long-term planning and investment.

As a result, whereas family budgets are usually in the range of thousands of dollars and years of time, large organizations routinely deal with millions and billions of dollars over decades and sometimes even centuries. The State of Georgia is an example. It has to finance the building of roads and bridges and operate institutions like colleges and universities over hundreds of years. It owns mountains, plains, river valleys, and park lands, and is a huge landlord of thousands of buildings and other facilities. Every year the state has to check its property and assess its value on the current market and decide how to manage it. In 2009 the Georgia State Government owned almost eighteen billion dollars ($17,687,608,810) in property and other assets. But sometimes it has to buy property, and takes out mortgages to do so. Or it may borrow money for maintenance and improvements to serve a growing population. As a result, the state government owes a lot of money, about fourteen and a half billion dollars ($14,616,131,557) in all. Figure 8.2 on the next page shows the bottom lines, our total assets and total debts in 2009.

While Figure 8.2 is useful for displaying the magnitude of the numbers involved when discussing Georgia's gross assets and debt obligations, the pie chart format is better used to compare how much of the State's property value is actually swallowed up by the debts and obligations. If some fantastic calamity happened, like foreign conquest, and the State of Georgia had to declare bankruptcy, it could sell all its assets and still end up with a little over three billion dollars in the bank. But unlike business organizations, public entities rarely go bankrupt, because their finances are watched very closely by a large number of public and private interest groups. And, of course, the State

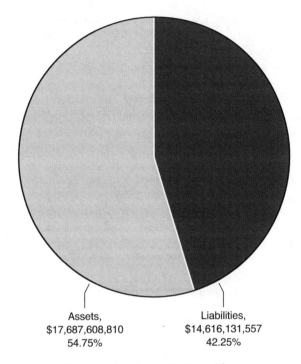

Assets,
$17,687,608,810
54.75%

Liabilities,
$14,616,131,557
42.25%

Figure 8.2   Some Bottom Lines

Source: Compiled by Authors from the Budgetary Compliance Report for the
Fiscal Year Ending Junes 30, 2009, page 6. The information was supplied
by the State Accounting Office, Georgia State Government.

would still have some cash inflow, particularly from tax revenues. It is because the State finances are watched so carefully that we own more than we owe, as displayed in Figure 8.3 on page 145. When so many billions of dollars are at stake, citizens need to watch their wallets carefully.

Taxes, Revenues, and Debts

Like all the citizens of the state, Georgia has to pay its bills. Unlike the United States Government, which does not separate its operational budgets from its capital budgets, all states, except Vermont, have to balance all their operational budgets. An operational budget includes the expenses for ongoing routine operations. In contrast, a capital budget is used for expensive long-term building projects such as highway and bridge construction. While it is recognized that building projects may have to be funded by bonds and other debt-creating instruments, State Constitutions usually require that on-going opera-

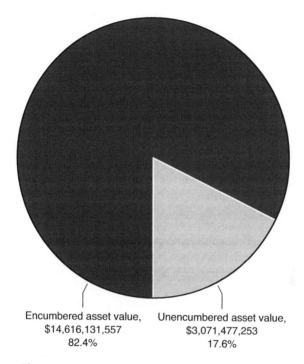

Encumbered asset value,   Unencumbered asset value,
$14,616,131,557 $3,071,477,253
82.4%   17.6%

Figure 8.3   Proportion of Assets Encumbered
Source: Compiled by Authors from the Budgetary Compliance Report for the Fiscal
Year Ending June 30, 2009, 6. The information was supplied by the
State Accounting Office, Georgia State Government.

tional budgets must be paid for on a cash flow basis. That is, states cannot spend more than they take in as revenue. Thus, they must have revenue sources that provide enough income for them to meet their needs and responsibilities each year.

Why does the state government have to live on a budget? Isn't it true that government doesn't have to budget because it has unlimited income, mainly from tax dollars? Actually, this myth about government could not be more wrong. The writers of the State Constitution, ratified by popular vote, decided that every year the government should carefully budget its money to pay as we go and not incur an annual deficit. All the states have done this, to force the government to spend the people's money wisely and not to get into debt. Nevertheless, states do go into debt, and the state indebted in Georgia is about as much as our total assets. If the state went bankrupt, we would be broke, but we would have prospects of continued revenues from tax and fee collections.

In fact, arguments over how to obtain budget money and how to spend it constitute the bulk of political conflict in Georgia. Politics can be defined as the struggle over who gets what, when, and how (Lasswell), but most political battles take place over *who pays* what, where, how, why, and when. The state's fiscal (budget) year runs from July 1 to June 30, and every day sees conflict over finances. There are lots of different sources for revenue, but the most important is taxes, so that is where any analysis must start.

The Georgia Constitution also addresses the matter of state debt. State Government is allowed to borrow money for several purposes. These may include crisis events, like debt to repel invasion, for suppression of insurrection; and of course for more routine problems such as temporary cash flow shortages or problems financing local governments. But the main reason is to sell bonds to finance big construction projects, like roads and bridges, or special projects.

The tax powers of the state are too valuable to be left only to the fads and fancies that buffet our politicians. Article VII of the Georgia Constitution deals with taxation and finance. It places the power to tax with the General Assembly, although that power may be delegated in part to local governments. Currently, the bulk of Georgia's revenue comes from three sources: ad valorem taxes, income taxes, and sales taxes.

Ad valorem is a Latin term meaning "according to the worth." An ad valorem tax is a tax determined by the value of that which is taxed. Those of you who own cars know that you have to buy license tags for your car each year. In addition to a small license tag fee, which varies from county to county in Georgia, you may be required to pay an ad valorem tax on the value of the automobile. If your car is an old "junker," there may be no ad valorem tax assessed. If, on the other hand, it is a new car, you may have to pay hundreds of dollars according to the value of your vehicle. So the amount that you pay can vary markedly from county to county.

Ad valorem taxes on automobiles are reported to be among the most popularly detested levies in the nation. When one Republican candidate for Governor of Virginia came up with the idea of eliminating the ad valorem tax on automobiles in the Commonwealth, his candidacy took off, and he won the 1997 race going away. In 1998, a number of gubernatorial candidates in several states, including Guy Milner, the GOP nominee in Georgia, followed Virginia Governor Gilmore's lead in running against this tax. Milner, however, lost the election. Voters knew that it was a reasonable tax that can be enforced. The county, acting as a subdivision of the state, also collects ad valorem taxes on tangible personal property and tangible real property. Tangible personal property includes all manner of possessions— jewelry, furs, boats, and even money itself. Tangible real property is real estate—land. Since land cannot be moved or hidden, it is a stable source of revenue for the government.

Over time, states have allowed local governments to assess a basic property tax and to keep the proceeds to defray their own expenses. Because land is used for a variety of purposes, and the purposes often determine its value, differently used property is taxed differently. For example, agricultural land may be taxed at seventy-five percent (75%) of the value of other land. Before the current budget crisis, the land on which many people lived was entitled to a homestead exemption, a reduction of the taxes you would otherwise pay.

Only a few states lack a state individual income tax. Georgia is certainly not one of them. In Georgia the personal income tax is a very important source of revenue for the state. Based, at least in theory, on the ability to pay, the income tax is progressive, meaning that the more income you earn, the more tax you pay. If a tax is designed so that people with large incomes pay a larger percentage, it is called a progressive tax. However, the tax scale in Georgia is somewhat flat, or regressive, so that income exceeding $7,000 may be taxed at a maximum rate of only 6.0%. Thus, a person earning over one million dollars a year might pay at the same rate as a person earning only $7,001.

Like the ad valorem tax, the income tax is also unpopular with many people. Republicans in the 1998 Session of the General Assembly promised to try to repeal the income tax over a period of several years. However, they could not muster the necessary votes, partly because they couldn't figure out how to replace all that lost revenue. They were no more successful in the next two sessions, where they barely mentioned what was clearly a scheme whose time had not yet come. In 2011 there is talk of repealing the corporate income tax, but not the individual income tax. Currently, in addition to the individual income tax, Georgia, like forty-six other states, levies an additional income tax on corporate profits.

Similarly, like forty-five other states, Georgia has a sales tax. When the sales tax was first enacted in Georgia, a miniscule tax was applied to most purchased goods, initially excluding services. Today, the early low sales tax has risen to about four percent, and as a result the state's lowest and middle income citizens pay higher percents of their total income into the state's coffers. This **"regressive tax"** (harder on poor people) has, however, become so critical to Georgia's budget that it is not anticipated that any substantial change will take place in the near future. Although it is officially set at four percent, counties may add an extra one percent local option sales tax (LOST).

In 1996, voters also approved an amendment to the Georgia Constitution permitting school districts to add another Special Local Option Sales Tax (SPLOST) if they could get a majority of the voters to agree to it. Agreement would allow one more penny to be added to the overall sales tax. Usage of the basic four percent sales tax and the one percent optional tax is fairly standard throughout the state; but the additional special one percent tax is earmarked for use only for special capital building projects—such as a new courthouse, a new jail, road construction—and has an automatic "sunset" provision which acts to terminate the tax within five years or less of its approval. The same provisions generally apply to school district SPLOST options.

With all these "piggy-back" sales taxes, many people in Georgia pay sales tax of seven percent. It is common for progressive states to try to exempt from sales taxes certain necessities such as food, medicine, and clothing so that sales taxes will be less burdensome on poor people. Although two decades ago Governor Zell Miller recommended, in 1990, that certain food items be exempted from the tax, and the Georgia legislature then passed laws to that effect, the wording of the law was subsequently challenged in court and the State Supreme Court invalidated part of the food exemption because the language was unclear and confusing. When the Governor and the General Assembly pass a tax or a revenue bill, the Supreme Court gets a shot at it, and of course eventually it can go full circle back to the legislature, which changes it again.

In 2009, the basic rate of the Georgia state sales tax was 4 percent, but local governments have been given authority to impose additional sales taxes. So the local counties and cities may impose additional sales taxes from one percent to three percent; therefore the sales taxes can range from 4 to 7 percent. To further complicate the picture, food is exempt from the state tax rate, but local jurisdictions can also levy sales tax on them. There are several types of local sales taxes. They include a local option tax, a homestead local option tax, an educational local option tax, the special purpose local option tax (SPOST), and, in Atlanta, a Metropolitan Atlanta Rapid Transit Authority (MARTA) tax and an additional one percent municipal options sales tax.

Due to politics, in 1996 the General Assembly again passed a law exempting food from the sales tax which would be fully effective by 1998. Thus, food joined some 60 other sales tax exemptions in Georgia, including Bibles and the fuel used to heat chicken houses. In the 1998 Session of the General Assembly, bills were introduced to exempt from sales taxes Boy Scout popcorn, wheelchairs, children's caskets, crop dusting planes, grass sod, and about a dozen other things (VD Times, February 12, 1998, p. 3-A). Although its sponsor argued that the Boy Scout popcorn provision would only result in a loss of about $11,000 a year in revenue, and besides it was only fair since Girl Scout cookies are exempt, all of these tax exemptions add up to a sizable amount. The exemption on food alone was estimated to cost the state treasury about half a billion dollars every year. But then the courts invalidated the Assembly-passed exemption! So food purchases were taxed again. Now, even with the Great Recession still impacting Georgia, several legislators are again calling for a renewed push to pass another food tax exemption.

The Georgia State Lottery

In addition to the major forms of taxes described above, Georgia also collects revenue from a variety of other types of taxes. These include the so-called "sin" taxes on alcohol and tobacco products, severance taxes on lumber products taken from state-owned lands, and motor fuels taxes on every gallon of gasoline sold in the state. The motor fuels tax revenues are then earmarked for building and maintaining the state's ever-expanding system of roads and highways.

In the 1980s many states joined a growing movement to derive some revenue from legalized gambling, but Georgia lawmakers at first resisted the temptation to establish a lottery or pari-mutuel betting on horse racing. The success of the lotteries in other states, however, put great pressure on Georgia legislators and in 1991 the General Assembly passed a bill placing a constitutional amendment for a state lottery on the November 1992 ballot, to allow the citizens to make their voices known on the issue. The voters spoke, and approved the budget amendment. Most of the revenue was originally dedicated to educational expenditures, such as the Hope Grant Program.

The lottery, passed by the voters as a constitutional amendment, has proven to be a phenomenal success, and was projected to be generating revenues, for 2009, from the Georgia Lottery Corporation of about $882,255,743 (BinB, FY 2008/2009, p. 12).

Faced with such figures, most of the die-hard opponents of the lottery plan just threw in the towel. As one writer said: *"accept it for what it is, . . . a voluntary, flat rate tax of 37% on every dollar spent on the lottery"* (Wooten, F7). That is pretty good for a "sin tax," in fact it is a heavier tax than state governments impose on any other *"bad habit."* This is also a big economic boom for the state treasury, and is likely to remain so, at least until all the other states adopt a similar lottery. While Georgia commits the money to educational purposes, some experts believe it would be wiser to shift the money into the general fund, or for special one-time projects (Wooten, F7). But however you cut the pie, it looks as though the lottery is here to stay.

In the first state budgetary period of operation, the proceeds from the lottery were over $879 million, including a surplus of income over expenditures of approximately $28 million in additional revenue for the state (Leg. Budg. Off.). This was a substantial vindication of the Governor's plan. However, financial experts cautioned us not to rely too heavily on these funds, because as the novelty of the new lottery wears off, sales might decline, so that future income from this source may be less than hoped for. In fact, by 1998 there were signs that interest in the Georgia lottery was indeed tapering off. However, by that time over $550 million a year was going to education in Georgia. Moreover, the anticipated decline in lottery interest was apparently premature. In FY 2006, the Georgia lottery had its best year ever. Unfortunately, current projections are that the growth of Hope Fund expenses will shortly begin to outstrip lottery revenues. More will be said about this topic in the chapter on education.

Are Georgians overtaxed or undertaxed? That may sound like a silly question, for whoever feels that he or she is undertaxed? Objectively, however, when Georgia is compared to other states, how does Georgia fare? In a recent year, per capita state and local tax revenue in Georgia was around $1,800, which placed Georgia 32nd among the states. And, when this per capita state and local revenue is examined as a percentage of personal income, Georgia ranked 37th. In other words, Georgia ranked below the median both in terms of the amount of taxes collected from the average person and according to the amount that each person could afford to pay (Dye, 508).

Tax-paying Georgia citizens can be thankful that, comparatively, Georgia ranks as a rather low-tax state. By signing into law the $100 million tax cut in 1994 and a $205 million reduction in 1998, Governor Miller reduced the tax burden even further. How about the distribution of the tax burden? Are Georgians fairly taxed according to income levels? Again, that might sound like a silly question, because no one ever thinks of his or her own tax in terms of tax progressivity (Gray, 314–315). That means that Georgia's burden is fair. And the fact that Georgia ranks twenty-seventh in the nation is slightly less fair than the average in assessing taxes in proportion to ability to pay.

Does Georgia need tax reform? Many economists and political scientists argue that it does. Although a study of state tax systems in 1990 showed that Georgia's system is particularly elastic and therefore likely to be able to withstand fiscal crises, by the time the study was published Georgia, like the rest of the nation, was in fact beginning to experience growing fiscal crisis (Gold, 31–33). Owing to the increasing severity of the recession of the 1990s, personal income in Georgia was down, while personal misery was on the rise.

With a decline in routine federal grants in aid to the states, a decline in state revenue collections, and large increases in necessary operating expenditures, Georgia, like most of the other states, was in serious fiscal trouble. To be sure, some other states were suffering worse, but the knowledge of that did not ease our pain very much. Editorials in major newspapers like the *Atlanta Journal/Constitution* and other influential voices around the Peach State raised the cry for meaningful fiscal and tax reform. But that crisis paled into insignificance compared to the crisis caused by the stock market meltdown and Great Recession of 2008.

Another suggestion for reforming Georgia's tax system is to tax services along with the sale of commodities. In an economy more and more dependent on services, it makes sense to tax car washing, dry cleaning, haircuts, lawyer's fees, dentist's fees, etc. Moreover, since those with higher incomes tend to spend more of their money on services than those with lower incomes, a tax on services would be more progressive than sales taxes on commodities. In what ways the General Assembly will seriously consider tax revision in 2011, especially if it entails new taxes, depends largely on the perception on the depth of the current crisis, or whether interest group ideology will triumph over the welfare of the entire state.

Unfortunately, it is a safe bet that we will not repeat what happened in 2002, when the Georgia General Assembly, at the urging of then-Governor Barnes, "gave back" $329 million to Georgians in the form of tax relief. Georgia did this not because the state's revenues were surging—in fact, they were lagging—but because the state, starting in 1994, embarked on a political policy of returning tax money to the taxpayers, because it had come to be expected. In other words politics, not sound financial policy, was steering the Ship of State. This political thinking has deep roots, even in supposedly conservative Georgia. For example, in introducing his own 1994 tax cut, then-Governor Miller announced: "In the old days, under the old ways, an increase in state revenues would have been treated as feeding time on the hog farm. I am giving this money back to the hardworking families and senior citizens of Georgia." (Miller, Feb. 24, 1994.)

That was fifteen years ago, and today surpluses are not just rare, but non-existent and still some of our politicians continue to demand cutting taxes. Why, when we have budget deficits and soaring demands for services? Well, one "solution" that the state has to fall back on when confronted with budgetary shortfalls is raising user fees or by borrowing. Some radicals suggest that as bankers love to lend money to states, their lobbyists actually work hard to promote economic crisis, just as the "bears" and "vultures" on New York's stock market sometimes deliberately undercut the more progressive "bull" market strategists.

Of course, there are many reasons why investment houses, bankers, and other business want to cut taxes, usually involving profitability of the enterprises. Another and more politically credible reason for cutting taxes is the belief that large scale government programs weaken the moral and business fiber of our citizens—that people should not expect government to help them but instead they should be aggressively seeking full employment. Argument over motives, means, and goals never end. There is a perpetual struggle of deciding what to do with the large amount of money that government can collect.

Operating Budgets—Revenues

State budgets are determined by current economic conditions and by the political aspirations of its people and leaders. In studying the budget we must look at 1) how money (revenues) are collected, and 2) how it is spent (appropriated). We should begin with how revenues are estimated and what the sources are. Later we can study to see how the money is spent. In 2008, the Georgia General Assembly responded to Governor Perdue's continuing state development plans and passed an anticipated $21.1 billion budget for FY 2009, based on revenue projections at the time. Figure 8.4 graphically compares most of the different expected revenues by sources for the year 2009. Pie charts provide visual comparisons

Total projected revenues for 2009 were *$21,165,882,616 (Ibid)*. The pie chart shows the biggest source of state revenues was expected to be the individual income tax, almost half (45.8%) of the total. The income tax is elastic, going up when income goes up and thus immediately responsive to the generally growing economy. And, because it is geared directly to the federal income tax, and collected after those federal taxes are calculated and reported, it is also a progressive tax,

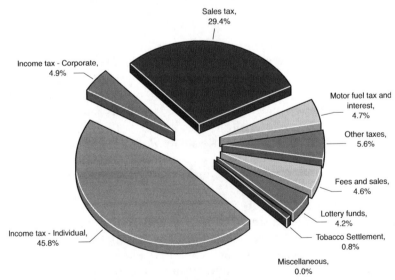

FIGURE 8.4 Projected Revenues—2009
Source: Georgia State Office of Planning and Budget. 2009.
Budget in Brief, Amended FY 2008 and FY 2009, p. 14.

slightly more of a burden on the wealthier taxpayers. But most importantly of all it is cheap to administer and operate because the federal government does most of the work. In contrast, the second largest source of revenue is the sales tax (almost 30%), which is designed, administered, and operated by state employees. But because it is a regressive tax, it is more of a burden on poorer people who have to spend most of their money on necessities. And sales taxes are collected and then submitted to the state by businesses (ideally; but sometimes not!), so the sales tax is unreliable, inelastic, and not very profitable. A wide variety of other taxes and fees and revenues are used, but none of them is as profitable as the income tax.

But while total projected revenues for 2009 were *$21,165,882,616, the actual dollar amount collected was over two million dollars less: only $18,903,699,531.* As shown in Table 8.2, the individual income tax collected only about eight billion dollars instead of the anticipated nine million dollars. And the other revenues were also less than was hoped for. As previously stated, the income tax is elastic, it goes down when income goes down and this happened in 2009. Tax cuts for corporations and higher income levels didn't help. The second largest source of revenue, the sales tax also declined by about three quarters of a billion dollars, even though it is inelastic and therefore less responsive to changes in the economy.

WHAT HAPPENED? In 2008 disaster had struck. Due to the Great Recession, state revenues drastically declined, and revenue fell below the level of projected expenditures. The Republican governor was probably surprised that the crisis had reached that point. Earlier, in

Table 8.2   Actual Revenues—2009

Revenue Source	Total Amount	Percent
Income Tax, Individual	$ 8,224,075,509	43.5%
Sales Taxes	5,432,736,812	28.7
Miscellaneous	1,234,992,394	6.5
Other Taxes	1,124,715,390	5.9
Motor Fuels Tax	993,534,395	5.2
Fees and Sales	983,955,285	5.2
Lottery	880,152,075	4.6
Income Tax, Corp.	695,434,000	3.6
Adjustment Reserve	187,278,126	0.9
Tobacco Settlement	159,069,341	0.8
Totals:	**$18,903,699,531**	**100.0%**

Source: Georgia State Office of Planning and Budget. 2010. Budget in Brief, Amended FY 2009 and FY 2010, p. 6.

2006, well into Georgia's "Republican Revolution," expecting that business deregulation would maintain an economic boom, Governor Perdue had recommended an increased budget of $17.4 billion, including $811 million in revenue from the lottery. This largesse may seem to be in violation of espoused conservative fiscal responsibility; but although our state's political parties may talk like they are worlds apart, in fact they tend to react similarly in meeting the needs and desires of our general population of almost two million people, even if sometimes recklessly, in terms of planning.

Whether financial error is due to recklessness or to willful disregard of economic cycles, political expediency, or maybe even more culpable special interest group manipulation, the structure of state revenues is only half of the annual budget battle. The other half is the perpetual struggle of deciding what to do with the money that is collected. The shortfalls in revenues would not have been a problem if the state had not budgeted itself to spend all the anticipated money. But the state had promised to spend it. If normal budget arguments are like arguing over distribution of peach cobbler, what do you do when the bread runs out first? That topic is further elaborated upon below.

Operating Budgets—Appropriations

Although there is a perpetual struggle of deciding what to do with state money, there are persistent patterns of appropriations. Public school education usually gets the biggest slice of the pie in Georgia, well over one-half. Large pieces also go to health care, human resources, and to higher education. Smaller pieces go to public safety and prisons and to roadway and heavy construction projects. A large portion of the budget goes to various miscellaneous projects within departmental agencies; how much is shown in Figure 8.5.

Appropriations and Expenditures

Although local school boards administer school district policies, the most funding is controlled by state authorities. One of the principal responsibilities of most state governments is public education, and Georgia is no exception. In fact, Georgia devotes more than half of its entire budget each year to primary, secondary, and higher education. The educational turf is divided between two major bureaucracies: the State Board of Education and the State Board of Regents. The great bulk of the state appropriations is allotted to the secondary and grade school institutions, most of which is supervised primarily by the State

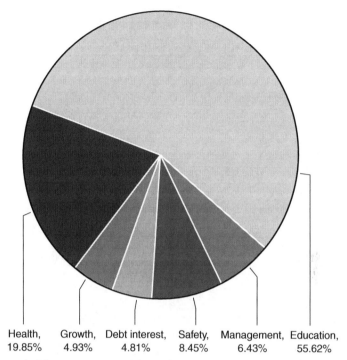

Health,	Growth,	Debt interest,	Safety,	Management,	Education,
19.85%	4.93%	4.81%	8.45%	6.43%	55.62%

Figure 8.5   Anticipated Appropriations—2009

Source: Derived by authors from Georgia State Office of Planning and Budget. 2009.
Budget in Brief, Amended FY 2008 and FY 2009, p. 14.
Total estimated amount: $21,165,882,616.

Board of Education (SBE), which has overall responsibility for administering Georgia's system of primary and secondary education. Together, the local primary and secondary schools, along with higher education, were budgeted to receive almost twelve billion dollars ($11,786,997,371) in 2009, or over half (55.62%) of the total state budget.

The State Board of Education (SBE) makes policy for the state's education systems, sets standards for teacher education programs, certifies teachers, establishes minimal salary levels, imposes graduation requirements, etc. Its members represent each of the congressional districts and are appointed by the Governor. Health care is also administered by a variety of state agencies, local health districts, and sometimes public hospitals.

The total amount budgeted for health care was over four billion dollars ($4,201,549,981), or almost twenty percent (19.85). Other basic institutional programs were positioned to receive another three billion dollars. The most important was public safety: state law

Table 8.3   Anticipated Appropriations—2009

Policy Areas	Amount	Percentage
Education	$11,786,997,371	55.62%
Health Care	4,201,549,981	19.85
Public Safety	1,783,300,947	8.45
Management	1,341,291,667	6.43
Growth	1,043,067,537	4.93
Debt Service	1,009,675,013	4.81
Total:	$21,165,882,616	100.00%

Source: Georgia State Office of Planning and Budget. 2009. Budget in Brief, Amended FY 2008 and FY 2009, p. 18.

Table 8.4   Amended Actual Appropriations—2009

Policy Areas	Expected	Actual	Result
Education Georgia	$11,786,997,371	$10,802,435,153	lower
Healthy Georgia	4,201,549,981	3,358,264,003	lower
Safe Georgia	1,783,300,947	1,590,147,440	lower
Best Managed State	1,341,291,667	1,218,849,495	lower
Growing Georgia	1,043,067,537	963,013,086	lower
General Obligation Debt	1,009,675,013	969,990,354	lower
Total:	$21,165,882,616	$18,903,699,531	$2B lower

Source: Adapted from Georgia State Office of Planning and Budget. Budget in Brief, Amended FY 2009 and FY 2010, p. 15.

enforcement operations, coordination with other police agencies, and particularly the large prison system together were scheduled to receive $1,783,300,947, or almost nine percent (8.5%). Other fundamental management operations were scheduled to receive $1,341,291,667 and various non-essential but important projects deemed to be important, too, were due to Georgia's well-being like state lands and tourism goals were supposed to receive just a little less than that: $1,043,067,537. And the payments on our large debt were set at another billion dollars ($1,009,675,013) or almost five percent (4.81%). In short: a total of over twenty-one billion dollars of public funding: $21,165,882,616. These figures are shown in Table 8.4.

On occasion, the estimated operating budget proves to be inaccurate after the start of the fiscal year. For example, school enrollments or welfare recipients may increase. Then the Governor may draw upon reserve funds from several sources, such as the Sinking Fund, Midyear Adjustment Reserve or the Rainy Day Fund, the Revenue Shortfall Reserve. If it is a serious problem, the Governor may even have to call the General Assembly back into special session to make changes, either to increase revenues by new taxes or by selling bonds, or by decreasing expenditures, or both. The reserve funds are usually fed by taking surplus funds in good years and saving them for emergencies in bad years. This was the case in 2009. Table 8.4 on page 156 shows how actual state appropriations for 2009 had to be reduced, a realistic adjustment to the "Great Recession."

Although the State does meet its constitutional limits in spending, by generally limiting itself to anticipated revenues it collects, each biennial session of the legislature, as well as the increasingly frequent special sessions, must resort to constant magician's tricks to balance the budget. The State Reserve fund may be used to fill in occasional gaps. One reform often suggested to control over-inflated budgets is the stronger exercise of the Governor's line item veto power. Former Governor Miller had used this power on several celebrated occasions, against the secret legislative educational slush fund (Lauth & Reese, 15–16) and against an indigent legal services fund and a provision involving excess federal funds (Ibid, 16). One study had shown that this may be an over-rated power. As the researchers indicated:

"The line-item veto is usually used in Georgia as an instrument for resolving inter-branch difference on appropriations bills, but it is not designed as an instrument of partisanship, and it is not primarily an instrument of fiscal restraint" (Lauth & Reese, 21).

Figure 8.6   Finding The Right Amount
Source: Original cartoon created by authors.

The major means of balancing the State's budget is established in the State's Constitution of 1983, which prohibits borrowing money for each year's current operating budget. All state operations are, therefore, on a pay-as-you-go system. Unfortunately, often revenues dribble in years behind times, because of structured payment schedules or because of delinquent taxpayers. This means that anticipated expenditures may have to be cut back if the hoped-for revenues do not materialize. And, on occasion, the estimated operating budget predictions prove to be inaccurate after the start of the fiscal year. This can happen when tax collections are lower than expected, because of economic slowdowns or natural disasters, or perhaps because school enrollments, prison populations, or welfare recipients may increase.

When this happens, the Governor may draw upon reserve funds from several sources, such as the Sinking Fund, Midyear Adjustment Reserve, or the Rainy Day Fund, the Revenue Shortfall Reserve. If it is a serious problem, the Governor may even have to call the General Assembly back into special session to make changes, either to increase revenues by new taxes or by selling assets or bonds, or by decreased expenditures, or both. The reserve funds are usually fed by taking surplus funds in good years and saving them for emergencies in bad years, a pattern set forth by Joseph millennia ago.

In 2008, disaster struck. Due to the Great Recession, not only did State revenues drastically decline, but the economic crisis put many people out of work and into the social safety net, leading to a great increase in the level of projected expenditures. Responding to the crisis, republican Governor Perdue took the unusual step of using his prerogative and vetoing $14.2 million dollars in outlays to keep the budget balanced. (Budget in Brief—FY 2009). Even then, another 187 million dollars had to be taken from the Midyear Adjustment Reserve. The actual revenues received were shown on Table 8.2 on page 153.

The republican Governor was probably surprised that the crisis had reached that point. Earlier, in 2006, well into Georgia's "Republican Revolution," still largely founded on Ronald Reagan's Laffer Curve economic slight-of-hand, Governor Perdue had recommended an increased budget of $17.4 billion, including $811 million in revenue from the lottery. This largesse may seem to be in violation of espoused conservative fiscal responsibility; but although our state's political parties may talk like they are worlds apart, in fact they tend to react similarly in meeting the needs and desires of our general population, even if it means correcting reckless assumptions.

For while total projected revenues for 2009 were *$21,165,882,616, the actual dollar amount collected was less by two million dollars: only $18,903,699,531.* As shown on the tables, the individual income tax collected only about eight billion dollars instead of the anticipated nine billion dollars. And the other revenues were also less than was hoped for. As previously stated, the income tax is elastic, it goes down when income goes down and this happened in 2009. Tax cuts for corporations and higher income levels didn't help. The sales tax, although slightly less elastic, also declined by about three quarters of a billion dollars.

The perpetual struggle of deciding what to do with money that is collected is greatly aggravated when hopes are dashed by realities. It is not easy to spend less for basic human resources and for health care which is desperately needed, and which is becoming more expensive each year as new medical technologies and higher population levels drive up the costs of health care services. And despite a slight reduction in crime levels, public safety and protection is still a very high priority in Georgia. Monies spent for miscellaneous activities, like economic development, agricultural programs, and for purchasing land is also hard to cut because of their investment values. In fact, it can almost be said to be the rule that budgets tend to grow, and are "sticky downward."

Why Budgets Tend To Grow

Why do budgets tend to grow? Is it because of some secret plot to steal money from the rich to give to the poor, or vice versa? No, the single most important reason for most increases in government budgeting is the growth in size of the population, not ideology. Yes, there are some other factors, such as technological progress (if you invent airplanes you need new aviation agencies), but basically population growth is the problem. Also, the economy and the businesses in it also change over time (see the Internet), and so the sources of state revenues also change over time, and so do state expenditures.

Within the last ten years, new challenges and demands for increased expenditures on various functions have occurred frequently. Most particularly, the issues of expenditures on health care and education have created political, as well as economic and legal, havoc within the state. On the other hand, because of primary expenditures of the state's budget on education, other functions of the state's government have been the recipients of too few expenditures, also creating very real immediate problems—such as prison and correctional facilities shortages. But most important of all, and in the near future even more so, the increasing demands expanded appropriations for health-related concerns are not so much due to new disease problems such as AIDS, but rather due to the rapidly aging Baby Boomers and their retirement needs.

Also, it should not be forgotten that there are over 1,320 local governments in Georgia. As explained in the next chapter, each of these local governments operative in Georgia is a taxing entity, funding and serving the variety of needs of the state's socio-economically diversified citizenry. Some of their money is locally raised and spent, but much of it comes from Georgia State funding. And since the shortest path to economic growth is to have larger populations employed by larger growing industries, almost every state tries to make money by spending money. And despite occasional complaints of state and federal mandates to spend money on selected programs, almost all local governments have the same "spending mania."

Local Government Expenditures

Sometimes opportunity knocks, and government must meet the demands of the increasingly competitive global economy. In 1996 the City of Atlanta played host to the International Olympic Games. The construction projects involved, but more importantly the increased global image of Atlanta (and Georgia) as an international economic player, were worth billions of dollars in trade and tourism in the future. To help the economy, the State of Georgia granted a charter to a special purpose entity named the Metropolitan Atlanta Olympic Games Authority, (MAOGA). Following the lead of Los Angeles, MAOGA was determined to support the Games by private financing and donations, without direct substantial governmental subsidies. The bulk of revenues came from selling television rights, corporate sponsorships, ticket sales, and merchandise proceeds; but, of course, some governmental support was necessary, even if it was only utility hook-ups and public safety protection.

Although city governments are mere creatures of the state, and are almost certain to lose in any power contests with the state or federal governments, they can at least take symbolic actions against what they perceive to be unfair laws or practices. For example, in 1994, Atlanta's city council passed a resolution declaring October 27th to be *"Unfunded Mandates Day"* (Banks, 7) as part of a highly visible effort to complain about the state and federal governments' tendency to enact laws requiring cities to provide services without providing financial resources to compensate the city for the new strains on its budget. State and local government budgets, like their policy areas, are closely intertwined and interdependent. Georgia is a state that takes pride in its local communities.

All local governments have budgets, and even relatively small cities receive revenues and make expenditures that make it apparent that even small municipal government are really big businesses. Local police and fire departments fall under the public safety function. The public works function includes a multitude of services, including sanitation, sewer and storm sewer, water, and the city's motor pools. Parks and recreation services include all the cultural and recreational activities that citizens demand and expect, but also the services provided by the municipal cemetery and city arborists. The general government function covers administration, including mayor and council, city manager, city attorney, and elections responsibilities, as well as human resources, finance, and engineering. And many cities and counties operate hospitals as well.

Local Expenditures
Most cities in Georgia rely on the same kinds of revenue sources that the state uses to provide them with the funds they need to allocate services. As we pointed out earlier on in this chapter, taxes are the principal sources of revenue for all governments, although there are several kinds of taxes. Atlanta derives its revenue mainly from several different taxes, supplemented by fees, fines, interest income, and intergovernmental revenue. The table below identifies each of the major areas of expenditures by the City of Atlanta in 2009.

Although not nearly as large as a state budget, a city such as Atlanta is a *really* big business. In the early 1990s, as described in the first edition of this textbook, Atlanta's General Fund Budget was listed at $375,760,947. And it's growing fast. Now, its total budget for FY 2009 is over half a billion dollars (see Table 8.5). That is the basic operational cost of running the city services and government, not counting such things as capitol building costs and special purpose fund expenses such as the great International

Airport, an expensive proprietary enterprise. When other fiduciary and proprietary funds are added, the total 2009 budget will approach many billions of dollars. Such costs as about two billion dollars for

Table 8.5   Atlanta Budget—2009

Functional Area	Amount	Percent
Public Safety	294,641,251	52.26
Non-Department	124,937,471	22.17
Public Works and Parks	53,865,633	9.55
Other	29,446,457	5.23
Council/Exec. Offices	24,774,133	4.39
Info. Technology	24,057,915	4.26
Finance and Procurement	12,090,754	2.14
Total:	**563,813,614**	**100%**

Source: City of Atlanta, Office of Budget Fiscal Policy, FY09 Adopted Budget, p. 54.

the initial start-up costs of the city's airport expansion program can add up rapidly. And of course the city's revenues are not as extensive as the city fathers would like them to be, and nowhere near as large as their ambitions and imaginations might place them if unchecked by public scrutiny.

A quick check of a search engine for results on Bell City, California, will show how public officials can run wild with the taxpayers' dollars. The reader may notice that the local budgets do not list judicial expenses. In part, they are subsumed within the context of public safety appropriations. In part, the local judicial function does not include the courts discussed in Chapter Seven because they are maintained by the State Government. The local judicial function generally applies only to the administration of Municipal Courts, which hears and decides all cases brought by the Police Department and the City Marshals, and which concern a violation of a local ordinance or misdemeanors under state law. Housing and Development Function encompasses Community Development.

Both the state and local governments get additional funds from other governments. These include such things as General Grants, Substandard Housing Grants, Main Street Program, Code Enforcement, Urban Redevelopment (Weed and Seed, Community Empowerment, Urban Development Action Grants, Community Development Block Grants), and Protective Inspection (Building, Plumbing, Electrical, as well as Planning and Zoning). An examination of the budget, therefore, not only tells us what a government **spends;** it also tells us what a government **does.** It is not always easy to accurately identify categories of expenditures. As priorities change, and as new political figures attempt to initiate new policies, the reporting categories of our budget documents are often revised, making comparisons from year to year difficult. For example, it should be noted that the personnel costs of government are kept down in part by the contracting out of services to private businesses.

Much governmental support was offered by state, county, and other city entities to the Atlanta City Council and Atlanta Committee for the Olympic Games (ACOG), a private sponsor. One measure of city participation in the Olympic effort was its support of negotiations between ACOG and the Atlanta Braves organization. The ACOG proposed to build a new stadium in downtown Atlanta, and then to lease it to the Braves for 20 years; but the Braves demanded that the city agree to maintain the facility for the duration of the contract. Faced with a threat to move the team from the downtown area if the new stadium deal was not approved, the city agreed, but only after the Braves' organization agreed to sweeten the pot with annual maintenance payments totaling about four million dollars during the course of the contract (Blackmon, H4). After this effort, similar talks

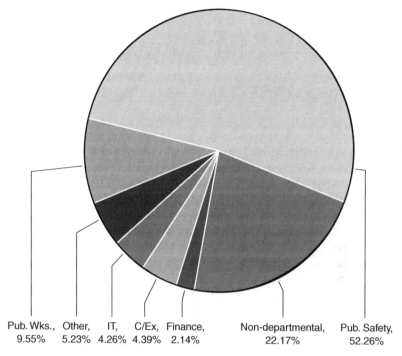

Pub. Wks.,	Other,	IT,	C/Ex,	Finance,	Non-departmental,	Pub. Safety,
9.55%	5.23%	4.26%	4.39%	2.14%	22.17%	52.26%

Figure 8.7   Atlanta City Budget—FY 2009
Source: City of Atlanta, Office of Budget Fiscal Policy, FY09 Adopted Budget, p. 54.

began with the Fulton County Commission, another player in this complex issue. The desire for economic growth binds Georgia governments together, often leading to representatives from one agency to sit as board members on other special purpose government authority's boards, and the operation of MAOGA was no exception to the rule. In short, population pressures, a shared desire for economic development, and competition for resources means that government budgets tend to grow from year to year, even when big projects are not underway.

Capital Budgets

Georgia has several different budgets, and not all of them have to be balanced like the operating budget, which pays for all of the normal, routine, and small budget items like employee salaries, program expenditures, and pass-through funds to other entities. Basically it is large only because it is comprised of so many little budget parts. The other most important state budget is the capital budget, which funds big property construction projects. For these types of expenses, the state borrows money and goes into debt, with interest. The state borrows money by selling bonds to investors and then pays back the face value and interest on those bonds. Each year roughly half a billion dollars is spent for capital construction projects, and for transportation construction and repairs.

Because Georgia sells bonds to borrow money for capital projects, the state is in fact in debt, like the other states, like the federal government, like most homeowners; and indeed, like most people. The total indebtedness of the State of Georgia in the fiscal year 2009 was over fourteen billion dollars ($14,616,131,557). The bulk of this debt is owned to its many creditors and bondholders, about nine billion dollars (9,689,903,540). Payment on this debt is supported directly by revenues from taxes, fees, and user fees. Much of the remaining debt is generated in the costs of self-supporting business operations, like rentals and contracts, and paid for by the same enterprises. It adds up fast. In fact, every Georgian owes almost a thousand dollars when per capita debt is calculated. Students can see this process in operation by going to the Debt Clock which tracks the debt. If you have not already done so, you should turn on your computer and go to *http://www.usdebtclock.org* and click on State Debt Clocks and then to Georgia to watch the numbers churn.

Capital budgets go through the same legislative processes as the operating budget, prepared first by the Governor's Office of Planning and Budget. The Georgia State Financing and Investment Commission, is responsible for implementing bond sales and debt management. The commission is composed of a mixed group of executive branch and legislative branch officials. On it are the Governor, Lieutenant Governor, the Speaker of the House, Attorney General, the State Auditor, the Director of the Office of Treasury and Fiscal Services, and even the Commissioner of Agriculture. Like the regular operating budget, the State Constitution is designed to limit the capital budget and debt process. But when the state gets a rare chance to show off on the world stage, our officials can get very creative. Look at the Atlanta Committee for the Olympic Games (ACOG), to see how the overlap between capital budgets and operations budgets can function, including inter-governmental financial exchanges all through the system. The same is generally true for cities, counties, and special districts like airports and development projects.

The instrument by which such debt is incurred is called a bond. When the state sells bonds, with a promise to buy them back with interest, it borrows money from bankers and bond brokers. Bonds may be either general obligation bonds or revenue bonds. A general obligation bond, in a sense, creates a lien on all the taxpayers of the state, since the guarantee of repayment to the buyers is placed on the "full faith and credit" of the entire state. This means that future tax revenues will be used to retire the bonds when they come due. A revenue bond, on the other hand, is retired with the revenues from particular money-making enterprises: e.g., tolls from bridges, fees from water and sewer systems, profits from education loans, and the like. Should those revenues fall short, however, the investors would be in danger of diminished or no returns, or even losing their investment entirely. For that reason, revenue bonds are riskier than general obligation bonds and must offer higher interest rates to capture investment capital. Allowable reasons for state debt are depicted on Table 8.6.

Article VII, Section IV of the Georgia Constitution addresses the matter of state debt. Paragraph I of that section contains a list of six purposes for which the state may incur debt. The purposes include crisis events, like debt to repel invasion, for suppression of insurrection; and more routine problems such as temporary cash flow shortages or problems financing local governments or special projects. The ability of a state to sell bonds to investors depends largely on a state's bond rating. The higher a state's rating, the more attractive its bonds are on the bond market. The two principal bond rating agencies are Moody's and Standard and Poor's. Moody's gives Georgia its highest rating

Table 8.6 Allowable State Indebtedness

1. Public debt without limit to repel invasion, suppress insurrection, and defend the state in time of war.
2. Public debt to cover for a temporary deficit in the state treasury in any fiscal year created by a delay in collecting the taxes of that year.
3. General obligation debt for:
   a. capital budgets to acquire and develop land, waters, highways, buildings, or facilities of the state and its agencies and authorities.
   b. educational facilities for school systems and public libraries.
   c. loans to political subdivisions and local authorities, for water or sewerage facilities.
4. Guaranteed revenue debt obligations issued by instrumentality of the state for:
   a. Toll bridges or toll roads,
   b. land public transportation facilities,
   c. water facilities or systems,
   d. sewage facilities or systems,
   e. loan programs for citizens for education.

Amended FY 2005/06 With FY 2009. *Source:* Compiled by authors.

(AAA), while Standard and Poor's put Georgia in its second highest rating category (AA+) (AJ/AC, Jan. 13, 1994). Repayment of bonded indebtedness is facilitated by the establishment of a general obligation debt Sinking Fund. Georgia's sinking fund is shown in Table 8.7 on page 167.

Emergency Funds

The State of Georgia also maintains an emergency fund. These are not usually used for budgeting purposes, but they can and are used when faced with a crisis like the Great Recession. More frequently, the fund is used for such things as natural disasters. But an interesting example of flexibility occurred in 2007 when Chief Justice Sears of the Georgia Supreme Court declared a funding crisis for the justice system, to cover the payroll costs of state-funded District Attorneys due to insufficient funding under the Amended FY 2007 budget. The judicial emergency declared by the Chief Justice resulted in Governor Perdue's executive order to transfer money out of the emergency fund (Perdue).

Stimulus Funds
Emergency funds come from both state and federal government sources. Income to the state from federal sources is substantial in Georgia, but because of the traditional reluctance of our citizens to accept the strings attached to federal money (and the penalty of increased federal control of state interests), the income from such sources is often not as much as it might be. In fact, the State of Georgia has been among the lowest ranking states in terms of federal funding from grants in the entire United States. According to the 2011 Statistical Abstract of the United States, as a result of the Great Recession, in 2009 the United States Government increased its grant-in-aid program by about 16%, to about five hundred and thirty seven billion dollars (Census). These stimulus funds were optional.

At first, then Governor Perdue was reluctant to apply for them, because he thought it might not be in the best long-term interest of the state to apply for them (AJC, 2/13/11, #). His remarks came as some of his his fellow southern republican governors were creating a stir by saying they would not accept some stimulus funds out of principle. Another stir was created earlier when one of Georgia's Senators, Johnny Isakson, suggested that state governments should consider bankruptcy when dealing with budget problems, including pension obligations to state employees (Haines). Today there is little doubt that capitalistic functioning is the most powerful tool for economic and social progress ever devised, as least as envisioned by Adam Smith. But the idea that government should be run like a business for

Table 8.7 Temporary Sinking Funds

State of Georgia General Obligation Debt Sinking Fund
Program Budget Financial Summary

	AMENDED FY 2009			FY 2010		
	Original Budget	Change	Final Budget	Original Budget	Change	Final Budget
Department Budget Summary						
State General Funds	$794,073,670	($10,804,092)	$783,269,578	$880,867,129	$26,241,256	$906,108,385
Motor Fuel Funds	216,601,343	(28,880,567)	186,720,776	215,601,343	9,080,000	224,681,343
Total State Funds	$1,009,675,013	($39,684,659)	$969,990,354	$1,096,468,472	$34,321,256	$1,130,789,728
Total Funds	$1,009,675,013	($39,684,659)	$969,990,354	$1,096,468,472	$34,321,256	$1,130,789,728
General Obligation Debt Sinking Fund—Issued						
State General Funds	$708,070,991	$32,913,599	$740,984,590	$794,864,450	($7,280,852)	$787,583,598
Motor Fuel Funds	195,062,643	(9,238,567)	185,824,076	195,062,643	20,538,700	215,601,343
Total Funds	$903,133,634	$23,675,032	$926,808,666	$989,927,093	$13,257,848	$1,003,184,941
General Obligation Debt Sinking Fund—New						
State General Funds	$86,002,679	($43,717,691)	$42,284,986	$86,002,679	$32,522,108	$118,524,787
Motor Fuel Funds	20,538,700	(19,642,000)	896,700	20,538,700	(11,458,700)	9,080,000
Total Funds	$106,541,379	($43,717,691)	$43,181,688	$106,541,379	$21,063,408	$127,604,787

Source: Office of Planning and Budget, Georgia State Government. 2010. Georgia Budget in Brief. P. 314.

profit dates back to the Persian Satrapies, and only the rankest of dictators in the third world still follow that model. Today, with the Great Recession still gripping our people, about one million seven hundred and eighty six thousand one hundred and sixty-eight people (1,786,168) depending on food stamps, we do have economic problems (*http://www.usdebtclock.org.*; 02/17/11). Some people who are simply anti-federal government would like to starve the beast and funnel national wealth into their plutocratic pockets while poor children go hungry.

Businessmen often go bankrupt, it is a routine, but vital tool for businessmen to cut their losses among themselves and continue to operate; it hardly ever hurts ordinary people earning a living in the professions, trades or public service for citizens dependent on continued government functioning for the good of the larger community. Government is not supposed to make a profit, and it is not supposed to benefit just part of the social matrix, or be so poorly run that it teeters into bankruptcy. Among the reasons our ancestors revolted against the British Government was because it used unelected judges to oppress people with tax and spending judgments so politicians could avoid responsibility for their corrupt profit taking. To get a little preachy, we should not go back down that path. So while it is true that our state is in some financial trouble, the solution is responsible decision-making by our elected legislative officials and the citizens who put them in office.

To his credit, therefore, Governor Perdue's legacy has proven itself to be more of a pragmatic political administrator than a myopic ideological extremist. In the end, Governor Perdue did in fact allow the state to apply for some of the stimulus funds, even though it was federal money from the democratic Obama administration. By mid-November, 2009, eighteen state agencies had spent over seven hundred million of the over three billion dollars allocated to the State of Georgia, helping to retain thousands of jobs, either retained or created by the fiscal stabilization grants (AJC, 02-13-2011, #). The bulk of the money went first to education, then to health, and then to transportation. Historically, Georgia prides itself on self-reliance, but it also prides itself on true fiscal responsibility, and its own brand of conservative American politics.

Conclusion

Each year, billions of dollars are spent by the Georgia State Government and its agencies for general secondary education, and additional billions are spent for human resources, health care programs, and for higher education. Law enforcement, corrections, capital construction projects, and transportation programs cost hundreds of thousands of dollars, and more money is spent for a wide variety of miscellaneous activities like purchasing land and for preserving environmental resources after cost/benefit analysis.

Budgetary politics is often a fierce struggle over who gets what, and who pays. But, in general, the people of Georgia in 1983 enacted a Constitution that creates a complex array of checks and balances to ensure that the powers of the state are used effectively to benefit the health and well-being of all the citizens, especially in times of crisis.

Key Terms

Capital Budget
Fiscal Budget
Income Tax
Indebtedness
Line-Item Veto
Operational Budget
Regressive Tax
Revenue Bond
Sales Tax
Sin Tax
Surplus
Unfunded Mandate
Valorem Tax

Essay Questions

1. Identify and explain the three sources contributing to the bulk of Georgia's revenue.
2. Why might a state exempt certain necessities such as food from sales tax? Has this approach ever been tried in the State of Georgia?
3. Explain why Georgians could be undertaxed or overtaxed. Either way is the distribution of tax burden fair? Support your answer with clear evidence to either side or to both sides of the issue.
4. What is the largest expenditure in the State of Georgia and how are these funds distributed?
5. What is the line-item veto? Does the Governor of Georgia have this power? If so, when may he exercise it? Why is this power considered by some scholars to be overrated?
6. Discuss why the *ad valorem tax* and the income tax are two of the most unpopular, if not resented, forms of taxation in the State of Georgia.

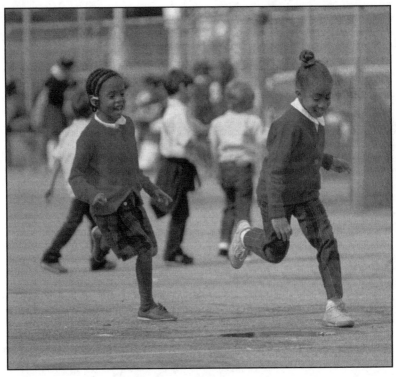

Figure 9.1 Children at Play

9

State Education Policy

The local government described in the last chapter has a lot in common with educational institutions in the State of Georgia as described in this chapter. Local, primary, and secondary school districts as well as college institutions have the power to tax and levy fees for services, to hire personnel, to make regulations and rules, to maintain public safety, and they all have the power to compel obedience. But it is common to think that they also have a higher mission, an idealistic duty to educate our children and to help society to continue to improve over time. And of course education and local government have something else in common: both are arenas of political conflict. In this chapter we will review the major educational institutions, their structures, their goals and policies, and their finances.

State Educational Structure

Public education is a principal responsibility of most state governments, and Georgia is no exception to the rule. Article VIII of the Georgia Constitution speaks to the view that education is the most important function of the state government. This article provides for the governance, administrative structure, and for the financial support of public education at the elementary and secondary and college levels. Thus, it no surprise that Georgia routinely devotes more than half of its entire budget each year to primary, secondary, and higher education. In 2010, the Georgia General Assembly took this responsibility seriously enough to allocate more than 58 percent of the state budget to funding all levels of education in the state even if that percentage has since witnessed a massive reduction for 2011. Traditionally, a distinction is made between the public schools offering of kindergarten through twelfth grade and post-secondary institutions. This division is reflected in two major bureaucracies: the State Board of Education and the State Board of Regents. The high levels of state appropriations to these two types of institutions reflect a commitment to providing a sound educational system for Georgia's students.

Overall responsibility for administering Georgia's system of primary and secondary education rests with the State Board of Education.

It makes policy for the state education systems, sets standards for teacher education programs, certifies teachers, establishes minimal salary levels, imposes graduation requirements, etc. Its members represent each of the 13 congressional districts and are appointed by the Governor and confirmed by the state senate. Members of the State Board of Education serve seven-year terms. As discussed in Chapter Five on Plural Executives, the State School Superintendent is the chief executive officer of the State Board of Education, but local school district superintendents actually control the schools' operations.

When the Going Gets Tough: Education and Massive Budget Cuts in Georgia

In a *Georgia Trend* article published in December 2009 titled "Georgia Schools Grapple with Massive State Budget Cuts," the Peach County School Superintendent Susan Clark bemoans Georgia's Education budget cuts of the 2009-2010 school year, a trend that continues. In late July 2009, when the budget news came down from Atlanta, the superintendent recalled that it was a week before teachers in the Peach County school system would report to work for the school year. School systems were told "to cut almost $800,000 from the budget." This cut, however, did not include furloughing teachers for three days, nor did it include the $2 million cut the Peach County School System had already made from their budget for that year, nor did it include the $8 million cut that was already slated over the previous six years.

To the Peach County School Superintendent, the budget cut news presented a dilemma as it did for 179 other school superintendents in the state of Georgia. Her immediate reaction was to call to meeting all school principals in Peach County as well as all of the central leadership. The intent of meeting was to figure out how to manage the sudden 3 percent budget cut in state funding on education as it continued from the initial spring 2009 massive cuts made during the legislative session.

According to Ms. Clark, "we brainstormed every possibility until we felt there were only two options which required either (a) to cut personnel, roughly 39 positions. What this meant also was that we had to cut kindergarten paraprofessionals and (b) cut elementary school music and physical education teachers. Since this option could not be seriously considered, we moved to the next option. The second option was no plan "B."" It consisted of moving to a four-day school week in order to save roughly $400,000 in transportation and energy costs. In the bigger picture, the 2009–2010 budget cuts were not in isolation. It was part of a seven consecutive year cut in the Georgia state funding for education initiated by Gov. Sonny Perdue and the Georgia state legislature.

Source: Compiled by authors from various sources and mostly from "How Low Can They Go?" *Georgia Trend. http://www.georgiatrend.com/cover-story/12_09_education.shtml,* December 2009.

As of 2008, approximately 1.6 million Georgia students were enrolled in prekindergarten through twelfth grade at more than 2,000 schools in 181 public school systems. There are approximately 114,000 full-time and nearly 5,000 part-time preK-12 teachers in Georgia; they are assisted by nearly 11,000 full-time and more than 2,000 part-time support personnel (paraprofessionals, nurses, speech pathologists, etc.) and more than 8,000 full-time and more than 1,500 part-time administrators.

In addition to the basic primary and secondary educational system, Georgia has an extensive college and university system encompassing over one hundred campuses. There are 35 public institutions of higher learning in the state, divided into five tiers: research universities, regional universities, state universities, four-year state colleges, and two-year colleges. Governance of the University System of Georgia is the responsibility of the State's Board of Regents. The 35 institutions managed by the State Board of Regents enrolls approximately 311,442 students and employs over 40,000 faculty and staff to provide teaching and related services to students and communities across the state. The University System of Georgia also oversees an independent research unit that employs faculty and hosts visiting students and interns but does not grant degrees.

Ultimately, the educational system in Georgia is comparable to that of other southern states in terms of structure and design. However, the Georgia educational system stands out by the large percentage of the state budget devoted to education. For example, Tennessee devotes approximately 46% of the state budget to education and while the University System of Florida and the Florida College System annually enroll over a million students combined, the total percentage of the Florida budget devoted to education is 32%.

Local School Districts

As noted above, members of the Georgia Board of Education represent 13 congressional districts. These districts are largely (but not entirely) defined by county lines. Each of Georgia's 159 counties maintains a separate school system, and 21 of the larger cities have independent school systems. The Georgia Constitution provides for separate Boards of Education to manage and control each of these many school systems and allows them to be either elected or appointed, as a local option. Most of the Boards of Education in Georgia are elected. Administration of school policy in each district is the responsibility of the state's Department of Education, the local School Boards, and their local school superintendent, who is appointed by the local board. Primary education is big business in Georgia, absorbing almost five billion dollars in state funds and perhaps as much or more in local funds.

In the early 1980s, the national government's publication of *A Nation at Risk—The Imperative for Educational Reform*, brought to light problems with proliferation of school districts, the amount and quality of their control and direction of the educational process, finally resulting in extensive reform of States' educational systems. By the late 1980s, challenges to funding reforms became the focus, particularly when it became apparent that the almost decade-old reforms of educational quality associated with teachers and students had produced little success—testing of students revealed that many students were still performing well below the national average.

School districts are the single most common type of special purpose district government in Georgia. School districts, both county-based and independent, or special combinations of the two, don't have to seek special permission from the state for every little thing they do, but they are constrained by their mission requirements and responsibilities, by the State Constitution, state statutes, and the state Department of Education. Some of these responsibilities are outlined in Table 9.1.

Funding for these basic elementary services is primarily derived from state formula funds, local option property taxes on residents' habitations and other privately-owned lands, and on businesses and from sales taxes and bond revenues. Generally, it is the locally-elected school boards and their professional staffs who are responsible for overseeing daily operations of local school budgets, and the boards

Table 9.1 School Responsibilities

1. Prepare children to join society.
2. Teach them the basic skills, the three r's.
3. Acquaint them with their historical heritage.
4. Strengthen their sense of morality.
5. Strengthen their interpersonal skills.
6. Ensure that they have a sense of self-worth.
7. Promote a sense of national patriotism.
8. Prepare them for a job or a career.
9. Give them guidance and counseling.
10. Strengthen their bodies as well as their minds.
11. Libraries and arts and sciences facilities.
12. Provide trained and dedicated teachers.
13. Train them to meet the new global challenges.
14. Prepare them for a changing future.

Source: Compiled by authors.

set appropriate tax rates for property in the district (within state constitutional limits).

Though parents and voters may not be familiar with every specialized aspect of the children's education, they are always aware of the level of taxation in the community, quick to fault any doubtful expenditures, and generally familiar with where responsibility rests— in the hands of the Board of Education. And at the local school district level, both blame and credit is quickly assessed and acted upon in the voting booth. Community satisfaction with budgetary and teaching policy is reflected in re-election; while failure in either area is usually reflected in community unrest and by voter election of a new school board at the first opportunity.

Of course, in Georgia, school districts are also closely accountable to state agencies. Like other local governments and special districts, school districts have no independent sovereignty, no right to exist independent of the authority and approval of the state government. In Georgia, the state Department of Education reviews local school districts to make sure that they comply with the requirements of the State Constitution.

A century ago many school districts were run directly by city officials, but sometimes politics got in the way of education. For example, in the City of Chicago, with a strong mayoral system of government, the mayor directly appointed the schoolteachers. Unfortunately, usually political supporters got the jobs because of their loyalty to political parties, and not because of their skills. In short patronage, and not merit or ability, determined who was hired as teachers. And in Chicago, with a large ethnic immigrant population, this often meant that the teachers often could not readily read or write English; it even meant that they sometimes could barely even speak the language, let alone teach it effectively to the students.

It has taken centuries to mold American schools into professional institutions instead of just megaphones for local prejudices. Unfortunately, this professionalism is now threatened on many levels. Ethnic and racial integration have less popular support for schools and teachers. And in a more subtle threat, the existence of the Internet, with its constantly changing blogs and doubtful (or hacked) data sources has damaged America'a common objective database. In George Orwell's novel *1984*, Big Brother loved to change wording and history. If less systematic and orchestrated, this phenomena is widespread today. So sometimes an Internet reference cannot be verified. Nevertheless, a scholar, like a police detective, can testify to his own observation of evidence, even if the suspect destroys it later.

The average local school board meets once or twice a month. Citizens and parents are invited to attend the sessions and to bring complaints and issues to the board meetings. Board members often work on committees, such as textbooks, curriculum, facilities, personnel, and budgeting. They review proposals and recommend policy to the board. But always the local citizens, and particularly the parents of the schoolchildren, are keenly sensitive to the costs of education and are anxious to make sure that they retain control over their schools, the teachers that are hired, and the skills, lessons, and attitudes that are inculcated. And since every community has differences of opinion over what should be taught, and how it should be taught and by whom, it is not uncommon to find people filing lawsuits to get their way if they find themselves outvoted at the local level. With billions of dollars at stake, and their children's future at risk, it is little wonder that passions over educational policies sometimes boil over into the political arena.

Much of the state funding for the primary and secondary levels of education is appropriated in the form of Quality Basic Education (QBE) funds. This grant program sets a number of requirements that include a statewide basic curriculum, incentives and rewards for teachers, and improved statewide performance standards. In 2010, Governor Sonny Perdue signed a state budget plan that included $393 million for all levels of education in the state signaling a continued commitment to education in spite of economic downturn (Office of Communications, June 8, 2010).

It is basically the job of the local community to raise more money to supplement the state funding, which may require taxation for operational costs and bond issues for capital expenditures (new classrooms). For society as a whole, and certainly for the parents of school-age youngsters, this system of free public education is a good deal; but there are also some who feel as though they are being taxed too heavily, and who may try to challenge the policy.

Usually school districts in Georgia try to downplay the politics as much as possible and try to focus on providing good educations for the children. Usually this is done by hiring a highly-trained professional education manager, the superintendent. In this type of system, the organization chart is very similar to the council/manager form of local government, but the influence of the professional manager, the Superintendent of Schools, is very closely related to the strength of their educational credentials, and usually a doctorate in educational administration is required. While an outstanding superintendent might seek to influence the board with their personal charisma, it is more likely to be their expertise in education, personnel management, and budgeting powers that determine their degree of success on the job. However, the superintendent does not make basic educational policy but only implements policies adopted by the board members.

Figure 9.2   Educational Burden

Educational systems, like all administrative systems, have a hier-archical structure. All hierarchies are identifiable from top to bottom, with decreasing control evident at the bottom of the chart. For instance, if one reviews a power chart of the school system in the fol-lowing graph, it is apparent that assigned power exists at the top of the hierarchy, while the least power in the system is associated with those at the bottom, the teaching faculty and the students. The hierarchical **"flow chart"** of the educational bureaucracy reveals that there are many levels of bureaucracies, but the main ones are the state level offi-cials, particularly the Georgia Department of Education (GaDOE), the eleven member State Board of Education, and its independently elected State School Superintendent, and the almost two hundred locally elected school boards. Each of these has thousands of career specialists who function as administrative, technical, or line level bureaucrats with complex duties.

The Georgia Department of Education (GaDOE) for example, oversees public education throughout the state. It ensures that laws and regulations pertaining to education are followed and that state and federal money appropriated for education is properly allocated to local school systems. That Department also provides education-related information to students, parents, teachers, educational staff, government officials, and the media. The Georgia Department of Education is comprised of five Offices under the State School Superintendent that include: the Office of External Affairs and Policy; the Office of Standards, Instruction and Assessment; the Office of Education Support and Improvement; the Office of Finance and Business Operations; and the Office of Technology Services.

Candidates for local school district boards are presumed to have appropriate abilities, skills, and interests to convince the voters that they will represent their interests. Of course, professionally-trained superintendents often have major impact on who will run for the positions on school boards. In theory, the voters constitute the clientele of the educational bureaucracy. Although displayed on the chart as a unitary entity, the *voters* are of course really a disparate collection of pressure groups, all with independent and often contradictory goals.

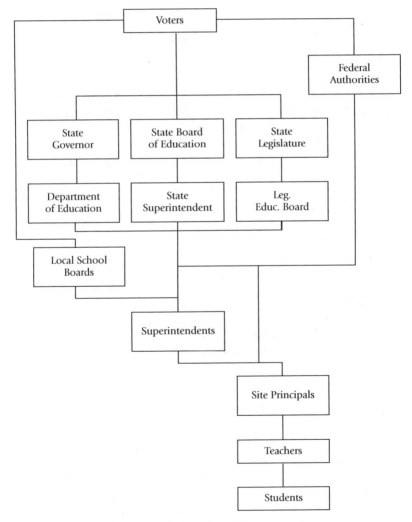

Figure 9.3 Educational Bureaucracies

Sources of Funds for School Districts

The vast majority of educational funds in Georgia are received from taxes (local property and sales taxes), local bonds, and state general revenue taxes. The State of Georgia limits the amount of property taxes the cities can adopt. Sometimes, parents may support increased requests for federal funding in the form of "**grants.**" However, other participants in the school's governance may be reluctant to do so, because the federal money may have strings attached to it that do not fit the goals and values of the local community, reflecting other national regions instead.

Federal grants for such things as demonstration projects in sex education are a prime example. School districts are less likely to object to state grants, however, because there is usually more compatibility of values at the local and state levels. For example, Georgia state law requires public schools to teach abstinence education in addition to providing information regarding sexually transmitted diseases and HIV as part of the health curriculum in the middle schools and high schools. Unfortunately, there are often funding disparities between and within school districts, so that some schools have more money than others. When this happens it is because when parents donate money to their children's schools, comparatively little attention is paid; but when public sector funds are not fairly distributed you can be sure that it will become a major political dispute.

Inner-city schools, especially in the Atlanta metropolitan area, are often the subject of discussion, research, and special funding requests. Though often receiving special attention and funds, these inner-city schools tend to deteriorate rapidly, because of the large numbers of pupils they try to serve. And since sometimes poverty-stricken families reside there, and as more and more wealthy people move to the suburbs, this weakens the revenue bases of the schools. In 2007, the state attempted to balance out the differences with additional funds, such as $278 million under the basic Equalization Formula and $245 million for pre-kindergarten programs.

Higher Education in Georgia

As noted above, the Georgia public school system (prekindergarten–grade 12) operates within districts governed by locally-elected school boards members and superintendents. The Georgia State Constitution requires that the state General Assembly provide a "free public education prior to college or postsecondary level." The State Constitution also notes that the required education shall be supported through taxation. Thus, the State of Georgia devotes more than half of its entire

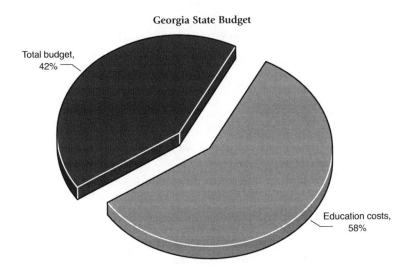

Georgia State Budget

Figure 9.4   Selected Budget Year—2007
Georgia's Education Costs: 58% of the State Budget. Compiled by Authors.

state budget each year to educational programs, including primary, secondary, and higher educational efforts (see Figure 9.4).

Governor Nathan Deal's proposed FY2012 budget totals $18.16 billion, or an increase of $273 million over FY2011. However, state university programs would see their funding cut about $300 million, down to a total of $1.74 billion for FY2012, over the next 18 months under Deal's amended 2011 and 2012 budgets. The total FY 2010 budget was approximately $18.57 billion. Education accounted for approximately $10.79 billion of the total budget of 58.10%. This included the state department of education, early care, teacher retirement system, the technical college system of Georgia, and the university system (AJC Jan 12 2011-02-17).

In the last legislative session, the Georgia General Assembly voted to appropriate nearly 1.8 billion dollars for post-secondary education, or higher education, in the state. Traditionally, a distinction is made between the colleges and universities, and the two-year colleges, technical colleges, and adult education training facilities. The higher levels of education are administered by the State Board of Regents, and there is little formal local community control, or local funding from the area. Instead of a local board, there is usually an institutional college president, often assisted by a faculty senate on campus. Political administration of Georgia's system of higher education rests with the State Board of Regents, and by the system chancellor, hired by the Regents. The Regents make policy for the state's academic institutions, set standards for faculty, establish salary levels, impose graduation requirements, etc. Its members are appointed by the Governor and confirmed by the state senate.

The Regents, in turn, select the Chancellor of the System, usually conducting a nationwide search to find a good professional educator. An effective administrator is needed, because Georgia has over a hundred college and university campuses. Hundreds of thousands of students attend the extensive system of public colleges and universities, studying a wide variety of subjects and academic disciplines. There are 35 public institutions of higher learning in the state, divided into four basic tiers: research universities, regional universities, four-year institutions, and two-year colleges. Georgia has a unified system of higher education, with a common core curriculum, with specialized programs on each campus.

Colleges and universities are vital to healthy economic growth, particularly in these times of global competition. Georgia has been putting large sums of money into higher education in the last decade. Under the guidance of former Chancellors Stephen R. Portch and Thomas C. Meredith and with funding made available from the Georgia lottery, the state legislature has provided not only adequate operations funding but also supported a multi-million dollar expansion and renovation campaign. In addition the state has adopted Governor Miller's Hope Scholarship Program, which basically pays the college tuition of any Georgia student who maintains a "B" or better grade point average. This program, linked to his original Georgia Rebound initiative which contained a number of economic initiatives outside of education, has allowed the state to also create a solid educational grant and loan program, which ensures that every student can pursue their educational dreams and be able to compete in the emerging global marketplace.

Insulated from political pressures and partisan bickering, the Board of Regents acts as trustee of Georgia's 35 public colleges and universities, with a nearly 1.5 billion dollar budget and a student population of about 302,000 students. The system chancellor is continuing to exhibit the kind of strong leadership Georgia enjoyed in the past, while working with a close-knit Board of Regents mostly appointed by Governor Barnes. Under this group, the number of institutions designated as universities has increased. However, the Governor and his predecessors have come under some criticism for appointing business and political elites to the board, movers, and shakers (often contributors to his campaigns), and predominantly white males (Vickers, Robert J., C11). These appointments can be tricky business, for although political pressures years ago led to the creation of special insulation against political tampering with the university system, politics of course continues to play a role in educational policy and administration.

Among Georgia state agencies, the Board of Regents is unique because its budget is not presented as a line-item budget. As discussed in an earlier chapter, after the Talmadge Administration tried to manipulate the university system for partisan advantages, the Constitution was rewritten to require the General Assembly to appropriate monies to the Board of Regents in a lump sum, to be used as the Board of Regents deems proper. The subtle disciplinary characteristics and features of higher education require special insulation from partisan politics. Thus, once money is appropriated, the system of higher education is generally placed out of the budgetary reach of both the executive and the legislative branches.

Educational Policy

Educational policy in Georgia continues to evolve, while searching for a way to improve the skills and score levels of the state's students. The Quality Basic Education grant noted above is rooted in the Georgia Quality and Basic Education Act of 1986. This educational reform was intended to enhance student and teacher performance but was challenged in 1995 on the grounds that it failed to significantly improve student achievement levels (Zanardi, 1). In 2003, a revision of the Quality Core Curriculum (QCC) was prompted by the results of an external audit conducted by Phi Delta Kappa International which revealed crucial gaps in the curriculum and a general lack of rigor. As a result of these findings, state teachers and other education experts developed a new curriculum, known as the *Georgia Performance Standards*. The implementation of the new standard began in 2005, focusing on English, math, science, and social studies (Mewborn, 2009).

Today, *Quality Basic Education* monies are still available to local school districts for various initiatives to improve education services. Additionally, the Georgia Board of Education has also decided to phase out the high school *"general diploma"* in favor of more rigorous programs in vocational education and college preparatory tracks. Until Georgia students' educational indicators improve, such as competency ratings and higher SAT scores (in 2009, a comparison of state SAT scores ranked Georgia 47 of 50 states and the District of Columbia), educational policy will continue in flux.

Few ideas about how to improve American education have generated as much controversy and struggle as public financial aid to private and religious education. America was founded in large part by refugees from religious wars, who determined to defuse the potential for strife by separating the powers and finances of church and state. But today, as the average quality of public education falls below acceptable levels, particularly with regard to the technical skills so

Funding Education in Georgia

Georgia public school systems are funded primarily through state and local dollars with the majority provided based on the Quality Basic Education (QBE) formula. Based on the number of full-time equivalent (FTE) students in a program, and the expense to educate students—it costs more to educate a severely disabled student in special education than it does to teach a ninth-grader taking a regular course load. The average total expenditure per student for FY 2008 (the latest year available from the Georgia Department of Education) was about $9,000.

However, this figure varies wildly from county to county. For example, the figure is just over $8,340 in Peach County, Georgia, but nearly $13,500 for the Atlanta Public Schools system. While there may be justifications for cost differences across the system due perhaps to "teacher and principal salaries, electric bills, insurance, text books, etc., there is no inflationary factor built into the formula" (Grillo 2009).

vital in an era of global competition, attacks on the public school system are mounting. The poor showing of students' test scores is probably attributable to several factors, such as open enrollment, grade inflation, poor discipline, and the decline of the traditional family in the post-industrial era. Among the reformers, some persons would like to create a private educational marketplace, in which both private and religious schools would be eligible to receive public funds in the form of certificates or *"portable vouchers"* for students (Delk, F2). Traditionally, this policy has had very strong opposition.

However, since the founding of the public school system, erosion of the so-called *"wall of separation"* between church and state has been slow and steady. While there are no public calls as yet for mandatory religious taxes, many supporters of *"school choice"* see a window of opportunity to gain publicly financed support of private and religious institutions. Some supporters claim that test scores in private institutions are higher; but critics attribute some of that to *"creaming,"* because the public schools have to admit all who apply, while private institutions can deny admission and services to persons at their discretion.

The cost of supporting private institutions through vouchers would require a tax boost of between three to seven percent according to former House Speaker Tom Murphy (A. Press, 11-15-93, 1); a cost of perhaps two billion dollars. A bill to do just this was introduced in the 1994 legislative session, in the form of a proposed constitutional amendment, but it failed to gain support and was not acted upon. In 2002, the U.S. Supreme Court addressed the constitutionality of a voucher plan in Cleveland, Ohio, and held that, despite the fact that most of the children attending private schools in that city would be attending church-related schools supported by the Roman Catholic Church, that fact alone did not violate the First Amendment requirement of separation of church and state (*Zelman v. Simmons-Harris, Hannah Perkins School v. Simmons-Harris, Taylor v. Simmons-Harris* (2000)). That ruling opens the door for voucher systems everywhere.

School boards serve to set policies such as property tax rates for their districts (under state limits); and to choose textbooks; to make capital improvement proposals; and a host of other decisions—but perhaps the most important work of the boards is the hiring of a professionally-trained superintendent who will implement the board's educational policies. Skilled professionals, focused on the technical and educational aspects of their jobs, are less likely to be imbued with outlandish ideas and political partisanship.

No Child Left Behind Act

The No Child Left Behind Act, enacted by Congress in 2001 and reauthorized in 2008, sets nationwide standards for improving public education by the end of the 2013–14 school year. When George Bush became the President of the United States in 2001, he announced this new initiative to improve the quality of education across the nation. While generally regarded as a state prerogative, education has also been regarded as a federal problem for at least the last fifty years. The President's initiative was known as the *No Child Left Behind Act* (NCLB). The NCLB requires states including Georgia to test students frequently to assess their progress. If schools repeatedly underperformed, their students may transfer to schools that do perform, and the underperforming school may be closed.

Teachers and school administrators in Georgia and elsewhere have complained bitterly that the NCLB is really a "no child left untested" program that require teachers to "teach to the test," instead of concentrating on knowledge acquisition and analytical and creative thinking. Moreover critics charge that the NCLB is an "undefined mandate," in that it requires states to make expenditures that are not compensated by the federal government. Despite the criticism, the Bush Administration insists that NCLB is working and there is some scant evidence that some provisions have been successful in improving the quality of public education.

In 2009, the Georgia General Assembly enacted HB 251, which provides additional choice options to parents. This law states that local school systems must offer parents the option to enroll their child(ren) in any school in the local school system, if space is available. School systems are not required to provide transportation for families opting to exercise the choice option. If there are more students requesting a school by choice than there are slots available, students are assigned by lottery.

Race to the Top

In 2010, Georgia and nine other states as well as the District of Columbia were selected as "Race to the Top" winners. Like No Child Left Behind, "Race to the Top" is a federal attempt to improve the quality of schools. This Obama administration initiative is rooted in the Reinvestment Act of 2009 and awards winning states a portion of $3.4 billion to improve education by, among other things, turning around low performing schools and implementing college standards. Georgia was awarded $400 million (over four years) of the "Race to the Top" funds in order to meet state goals such as increasing the high school graduation rate, improving college entrance exam and achievement scores, strengthening teacher quality, and improving workforce readiness. The State Board of Education adopted these standards in July of 2010 (see, The Georgia Department of Education [GaDOE], "Georgia Wins Race to the Top, GaDOE Communications Office, August 24, 2010).

Educational Morality

Plato said that those in charge of a city must see that education is not corrupted without their noticing it. If a school graduates many people with high school diplomas who cannot read or write, then those in charge are not doing their jobs. Who is in charge of our educational policy? State level participants include the legislators who are members of educational oversight committees in the General Assembly, members of the Board of Regents and its staff, members of the Department of Education and its staff, the Governor's appointed officials in the Department of Education, and occasionally members of the judiciary, who hear policy disputes in their courtrooms. The Legislative Education Board and many individual committees are responsible for reviewing all aspects of educational policies and finances, including reactions to policy initiatives introduced by other participants.

At the local secondary level, influential persons associated with policy formation and implementation in the education system are primarily the various locally-elected Boards of Education, the administrators hired by them and the professional faculty of the technical schools and colleges and the universities. These experts serve with the explicit responsibility for carrying out policies established by these boards and implicitly with the policy mandates of more distant representatives of the public's wishes, such as state agency personnel, the state school superintendent, and the members of the General Assembly. The superintendents of the school districts, school principals, and finally the professional faculty members of the schools implement the lowest level of policy, line level interaction with the students. The professional administrative and bureaucratic levels, which are not elected, may actually hold major power over the public bodies nominally responsible for making policy, because they inform their respective elected bodies of the direction local policies should take. In addition, the faculty and teachers themselves, sometimes individually, and sometimes through their representatives, such as the Georgia Association of Educators, often affect educational policy as well.

The educational establishment is the largest bureaucracy in the state, as it is in many states, and examining the successes and failures inherent to the system may clarify general understanding of bureaucracies throughout the state. Candidates for local independent school districts are also presumed to have such abilities, skills, and interests as are needed for them to be selected by the voters to represent their interests. An English philosopher and legislative leader, Edmund Burke, described two fundamental types of representatives, the delegate, faithfully executing the desires of constituents; and the trustee, who uses personal wisdom on behalf of constituents if for some reason they are unaware of their own best interests. Thus, the primary factor in the success in this hierarchical model is the voters, and one hopes their responsible selection of those who will make policy for the educational bureaucracy. When the voters are informed of the facts and sensitive to their own best interests, and act responsibly on that knowledge, this is an ideal system. All we need to do then is to allow voters to select good delegates as their representatives on local school boards, and they will provide the professional educators with local community input on value preferences. But whenever these professionals raise questions of expertise and superior judgment that runs counter to local culture, the political hackles of the school board and the general public is certain to rise.

Conclusion

Amidst the complexity of the system of public education in the State of Georgia is the obvious fact that it functions inter-dependently. Yet, while one may be tempted to draw hasty conclusions about the state of education in the state, we cannot just look at the secondary and higher education systems themselves for any conclusive understanding of how they function. The responsibility for making sure that the state's younger generations are adequately prepared for the challenges of the future and that current institutions are well-equipped to train them rests on a wide variety of people: the general citizenry, elected officials, professional educators, the students themselves, and the parent especially. In our emerging climate of global economic competition, the need for strong educational institutions has never been greater.

Key Terms

Creaming
Chancellor
Grant
Georgia Rebound Initiative
No Child Left Behind Act
Portable voucher
Quality Basic Education Funds
Race to the Top
School choice
State Board of Education
State Board of Regent
Voucher System
Wall of Separation

Essay Questions

1. Explain the hierarchical structure of the basic educational system in Georgia.
2. Explain the structure of the University System of Georgia. How has higher education in Georgia been impacted by the use of a lottery?
3. Georgia contributes more than half of its budget to education. Can this devotion to education be seen in the performance of Georgia students compared to those from other states?
4. How might incompatibility between national and state values impact funding for education in Georgia?
5. Among Georgia state agencies, the Board of Regent is unique because its budget is not presented as a line item budget. Discuss how this historical arrangement came about and the measure that was taken.

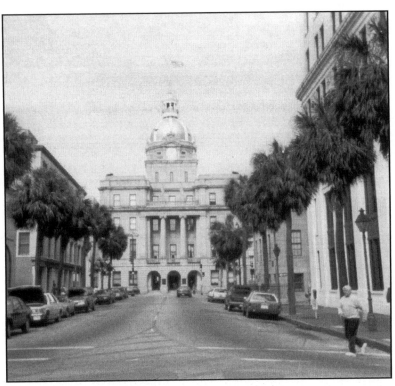

Figure 10.1 Savannah City Hall

Local Government

Local Government

The primary local level of government is the county, which often functions as a subdivision of the state, and is subject to the actions of the state legislature and the limitations of the State Constitution. Only the states of Connecticut and Rhode Island lack county government, although in Louisiana and Alaska similar local structures exist, called, respectively, parishes and boroughs. In addition, all states have municipal corporations, although they may be variously called cities, towns, or villages. Many states classify cities according to first class status, second class, or third class status, specifying the types of municipal structure and degree of local autonomy they enjoy. In addition, all states have created various single purpose special districts to provide specific services to local communities. School districts are the single most common type of special purpose district, and public utilities are the second most numerous, like water and health districts.

Counties and municipalities, or permitted combinations of the two, are given home rule, meaning that they don't have to seek special permission from the state for every little thing they do. General local government entities are given supplementary powers by Article IX, Section II of the Georgia Constitution. These powers are listed in Table 10.1.

The General Assembly may (and often does) expand these powers, and in addition may regulate, restrict, or limit them. In other words, local government in Georgia is very much state government applied locally. Currently, a lot of activity centers on special single purpose districting. Special districts have proliferated all over the country, and Georgia is no exception. While the school district is still the most common type of special district, it is also the one kind of special district that is actually declining in terms of real numbers, because of consolidation. Also called authorities, special districts have been created to provide transportation, soil conservation, libraries, water, sewage disposal, etc. In short, because they can be empowered

Table 10.1 Municipal Responsibilities

1. Authority for police and fire protection.
2. Garbage and solid waste collection and disposal.
3. Public health facilities and services, including hospitals, emergency services, animal control.
4. Street and road construction and maintenance.
5. Parks and recreational programs and facilities.
6. Storm water and sewage and disposal systems.
7. Water storage, treatment, and distribution.
8. Create and maintain public housing.
9. Provide public transportation.
10. Libraries, and arts and sciences facilities.
11. Terminal and dock and parking facilities.
12. Codes for building, plumbing, and electricity.
13. Air quality control.

Source: Compiled by authors.

to collect taxes and to make expenditures, these special purpose governments are in fact just as much governments as are the more common and traditional general purpose governments, such as counties and municipalities.

County Government

Georgia has 159 counties, more than that of any other state except Texas. The Georgia Constitution in Article IX states that there shall not be more than 159, but within that framework counties may merge or consolidate, providing that a majority of the voters in each of the counties approve. This is an unlikely event given the attachment that Georgians have to their counties. The Constitution requires a degree of uniformity in county government. Each county must elect a clerk of the superior court, a judge of the probate court, a sheriff, and tax officials. Traditionally, the tax officials have been a tax collector and a tax receiver, but in some counties these offices have been replaced by a single tax commissioner. Of course, each county elects a set of county commissioners, and may elect a variety of other county officials. Generally, Georgia's political sub-divisions enjoy home rule jurisdiction. The county commissioners, and any other elected officials, are subject to the home rule provisions of Article IX. The idea of home rule is that a municipal government is allowed to conduct its own affairs with a minimum amount of interference from state authorities, as long as the local options are consistent with the Georgia

Constitution and the general laws enacted by the General Assembly of the State.

In general, the powers of local government in cities and counties are defined in their official state charters. The form or structure is the primary determining factor in how power is distributed and in how both personnel and budgets will be managed. If the form allows primary power with one individual (a strong mayor) the individual will be held accountable for conditions and issues associated with personnel and budget matters; the reverse is true when the form provides for responsibility divided among an entire city council or on the county commission.

Georgia County Government

In Georgia, the 159 separate counties are run by county commissioners who function as a legislative body, although they may have executive responsibilities as well. Actually, Georgia county government can take a variety of forms (Ammons and Campbell, 1993). The most common type of county government is the traditional form which is found in 93 of Georgia's counties. In the traditional form, commissioners serve as both legislators and executives, although they may entrust more of the executive authority to the chairperson, who may serve either in a part-time or a full-time capacity.

The second most frequently used form of county government in Georgia is the commission-administrator form. In the 34 counties that employ this system, the commissioners appoint a full-time administrator to administer the day-to-day activities of the county. While the administrator may have some power over budgetary matters and may hire and fire some county employees, those powers are somewhat limited.

Limited, that is, by comparison to the powers of a county manager. The commission-manager form is the third most popular form of county government in Georgia. Employed in 20 counties, the commission appoints the manager (just as it does in a county-administrator system), but the managers' duties are somewhat more substantial than they are in the county-administrator system. The manager has the power to hire and fire all department heads, prepare and submit the budget to the commission and generally administer the county's affairs in the same manner that a city manager manages the city government.

Georgia is unique among the states in having single commissioner county governments. As of 1995, 13 Georgia counties utilized the single commissioner system (ACCG, Survey of County Governments, 1995). In such a system, found only in small rural counties, the commissioner is both the legislator and the executive. Challenged in 1994 as a violation of the 1965 Voting Rights Act, the single commissioner system in Bleckley County was upheld by the U.S. Supreme Court (**Holder v. Hall,** no. 91-2012, 1994). The court held that Bleckley County, which was 22 percent African-American, did not dilute minority voting strength by having only one county commissioner.

DeKalb County is the sole example of the final form of county government in Georgia. In 2010, it had an elected executive, much like a president or a governor or a strong mayor, who has the power to appoint and remove department heads, prepare and submit the budget, and who can also veto ordinances passed by the commission. The rest of the commissioners serve as the legislative branch of county government. Five of the seven are elected in county districts, the other two commissioners are elected at-large within the county. With the obvious exception of single commissioner county government, county commissions in Georgia range in size from two to eleven commissioners (see Table 10.2). With the exception of counties that have only one commissioner, 97 counties' commissioners serve staggered terms, while 49 serve concurrent terms.

The County Commission creates a budget to manage the services necessary to respond to citizen demands, such as road and bridge building, health services, law enforcement, and legal services. Funding for these elementary services is primarily derived from property taxes on residents' habitations and owned lands. The Commissioners are responsible for setting the tax rate for property in the county, within state constitutional limits. They are also responsible for contracting to build roads, bridges, county facilities—including jails, libraries, hospitals, and other health facilities, as well as provision for fire protection, sanitation, and emergency and disaster relief.

Table 10.2 County Commission Size

No. of Commissioners	No. of Counties
1	13
3	18
4	2
5	98
6	12
7	10
8	3
9	1
11	2

Source: ACCG Survey on County Governments, 1995.

Many other individuals charged with responsibility for implementation of the many functions of the county level of government are publicly elected, including the Clerk of the Superior Court, the Tax Commissioner, the Sheriff, and the Judge of the Probate court. And of course the County Commissioners also hire a wide array of professionals to staff the bureaucracies and offices to meet the citizens' needs.

Though voters may not specifically be familiar with the broad allocation of powers given in the commission's charter, they are familiar, almost intuitively, with where responsibility rests; and at the county level blame and credit are quickly assessed in the voting booth. Success in budget and personnel power is reflected by repeated reelections; while failure in either area is often reflected by rejection of a county commissioner or a county sheriff. For example, in the authors' home county, Lowndes, the entire county commission was defeated for reelection in 1996 in either the primary or the general election. Disgruntlement within the electorate over the manner in which the incumbent commissioners handled the financial and infrastructure arrangements for a new chemical plant to locate in Lowndes County resulted in this clean sweep. Four years later, all but one of them were out of office, either deciding not to run for reelection, or having been defeated. And, in 2010, community discontent over the decision to build a new wood biomass incineration plant, with probable pollution, threatens to result in similar political turmoil (Bergstrom, 9-29-10).

City Government

Unlike some states, Georgia does not differentiate among its municipalities by labeling them as first, second, or third class according to population size. In general, all municipal corporations are treated equally, but occasionally the General Assembly may make laws that are applicable only to cities of a certain population size. Officially, all urban areas are simply called *municipalities* without the distinctions found in other states which designate municipal government as, for examples, towns, townships, boroughs, etc. Of course, many local officials like to call their home towns "cities," but that is a matter of local concern, and not a reflection of any state policy.

Local Government in Georgia

In ancient times, cities were often free and independent states, city-states exercising sovereign power. But in the modern world and certainly in Georgia, cities are mere creatures of the state. That is, local governments have no independent sovereignty, no right to exist independent of the authority and approval of the state government. The mechanism by which this authority is granted, and the precise powers and geographical scope of the city is the city charter. The city charters can be granted, and a new local government will come into existence.

An old standing joke in Georgia says that every town (remember that "town" is not a legal designation) is a county seat. Certainly most towns want to be known as viable and important centers of population and commerce. But if a town starts off well, but then declines in population, or fails to provide enough services to justify its continued existence, it may actually lose its charter. In Georgia, the state reviews local governments to make sure that municipal entities continue to be worthy of their charters.

The City Charter in Georgia
In the early 1990s, the town of Good Hope in Walton County had a population of 181 persons; the town of Newborn in Newton County had a population of 404 people; and Deepstep in Washington County had a population of 120 inhabitants. All three of these communities were among the hundreds of small cities examined to determine if they should have their municipal charters revoked. This review was conducted by a special government commission established by former governor Joe Frank Harris. A recent law passed by the state General Assembly authorized the Local Government Commission to survey small cities in rural Georgia to determine whether they remain viable. The criteria enacted require providing, or contracting for, a minimum of three municipal services: such as water, sewers, or zoning (Osinski, 1994). If cities are losing too much population to be viable, and lapse on such services, they might be culled from the ranks of Georgia municipalities. Update in 2010: according to a recent google search of their modern websites, Goodhope has grown to 210 persons and Newborn has increased up to 520 persons. As for Deepstep, students may conduct their own research to determine its status.

State officials say that problems that might lead to revocation of a city charter include not only declining population and dwindling services, but also cities which are inefficient, or providing duplicate services that could be provided by an alternative local government (Osinski, 1994). However, no one predicts the wholesale revocation of hundreds of city charters in Georgia. Where the commission does detect a problem, the city is formally notified and given at least a year to mend its ways or justify its existence. Given the loyalties many Georgians feel toward their hometowns, few observers expect that the commission will, in fact, recommend the demise of many cities. In fact, some of these cities, like Good Hope, have weathered the storm, and because they lie close to growing metropolitan areas, are becoming merged into suburban developments and soon can expect to start to grow again.

If there is any doubt that Georgians are loyal to homeplace, the reaction to a decision by the State Department of Transportation to remove hundreds of place names from the official roadmap of Georgia in 2006, because those places were not incorporated and added "clutter" to the map, should remove that doubt. The clatter over the clutter was heard from one end of the state to the other. Even Governor Perdue weighed in, sending a letter to the State Transportation Board and the Transportation Commissioner, protesting the deletion of these tiny dots on the map. The DOT responded by promising to restore the dots.

City Government Forms

Throughout the United States there are four fundamental forms of city government. Georgia has examples of each of the major forms. The most basic form is some kind of a combination of a Mayor and Council Government. This form of government is the oldest in the United States, dating to its heritage from the British system more than 400 years ago. This form has had many modifications over the centuries, but basically there are two versions, depending on whether the formal powers of the mayor are strong or weak.

Strong Mayor/(Weak) Council

In the strong mayor/council form of city government the mayor has major powers particularly associated with personnel and budget. The mayor can "hire or fire" city personnel without approval by the city's council—regardless of the number of the council or the employee's position in the city. However, rarely does this occur even in settings in which mayors are identified as "strong." Political havoc can occur; the mayor needs council support both publicly and politically. Thus, even with strong personnel powers granted by a city's charter, few mayors would consistently circumvent the powers delegated a city's council and risk losing wide-ranging public support over repeated elections. Atlanta is often depicted as a clearly identifiable "strong" mayor/council city, which like both Chicago and New York have a city charter giving both personnel and budgeting power to their mayors. Effectively, the publics' voices are limited to what the mayor perceives as essential to the city's needs. Council members in such cities must rely on either advocating or rejecting the mayor's position, and suffer the consequences of the public's interpretation of the mayor's impact on each area's resident's life. The standard type of organization chart for a strong mayor system is shown in Figure 10.2 on page 196.

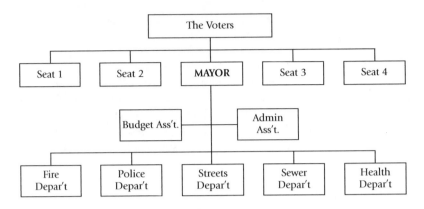

Mayor (elected at-large)
Council Members (at-large or district member, or both)
Department Heads (Appointed)

Figure 10.2 Strong Mayor Organization Chart

The flow of power, the vertical and horizontal lines, indicates the form of the cities' government, whether it is strong or weak mayor or council, or modifications where other elected positions intersect either budget, personnel, or both.

The City of Atlanta
Atlanta is the largest city in the State of Georgia, and in fact serves as a transportation, communication, and cultural hub of the southeastern United States. The City of Atlanta serves as the state capitol, and with a total population of 416,474, ranks 39th in size among the nation's great cities.

During the political and constitutional reform movements in Georgia of the mid-1970s, the Atlanta city charter was redrafted, and various changes and improvements reforms took effect in 1974. The old Board of Aldermen was reorganized as a City Council, and a mayor/council form of government was instituted. Instead of electing all of the members at-large, two-thirds of the eighteen new city council members were elected (four-year terms) from twelve districts to foster better urban representation; among the remaining six at-large posts was the position of President of the Council, the former vice-mayor position, which today serves as the council's presiding legislative leader.

As a political rule of thumb, the bigger the city, the stronger the mayor, and Atlanta is no exception to the rule. The mayoralty of Atlanta is a qualified **strong mayor**/city council system. The mayor operates as the city's chief executive officer, enjoys a veto power over council actions, and prepares the annual city budgets for the council's review and approval. Although in the past council members have not succeeded to the mayoralty position, that was changed when District Two Councilman Bill Campbell ran on a platform of "**make the system work**" and was inaugurated as mayor on January 3, 1994 (Campbell was reelected in 1997). In 2001 Campbell was replaced with Shirley Franklin, who has been designated as one of the nation's best mayors. In 2006, Campbell was convicted on corruption charges.

Some of the complexity of local government functioning and intergovernmental relations is seen by the linkages between the city government and special purpose governments in the area. At the sub-local level, dozens of neighborhoods planning units are incorporated in the council districts, influencing the elections to the council and serving as a focus for the council's legislative focus and planning efforts. Expanding its geographical focus, the City Council also elects a number of its members to be directors and board members of various special purpose government authorities. These include such entities as the Atlanta Regional Commission (ARC) and the Solid Waste Management Authority (SWMA).

The Atlanta City Council meets twice a month. Citizens are invited to attend the sessions and to bring complaints, issues, and sometimes even "**thank-you's**" to the council meetings. Here is local government in the raw: vital, emotional, and sometimes characterized by hot-tempered exchanges of opinion and viewpoint. Council members are assigned to various functional committees, which meet twice a month, and whose function is to review proposals, recommend legislation to the council, and oversee daily departmental operations. These committees are concerned with such areas as public utilities, finance, human resources, zoning, and transportation. Members may serve on three or four such committees, including the Committee on Council, the executive committee of the city council. Of course, the exact powers of the mayor and the council will vary with the personalities of the people involved. A mayor with a strong personality and a canny political style may be able to gain power even when the city council is designed to be dominant.

For their part-time, but politically intensive jobs, the city council members in 2009 received salaries of close to forty thousand dollars a year, and were responsible to the operation of the city and its annual budget of nearly one billion dollars, including bonds and the capital construction projects of water and sewer connections under the streets and also the Airport Authority budget allotments. As is routine in Georgia, the mayor receives a higher salary. But when a five member citizen commission appointed by Mayor Franklin recommended that the Mayor's salary be raised by more than 50%, from $147,500 to $225,000, with concomitant raises of 17% for council members, from

$39,473 to $46,183, there was opposition. Because of the 'Great recession' of 2008, money was getting very tight, so the council opposed the plan (AJC, 01-06-09).

The city government exercises two types of legislative enactments: ordinances and resolutions. Ordinances are the ordinary laws of a city, binding on the citizens and business of daily life. In contrast, resolutions are non-binding, used to project a sense of the local government's feelings on various issues.

Weak Mayor/(Strong) Council

Mayor/council relationships are similar to the strong mayor/council, systems, but effectively the power of the government as identified in the city's charter is held in the hands of the city's council as a group instead of concentrated in the mayor's hands. Like any Governor, the mayors of such cities must **"rule"** by political skill, charisma, or both. Cities with a weak mayor system have both personnel and funding power chartered to the city's council members. The mayor can only seek public support politically, and seek to acquire support of the city's council members through use of political manipulation and personal charisma.

In this type of system, the organization chart is very similar to the strong mayor system, but the power of the mayor is considerably reduced. The mayor generally is little more than a typical council member, and all decisions must be by majority vote. The mayor must either submit to the council's decision, or seek to influence the council with personal charisma and political influence. In particular, the personnel and budgeting powers of the mayor are greatly reduced, and usually the mayor will not control the agenda of the meetings. Organizational depictions of this form of government will not reveal a general structural difference, but the flow of power will be significantly modified to the benefit of the council. Essentially, the weak mayor system results in a legislatively-dominated political system.

There is little information from various municipalities in Georgia as to whether they have a strong mayor/council or a weak mayor/council form of government. We do know, however, that regardless of the strength of the mayor, some form of mayor-council government is considerably more popular than any other type of municipal government in Georgia. In one study, 85% of the cities responding indicated that they had a mayor-council form (see Weeks and Hardy, Handbook for Georgia Mayors and Councilmembers, 1993). By contrast, fewer than thirteen percent of Georgia's cities employed the next most popular of the municipal government types, the council-manager form, although half of all responding larger cities (with more than 10,000 population) did.

Council-Manager Form of City Government

Moving to become one of the most popular forms of government after World War II, with expansion of expectations for professionalism by the public, the council-manager form of government rapidly increased. This form is also referred to as the **"corporate"** form of government, in that it splits the responsibility for directing policy-making and implementation of policy. Elected city leaders are charged with responsibility for making policy, while an individual they collectively hire, the city manager, is charged with implementing the mayor and council's policies.

The operation of this form of government is similar to the form of special district governments, especially school districts, which are discussed below; and it reflects the business management style of many major corporations. For instance, the council and mayor are comparable to the corporation's Board of Directors, as policymakers, while the city manager is comparable to the chief executive officer (CEO) of a corporation.

According to this model, the city manager does not make policy but only implements policies adopted by elected leaders. However, in reality, the city manager may acquire a substantial amount of power and be requested to provide major input to council members and the mayor in decisions associated with both personnel and budgets. Unfortunately, because the council and mayor must stand for election periodically, the city manager's position is subject to the stability of the council. When the council and/or mayor are changed in the majority that hired the manager, a high probability occurs that the manager will be terminated from his or her position; another hired, and the process continues.

The Council-Manager system may be popular today, but there was a time when it had to compete for popularity with a form of municipal government that is now all but extinct. That is the commission form of city government.

Commission

It is said that "necessity is the mother of invention," and that is no less true in government than elsewhere. A devastating flood destroyed Galveston, Texas, in 1900. This disaster provided the opportunity for Galveston to experiment with a brand new form of local government, the commission. In the commission form of municipal government executive and legislative functions are entrusted to the same persons, who, in effect, wear two hats. When they're wearing their legislative hats, commissioners are policy-makers. But when they switch to their executive hats, they are department heads. Thus, one commissioner will head the Department of Public Safety, another the Public Works

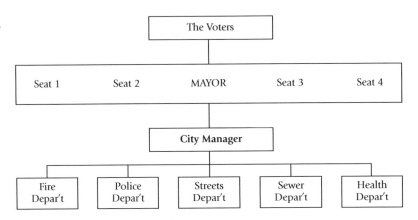

Figure 10.3 Council Manager Organization Chart

Department, a third will be mayor, and so on. The problem with this system is that there is relatively weak executive control. Today most former commission cities have abandoned that form. Georgia is no exception; in the study cited above, only three responding cities retained the commission form of government (less than one percent).

Americans in general and many Georgians treat politics and government with a wry sense of humor; they are a necessary evil and we can't live with them and we can't live without them. About the best thing we can do is to remember Winston Churchill's quip to the effect that democracies are the worst form of government, except that the alternatives are even worse! Politicians will always make more promises than they can keep, and we just have to grin and bear it.

Special District Governments

The State of Georgia has over 600 governments identified as **special districts**. Special district governments are governments associated with singular interests. Thus, special district governments may be seen throughout the state, both statewide and at regional levels, served by both appointed or elected boards. The forms of the boards vary as much as do the geographical areas and specialized topics they manage. Included in the varieties of special government districts are school districts, airports, sanitation, housing, and soil conservation districts. Some, such as an airport authority, require a big investment for construction and operation. As a general rule, the board or commission that is elected or appointed to manage the concern of the single purpose government is accorded a major degree of autonomy, but is usually cross-linked to adjoining city and county governments by appointed board memberships.

Figure 10.4   Local Government Promises Revealed

Organizational Structure

The special purpose form of government, focusing on a particular type of service, usually relies heavily on a professional ethic and organizational style. It is most similar to the council-manager form of government, and was first used in the nineteenth century to reform the Chicago school district by removing it from the corrupt political practices of the big city "party machine." In this form, the responsibility for directing policy-making is placed in an elected board, which then appoints an expert administrator for implementation of policy. Often the administrative director will dominate the board because of his or her expertise as well as the administrator's operational control. Figure 10.5 on page 202 shows this type of organization.

Special District Funding

Each district also has independent local taxing power, judicial power, and executive power, in addition to its primary allocated lawmaking powers in its special purpose area or function. A high degree of growth in special districts has proliferated across the nation, as well as in Georgia. Much of the reason for the growth is linked to the so-called taxpayer revolt; citizens won't vote for general tax increases, but they understand and tolerate tax burdens for identifiable and needed services.

Today, it seems as if there is a **"fad"** to create local special districts; it almost seems as if such fads come along periodically, with new

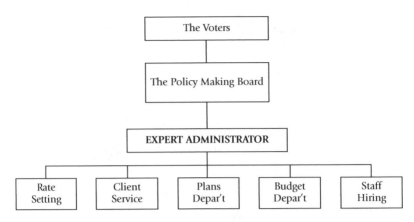

Figure 10.5 Special Purpose Government Chart

types of special districts being established whenever opportunity to do so arises. But in reality such special districts are cold, rational decisions to counter increasing taxpayer opposition to government programs. In the past, voters trusted government and supported its efforts with broad based tax revenues; but now planners are instead attaching fees for the use of such things as bridges built by these special districts. Even the most reactionary taxpayer understands the need for building and maintaining new transportation projects. (It is noted by the authors that rarely do the special districts *"go out of business"* even when the **"fad"** passes). That is because the special projects can more easily justify their budgets. The multiplicity of special districts throughout the state comprises another tier of taxing and governing entities. Each special entity carries responsibility to the people of Georgia both for service and for efficient use of public monies.

Educational Districts
It should be mentioned that school districts are a particular example of local special purpose governments. Traditionally, a distinction is made between the public schools offering of kindergarten through twelfth grade, and the higher educational, or college institutions. This division is reflected in two major bureaucracies: the State Board of Education and the State Board of Regents. These agencies and local governments are discussed in more detail in Chapter 9.

Too Many Governments?

One frequently heard criticism of local government in Georgia and everywhere is that there are simply too many governments. Why do we need 159 counties, 531 municipalities, 180 school districts, and hundreds of other special districts? The simple answer is that we probably don't, but how do we get rid of governments that may no longer be necessary?

It is probably safe to say that no plan to eliminate or merge counties will succeed in Georgia. The attachment to county is just too strong. But annexation and consolidation are still possible approaches to the problem of too many governments. Georgia law provides for four methods of annexation, where one government absorbs people and property in immediate proximity to it. A municipal corporation can annex if its local legislative delegation can get the General Assembly to pass a local act, or if it passes a resolution to annex and holds a referendum in the to-be-annexed area or areas, or by one of two petition procedures. The first procedure allows the municipality to annex if all the owners of all of the land in the area to be annexed petition for annexation. The second procedure allows the municipality to annex land where sixty percent of the landowners and sixty percent of the others petition for annexation. In either case, there must be a public hearing and the passage of an ordinance for the annexation to be completed. In cases where a municipality completely surrounds an unincorporated area of fewer than fifty acres, the municipality may annex the "island."

Consolidation is a process by which a county, its municipalities, and perhaps its special districts become one government. Successful consolidation of school districts has taken place all over the country, with the number of independent school districts declining quite dramatically. Consolidation of counties, cities, and special districts, however, has been quite rare. Although there have been 27 proposals for city-county consolidation in Georgia between 1933 and 1997, only three have succeeded: Columbus-Muscogee County, Athens-Clarke County, and Augusta-Richmond County. Probably the principal obstacle to successful consolidation in Georgia is the requirement that there must be a majority vote in support of consolidation in each of the governmental entities to be consolidated, even if the overall vote is in favor of a merger. In 1987, for example, a proposed consolidation of Brunswick and Glynn County failed because the residents of Brunswick opposed it, even though a majority of the residents on the Islands (St. Simons, Sea Island, and Jekyll Island) supported it along with the residents of rural Glynn County. In fact, this was a "textbook case" of the failure of consolidation proposals. African-Americans, who had established a power base in Brunswick were reluctant to have that power diluted by merging with majority white unincorporated communities in the County. Arguments that consolidation would eliminate duplication of services and reduce expenses, and ultimately taxes, largely fell on deaf ears in the city.

Conclusion

Under America's "apple pie" system of federalism, there is no easy way to separate one government's functioning from another, as none functions independently. Yet, ultimately, each entity must also be viewed in isolation if we are to understand it. The complexity of viewing all levels of our state's government is properly the enterprise of a substantial number of books, and a substantial number of researchers; far more than the scope appropriate to this small volume on Georgia state government. In our hectic day and age, the need for strong local governments has been met by continued growth and evolution of local government forms, meeting the modern challenges.

Key Terms

Corporate
Commission
Council-Manager or Corporate form of Government
Consolidation
County government
Home Rule
Mayor/Strong Council
Municipalities
Party Machine
Single Commissioner System
Single Commission Commissioner
School district
Special purpose District
Strong Mayor/Weak Council

Essay Questions

1. Identify responsibilities of local governments in Georgia.
2. In what ways are municipal governments "creatures of the state"?
3. Explain why a city might lose its municipal status.
4. Compare and contrast the Strong Mayor/(Weak) Council model, the Weak Mayor/(Strong) Council model, and the Council-Manager form of city government.
5. What are the arguments for and against consolidation?
6. One of the frequently heard criticisms of local government in Georgia and everywhere is that there are too many governments. Why do we need 159 counties, 531 municipalities, 180 school districts, and hundreds of other special districts?
7. List and discuss in detail the four forms of city governments in Georgia.

Figure 11.1   Statue of Herman Eugene Talmadge

The State Constitution

Reflecting State Diversity

It is well-known in academic circles that much of Georgia's Constitution reflects the political theories of an Englishman, John Locke, as adapted by the American experience after the British monarchy was rejected by the colonies over two hundred years ago. It is less well-known and understood that Georgia's Constitution is also indebted to the French theorist Jean J. Rousseau, for his theory of the general will. Rousseau argued that in a democracy the structure of government, and its functioning and policies, should reflect the general will of all the people. This is the essential basis of democratic theory, that the government should represent the people and their desires. And if we had a simple society, and a simple undifferentiated economy, and if we had ethnic and cultural unity, then our Constitution could be simple, too. However, those are a lot of ifs, and unfortunately, none of them are true.

Georgia is, in fact, a large and complex state, the biggest east of the Mississippi River and with a correspondingly rich and complicated economy and multifaceted culture. Therefore, we should expect lots of diversity, and that as a result our Constitution would be complex also, as in fact it is. But underlying that political complexity is an orderly and rational system of government that reflects Georgia's civilization and culture, and the general will of its citizens. This chapter focuses on explaining how our system of government does reflect the will of the people of Georgia, but that it does so by reflecting the varied desires and policy preferences of many different groups of people, as they were described in Chapter Three. How can the wills and desires of different people, with different ideas, be incorporated into one government and one constitution? One definition of politics is that it is the process that determines who gets what, when, and how (Lasswell); it should be expanded to include who is and who is not taxed.

207

James Q. Wilson describes how a complicated federal government can have several different types of public policies. His typology is based on an analysis of winners and losers in political conflict, who benefits from a policy and who has to pay for it. Generally his model can be used to describe not only financial cost/benefit situations, but regulatory cost/benefit situations as well. He derives four scenarios: majority benefits and it incurs the cost; the majority benefits and a minority incurs the cost; the minority benefits and the majority incurs the costs; and finally isolated policies. Wilson names these four types of policies: majoritarian, interest-group policies, client centered policies, and entrepreneurial policies. These are depicted in Table 11.1.

Within Wilson's typology, Rousseau's concept of the general will is best expressed in majoritarian policies, ones that benefit all of the people, and are paid for all of the people. An example of majoritarian policy is when the state capitol building's construction and maintenance is paid for out of general revenues. In contrast, interest-group policies benefit one smaller group of people and are paid for only by that group of people, who thus incur both the costs and the benefits of that program. A good example can be found in the hunting and fishing laws of the state. Hunters and fishermen pay fees for their hunting and fishing licenses, and the money collected from them is used to regulate wildlife and to stock the forests and rivers with game. Few people seriously contest the equity of either the majoritarian or special-interest policies as described by Wilson.

However, the other two types of policies: client centered policies, and entrepreneurial policies, generate a great deal of controversy and constitutional activity. That is because both of them involve taking

Table 11.1 Wilson's Typology

		BENEFIT	
		Majority	Minority
COST	Majority	Majoritarian	Client Politics
	Minority	Entrepreneurial	Interest Group

money or resources from one group of people and redistributing money or benefits to other groups of people. When government collects money from the majority of the people and gives to a small group of people, Professor Wilson calls it client politics. An example might be welfare programs, or food distribution programs; the larger part of society pays the cost of helping out a smaller part. On the other hand, when government collects money from a small group of people and uses it to give benefits to a larger group or to the majority, Professor Wilson calls that entrepreneurial politics. An example might be taxes levied on businessmen who own manufacturing facilities which pollute our air and water, and then uses the money to protect the environment. Society wants strong industry, of course, but we need good air and water, too, so we tax the small number of big polluters and use the revenues to benefit society as a whole. Every element of our State Constitution reflects one or more of these four types of policies.

All of the different provisions of the Constitution of the State of Georgia can also be looked at as policies which are so important that they have been lodged within the Constitution to protect them from routine political maneuvering. And each policy generally falls into one of the four categories of policies described by Professor Wilson, depending on who benefits from the policy, and who bears the cost of the policy. So while it is true that in a democratic society the will of the people usually determines the substantive policies and procedures of the state, it is also true that the politics of state government reflects all of the different interest groups, and so can sometimes be controversial, benefiting only a few of our citizens, and result in complex laws and constitutional provisions.

The more the variation in regions, industries, peoples and activities that a state encompasses, the more and varied the representatives of the interest groups will be. In Georgia, they may be called lobbyists, interest groups, special interest groups, or pressure groups, but they are all concerned with pursuing their own agendas and policy preferences. These interest groups have two major ways of pursuing their political goals: financing the political campaigns of their representatives and supporters, and lobbying for regulations, laws, and constitutional amendments that institutionalize their policy preferences. Groups which are not effective in lobbying for their preferred policies are unlikely to be well-served by the policies which are enacted.

This chapter is not concerned with the variety of techniques interest groups use to influence policymaking, but rather in describing the end results: the extent to which the Constitution is fundamentally majoritarian or not. Are the people of Georgia generally receiving their fair share of the state's budget? Have they succeeded in maintaining their democratic political influence, and changing the law and the state's Constitution to reflect their changing needs? As we discussed in Chapter Four supra, Georgia's General Assembly is quite sensitive to the needs of interest groups; but constitutional provisions require popular ratification, and an analysis of the policy types within the Constitution will enable us to determine the extent to which the people of the state favor majoritarian policies. The relative power of all of the contending interest groups in Georgia is reflected in the Constitution and its recent amendments.

The Constitution of 1983

The present Constitution of the State of Georgia, as ratified in 1983 and amended over the last twenty years, is short, just over 40,000 words as measured on a word processor. In structure, it consists of a preamble and eleven articles. Cursory overview of the Constitution shows that most of its provisions are intended to be majoritarian in conception and function. However, there are sections which seem to indicate that interest-group policies, client-centered policies, and even some entrepreneurial policies exert significant influence in the Constitution.

The preamble is a short positive invocation expressing the hope of all Georgians that the Constitution will serve our overall needs and desires for freedom and justice. Article One of the Constitution of the State of Georgia begins basically as a Bill of Rights emphasizing the powers of the people and their rights and privileges *vis-à-vis* the government; it also has a second section on the origin and structure of government and a third section focusing on property rights. The basic organization of this article is clearly majoritarian oriented, as is Article II, which continues the theme of popular sovereignty, detailing the requirements of popular voting, elections for the most important state offices, and procedures for removal of public officials. Both of these articles are designed to benefit the majority of the population.

Articles III through VI, discussing the four branches of state government, also clearly convey the general intent that the government is designed to be under general popular control, and can thus be categorized as majoritarian as well. All of these articles illustrate the importance of the representatives of the people in framing the laws of the state, and reflecting the wills and desires of the people as a whole.

In contrast, Article VII is a very different story altogether. Article VII is the taxation article, granting the power to tax, the power to exempt from taxation, and it describes the purposes for which debt may be incurred. Let us look at the various sections of that article. Section One describes the general power of taxation, including taxes on tangible and intangible property (including the income tax). It should be noted that most of the language of this section is extremely detailed as to what types of tangible property are to be taxed, such as trailers, motor vehicles, real property, and agricultural products. The specifications here, and the fact that the section allows the General Assembly to modify the tax rates and methods for these categories, indicates that interest group competition over policy is probably intense, and probably not simply majoritarian in operation.

This is even more noticeable in Section Two, which lists specific exemptions from the state's ad valorem taxation. There are primarily four categories of exemption: homesteads, locally granted exemptions, holdover exemptions from the prior Constitution and laws, and an exemption for disabled veterans. These exemptions are clearly designed to benefit their respective groups, and are thus not majoritarian. The toleration for locally granted exemptions, when multiplied by the hundreds of governmental taxing entities in Georgia, makes it certain that interest-group policies, client-centered policies, and entrepreneurial policies could each be identified with a minimum of additional research.

Similarly, Sections Three and Four of Article VII provide explicit exceptions to the majoritarian principle. Section III creates the basic practice of putting all revenues in the state's general fund. However, it allows agricultural revenues to be treated differently and used for the promotion of agricultural produce, a clear example of interest-group policy. Of course, most people will agree that the special conditions and hazards of agricultural productivity and perishability justify this exception to the majoritarian principle. Section III also allows general revenue funds to be dispensed as grants to counties and municipalities, a clear example of client-centered policy embedded in the Constitution. These are usually justified in terms of disaster relief programs and in promoting economic growth.

Section IV, detailing the purposes and guarantees for public debt in Georgia, both at the state and local levels, by underwriting special programs and capital building projects, also creates a wide variety of client-centered policies and expenditures. This section basically allows counties and other local entities to borrow money for large construction projects and public improvement programs. Although Article VII is obviously not simply majoritarian in its operation, it allows local flexibility in responding to the needs of the people of the State of Georgia, and so allows our Georgia government to respond to needs on a priority basis.

Article VIII, concerning public education is, in monetary terms, the largest and most important function of state government. This article provides for the governance, administrative structure, and for the financial support of public education at the elementary, secondary, and college levels. Since it takes general revenue funds and allocates them to specific educational entities, school districts and colleges, it is clearly an example of client-centered policy. And since some paragraphs allow the use of lottery money to support education, this article also provides an example of entrepreneurial policy, by taxing one group, the lottery gamblers, for the benefit of another group, students in the State of Georgia. Gambling, although occasionally leading to excess, is in essence *malum prohibitum*, that is not bad in and of itself, usually a victimless crime except as it might damage the economic security of an addict's children. Dedicating the proceeds of a lottery to the children and students of the state displays a sophisticated understanding of the problems in forging public policy.

As discussed in Chapter One of this textbook, Georgia's political culture is a blend of traditionalistic and individualistic elements, with a moralistic tinge, that would generally be hostile to state-approved gambling activities. However, in this case the need to secure adequate levels of funding for education overrides minor moral considerations, and having gamblers pay a "sin tax" marks this entrepreneurial tax policy as an understandable exception to the tendency of moralistic cultures to outlaw everything that does not conform to their particular perception and interpretation of the world around them.

Article IX deals with counties and municipal corporations. Lacking sovereignty, these local governments are creatures of the state, and subject to the State Constitution and to state laws. The article describes the allowable structures, powers and governance of county, city, and special purpose governments; and relations among these and between them and the state as a whole. In Wilson's typology, perhaps the essential significance of a multiplicity of little governments is that it allows small regional populations to control themselves, enjoying their own unique political and cultural lifestyles. In this view, the entire article is an example of interest group politics, centered not so much on financial policies, but upon other political values, primarily freedom and diversity. Home rule is a very comforting policy to many of the citizens of the State of Georgia. In short, the Constitution clearly reflects our respect for individuals and local traditions.

The Amending Process

Article X is the amending article. It allows amendments to the Constitution to be proposed either by the General Assembly or by a constitutional convention. It is based on the Madisonian idea that frequent elections to facilitate change is superior to suppressing dissent, and thus risking subsequent violent change. It provides for amendments to be submitted to the voters, with a majority of those voting necessary for ratification. In Wilson's typology, this article is clearly majoritarian in conception. It underscores Georgia's commitment to

Figure 11.2   Safety Improved Baby Carriage

democratic governance, so that if it is the general will of the people to change their Constitution, then they may do so through the ballot box.

Article X establishes identical procedures for either amending the existing Constitution or for replacing it with a totally new one. An amendment or an entirely new Constitution may be proposed either by a two-thirds vote on a resolution by both houses of the General Assembly or by a convention called by a two-thirds vote of the General Assembly. Under the 1983 Constitution, however, all amendments have been proposed by a two-thirds vote on a resolution in the General Assembly, not by a convention process.

Should a convention route be taken, the General Assembly determines the procedures by which it would be called and the procedures by which it would operate. Whichever process is used, once proposed, an amendment or a new Constitution must be submitted to the electorate for ratification. A simple majority (50% + 1) of those actually voting in the first general election in an even-numbered year following the proposal is all that is required for ratification. The Governor has no official veto power over amendments or new Constitutions, so the decision of the people is final. Hopefully, only necessary amendments should be ratified, otherwise the Constitution may become cluttered up with frills that may look ridiculous or unfair, but that "lock in" some special benefit to an interest group enjoying temporary political power.

Finally, Article XI is the effective implementing article for the effectuation of the 1983 Constitution, concluding in Paragraph VI: "this Constitution shall become effective on July 1, 1983; and except as otherwise provided in this Constitution, all previous Constitutions and all amendments thereto shall thereupon stand repealed." Now that the 1983 Constitution has in fact been adopted, this section is inoperative, except as perhaps a model for the next time a similar process occurs.

Constitutional Changes

What changes have been made in the Constitution of the State of Georgia since it was ratified in 1983? The reader can tell by comparing the original version and then by looking at the most up-to-date version of the Constitution. There are several ways to do so. The state has a contractor who services the updating and printing of the document, but attempts to get copies can be cumbersome. There is also a Web site that lists all of the Constitutions and even colonial charters of the state, it can be found at: *http://georgiainfo.galileo.usg.edu/>* *<contents.htm.* Alternatively, the unabridged and instructor's editions of this textbook included the text of the Constitution in the appendix. If the reader has a copy of one of the unabridged editions, and reads it, it should also be noted that original contents remaining from the 1983 wording are in normal font, but other sections are in an italic font; to represent any new additions to the Constitution ratified after 1983 (deleted and omitted portions may be annotated in the appendix).

What are the significant changes since 1983? This is not always easy to determine, because several of its sections have been amended as many as five times, so the individual provisions may vary from year to year, and sometimes even our elected officials have trouble keeping track. This is not surprising, because as researchers know, one of the many problems of identifying the law at any level is its lack of coherency (Elza, 162). However, every constitutional amendment is noted in the Official Code of Georgia, Annotated, affectionately known as the "mickey code" as a mnemonic for its publisher, the Michie company.

A perusal of the Code showed that in the last thirty or so years there have been many proposed amendments. As of 2010, a total of ninety-four (94) proposed amendments have been sent to the citizens for consideration. Of those, seventy-two (72) have been ratified, and the remaining twenty-two (22) rejected by the voters. In percentage terms, the substance of the Constitution has been changed by about 35 percent.

Summary Analysis

A casual inspection of Table 11.2 below shows that the pace of amendment is slowing down, and that when the General Assembly has offered proposed amendments to the people the likelihood is that they will be ratified. Further analysis led the authors to conclude that many of the amendments are the sort of technical trivia that scholars love to criticize as being too minor to deserve to be elevated to constitutional status.

Minor changes in the tax code, restrictions on offenders as voters and office-holders, procedures for suspending indicted officials, punishments for accepting gratuities, and perhaps instructions on how to appoint replacements for vacant offices could be handled by statute. Many others, such as the creation of re-development zones and community improvement districts do represent progress in creating new governmental entities and probably do belong in the Constitution.

Table 11.3 on the following page shows some of the major structural page changes in the Constitution since it was adopted in 1983. Of the eleven Articles, the ones most significantly amended have been the voting Article II (84.0% ±) reflecting restricting the right to vote and serve in office of public offenders; the tax and finance Article VII

Table 11.2 Constitutional Changes Proposed

YEAR	Proposed	Rejected	Ratified
1984	11	1	10
1986	9	1	8
1988	15	9	6
1990	9	1	8
1992	8	1	7
1994	6	1	5
1996	5	1	4
1998	5	1	4
2000	7	1	6
2002	6	2	4
2004	2	0	2
2006	3	0	3
2008	3	1	2
2010	5	1	4
Totals	**94**	**22**	**72**

Source: Compiled by authors, 2010.

Table 11.3 Changes Listed by Sections

Portion	Topic	# New Pages	% Change
ARTICLE I	Lottery Allowed	2 of 6	+ 30%
ARTICLE II	Ineligible Voters	4 of 5	+ 80%
ARTICLE III	Powers of Leg.	7 of 18	+ 40%
ARTICLE IV	Powers of Bds.	0.5 of 4	+ 12%
ARTICLE V	no change	—	0%
ARTICLE VI	Court Organization	3 of 10	+ 28%
"	& jud. discipline		
ARTICLE VII	Classif. of Prop.	6 of 13	+ 45%
"	& local options		
"	& public debt		
ARTICLE VIII	Bds of Educat.		
"	& tax options	3 of 8	+ 36%
ARTICLE IX	Re-devel. Zones		
"	Inter-gov't Relat.		
"	Regional Facil.		
"	Comm. Imp. Dist.	5.5 of 17	+ 32%
ARTICLE X	—	—	0%
ARTICLE XI	Indust. Parks	.5 of 3	+ 15%
Totals:	**all changes**	**27.5 of 97**	**+ 28%**

Source: Compiled by authors, 2010.

(45% ±) detailing tax classifications and debt provisions; and Article III (45% ±) increasing the powers of the legislative branch of government. Similar expansion of taxing and operational changes for boards of education (Article VIII); local government (Article IX); and the judicial branch (Article VI) were ratified. One outstanding trend of the last decade or so toward improved funding of education in Georgia was reflected in Hope grants and substantial increases in the powers of boards of education to levy taxes and issue bonds, subject of course to voter approval.

Significant changes were also made in the area of special purpose districts and operations. Article IX was amended to allow the creation of local community improvement districts with local revenue sources; this built on other amendments that approved the creation of regional facilities such as industrial parks and re-development zones. In comparison, Articles V (Executive) and X (Amending) were not changed. A summary depiction of the number of proposed amendments and the years for their consideration by the voters and subsequent ratification is depicted in Table 11.3.

Other significant changes are the amendments establishing, in great detail, procedures for dealing with judges who have earned official sanctions and changing the structure of the courts by allowing the creation of special court projects. There were technical changes in the replacement appointive duties of the Governor to fill vacancies. On a more positive note, one amendment gives increased power to local governments to contract with each other to provide services. By using memorandums of understanding (MoU's) and memoranda of agreement (MoA's) or simple contracts for services, the field of intergovernmental cooperation was much strengthened.

In terms of intergovernmental relations, perhaps the single most interesting amendment to be ratified involved the amendment that established The Georgia State Finance and Investment Commission, the "super commission" responsible for approving general obligation bonds. The Constitutional Commission's members include the Governor, the Lt. Governor, The Speaker, The Attorney General, the Commissioner of Agriculture, and the State Auditor. See Article VII, Section IV, Paragraph VII, which passed on November 4, 1986. An attempt by Governor Perdue to establish a similar commission to evaluate the entire revenue and expenditure picture and make recommendations has not met with similar success.

In terms of policy politics, some of the most interesting amendments are changes in the tax and appropriations provisions, intended for a variety of purposes. In main they allow for more flexible legislative appropriations for children, injured workers, and indigent persons. They also allow more latitude for allotments to entrepreneurial efforts in technology, manufacturing, and agriculture. Investment "seed capital" is offered for new small business ventures, as are provisions for a new agricultural crop fund. One hopes that the majority of these amendments will help to alleviate misery and to spur economic development. To enable readers to more easily identify these amendments, the sections of the Constitution which have been amended recently are italicized in the Appendix containing the Constitution of the State of Georgia.

Annotations on Selected Amendments

Ratification of an amendment to Article I, Section II, Paragraph VII (d), which took effect on and after January 1, 1995, now allows the holding of raffles by nonprofit organizations and repeals contrary laws enacted prior to January 1, 1995. Since the state government is allowed to hold a lottery, this gives other local governments and organizations the power to hold revenue raising raffles. This provision maintains the power of the state to regulate such activities by saying that laws which may be enacted by the General Assembly may restrict, regulate, or prohibit the operation of such raffles.

Article III, Section VI was amended by adding Paragraph VII, on the regulation of alcoholic beverages, particularly in the counties and municipalities of the state for the purpose of regulating, restricting, or prohibiting the exhibition of nudity, partial nudity, or depictions of nudity in connection with the sale or consumption of alcoholic beverages. It provides delegated regulatory authority for the adoption and enforcement of regulatory ordinances by the counties and municipalities of this state. It helps to control the spread of "red light" districts. Although some would argue that these types of activities are mere *malum prohibitum*, there is little doubt that every culture needs to have some control over such activity, and keep its visibility at a low profile.

Despite the fact that overall crime rates have been declining for years, the "tough-on-crime" mentality continues to be a popular choice for many Georgia political elements. Article IV, Section II was amended restricting the powers of the courts and of the Board of Pardons and Paroles. The new Paragraph II (b) (2) provides that the General Assembly may by general law provide for minimum mandatory sentences and for sentences which are required to be served in their entirety for persons convicted of armed robbery, kidnapping, rape, aggravated child molestation, aggravated sodomy, or aggravated sexual battery. And sub-section (3) provides that the General Assembly may similarly provide for the imposition of sentences of life without parole for persons convicted of murder, and for anyone who is twice convicted of murder, armed robbery, kidnapping, rape, aggravated child molestation, aggravated sodomy, or aggravated sexual battery, the so-called "two-strikes law." These types of offenses are universally recognized as *malum in se*, bad and evil in and of themselves, with clearly identifiable victims. When and if the General Assembly specifies, the board of pardons and parole shall not have the authority to consider categories of such persons for pardon, parole, or commutation from any portion of such sentence.

One result of this policy has been a great increase in the size of the prison population, one of the highest in the world. In contrast, the next article was amended by a new paragraph, Paragraph X of Article VI, Section I, which authorizes pilot projects in the courts. This substantially modifies the court structure of the state, by allowing the General Assembly to enact legislation providing for, as pilot programs of limited duration, courts which are not uniform within their classes in jurisdiction, powers, rules of practice and procedure, and also the selections, qualifications, terms, and discipline of judges for such pilot courts. Some of these were intended to deflect persons accused of minor offenses to community treatment facilities instead of hard core penitentiaries. This can have particular application to status offenses, *malum prohibitum*. These can be young persons experimenting with controlled substances. The hope is that treatment is more likely to salvage them as useful citizens, instead of placing them among hardened criminals after which they may become unsalvageable.

Article VIII, Section VI was modified so that boards of education may impose new sales and use taxes for educational purposes, as long as they are approved by a majority of the local voters. The voters have to be given information about which capital outlay projects the money is for, the maximum cost of such projects, with the maximum period of time not to exceed five years. Nothing in this amendment prohibits counties and municipalities from imposing additional local sales and use taxes authorized by general law.

In these days of continued taxpayer revolt, ways to finance public improvement without new taxes has led to a variety of budget cutting and privatization initiatives. One amendment, altering Article IX, Section II, Paragraph VII authorized the General Assembly to provide for the creation of enterprise zones by counties or municipalities, or both. This allows for exemptions, credits, or reductions of any tax or taxes levied within such zones by the state, a county, or any municipality, or any combination thereof, if persons, firms, or corporations create job opportunities within the enterprise zone for unemployed, low, and moderate income persons.

Similarly Article IX, Section IV was amended to allow the creation of "regional facilities." These regional facilities mean industrial parks, business parks, conference centers, convention centers, airports, athletic facilities, recreation facilities, jails or correctional facilities, or other similar or related economic development facilities. Counties and municipalities are authorized to enter into contracts with contiguous counties for the purpose of allocating the proceeds of ad valorem taxes assessed and collected on real property for development purposes. Unless otherwise provided by law, the regional facilities can qualify for any income tax credits, regardless of where the business is located.

Finally, in one amendment that looked as if it were very narrowly drawn, Article XI, Section I was amended so that any person owning property in an industrial area may voluntarily remove the property from that industrial area, by filing a certificate to that effect with the clerk of the superior court in that county. Once the certificate is filed, the property described in the certificate, together with all public streets and public rights of way within the property, abutting the property, or connecting the property to property outside the industrial area may be annexed by an adjacent city.

Recent Constitutional Amendments

In 2006, three proposed constitutional amendments were on the general ballot, and all three were ratified by the voters. Probably the most important one was to restrict the use of the power of eminent domain; it passed by an overwhelming vote. The other two also passed easily; one was to protect the traditional rights of fishing and hunting by managing natural resources for the public good; the other to authorize the General Assembly to dedicate revenue from special motor vehicle license plates. These new amendments have been finally incorporated into the official copy of the Constitution posted on the Web site maintained by the Secretary of State's Office, and are highlighted in the instructor's edition of the textbook.

In 2008, Georgia voters had an opportunity to vote to ratify three more possible amendments. As usual, they covered a multitude of issues, but two of them involved taxes, which was passed by the voters, and the third on new special purpose districts, which did not pass muster. The first of the tax measures was an amendment on encouraging the preservation of Georgia's forests through a conservation use property tax reduction program. It was ratified and the formal language will eventually be found in Article VII, Section I, Paragraph III. The second offered amendment to authorize local school districts to use tax funds for community redevelopment purposes was also ratified and will eventually be found in Article IX, Section II, Paragraph VIII. However, the third offered amendment to authorize the creation of special Infrastructure Development Districts, to oversee the provision of new infrastructure to underserved areas was defeated.

And in 2010, Georgia voters had an opportunity to vote to ratify five more possible amendments. As usual, they covered a multitude of issues, but as we might expect, five of them had a link to taxes. The first proposed amendment was to allow competitive contracts to be enforced in Georgia Courts. With 100% of precincts reporting on election night, it was ratified and should soon be formally written up to be placed in Article III, Section VI, Paragraph V; and in particular subparagraph C will be substantially re-written. It had a plurality of 1,633,066 non-partisan votes (67.6%) of the total of 2,416,456 votes cast (Hinton).

However, the proposed amendment listed as second on the ballot, to add an extra $10 tag fee on private passenger vehicles for the benefit of statewide trauma care expansion, was defeated. With 100% of precincts reporting, the No votes were 1,342,555 (52.6%) out of the 2,550,391 total votes cast on the issue. The third amendment, to allow the state to execute multiyear contracts for projects to improve energy efficiency and conservation, appeared to be doing well on election night. But despite this early lead, later events indicated that it was not to be ratified and incorporated within the Constitution (Ibid).

In contrast, amendment number four was *barely ratified*. Its purpose was to allow state agencies to execute multiyear contracts for long-term transportation projects. This would remove it from the normal budgeting cycle, thus limiting legislative oversight. With 100% of precincts reporting, the original votes were tending toward No, at 1,216,780 (50.1%); as against the Yes votes, which numbered 1,212,863 (49.9%). As sometimes happens with such close tallies, the final count reversed the outcome, as it was determined to be in favor of the amendment passing. The exact wording will be placed in Article VII, Section IV, Paragraph XII (Ibid).

Finally, in 2010, the fifth amendment, intended to allow owners of industrial-zoned property to choose to remove the industrial designation from their property, was overwhelmingly passed by the voters. With 100% of the precincts reporting, the yes votes numbered 1,520,636 (63.5%) out of the total of 2,394,526 votes cast. It will be placed in Article XI, Section 1, Paragraph IV (Ibid).

Also in 2010, a special statewide referendum was placed on the ballot, designed to get voter approval for the legislature to provide for inventory of businesses to be exempt from state property tax. With 100% of precincts reporting it attained a healthy majority of yes votes, 1,310,116 (54.0%) out of 2,425,702 votes cast (Ibid).

Conclusions

By applying Wilson's classification of policy model, it can be confidently asserted that Georgia's State Constitution with its amendments is fundamentally majoritarian, except as tax and local options are structured to allow narrower interest-group policies to flourish, hopefully for general economic improvement. While there are examples of client policies (taxing the many to benefit the few) and even entrepreneurial policies (taxing the few to benefit the many) these are generally justified in promoting the public good. Generally, the Constitution of the State of Georgia is an accurate reflection of the fundamental structure of the state's economics and politics. Unlike some states, with antiquated and outmoded government systems, the Georgia State Government, responding to the voice of the people in their varied interest groups, has attempted to create a modern flexible system of functional branches and specialized agencies to meet the growing needs of an increasingly sophisticated urban society.

It is certain that the traditionalistic elements of our people are yielding to the disruptive demands of an increasingly individualistic economic and social setting. It is the genius of the State of Georgia that a regional leader can move into the age of mass bureaucracy, and yet retain the traditional style that has always made the Peach State a symbol of well-managed change. Having already had ten Constitutions in its history, it is unlikely that the 1983 Constitution will be the last.

It is the contention of the authors that the political culture of the state is evolving from traditionalistic to individualistic, and with the approval of gambling venues, perhaps a decreasing element of moral responsibility. This can be attributed to three main factors: 1) in part to the large numbers of northern professionals and managers migrating southward to the Peach State; 2) increasing numbers of foreign derived workers (mostly Hispanic); and 3) in part to the undeniable modernization of the state's economy. Whatever the proportion, Georgia is in a state of transition. As a result, it can be expected that the current Constitution will continue to gradually reflect the changing demographics of the state and will undergo such dichotomous amendment that within another two decades, or even sooner, it may need another complete revision.

It is important enough to repeat: the state is undergoing economic changes and new people are moving into Georgia, bringing their new ideas with them. The new emphasis on enterprise zones and redevelopment districts exemplifies the dramatic professionalization of our emerging administrative government; and until recently merit systems had all but completely replaced the earlier system of political patronage. Now the pendulum is swinging back. The merit system has been weakened, and the current attack on public sector workers across the United States, particularly in the Great Lakes region, is sure to be reflected in new proposed amendments in 2012.

While the 1998 session of the General Assembly hinted at the declining power of the "good old boy" legislative network and the emphatic participation by new, more professional legislators oriented to the Republican Party, the recently re-achieved one-party dominance by republicans may yet disappoint reformers. 'Good old boy' republicans are not going to be very different. One thing is sure: the times are changing in Georgia. And if history provides any one lesson, it is this: when the times change in Georgia, so does the Constitution.

Key Terms

Amendment
Client Policies
Client-Centered Policies
Entrepreneurial Policies
General Will
Interest Group-type
Majoritarian Policies
Special Interest Policies
The Amending Process
Rousseau theory of general will

Essay Questions

1. Explain James Q. Wilson's policy typology. How does it relate to the will of the people impacting policies?
2. How might the Georgia Constitution be amended?
3. Compare and contrast the U.S. Constitution and the Constitution of the State of Georgia. What are the similarities and dissimilarities?
4. State and discuss the most amended Article of the Georgia Constitution and please comment on the various (historical) reasons stated or inferred for this frequent revision.
5. What changes have been made by the Constitution of the State of Georgia since it was ratified in 1933?
6. List and discuss the procedure provided by Article X of the Georgia Constitution for Amending the Constitution. Further explain why your authors believe that the process is based on Madisonian idea and Wilson's typology.

Georgia State Questions

Chapter 1: Introduction to Georgia Politics

1. Which of the following is not a state power?
   a. Education
   b. Transportation
   c. Police protection
   d. Mail delivery

2. State laws must be compatible with all of the following, except:
   a. State constitutions
   b. The U.S. Constitution
   c. Federal laws
   d. The U.N. Charter

3. The U.S. Constitution:
   a. Is longer than Georgia's
   b. Is shorter than Georgia's
   c. Has fewer amendments than Georgia's
   d. Has more amendments than Georgia's
   e. Both b and c are correct

4. Only one state has had more Constitutions in its history than Georgia. That state is:
   a. Alabama
   b. New York
   c. Louisiana
   d. Massachusetts

5. The current Georgia Constitution can best be described as the:
   a. Restoration Constitution
   b. Bureaucratic Constitution
   c. Secession Constitution
   d. Reconstruction Constitution

6. As of 2006, the number of amendments to Georgia's Constitution stood at:
   a. 27
   b. 66
   c. 432
   d. 1,000-plus

7. The body of the Georgia Constitution contains:
   a. A preamble and eleven articles
   b. A preamble and seven articles
   c. A preamble and thirty-two articles
   d. Sixteen articles

8. Amendments to the Georgia Constitution are ratified by:
   a. The county commissions
   b. County commissions and city councils
   c. The people in a referendum
   d. The Governor of Georgia

9. Georgia has a plural executive, which means:
   a. Georgia has two Governors, one for domestic affairs, one for foreign affairs
   b. Georgia has a constitutional relationship between the Governor and the CEOs of major businesses like Coca-Cola
   c. Georgia has many independently elected executives
   d. The Georgia Governor appoints all the other executive officers to his cabinet

10. Which of these is not an executive officer in Georgia?
    a. Lieutenant Governor
    b. Attorney General
    c. Commissioner of Agriculture
    d. State auditor

11. Georgia is closest to which of Daniel Elazar's types of political culture?
    a. Traditionalistic
    b. Individualistic
    c. Moralistic
    d. Communistic

12. Where would one find Georgia's Bill of Rights?
    a. Georgia Declaration of the Rights of Man
    b. Article I of the Georgia Constitution
    c. Amendments I through XI of the Georgia Constitution
    d. Georgia has no written Bill of Rights

13. "Devolution" means:
    a. Transferring power from the national government to the state governments
    b. Transferring power from the state governments to the national government
    c. Devil worship
    d. Transferring power from local governments to the national government

14. States are free:
    a. To exceed federal constitutional protections
    b. To supersede federal constitutional protections
    c. To deny, disparage, or abuse peoples' rights
    d. To ignore the federal government whenever it suits them

15. According to the authors of the text, an understanding of Georgia's political culture helps us understand:
    a. that the political culture is evolving from individualistic to traditional
    b. why the State of Georgia for so long was a one party system
    c. that the Georgia State Constitution is fundamentally more principle than other state Constitutions
    d. the U.S. Constitution is more pluralistic than it is majoritarian

Chapter 6: Administration and Agencies

1. Max Weber's "succession crisis" is:
   a. A typology of historical change in government organizations
   b. What happens when a newly appointed bureaucrat replaces one who is stepping down
   c. A model of bureaucratic inertia
   d. Probably the major problem with bureaucracies today

2. The Article of the Georgia Constitution that establishes the Bureaucracy is:
   a. Article I
   b. Article II
   c. Article III
   d. Article IV

3. The Georgia Public Service Commission regulates:
   a. The Insurance Industry
   b. Electric Power Companies and Railroad Companies
   c. Certification for Insurance Practice
   d. The Cable and Satellite Companies

4. Members of the State Transportation Board:
   a. Are appointed by the Governor
   b. Are chosen by the General Assembly
   c. Are elected by the people
   d. Are appointed by their U.S. Congressmen

5. The State Board of Pardons and Paroles:
   a. Has the power to grant reprieves, pardons, and paroles
   b. Has the power to communicate sentences
   c. Has the power to impose sentences
   d. Has the power to build prisons

6. The State Personnel Board includes all of the following except:
   a. Consists of five members nominated by the Governor
   b. Sets policy for the State Merit System
   c. Selects its own chairman
   d. Tracks employment demands for the State of Georgia

7. Veterans preference means that veterans:
   a. Don't have to take state merit exams
   b. Automatically get the state jobs for which they apply
   c. Get bonus points on merit exams
   d. Prefer public sector jobs to private sector jobs

8. The Georgia Board of Natural Resources:
   a. Has a complicated task of policing Georgia's rivers and lakes
   b. Is charged with environmental protection
   c. Primarily engages in oil exploration
   d. Operates all the state's zoos and lakes

9. Special Authorities are created in Georgia with the purpose:
   a. To finance an enterprise to get around debt limitations
   b. To avoid raising taxes
   c. To serve the needs that cut across traditional governmental boundaries
   d. All of the above

10. The number of state bureaucrats in Georgia:
    a. Is approximately 114,000
    b. Is approximately 184,000
    c. Is approximately 344,000
    d. Is in the millions

11. The Commissioner of Insurance does all of the following except:
    a. Sets criteria for licensing insurance companies
    b. Sets standards for performance of insurance companies
    c. Sets rates for insurance policies
    d. Mandates that all pre-school through 8th grade are properly insured

12. Who selects Georgia's State Superintendent of Schools?
    a. State Board of Education
    b. Governor
    c. General Assembly
    d. Voters

13. The Georgia Secretary of State does the following, except:
    a. Oversees the elections process
    b. Carries out Georgia's foreign policy with other countries
    c. Records financial statements from candidates for office
    d. Grants charters to corporations

14. All of the following applies to the "State Financing and Investment Commission" except:
    a. Is an example of a "Super Commission"
    b. Includes among its members the Governor, Speaker of the House, Agriculture Commissioner
    c. Tries to ensure that Special Authorities contribute to efficient government
    d. Includes among its members the Speaker of the House and the Attorney General of the State of Georgia

15. It is the contention of the authors of the text that:
    a. The political culture is evolving from individualistic to traditional
    b. Georgia is in the state of transformation
    c. The Georgia State Constitution is fundamentally more majoritarian than it is pluralistic
    d. The U.S. Constitution is more pluralistic than it is majoritarian

Chapter 8: Budgeting and Finance

1. In Fiscal Year 2009, the total indebtedness of the State of Georgia was:
   a. Over nine billion dollars
   b. Nothing, because the State is required to pay as it goes
   c. Nearly three trillion dollars
   d. Approximately ten million dollars

2. The bulk of Georgia's revenue comes from all of the following sources, except:
   a. Ad valorem taxes
   b. Income taxes
   c. Sales taxes
   d. The lottery

3. Comparatively, Georgia is considered:
   a. A high-tax state
   b. A low-tax state
   c. A fair-tax state
   d. An unfair-tax state

4. A revenue bond:
   a. Is retired with the revenues from money-making enterprises and is usually a risky undertaking
   b. Is based on the "full faith and credit" of the state
   c. Is a tie that links a taxpayer to his state government
   d. Affects the retired and older and affluent population

5. The largest single expenditure in the Georgia State Budget is:
   a. Transportation
   b. Education
   c. Welfare
   d. Corrections

6. In 2002, the Georgia General Assembly "gave back" about _____ in tax relief to the people of Georgia.
   a. Less than $100 million
   b. Less than $200 million
   c. More than $300 million
   d. More than $400 million

7. Georgia's bond ratings are:
   a. very high
   b. very low
   c. set by the General Assembly
   d. dictated by the Governor

8. Income of over $7,000 a year is taxed in Georgia at a rate of:
   a. 6%
   b. 28%
   c. 35%
   d. 62%

9. Exempted from Georgia's sales tax are all of the following, except:
   a. Bibles
   b. Food
   c. Fuel used to heat chicken houses
   d. Girl Scout cookies
   e. Raincoats for pre-school kids

10. Georgia's sales tax rate varies from:
    a. 3–6%
    b. 4–7%
    c. 8–10%
    d. 11–15%

11. Georgia's fiscal (budget) year runs from:
    a. October to September
    b. January to December
    c. July to June
    d. May to September

12. A capital budget is:
    a. Used for maintenance of the capitol building
    b. Used to fund routine operations
    c. Used for expensive long-term building projects
    d. Used to fund capital death penalty appeals

13. By 2009, the Georgia lottery was producing $_____ for education.
    a. Under $100 million
    b. Over $800 million
    c. Over $1 billion
    d. Over $5 billion

14. Elementary, secondary, and higher education together consume what percent of the Georgia State annual budget?
    a. Nearly 40%
    b. Nearly 56%
    c. Nearly 75%
    d. Nearly 25%

15. According to Article VII, Section IV, which of the following is not the purpose for which the State of Georgia may incur debt:
    a. Crises event
    b. Debt to repel invasion
    c. Debt for the suppression of insurrection
    d. Debt for temporal cash flow shortages
    e. Debt for state of transformation

Chapter 10: Local Government

1. A Georgia county with a single member county commission is:
   a. Fulton
   b. Cobb
   c. Bleckley
   d. Lowndes

2. The City of Atlanta is closest to this form of municipal government:
   a. Strong mayor/weak council
   b. Weak mayor/strong council
   c. Council-Manager
   d. Commission

3. Once granted, a municipal charter may:
   a. Never be revoked
   b. Be revoked only if population declines
   c. Be revoked if population declines and services stop
   d. Be revoked without cause

4. The current number of special districts in Georgia is about:
   a. 34
   b. 125
   c. 436
   d. 627

5. Local governments in Georgia are known as:
   a. Counties
   b. Municipalities
   c. Special districts
   d. Townships

6. The number of counties in Georgia is:
   a. 46
   b. 93
   c. 159
   d. 227

7. Each county in Georgia must elect the following except:
   a. A clerk of the superior court
   b. A sheriff
   c. A judge of the probate court
   d. A dogcatcher

8. Which of the following services is a "special district" most likely to carry out?
   a. Provision of water utility service to a group of contiguous local communities
   b. Regulation of interstate commerce
   c. Administration of prison facilities for the state government
   d. Election of state legislators

9. What is the purpose of a special district?
   a. To provide services to several neighboring communities
   b. To decide disputes between city department heads
   c. To elect a delegate to a convention
   d. To serve as a state capital or county seat

10. The most common type of county government in Georgia is:
    a. The commission-administrator form
    b. The traditional form
    c. The commission-manager form
    d. The single commissioner form

11. Consolidation of cities and counties in Georgia:
    a. Is a very popular process
    b. Is never used
    c. Has been used three times in over 60 years
    d. Has been used 60 times in three years

12. What is "home rule"?
    a. The principle that police need a warrant to search one's residence
    b. The principle that any state should be able to secede
    c. The principle that justifies geographic representation
    d. The principle that local governments should be given substantial governing authority

13. The system of municipal government most like a Business Corporation is:
    a. Council-Manager
    b. Weak mayor-Council
    c. Strong mayor-Council
    d. Commission

14. The City of Atlanta is:
    a. A Class A City
    b. A Class I City
    c. A Class B City
    d. A municipality as is every other municipal corporation in Georgia

15. It is the contention of the authors of the text that in this chapter:
    a. The political culture is evolving from individualistic to traditional
    b. Georgia is in the state of transformation
    c. Georgia's educational system fails to meet Edmond Burke's theory of delegate and trustee
    d. Georgia's Constitution guarantees each Georgian the right to be educated in an institution of their choice

Chapter 11: The State Constitution

1. How many articles are there in the Georgia Constitution?
   a. Seven
   b. Eleven
   c. Seventeen
   d. Twenty-five

2. The present Constitution of the State of Georgia was basically written in:
   a. 1777
   b. 1860
   c. 1945
   d. 1983

3. Which of the following constitutional statements is mostly true?
   a. John Locke is the exclusive source for basic theory
   b. Constitutional theory is extremely complex
   c. Jean Rousseau is the exclusive source for basic theory
   d. Georgia is a simple state and needs a simple constitution

4. Which of the following is *not* one of James Q. Wilson's types?
   a. Capitalistic policies
   b. Majoritarian policies
   c. Interest-group policies
   d. Entrepreneurial policies

5. Which of the following is a good example of Wilson's majoritarian policy?
   a. Welfare policy
   b. Hunting and fishing
   c. The Capitol Building
   d. Pollution taxes

6. Which is a good example of Wilson's client-centered type?
   a. Welfare policy
   b. Hunting and fishing
   c. The Capitol Building
   d. Pollution taxes

7. Which is a good example of Wilson's interest group-type?
   a. Welfare policy
   b. Hunting and fishing
   c. The Capitol Building
   d. Pollution taxes

8. Which is a good example of Wilson's entrepreneurial type?
   a. Welfare policy
   b. Hunting and fishing
   c. The Capitol Building
   d. Pollution taxes

9. In the Georgia State Constitution, true majoritarian policies:
   a. Are the prevailing type
   b. Exist only in the Civil Rights article
   c. Exist only in the taxation article
   d. Hardly exist at all

10. The belief that government should serve the general public is in:
    a. Client-Group policies
    b. Majoritarian policies
    c. Interest Group policies
    d. Entrepreneurial policies

11. Generally, the Georgia State Constitution rejects all of the following ideas, except:
    a. Right of governing comes from conquest
    b. Right of governing comes from divine will
    c. Right of governing comes from ethnic superiority
    d. Right of governing comes from the will of the people

12. Which of the following is NOT specifically authorized in the Georgia State Constitution?
    a. The rights of the people
    b. Limits on government power
    c. Limits on government officials
    d. A blend of traditional and individualistic culture with a moralistic tinge

13. Since the adoption of the current Georgia Constitution in the 1980s:
    a. Over 80 amendments have been proposed
    b. Over 60 amendments have been ratified
    c. Over 19 amendments have been rejected
    d. All of its eleven articles have been amended by the state legislature

14. The _____ article of the Georgia Constitution that is most amended.
    a. The Second
    b. The Fourth
    c. The Eighth
    d. The Last

15. It is the contention of the authors of the text that:
    a. The political culture is evolving from individualistic to traditional
    b. Georgia is in the state of transformation
    c. The Georgia State Constitution is fundamentally more majoritarian than it is pluralistic
    d. The U.S. Constitution is more pluralistic than it majoritarian

Appendix

The Georgia State Constitution

Georgia State Politics:
The Constitutional Foundation
(From 1983 as Revised through January 2011)

Table of Contents

Sources

Compiled by authors from various sources including: Ga. Laws 1981 Ex. Session, p. 141, as amended by Ga. Laws 1982, p. 2551. Some source notes are retained from earlier editions. Present textual material is also a merger of the 1983 Constitution and the one posted as of January 2010, using MS Office Review for text materials downloaded from the official Georgia Constitution website page Georgia Info Home. All changes from the 1983 Constitution are presented in italics.

The final format and presentation, as well as comments made regarding the purpose of amendments and the placement of pending recent amendments were designed for academic purposes and are the sole responsibility of the authors. This particularly includes sub-paragraph notation. And Georgia students please see:

http://georgiainfo.galileo.usg.edu/><contents.htm.

The Georgia State Constitution

Preamble

To perpetuate the principles of free government, insure justice to all, preserve peace, promote the interest and happiness of the citizen and of the family, and transmit to posterity the enjoyment of liberty, we the people of Georgia, relying upon the protection and guidance of Almighty God, do ordain and establish this Constitution.

Article I.
Bill of Rights

Section I.
Rights of Persons

Paragraph I. Life, liberty, and property. No person shall be deprived of life, liberty, or property except by due process of law.

Paragraph II. Protection to person and property; equal protection. Protection to person and property is the paramount duty of government and shall be impartial and complete. No person shall be denied the equal protection of the laws.

Paragraph III. Freedom of conscience. Each person has the natural and inalienable right to worship God, each according to the dictates of that person's own conscience; and no human authority should, in any case, control or interfere with such right of conscience.

Paragraph IV. Religious opinions; freedom of religion. No inhabitant of this state shall be molested in person or property or be prohibited from holding any public office or trust on account of religious opinions; but the right of freedom of religion shall not be so construed as to excuse acts of licentiousness or justify practices inconsistent with the peace and safety of the state.

Paragraph V. Freedom of speech and of the press guaranteed. No law shall be passed to curtail or restrain the freedom of speech or of the press. Every person may speak, write, and publish sentiments on all subjects but shall be responsible for the abuse of that liberty.

Paragraph VI. Libel. In all civil or criminal actions for libel, the truth may be given in evidence; and, if it shall appear to the trier of fact that the matter charged as libelous is true, the party shall be discharged.

Paragraph VII. Citizens, protection of. All citizens of the United States, resident in this state, are hereby declared citizens of this state; and it shall be the duty of the General Assembly to enact such laws as will protect them in the full enjoyment of the rights, privileges, and immunities due to such citizenship.

Paragraph VIII. Arms, right to keep and bear. The right of the people to keep and bear arms shall not be infringed, but the General Assembly shall have power to prescribe the manner in which arms may be borne.

Paragraph IX. Right to assemble and petition. The people have the right to assemble peaceably for their common good and to apply by petition or remonstrance to those vested with the powers of government for redress of grievances.

Paragraph X. Bill of attainder; ex post facto laws; and retroactive laws. No bill of attainder, ex post facto law, retroactive law, or laws impairing the obligation of contract or making irrevocable grant of special privileges or immunities shall be passed.

Paragraph XI. Right to trial by jury; number of jurors; selection and compensation of jurors.

(a) The right to trial by jury shall remain inviolate, except that the court shall render judgment without the verdict of a jury in all civil cases where no issuable defense is filed and where a jury is not demanded in writing by either party. In criminal cases, the defendant shall have a public and speedy trial by an impartial jury; and the jury shall be the judges of the law and the facts.

(b) A trial jury shall consist of 12 persons; but the General Assembly may prescribe any number, not less than six, to constitute a trial jury in courts of limited jurisdiction and in superior courts in misdemeanor cases.

(c) The General Assembly shall provide by law for the selection and compensation of persons to serve as grand jurors and trial jurors.

Paragraph XII. Right to the courts. No person shall be deprived of the right to prosecute or defend, either in person or by an attorney, that person's own cause in any of the courts of this state.

Paragraph XIII. Searches, seizures, and warrants. The right of the people to be secure in their persons, houses, papers, and effects against unreasonable searches and seizures shall not be violated; and no warrant shall issue except upon probable cause supported by oath or affirmation particularly describing the place or places to be searched and the persons or things to be seized.

Paragraph XIV. Benefit of counsel; accusation; list of witnesses; compulsory process. Every person charged with an offense against the laws of this state shall have the privilege and benefit of counsel; shall be furnished with a copy of the accusation or indictment and, on demand, with a list of the witnesses on whose testimony such charge is founded; shall have compulsory process to obtain the testimony of that person's own witnesses; and shall be confronted with the witnesses testifying against such person.

Paragraph XV. Habeas corpus. The writ of habeas corpus shall not be suspended unless, in case of rebellion or invasion, the public safety may require it.

Paragraph XVI. Self-incrimination. No person shall be compelled to give testimony tending in any manner to be self-incriminating.

Paragraph XVII. Bail; fines; punishment; arrest, abuse of prisoners. Excessive bail shall not be required, nor excessive fines imposed, nor cruel and unusual punishments inflicted; nor shall any person be abused in being arrested, while under arrest, or in prison.

Paragraph XVIII. Jeopardy of life or liberty more than once forbidden. No person shall be put in jeopardy of life or liberty more than once for the same offense except when a new trial has been granted after conviction or in case of mistrial.

Paragraph XIX. Treason. Treason against the State of Georgia shall consist of insurrection against the state, adhering to the state's enemies, or giving them aid and comfort. No person shall be convicted of treason except on the testimony of two witnesses to the same overt act or confession in open court.

Paragraph XX. Conviction, effect of. No conviction shall work corruption of blood or forfeiture of estate.

Paragraph XXI. Banishment and whipping as punishment for crime. Neither banishment beyond the limits of the state nor whipping shall be allowed as a punishment for crime.

Paragraph XXII. Involuntary servitude. There shall be no involuntary servitude within the State of Georgia except as a punishment for crime after legal conviction thereof or for contempt of court.

Paragraph XXIII. Imprisonment for debt. There shall be no imprisonment for debt.

Paragraph XXIV. Costs. No person shall be compelled to pay costs in any criminal case except after conviction on final trial.

Paragraph XXV. Status of the citizen. The social status of a citizen shall never be the subject of legislation.

Paragraph XXVI. Exemptions from levy and sale. The General Assembly shall protect by law from levy and sale by virtue of any process under the laws of this state a portion of the property of each person in an amount of not less than $1,600.00 and shall have authority to define to whom any such additional exemptions shall be allowed; to specify the amount of such exemptions; to provide for the manner of exempting such property and for the sale, alienation, and encumbrance thereof; and to provide for the waiver of said exemptions by the debtor.

Paragraph XXVII. Spouse's separate property. The separate property of each spouse shall remain the separate property of that spouse except as otherwise provided by law.

Paragraph XXVIII. *Fishing and hunting. The tradition of fishing and hunting and the taking of fish and wildlife shall be preserved for the people and shall be managed by law and regulation for the public good. NOTE: THIS REFLECTS THE AMENDMENT AS PASSED IN 2006.*

Paragraph XXVIX. **Enumeration of rights not denial of others.** The enumeration of rights herein contained as a part of this Constitution shall not be construed to deny to the people any inherent rights which they may have hitherto enjoyed.

Section II.
Origin and Structure of Government

Paragraph I. Origin and foundation of government. All government, of right, originates with the people, is founded upon their will only, and is instituted solely for the good of the whole. Public officers are the trustees and servants of the people and are at all times amenable to them.

Paragraph II. Object of government. The people of this state have the inherent right of regulating their internal government. Government is instituted for the protection, security, and benefit of the people; and at all times they have the right to alter or reform the same whenever the public good may require it.

Paragraph III. Separation of legislative, judicial, and executive Powers. The legislative, judicial, and executive powers shall forever remain separate and distinct; and no person discharging the duties of one shall at the same time exercise the functions of either of the others except as herein provided.

Paragraph IV. Contempts. The power of the courts to punish for contempt shall be limited by legislative acts.

Paragraph V. What acts void. Legislative acts in violation of this Constitution or the Constitution of the United States are void, and the judiciary shall so declare them.

Paragraph VI. Superiority of civil authority. The civil authority shall be superior to the military.

Paragraph VII. Separation of church and state. No money shall ever be taken from the public treasury, directly or indirectly, in aid of any church, sect, cult, or religious denomination or of any sectarian institution.

Paragraph VIII. Lotteries *and nonprofit bingo games.*

(a) *Except as herein specifically provided in this Paragraph VIII,* all lotteries, and the sale of lottery tickets, *and all forms of pari-mutuel betting and casino gambling* are hereby prohibited; and this prohibition shall be enforced by penal laws.

(b) The General Assembly may by law provide that the operation of a nonprofit bingo game shall not be a lottery and shall be legal in this state. The General Assembly may by law define a nonprofit bingo game and provide for the regulation of nonprofit bingo *games.*

(c) *The General Assembly may by law provide for the operation and regulation of a lottery or lotteries by or on behalf of the state and for any matters relating to the purposes or provisions of this subparagraph. Proceeds derived from the lottery or lotteries operated by or on behalf of the state shall be used to pay the operating expenses of the lottery or lotteries, including all prizes, without any appropriation required by law, and for educational programs and purposes as hereinafter provided. Lottery proceeds shall not be subject to Article VII, Section III, Paragraph II; Article III, Section IX, Paragraph VI(a); or Article III, Section IX, Paragraph IV(c), except that the net proceeds after payment of such operating expenses shall be subject to Article VII, Section III, Paragraph II. Net proceeds after payment of such operating expenses shall be separately accounted for and shall be specifically identified by the Governor in his annual budget presented to the General Assembly as a separate budget category entitled "Lottery Proceeds" and the Governor shall make specific recommendations as to educational programs and educational purposes to which said net proceeds shall be appropriated. In the General Appropriations Act adopted by the General Assembly, the General Assembly shall appropriate all net proceeds of the lottery or lotteries by such separate budget category to educational programs and educational purposes. Such net proceeds shall be used to support improvements and enhancements for educational programs and purposes and such net proceeds shall be used to supplement, not supplant, non-lottery educational resources for educational programs and purposes. The educational programs and educational purposes for which proceeds may be so appropriated shall include only the following:*

(1) *Tuition grants, scholarships, or loans to citizens of this state to enable such citizens to attend colleges and universities located within this state, regardless of whether such colleges or universities are operated by the board of regents, or to attend institutions operated under the authority of the Department of Technical and Adult Education;*

(2) *Voluntary pre-kindergarten;*

(3) One or more educational shortfall reserves in a total amount of not less than 10 percent of the net proceeds of the lottery for the preceding fiscal year;

(4) Costs of providing to teachers at accredited public institutions who teach levels K–12, personnel at public postsecondary technical institutes under the authority of the Department of Technical and Adult Education, and professors and instructors within the University System of Georgia the necessary training in the use and application of computers and advanced electronic instructional technology to implement interactive learning environments in the classroom and to access the state-wide distance learning network; and

(5) Capital outlay projects for educational facilities; provided, however, that no funds shall be appropriated for the items listed in paragraphs (4) and (5) of this subsection until all persons eligible for and applying for assistance as provided in paragraph (1) of this subsection have received such assistance, all approved pre-kindergarten programs provided for in paragraph (2) of this subsection have been fully funded, and the education shortfall reserve or reserves provided for in paragraph (3) of this subsection have been fully funded. AMENDMENT APPROVED 1998, CVIG.

(d) On and after January 1, 1995, the holding of raffles by nonprofit organizations shall be lawful and shall not be prohibited by any law enacted prior to January 1, 1994. Laws enacted on or after January 1, 1994, however, may restrict, regulate, or prohibit the operation of such raffles. (Source: Sec. St. 1997)

Paragraph IX. Sovereign immunity *and waiver thereof; claims against* the state *and its departments, agencies, officers, and employees.*

(a) The General Assembly may waive the state's sovereign immunity from suit by enacting a State Tort Claims Act, in which the General Assembly may provide by law for procedures for the making, handling, and disposition of actions or claims against the state and its departments, agencies, officers, and employees, upon such terms and subject to such conditions and limitations as the General Assembly may provide.

(b) The General Assembly may also provide by law for the processing and disposition of claims against the state which do not exceed such maximum amount as provided therein.

(c) The state's defense of sovereign immunity is hereby waived as to any action ex contractu for the breach of any written contract now existing or hereafter entered into by the state or its departments and agencies.

(d) Except as specifically provided by the General Assembly in a State Tort Claims Act, all officers and employees of the state or its departments and agencies may be subject to suit and may be liable for injuries and damages caused by the negligent performance of, or negligent failure to perform, their ministerial functions and may be liable for injuries and damages if they act with actual malice or with actual intent to cause injury in the performance of their official functions. Except as provided in this subparagraph, officers and employees of the state or its departments and agencies shall not be subject to suit or liability, and no judgment shall be entered against them, for the performance or nonperformance of their official functions. The provisions of this subparagraph shall not be waived.

(e) Except as specifically provided in this Paragraph, sovereign immunity extends to the state and all of its departments and agencies. The sovereign immunity of the state and its departments and agencies can only be waived by an Act of the General Assembly which specifically provides that sovereign immunity is thereby waived and the extent of such waiver.

(f) No waiver of sovereign immunity under this Paragraph shall be construed as a waiver of any immunity provided to the state or its departments, agencies, officers, or employees by the United States Constitution. (Authority: OLC pp. 44-45).

Section III.
General Provisions

Paragraph I. Eminent domain.

(a) Except as otherwise provided in this Paragraph, private property shall not be taken or damaged for public purposes without just and adequate compensation being first paid.

(b) When private property is taken or damaged by the state or the counties or municipalities of the state for public road or street purposes, or for public transportation purposes, or for any other public purposes as determined by the General Assembly, just and adequate compensation therefore need not be paid until the same has been finally fixed and determined as provided by law; but such just and adequate compensation shall then be paid in preference to all other obligations except bonded indebtedness.

(c) The General Assembly may by law require the condemnor to make prepayment against adequate compensation as a condition precedent to the exercise of the right of eminent domain and provide for the disbursement of the same to the end that the rights and equities of the property owner, lien holders, and the state and its subdivisions may be protected.

(d) The General Assembly may provide by law for the payment by the condemnor of reasonable expenses, including attorney's fees, incurred by the condemnee in determining just and adequate compensation.

(e) Notwithstanding any other provision of the Constitution, the General Assembly may provide by law for relocation assistance and payments to persons displaced through the exercise of the power of eminent domain or because of public projects or programs; and the powers of taxation may be exercised and public funds expended in furtherance thereof.

Paragraph II. Private ways. In case of necessity, private ways may be granted upon just and adequate compensation being first paid by the applicant.

Paragraph III. Tidewater titles confirmed. The Act of the General Assembly approved December 16, 1902, which extends the title of ownership of lands abutting on tidal water to low water mark, is hereby ratified and confirmed.

Section IV.
Marriage

Paragraph I. Recognition of marriage.

(a) This state shall recognize as marriage only the union of man and woman. Marriages between persons of the same sex are prohibited in this state.

(b) No union between persons of the same sex shall be recognized by this state as entitled to the benefits of marriage. This state shall not give effect to any public act, record, or judicial proceeding of any other state or jurisdiction respecting a relationship between persons of the same sex that is treated as a marriage under the laws of such other state or jurisdiction. The courts of this state shall have no jurisdiction to grant a divorce or separate maintenance with respect to any such relationship or otherwise to consider or rule on any of the parties' respective rights arising as a result of or in connection with such relationship. (Source: Sec. St. 2006).

Article II.
Voting and Elections

Section I.
Method of Voting; Right to Register and Vote

Paragraph I. Method of voting. Elections by the people shall be by secret ballot and shall be conducted in accordance with procedures provided by law.

Paragraph II. Right to register and vote. Every person who is a citizen of the United States and a resident of Georgia as defined by law, who is at least 18 years of age and not disenfranchised by this article, and who meets minimum residency requirements as provided by law shall be entitled to vote at any election by the people. The General Assembly shall provide by law for the registration of electors.

Paragraph III. Exceptions to right to register and vote.
(a) No person who has been convicted of a felony involving moral turpitude may register, remain registered, or vote except upon completion of the sentence.
(b) No person who has been judicially determined to be mentally incompetent may register, remain registered, or vote unless the disability has been removed.

Section II.
General Provisions

Paragraph I. Procedures to be provided by law. The General Assembly shall provide by law for a method of appeal from the decision to allow or refuse to allow any person to register or vote and shall provide by law for a procedure whereby returns of all elections by the people shall be made to the Secretary of State.

Paragraph II. Run-off election. A run-off election shall be a continuation of the general election and only persons who were entitled to vote in the general election shall be entitled to vote therein; and only those votes cast for the persons designated for the runoff shall be counted in the tabulation and canvass of the votes cast.

Paragraph III. Persons not eligible to hold office. No person who is not a registered voter; who has been convicted of a felony involving moral turpitude, unless that person's civil rights have been restored *and at least ten years have elapsed from the date of the completion of the sentence without a subsequent conviction of another felony involving moral turpitude; who is a defaulter for any federal, state, county, municipal, or school system taxes required of such officeholder or candidate if such person has been finally adjudicated by a court of competent jurisdiction to owe those taxes, but such ineligibility may be removed at any time by full payment thereof, or by making payments to the tax authority pursuant to a payment plan, or under such other conditions as the General Assembly may provide by general law;* or who is the holder of public funds illegally shall be eligible to hold any office or appointment of honor or trust in this state. Additional conditions of eligibility to hold office for persons elected on a write-in vote and for persons holding offices or appointments of honor or trust other than elected offices created by this Constitution may be provided by law.

Paragraph IV. Recall of public officials holding elective office. The General Assembly is hereby authorized to provide by general law for the recall of public officials who hold elective office. The procedures, grounds, and all other matters relative to such recall shall be provided for in such law.

Paragraph V. Vacancies created by elected officials qualifying for other office. The office of any state, county, or municipal elected official shall be declared vacant upon such elected official qualifying, in a general primary or general election, or special primary or special election, for another state, county, or municipal elective office or qualifying for the House of Representatives or the Senate of the United States if the term of the office for which such official is qualifying for begins more than 30 days prior to the expiration of such official's present term of office. The vacancy created in any such office shall be filled as provided by this Constitution or any general or local law. This provision shall not apply to any elected official seeking or holding more than one elective office when the holding of such offices simultaneously is specifically authorized by law. (Authority: OLC p. 58).

Section III.
Suspension and Removal of Public Officials

Paragraph I. Procedures for and effect of suspending or removing public officials upon felony indictment.
  (a) As used in this Paragraph, the term "public official" means the Governor, the Lieutenant Governor, the Secretary of State, the Attorney General, the State School Superintendent, the Commissioner of Insurance, the Commissioner of Agriculture, the Commissioner of Labor, and any member of the General Assembly.
  (b) Upon indictment for a felony by a grand jury of this state or by the United States, which felony indictment relates to the performance or activities of the office of any public official, the Attorney General or district attorney shall transmit a certified copy of the indictment to the Governor or, if the indicted public official is the Governor, to the Lieutenant Governor who shall, subject to subparagraph (d) of this Paragraph, appoint a review commission. If the indicted public official is the Governor, the commission shall be composed of the Attorney General, the Secretary of State, the State School Superintendent, the Commissioner of Insurance, the Commissioner of Agriculture, and the Commissioner of Labor. If the indicted public official is the Attorney General, the commission shall be composed of three other public officials who are not members of the General Assembly. If the indicted public official is not the Governor, the Attorney General, or a member of the General Assembly, the commission shall be composed of the Attorney General and two other public officials who are not members of the General Assembly. If the indicted public official is a member of the General Assembly, the commission shall be composed of the Attorney General and one member of the Senate and one member of the House of Representatives. If the Attorney General brings the indictment against the public official, the Attorney General shall not serve on the commission. In place of the Attorney General, the Governor shall appoint a retired Supreme Court Justice or a retired Court of Appeals Judge. The commission shall provide for a speedy hearing, including notice of the nature and cause of the hearing, process for obtaining witnesses, and the assistance of counsel. Unless a longer period of time is granted by the appointing authority, the commission shall make a written report within 14 days. If the commission determines that the indictment relates to and adversely affects the administration of the office of the indicted public official and that the rights and interests of the public are adversely affected thereby, the Governor or, if

the Governor is the indicted public official, the Lieutenant Governor shall suspend the public official immediately and without further action pending the final disposition of the case or until the expiration of the officer's term of office, whichever occurs first. During the term of office to which such officer was elected and in which the indictment occurred, if a nolle prosequi is entered, if the public official is acquitted, or if after conviction the conviction is later overturned as a result of any direct appeal or application for a writ of certiorari, the officer shall be immediately reinstated to the office from which he was suspended. While a public official is suspended under this Paragraph and until initial conviction by the trial court, the officer shall continue to receive the compensation from his office. After initial conviction by the trial court, the officer shall not be entitled to receive the compensation from his office. If the officer is reinstated to office, he shall be entitled to receive any compensation withheld under the provisions of this Paragraph.

(c) Unless the Governor is the public officer under suspension, for the duration of any suspension under this Paragraph, the Governor shall appoint a replacement officer except in the case of a member of the General Assembly. If the Governor is the public officer under suspension, the provisions of Article V, Section I, Paragraph V of this Constitution shall apply as if the Governor were temporarily disabled. Upon a final conviction with no appeal or review pending, the office shall be declared vacant and a successor to that office shall be chosen as provided in this Constitution or the laws enacted in pursuance thereof.

(d) No commission shall be appointed for a period of 14 days from the day the indictment is received. This period of time may be extended by the Governor. During this period of time, the indicted public official may, in writing, authorize the Governor or, if the Governor is the indicted public official, the Lieutenant Governor to suspend him from office. Any such voluntary suspension shall be subject to the same conditions for review, reinstatement, or declaration of vacancy as are provided in this Paragraph for a nonvoluntary suspension.

(e) After any suspension is imposed under this Paragraph, the suspended public official may petition the appointing authority for a review. The Governor or, if the indicted public official is the Governor, the Lieutenant Governor may reappoint the commission to review the suspension. The commission shall make a written report within 14 days. If the commission recommends that the public official be reinstated, he shall immediately be reinstated to office.

(f) The report and records of the commission and the fact that the public official has or has not been suspended shall not be admissible in evidence in any court for any purpose. The report and record of the commission shall not be open to the public.

(g) The provisions of this Paragraph shall not apply to any indictment handed down prior to January 1, 1985.

(h) If a public official who is suspended from office under the provisions of this Paragraph is not first tried at the next regular or special term following the indictment, the suspension shall be terminated and the public official shall be reinstated to office. The public official shall not be reinstated under this subparagraph if he is not so tried based on a continuance granted upon a motion made only by the defendant. (Authority: OLC pp. 59–61)

Paragraph II. Suspension upon felony conviction. Upon initial conviction of any public official designated in Paragraph I of this section for any felony in a trial court of this state or the United States, regardless of whether the officer has been suspended previously under Paragraph I of this section, such public official shall be immediately and without further action suspended from office. While a public official is suspended from office under this Paragraph, he or she shall not be entitled to receive the compensation from his or her office. If, during the remainder of the elected official's term of office, the conviction is later overturned as a result of *any direct appeal or application for a writ of certiorari, the public official shall be immediately reinstated to the office from which he or she was suspended and shall be entitled to receive any compensation withheld under the provisions of this Paragraph. Unless the Governor is the public official under suspension, for the duration of any suspension under this Paragraph, the Governor shall appoint a replacement official except in the case of a member of the General Assembly. If the public officer under suspension is a member of the Senate or House of Representatives, then a replacement member for the duration of the suspension shall be elected as now or hereafter provided by law, in a manner the same as or similar to the election of a member to fill a vacancy in the General Assembly but to serve only for the duration of the suspension. If the Governor is the public officer under suspension, the provisions of Article V, Section I, Paragraph V of this Constitution shall apply as if the Governor were temporarily disabled. Upon a final conviction with no appeal or review pending, the office shall be declared vacant and a successor to that office shall be chosen as provided in this Constitution or the laws enacted in pursuance thereof. The provisions of this Paragraph shall not apply to any conviction rendered prior to January 1, 1987. (Authority: OLC p. 61)*

Article III.
Legislative Branch

Section I.
Legislative Power

Paragraph I. Power vested in General Assembly. The legislative power of the state shall be vested in a General Assembly which shall consist of a Senate and a House of Representatives.

Section II.
Composition of General Assembly

Paragraph I. Senate and House of Representatives.

(a) The Senate shall consist of not more than 56 Senators, each of whom shall be elected from single-member districts.

(b) The House of Representatives shall consist of not fewer than 180 Representatives apportioned among representative districts of the state.

Paragraph II. Apportionment of General Assembly. The General Assembly shall apportion the Senate and House districts. Such districts shall be composed of contiguous territory. The apportionment of the Senate and of the House of Representatives shall be changed by the General Assembly as necessary after each United States decennial census.

Paragraph III. Qualifications of members of General Assembly.

(a) At the time of their election, the members of the Senate shall be citizens of the United States, shall be at least 25 years of age, shall have been citizens of this state for at least two years, and shall have been legal residents of the territory embraced within the district from which elected for at least one year.

(b) At the time of their election, the members of the House of Representatives shall be citizens of the United States, shall be at least 21 years of age, shall have been citizens of this state for at least two years, and shall have been legal residents of the territory embraced within the district from which elected for at least one year.

Paragraph IV. Disqualifications.

(a) No person on active duty with any branch of the armed forces of the United States shall have a seat in either house unless otherwise provided by law.

(b) No person holding any civil appointment or office having any emolument annexed thereto under the United States, this state, or any other state shall have a seat in either house.

(c) No Senator or Representative shall be elected by the General Assembly or appointed by the Governor to any office or appointment having any emolument annexed thereto during the time for which such person shall have been elected unless the Senator or Representative shall first resign the seat to which elected; provided, however, that, during the term for which elected, no Senator or Representative shall be appointed to any civil office which has been created during such term.

Paragraph V. Election and term of members.
(a) The members of the General Assembly shall be elected by the qualified electors of their respective districts for a term of two years and shall serve until the time fixed for the convening of the next General Assembly.
(b) The members of the General Assembly in office on June 30, 1983, shall serve out the remainder of the terms to which elected.
(c) The first election for members of the General Assembly under this Constitution shall take place on Tuesday after the first Monday in November, 1984, and subsequent elections biennially on that day until the day of election is changed by law.

Section III.
Officers of the General Assembly

Paragraph I. President and President Pro Tempore of the Senate.
(a) The presiding officer of the Senate shall be styled the President of the Senate.
(b) A President Pro Tempore shall be elected by the Senate from among its members. The President Pro Tempore shall act as President in case of the temporary disability of the President. In case of the death, resignation, or permanent disability of the President or in the event of the succession of the President to the executive power, the President Pro Tempore shall become President and shall receive the same compensation and allowances as the Speaker of the House of Representatives. The General Assembly shall provide by law for the method of determining disability as provided in this Paragraph.

Paragraph II. Speaker and Speaker Pro Tempore of the House of Representatives.
(a) The presiding officer of the House of Representatives shall be styled the Speaker of the House of Representatives and shall be elected by the House of Representatives from among its members.
(b) A Speaker Pro Tempore shall be elected by the House of Representatives from among its members. The Speaker Pro Tempore shall become Speaker in case of the death, resignation, or permanent disability of the Speaker and shall serve until a Speaker is elected. Such election shall be held as provided in the rules of the House. The General Assembly shall provide by law for the method of determining disability as provided in this Paragraph.

Paragraph III. Other officers of the two houses. The other officers of the two houses shall be a Secretary of the Senate and a Clerk of the House of Representatives.

Section IV.
Organization and Procedure of the General Assembly

Paragraph I. Meeting, time limit, and adjournment.
(a) The Senate and House of Representatives shall organize each odd-numbered year and shall be a different General Assembly for each two-year period. The General Assembly shall meet in regular session on the second Monday in January of each year, or otherwise as provided by law, and may continue in

session for a period of no longer than 40 days in the aggregate each year. By concurrent resolution, the General Assembly may adjourn any regular session to such later date as it may fix for reconvening. Separate periods of adjournment may be fixed by one or more such concurrent resolutions.

(b) Neither house shall adjourn during a regular session for more than three days or meet in any place other than the state capitol without the consent of the other. Following the fifth day of a special session, either house may adjourn not more than twice for a period not to exceed seven days for each such adjournment. In the event either house, after the thirtieth day of any session, adopts a resolution to adjourn for a specified period of time and such resolution and any amendments thereto are not adopted by both houses by the end of the legislative day on which adjournment was called for in such resolution, the Governor may adjourn both houses for a period of time not to exceed ten days.

(c) If an impeachment trial is pending at the end of any session, the House shall adjourn and the Senate shall remain in session until such trial is completed.

Paragraph II. Oath of members. Each Senator and Representative, before taking the seat to which elected, shall take the oath or affirmation prescribed by law.

Paragraph III. Quorum. A majority of the members to which each house is entitled shall constitute a quorum to transact business. A smaller number may adjourn from day to day and compel the presence of its absent members.

Paragraph IV. Rules of procedure; employees; interim committees. Each house shall determine its rules of procedure and may provide for its employees. Interim committees may be created by or pursuant to the authority of the General Assembly or of either house.

Paragraph V. Vacancies. When a vacancy occurs in the General Assembly, it shall be filled as provided by this Constitution and by law. The seat of a member of either house shall be vacant upon the removal of such member's legal residence from the district from which elected.

Paragraph VI. Salaries. The members of the General Assembly shall receive such salary as shall be provided for by law, provided that no increase in salary shall become effective prior to the end of the term during which such change is made.

Paragraph VII. Election and returns; disorderly conduct. Each house shall be the judge of the election, returns, and qualifications of its members and shall have power to punish them for disorderly behavior or misconduct by censure, fine, imprisonment, or expulsion; but no member shall be expelled except by a vote of two-thirds of the members of the house to which such member belongs.

Paragraph VIII. Contempts, how punished. Each house may punish by imprisonment, not extending beyond the session, any person not a member who shall be guilty of a contempt by any disorderly behavior in its presence or who shall rescue or attempt to rescue any person arrested by order of either house.

Paragraph IX. Privilege of members. The members of both houses shall be free from arrest during sessions of the General Assembly, or committee meetings thereof, and in going thereto or returning therefrom, except for treason, felony, or breach of the peace. No member shall be liable to answer in any other place for anything spoken in either house or in any committee meeting of either house.

Paragraph X. Elections by either house. All elections by either house of the General Assembly shall be by recorded vote, and the vote shall appear on the respective journal of each house.

Paragraph XI. Open meetings. The sessions of the General Assembly and all standing committee meetings thereof shall be open to the public. Either house may by rule provide for exceptions to this requirement.

Section V.
Enactment of Laws

Paragraph I. Journals and laws. Each house shall keep and publish after its adjournment a journal of its proceedings. The original journals shall be the sole, official records of the proceedings of each house and shall be preserved as provided by law. The General Assembly shall provide for the publication of the laws passed at each session.

Paragraph II. Bills for revenue. All bills for raising revenue, or appropriating money, shall originate in the House of Representatives.

Paragraph III. One subject matter expressed. No bill shall pass which refers to more than one subject matter or contains matter different from what is expressed in the title thereof.

Paragraph IV. Statutes and sections of Code, how amended. No law or section of the Code shall be amended or repealed by mere reference to its title or to the number of the section of the Code; but the amending or repealing Act shall distinctly describe the law or Code section to be amended or repealed as well as the alteration to be made.

Paragraph V. Majority of members to pass bill. No bill shall become law unless it shall receive a majority of the votes of all the members to which each house is entitled, and such vote shall so appear on the journal of each house.

Paragraph VI. When roll-call vote taken. In either house, when ordered by the presiding officer or at the desire of one-fifth of the members present or a lesser number if so provided by the rules of either house, a roll-call vote on any question shall be taken and shall be entered on the journal. The yeas and nays in each house shall be recorded and entered on the journal upon the passage or rejection of any bill or resolution appropriating money and whenever the Constitution requires a vote of two-thirds of either or both houses for the passage of a bill or resolution.

Paragraph VII. Reading of general bills. The title of every general bill and of every resolution intended to have the effect of general law or to amend this Constitution or to propose a new Constitution shall be read three times and on three separate days in each house before such bill or resolution shall be voted upon; and the third reading of such bill and resolution shall be in their entirety when ordered by the presiding officer or by a majority of the members voting on such question in either house.

Paragraph VIII. Procedure for considering local legislation. The General Assembly may provide by law for the procedure for considering local legislation. The title of every local bill and every resolution intended to have the effect of local law shall be read at least once before such bill or resolution shall be voted upon; and no such bill or resolution shall be voted upon prior to the second day following the day of introduction.

Paragraph IX. Advertisement of notice to introduce local legislation. The General Assembly shall provide by law for the advertisement of notice of intention to introduce local bills.

Paragraph X. Acts signed. All Acts shall be signed by the President of the Senate and the Speaker of the House of Representatives.

Paragraph XI. Signature of Governor. No provision in this Constitution *for a* two-thirds' vote of both houses of the General Assembly shall be *construed to waive the* necessity for the signature of the Governor as in *any other case, except in the case of the* two-thirds' vote required to override the veto or to submit proposed constitutional amendments or a proposal for a new Constitution.

Paragraph XII. Rejected bills. No bill or resolution intended to have *the effect of law* which shall have been rejected by either house shall again be proposed during the same regular or special session under the same or any other title without the consent of two-thirds of the house by which the same was rejected.

Paragraph XIII. Approval, veto, and override of veto of bills and resolutions.
(a) All bills and all resolutions which have been passed by the General Assembly intended to have the effect of law shall become law if the Governor approves or fails to veto the same within six days from the date any such bill or resolution is transmitted to the Governor unless the General Assembly adjourns sine die or adjourns for more than 40 days prior to the expiration of said six days. In the case of such adjournment sine die or of such adjournment for more than 40 days, the same shall become law if approved or not vetoed by the Governor within 40 days from the date of any such adjournment.
(b) During sessions of the General Assembly or during any period of adjournment of a session of the General Assembly, no bill or resolution shall be transmitted to the Governor after passage except upon request of the Governor or upon order of two-thirds of the membership of each house. A local bill which is required by the Constitution to have a referendum election conducted before it shall become effective shall be transmitted immediately to the Governor when ordered by the presiding officer of the house wherein the bill shall have originated or upon order of two-thirds of the membership of such house.
(c) The Governor shall have the duty to transmit any vetoed bill or resolution, together with the reasons for such veto, to the presiding officer of the house wherein it originated within three days from the date of veto if the General Assembly is in session on the date of transmission. If the General Assembly adjourns sine die or adjourns for more than 40 days, the Governor shall transmit any vetoed bill or resolution, together with the reasons for such veto, to the presiding officer of the house wherein it originated within 60 days of the date of such adjournment.
(d) During sessions of the General Assembly, any vetoed bill or resolution may upon receipt be immediately considered by the house wherein it originated for the purpose of overriding the veto. If two-thirds of the members to which such house is entitled vote to override the veto of the Governor, the same shall be immediately transmitted to the other house where it shall be immediately considered. Upon the vote to override the veto by two-thirds of the members to which such other house is entitled, such bill or resolution shall become law. All bills and resolutions vetoed during the last three days of the session and not considered for the purpose of overriding the veto and all bills and resolutions vetoed after the General Assembly has adjourned sine die may be considered at the next session of the General Assembly for the purpose of overriding the veto in the manner herein provided. If either house shall fail to override the Governor's veto, neither house shall again consider such bill or resolution for the purpose of overriding such veto.

(e)   The Governor may approve any appropriation and veto any other appropriation in the same bill, and any appropriation vetoed shall not become law unless such veto is overridden in the manner herein provided.

Paragraph XIV. Jointly sponsored bills and resolutions. The General Assembly may provide by law for the joint sponsorship of bills and resolutions.

Section VI.
Exercise of Powers

Paragraph I. General powers. The General Assembly shall have the power to make all laws not inconsistent with this Constitution, and not repugnant to the Constitution of the United States, which it shall deem necessary and proper for the welfare of the state.

Paragraph II. Specific powers.
(a)   Without limitation of the powers granted under Paragraph I, the General Assembly shall have the power to provide by law for:
   (1)   Restrictions upon land use in order to protect and preserve the natural resources, environment, and vital areas of this state.
   (2)   A militia and for the trial by courts-martial and nonjudicial punishment of its members, the discipline of whom, when not in federal service, shall be in accordance with law and the directives of the Governor acting as commander in chief.
   (3)   The participation by the state and political subdivisions and instrumentalities of the state in federal programs and the compliance with laws relating thereto, including but not limited to the powers, which may be exercised to the extent and in the manner necessary to effect such participation and compliance, to tax, to expend public money, to condemn property, and to zone property.
   (4)   The continuity of state and local governments in periods of emergency resulting from disasters caused by enemy attack including but not limited to the suspension of all constitutional legislative rules during such emergency.
   (5)   The participation by the state with any county, municipality, nonprofit organization, or any combination thereof in the operation of any of the facilities operated by such agencies for the purpose of encouraging and promoting tourism in this state.
   (6)   The control and regulation of outdoor advertising devices adjacent to federal aid interstate and primary highways and for the acquisition of property or interest therein for such purposes and may exercise the powers of taxation and provide for the expenditure of public funds in connection therewith.
(b)   The General Assembly shall have the power to implement the provisions of Article I, Section III, Paragraph I(2.); Article IV, Section VIII, Paragraph II; Article IV, Section VIII, Paragraph III; and Article X, Section II, Paragraph XII of the Constitution of 1976 in force and effect on June 30, 1983; and all laws heretofore adopted thereunder and valid at the time of their enactment shall continue in force and effect until modified or repealed.
(c)   *The distribution of tractors, farm equipment, heavy equipment, new motor vehicles, and parts therefor in the State of Georgia vitally affects the general economy of the state and the public interest and public welfare. Notwithstanding the provisions of*

Article I, Section I, Paragraphs I, II, and III or Article III, Section VI, Paragraph V (c) of this Constitution, the General Assembly in the exercise of its police power shall be authorized to regulate tractor, farm equipment, heavy equipment, and new motor vehicle manufacturers, distributors, dealers, and their representatives doing business in Georgia, including agreements among such parties, in order to prevent frauds, unfair business practices, unfair methods of competition, impositions, and other abuses upon its citizens. Any law enacted by the General Assembly shall not impair the obligation of an existing contract but may apply with respect to the renewal of such a contract after the effective date of such law (Source: GA.L. 1962, p. 3342). NOTE: THIS SECTION IS ALSO SUPPOSED TO BE RE-WRITTEN TO REFLECT THE AMENDMENT ON COMPETITIVE AGREEMENTS AS PASSED IN 2010.

Paragraph III. Powers not to be abridged. The General Assembly shall not abridge its powers under this Constitution. No law enacted by the General Assembly shall be construed to limit its powers.

Paragraph IV. Limitations on special legislation.

(a) Laws of a general nature shall have uniform operation throughout this state and no local or special law shall be enacted in any case for which provision has been made by an existing general law, except that the General Assembly may by general law authorize local governments by local ordinance or resolution to exercise police powers which do not conflict with general laws.

(b) No population bill, as the General Assembly shall define by general law, shall be passed. No bill using classification by population as a means of determining the applicability of any bill or law to any political subdivision or group of political subdivisions may expressly or impliedly amend, modify, supersede, or repeal the general law defining a population bill.

(c) No special law relating to the rights or status of private persons shall be enacted.

Paragraph V. Specific limitations.

(a) The General Assembly shall not have the power to grant incorporation to private persons but shall provide by general law the manner in which private corporate powers and privileges may be granted.

(b) The General Assembly shall not forgive the forfeiture of the charter of any corporation existing on August 13, 1945, nor shall it grant any benefit to or permit any amendment to the charter of any corporation except upon the condition that the acceptance thereof shall operate as a novation of the charter and that such corporation shall thereafter hold its charter subject to the provisions of this Constitution.

(c) The General Assembly shall not have the power to authorize any contract or agreement which may have the effect of or which is intended to have the effect of defeating or lessening competition, or encouraging a monopoly, which are hereby declared to be unlawful and void. NOTE: THIS SECTION WILL BE RE-WRITTEN AS A RESULT OF THE AMENDMENT ON COMPETITIVE CONTRACTS RATIFIED IN 2010.

(d) The General Assembly shall not have the power to regulate or fix charges of public utilities owned or operated by any county or municipality of this state, except as authorized by this Constitution.

(e) *No municipal or county authority which is authorized to construct, improve, or maintain any road or street on behalf of, pursuant to a contract with, or through the use of taxes or other revenues of a county or municipal corporation shall be created by any local Act or pursuant to any general Act nor shall any law specifically relating to any such authority be amended unless the creation of such authority or the amendment of such law is conditioned upon the approval of a majority of the qualified voters of the county or municipal corporation affected voting in a referendum thereon. This subparagraph shall not apply to or affect any state authority* (Authority: OLC, pp. 70–71).

Paragraph VI. Gratuities.

(a) Except as otherwise provided in the Constitution, (1) the General Assembly shall not have the power to grant any donation or gratuity or to forgive any debt or obligation owing to the public, and (2) the General Assembly shall not grant or authorize extra compensation to any public officer, agent, or contractor after the service has been rendered or the contract entered into.

(b) All laws heretofore adopted under Article III, Section VIII, Paragraph XII of the Constitution of 1976 in force and effect on June 30, 1983, shall continue in force and effect and may be amended if such amendments are consistent with the authority granted to the General Assembly by such provisions of said Constitution.

(c) *The General Assembly may provide by law and may expend or authorize the expenditure of public funds for a health insurance plan or program for persons and the spouses and dependent children of persons who are retired former employees of public schools or public school systems of this state.*

(d) *The General Assembly may provide by law for indemnification with respect to licensed emergency management rescue specialists who are or have been killed or permanently disabled in the line of duty on or after January 1, 1991, and publicly employed emergency medical technicians who are or have been killed or permanently disabled in the line of duty on or after January 1, 1987.*

(e) *(1) The General Assembly may provide by law for a program of indemnification with respect to the death or permanent disability of any law enforcement officer, fireman, prison guard, or publicly employed emergency medical technician who is or at any time in the past was killed or permanently disabled in the line of duty. Funds shall be appropriated as necessary for payment of such indemnification or for the purchase of insurance for such indemnification or both.*

(2) The General Assembly may provide by law for a program of compensation for injuries incurred by law enforcement officers and firemen in the line of duty. A law enforcement officer who becomes physically disabled, but not permanently disabled, as a result of a physical injury incurred in the line of duty and caused by a willful act of violence and a fireman who becomes physically disabled, but not permanently disabled, as a result of a physical injury incurred in the line of duty while fighting a fire shall be entitled to receive monthly compensation from the state in an amount equal to any such person's regular compensation for the period of time that the law enforcement officer or fireman is physically unable to perform the duties of his or her employment; provided, however, that such benefits provided in this subparagraph shall not be granted for more than a total of 12 months for injuries resulting from a single incident. A law enforcement officer or fireman shall be required to submit to a state agency satisfactory evidence of such disability. Benefits made available under this subparagraph shall be subordinate to workers' compensation benefits, disability and other compensation benefits from an employer which the law enforcement officer or fireman is awarded and shall be limited to the difference between the amount of workers' compensation benefits, disability and other compensation benefits actually paid and the amount of the law enforcement officer's or fireman's regular compensation. Any law enforcement officer or fireman who receives indemnification under subparagraph (1) of this subparagraph (e) shall not be entitled to any compensation under this subparagraph.

(f) *The General Assembly is authorized to provide by law for compensating inno-cent victims of crimes which occur on and after July 1, 1989. The General Assembly is authorized to define the types of victims eligible to receive com-pensation and to vary the amounts of compensation according to need. The General Assembly shall be authorized to allocate certain funds, to appropriate funds, to provide for a continuing fund, or to provide for any combination thereof for the purpose of compensating innocent victims of crime and for the administration of any laws enacted for such purpose.*

(g) *The General Assembly may provide by law for indemnification with respect to public school teachers, administrators, and employees who are killed or per-manently disabled by an act of violence in the line of duty, a nonlapsing indemnification fund for such purposes, and dedication of revenue from spe-cial and distinctive motor vehicle license plates honoring Georgia educators to such fund. (NOTE DUPLICATE NOMENCLATURE.)*

(g) *The General Assembly may provide by law for a program of indemnification with respect to the death or permanent disability of any state highway employee who is or at any time in the past was killed or permanently disabled in the line of duty. Funds shall be appropriated as necessary for payment of such indemnification or for the purchase of insurance for such indemnification or both (NOTE: DUPLICATE NOMENCLATURE STILL FOUND IN OFFI-CIAL SOURCE AS OF JANUARY 2010).* (Source: Sec. St. 1997).

Paragraph VII. Regulation of alcoholic beverages. *The State of Georgia shall have full and complete authority to regulate alcoholic beverages and to regulate, restrict, or prohibit activ-ities involving alcoholic beverages. This regulatory authority of the state shall include all such regulatory authority as is permitted to the states under the Twenty-First Amendment to the United States Constitution. This regulatory authority of the state is specifically delegated to the counties and municipalities of the state for the purpose of regulating, restricting, or prohibiting the exhibition of nudity, partial nudity, or depictions of nudity in connection with the sale or consumption of alcoholic beverages; and such delegated regulatory authority may be exercised by the adoption and enforcement of regulatory ordinances by the counties and municipalities of this state. A general law exercising such regulatory authority shall control over conflicting pro-visions of any local ordinance but shall not preempt any local ordinance provisions not in direct conflict with general law.* (Source: Sec. St. 1997).

Section VII.
Impeachments

Paragraph I. Power to impeach. The House of Representatives shall have the sole power to vote impeachment charges against any executive or judicial officer of this state or any member of the General Assembly.

Paragraph II. Trial of impeachments. The Senate shall have the sole power to try impeachments. When sitting for that purpose, the Senators shall be on oath, or affir-mation, and shall be presided over by the Chief Justice of the Supreme Court. Should the Chief Justice be disqualified, then the Presiding Justice shall preside. Should the Presiding Justice be disqualified, then the Senate shall select a Justice of the Supreme Court to preside. No person shall be convicted without concurrence of two-thirds of the members to which the Senate is entitled.

Paragraph III. Judgments in impeachment. In cases of impeachment, judgments shall not extend further than removal from office and disqualification to hold and enjoy any office of honor, trust, or profit within this state or to receive a pension there-from, but no such judgment shall relieve any party from any criminal or civil liability.

Section VIII.
Insurance Regulation

Paragraph I. Regulation of insurance. Provision shall be made by law for the regulation of insurance.

Paragraph II. Issuance of licenses. Insurance licenses shall be issued by the Commissioner of Insurance as required by law.

Section IX.
Appropriations

Paragraph I. Public money, how drawn. No money shall be drawn from the treasury except by appropriation made by law.

Paragraph II. Preparation, submission, and enactments of general appropriations bill.

(a) The Governor shall submit to the General Assembly within five days after its convening in regular session each year a budget message and a budget report, accompanied by a draft of a general appropriations bill, in such form and manner as may be prescribed by statute, which shall provide for the appropriation of the funds necessary to operate all the various departments and agencies and to meet the current expenses of the state for the next fiscal year.

(b) The General Assembly shall annually appropriate those state and federal funds necessary to operate all the various departments and agencies. To the extent that federal funds received by the state for any program, project, activity, purpose, or expenditure are changed by federal authority or exceed the amount or amounts appropriated in the general appropriations Act or supplementary appropriation Act or Acts, or are not anticipated, such excess, changed or unanticipated federal funds are hereby continually appropriated for the purposes authorized and directed by the federal government in making the grant. In those instances where the conditions under which the federal funds have been made available do not provide otherwise, federal funds shall first be used to replace state funds that were appropriated to supplant federal funds in the same state fiscal year. The fiscal year of the state shall commence on the first day of July of each year and terminate on the thirtieth of June following.

(c) The General Assembly shall by general law provide for the regulation and management of the finance and fiscal administration of the state.

Paragraph III. General appropriations bill. The general appropriations bill shall embrace nothing except appropriations fixed by previous laws; the ordinary expenses of the executive, legislative, and judicial departments of the government; payment of the public debt and interest thereon; and for support of the public institutions and educational interests of the state. All other appropriations shall be made by separate bills, each embracing but one subject.

Paragraph IV. General appropriations Act.

(a) Each general appropriations Act, now of force or hereafter adopted with such amendments as are adopted from time to time, shall continue in force and effect for the next fiscal year after adoption and it shall then expire, except for the mandatory appropriations required by this Constitution and those required to meet contractual obligations authorized by this Constitution and the continued appropriation of federal grants.

(b) The General Assembly shall not appropriate funds for any given fiscal year which, in aggregate, exceed a sum equal to the amount of unappropriated surplus expected to have accrued in the state treasury at the beginning of the fiscal year together with an amount not greater than the total treasury receipts from existing revenue sources anticipated to be collected in the fiscal year, less refunds, as estimated in the budget report and amendments thereto. Supplementary appropriations, if any, shall be made in the manner provided in Paragraph V of this section of the Constitution; but in no event shall a supplementary appropriations Act continue in force and effect beyond the expiration of the general appropriations Act in effect when such supplementary appropriations Act was adopted and approved.

(c) All appropriated state funds, except for the mandatory appropriations required by this Constitution, remaining unexpended and not contractually obligated at the expiration of such general appropriations Act shall lapse.

(d) *Funds appropriated to or received by the State Housing Trust Fund for the Homeless shall not be subject to the provisions of Article III, Section IX, Paragraph IV(c), relative to the lapsing of funds, and may be expended for programs of purely public charity for the homeless, including programs involving the participation of churches and religious institutions, notwithstanding the provisions of Article I, Section II, Paragraph VII.* (Authority: OLC, p. 76)

Paragraph V. Other or supplementary appropriations. In addition to the appropriations made by the general appropriations Act and amendments thereto, the General Assembly may make additional appropriations by Acts, which shall be known as supplementary appropriation Acts, provided no such supplementary appropriation shall be available unless there is an unappropriated surplus in the state treasury or the revenue necessary to pay such appropriation shall have been provided by a tax laid for such purpose and collected into the general fund of the state treasury. Neither house shall pass a supplementary appropriation bill until the general appropriations Act shall have been finally adopted by both houses and approved by the Governor.

Paragraph VI. Appropriations to be for specific sums.

(a) Except as hereinafter provided, the appropriation for each department, officer, bureau, board, commission, agency, or institution for which appropriation is made shall be for a specific sum of money; and no appropriation shall allocate to any object the proceeds of any particular tax or fund or a part or percentage thereof.

(b) An amount equal to all money derived from motor fuel taxes received by the state in each of the immediately preceding fiscal years, less the amount of refunds, rebates, and collection costs authorized by law, is hereby appropriated for the fiscal year beginning July 1, of each year following, for all activities incident to providing and maintaining an adequate system of public roads and bridges in this state, as authorized by laws enacted by the General Assembly of Georgia, and for grants to counties by law authorizing road construction and maintenance, as provided by law authorizing such grants. Said sum is hereby appropriated for, and shall be available for, the aforesaid purposes regardless of whether the General Assembly enacts a general appropriations Act; and said sum need not be specifically stated in any general appropriations Act passed by the General Assembly in order to be available for such purposes. However, this shall not preclude the General Assembly from appropriating for such purposes an amount greater than the sum specified above for such purposes. The expenditure of such funds shall be subject to all the rules, regulations, and restrictions imposed on the expenditure of appropriations by provisions of the Constitution and laws of this state, unless such provisions are in conflict with the provisions of this paragraph.

And provided, however, that the proceeds of the tax hereby appropriated shall not be subject to budgetary reduction. In the event of invasion of this state by land, sea, or air or in case of a major catastrophe so proclaimed by the Governor, said funds may be utilized for defense or relief purposes on the executive order of the Governor.

(c) A trust fund for use in the reimbursement of a portion of an employer's workers' compensation expenses resulting to an employee from the combination of a previous disability with subsequent injury incurred in employment may be provided for by law. As authorized by law, revenues raised for purposes of the fund may be paid into and disbursed from the trust without being subject to the limitations of subparagraph (a) of this Paragraph or of Article VII, Section III, Paragraph II.

(d) As provided by law, additional penalties may be assessed in any case in which any court in this state imposes a fine or orders the forfeiture of any bond in the nature of the penalty for all offenses against the criminal and traffic laws of this state or of the political subdivisions of this state. The proceeds derived from such additional penalty assessments may be allocated for the specific purpose of meeting any and all costs, or any portion of the cost, of providing training to law enforcement officers and to prosecuting officials.

(e) The General Assembly may by general law approved by a three-fifths' vote of both houses designate any part or all of the proceeds of any state tax now or hereafter levied and collected on alcoholic beverages to be used for prevention, education, and treatment relating to alcohol and drug abuse.

(f) *The General Assembly is authorized to provide by law for the creation of a State Children's Trust Fund from which funds shall be disbursed for child abuse and neglect prevention programs. The General Assembly is authorized to appropriate moneys to such fund and such moneys paid into the fund shall not be subject to the provisions of Article III, Section IX, Paragraph IV(c), relative to the lapsing of funds.*

(g) *The General Assembly is authorized to provide by law for the creation of a Seed-Capital Fund from which funds shall be disbursed at the direction of the Advanced Technology Development Center of the University System of Georgia to provide equity and other capital to small, young, entrepreneurial firms engaged in innovative work in the areas of technology, manufacturing, or agriculture. Funds shall be disbursed in the form of loans or investments which shall provide for repayment, rents, dividends, royalties, or other forms of return on investments as provided by law. Moneys received from returns on loans or investments shall be deposited in the Seed-Capital Fund for further disbursement. The General Assembly is authorized to appropriate moneys to such fund and such moneys paid into the fund shall not be subject to the provisions of Article III, Section IX, Paragraph IV(c) relative to the lapsing of funds. The General Assembly shall be authorized to provide by law for any matters relating to the purpose or provisions of this subparagraph.*

(h) *The General Assembly is authorized to provide by general law for additional penalties or fees in any case in any court in this state in which a person is adjudged guilty of an offense against the criminal or traffic laws of this state or an ordinance of a political subdivision of this state. The General Assembly is authorized to provide by general law for the allocation of such additional penalties or fees for the construction, operation, and staffing of jails, correctional institutions, and detention facilities by counties.*

(i) *The General Assembly is authorized to provide by general law for the creation of an Indigent Care Trust Fund. Any hospital, hospital authority, county, or municipality is authorized to contribute or transfer moneys to the fund and any other person or entity specified by the General Assembly may also contribute to the fund. The*

General Assembly may provide by general law for the dedication and deposit of revenues raised from specified sources for the purposes of the fund into the fund. Moneys in the fund shall be exclusively used for primary health care programs for medically indigent citizens and children of this state, for expansion of Medicaid eligibility and services, or for programs to support rural and other health care providers, primarily hospitals, who disproportionately serve the medically indigent. Any other appropriation from the Indigent Care Trust Fund shall be void. Contributions and revenues deposited to the fund shall not lapse and shall not be subject to the limitations of subparagraph (a) of this Paragraph or of Article VII, Section III, Paragraph II. Contributions in the fund which are not appropriated as required by this subparagraph shall be refunded pro rata to the contributors thereof, as provided by the General Assembly.

(j) The General Assembly is authorized to provide by general law for the creation of an emerging crops fund from which to pay interest on loans made to farmers to enable such farmers to produce certain crops on Georgia farms and thereby promote economic development. The General Assembly is authorized to appropriate moneys to such fund and moneys so appropriated shall not be subject to the provisions of Article III, Section IX, Paragraph IV(c), relative to the lapsing of appropriated funds. Interest on loans made to farmers shall be paid from such fund pursuant to such terms, conditions, and requirements as the General Assembly shall provide by general law. The General Assembly may provide by general law for the administration of such fund by such state agency or public authority as the General Assembly shall determine.

(k) The General Assembly is authorized to provide by general law for additional penalties or fees in any case in any court in this state in which a person is adjudged guilty of an offense involving driving under the influence of alcohol or drugs. The General Assembly is authorized to provide by general law for the allocation of such additional penalties or fees to the Brain and Spinal Injury Trust Fund, as provided by law, for the specified purpose of meeting any and all costs, or any portion of the costs, of providing care and rehabilitative services to citizens of the state who have survived neurotrauma with head or spinal cord injuries. Moneys appropriated for such purposes shall not lapse. The General Assembly may provide by general law for the administration of such fund by such authority as the General Assembly shall determine.

(l) The General Assembly is authorized to provide by general law for the creation of a roadside enhancement and beautification fund from which funds shall be disbursed for enhancement and beautification of public rights of way; for allocation and dedication of revenue from tree and other vegetation trimming or removal permit fees, other related assessments, and special and distinctive wildflower motor vehicle license plate fees to such fund; that moneys paid into the fund shall not lapse, the provisions of Article III, Section IX, Paragraph IV(c) notwithstanding; and for any matters relating to the purpose or provisions of this subparagraph. An Act creating such fund and making such provisions effective January 1, 1999, or later may originate or have originated in the Senate or the House of Representatives. (AMENDMENT APPROVED 1998, CVIG)

(m) There shall be within the Department of Agriculture a dog and cat reproductive sterilization support program to control dog and cat overpopulation and thereby reduce the number of animals housed and killed in animal shelters, which program shall be administered by the Commissioner of Agriculture. In order to fund the program, there shall be issued beginning in 2003 specially designed license plates promoting the program. The General Assembly shall provide by law for the issuance of such license plates and for dedication of certain revenue derived from fees for such plates to the support of the program. All such dedicated revenue derived from special license plate fees, any funds appropriated to the department for such purposes, and any voluntary contributions or other funds made available to the department for *such purposes and all interest thereon shall be deposited in a special fund for support of the program, shall not be used for any purpose other than support of the program, and shall not lapse. The General Assembly may provide by law for all matters necessary or appropriate to the implementation of this paragraph.*

(n) *The General Assembly may provide by law for the issuance and renewal of special motor vehicle license plates that motor vehicle owners may optionally purchase and renew for additional fees. The General Assembly may provide for all or a portion of the net revenue, as defined by the General Assembly, derived from the additional fees charged for any such special license plate to be dedicated to an agency, fund, or nonprofit corporation to implement or support programs related to the nature of the special license plate, as intended by the authorizing statute. Any dedication of funds enacted pursuant to the authority of this subparagraph may be in whole or in part for the ultimate use of a nonprofit corporation, without limitation by Article III, Section VI, Paragraph VI, if the General Assembly determines that the license plate program and such appropriation will benefit both the state and the nonprofit corporation . Any law enacted pursuant to the authority of this subparagraph may provide that funds dedicated pursuant to such law shall not lapse as otherwise required by Article III, Section IX , Paragraph IV(c). Any law enacted pursuant to the authority of this subparagraph shall be required to receive a two thirds' majority vote in both the Senate and the House of Representatives.* (AMENDMENT APPROVED 2006, CVIG)

Paragraph VII. **Appropriations void, when.** Any appropriation made in conflict with any of the foregoing provisions shall be void.

Section X.
Retirement Systems

Paragraph I. Expenditure of public funds authorized. Public funds may be expended for the purpose of paying benefits and other costs of retirement and pension systems for public officers and employees and their beneficiaries.

Paragraph II. Increasing benefits authorized. Public funds may be expended for the purpose of increasing benefits being paid pursuant to any retirement or pension system wholly or partially supported from public funds.

Paragraph III. Retirement systems covering employees of county boards of education. Notwithstanding Article IX, Section II, Paragraph III(a)(14), the authority to establish or modify heretofore existing local retirement systems covering employees of county boards of education shall continue to be vested in the General Assembly.

Paragraph IV. Firemen's Pension System. The powers of taxation may be exercised by the state through the General Assembly and the counties and municipalities for the purpose of paying pensions and other benefits and costs under a firemen's pension system or systems. The taxes so levied may be collected by such firemen's pension system or systems and disbursed therefrom by authority of the General Assembly for the purposes therein authorized.

Paragraph V. Funding standards. It shall be the duty of the General Assembly to enact legislation to define funding standards which will assure the actuarial soundness of any retirement or pension system supported wholly or partially from public funds and to control legislative procedures so that no bill or resolution creating or amending any such retirement or pension system shall be passed by the General Assembly without concurrent provisions for funding in accordance with the defined funding standards.

Paragraph V-A. Limitation on involuntary separation benefits for Governor of the State of Georgia. Any other provisions of this Constitution to the contrary notwithstanding, no past, present, or future Governor of the State of Georgia who ceases or ceased to hold office as Governor for any reason, except for medical disability, shall receive a retirement benefit based on involuntary separation from employment as a result of ceasing to hold office as Governor. The provisions of any law in conflict with this Paragraph are null and void effective January 1, 1985. (Authority: OLC, p. 81)

Paragraph VI. Involuntary separation; part-time service.

(a) *Any public retirement or pension system provided for by law in existence prior to January 1, 1985, may be changed by the General Assembly for any one or more of the following purposes:*

(1) *To redefine involuntary separation from employment; or*

(2) *To provide additional or revise existing limitations or restrictions on the right to qualify for a retirement benefit based on involuntary separation from employment.*

(b) *The General Assembly by law may define or redefine part-time service, including but not limited to service as a member of the General Assembly, for the purposes of any public retirement or pension system presently existing or created in the future and may limit or restrict the use of such part-time service as creditable service under any such retirement or pension system.*

(c) *Any law enacted by the General Assembly pursuant to subparagraph (a) or (b) of this Paragraph may affect persons who are members of public retirement or pension systems on January 1, 1985, and who became members at any time prior to that date.*

(d) *Any law enacted by the General Assembly pursuant to subparagraph (a) or (b) of this Paragraph shall not be subject to any law controlling legislative procedures for the consideration of retirement or pension bills, including, but not limited to, any limitations on the sessions of the General Assembly at which retirement or pension bills may be introduced.*

(e) *No public retirement or pension system created on or after January 1, 1985, shall grant any person whose retirement is based on involuntary separation from employment a retirement or pension benefit more favorable than the retirement or pension benefit granted to a person whose separation from employment is voluntary.* (Authority, OLC, pp. 81–82)

Article IV.
Constitutional Boards and Commissions

Section I.
Public Service Commission

Paragraph I. Public Service Commission.

(a) There shall be a Public Service Commission for the regulation of utilities which shall consist of five members who shall be elected by the people. The Commissioners in office on June 30, 1983, shall serve until December 31 after the general election at which the successor of each member is elected. Thereafter, all succeeding terms of members shall be for six years. Members shall serve until their successors are elected and qualified. A chairman shall be selected by the members of the commission from its membership.

(b) The commission shall be vested with such jurisdiction, powers, and duties as provided by law.

(c) The filling of vacancies and manner and time of election of members of the commission shall be as provided by law.

Section II.
State Board of Pardons and Paroles

Paragraph I. State Board of Pardons and Paroles. There shall be a State Board of Pardons and Paroles which shall consist of five members appointed by the Governor, subject to confirmation by the Senate. The members of the board in office on June 30, 1983, shall serve out the remainder of their respective terms, provided that the expiration date of the term of any such member shall be December 31 of the year in which the member's term expires. As each term of office expires, the Governor shall appoint a successor as herein provided. All such terms of members shall be for seven years. A chairman shall be selected by the members of the board from its membership.

Paragraph II. Powers and authority.

(a) Except as otherwise provided in this Paragraph, the State Board of Pardons and Paroles shall be vested with the power of executive clemency, including the powers to grant reprieves, pardons, and paroles; to commute penalties; to remove disabilities imposed by law; and to remit any part of a sentence for any offense against the state after conviction.

(b) (1) When a sentence of death is commuted to life imprisonment, the board shall not have the authority to grant a pardon to the convicted person until such person has served at least 25 years in the penitentiary; and such person shall not become eligible for parole at any time prior to serving at least 25 years in the penitentiary.

(2) *The General Assembly may by general law approved by two-thirds of the members elected to each branch of the General Assembly in a roll-call vote provide for minimum mandatory sentences and for sentences which are required to be served in their entirety for persons convicted of armed robbery, kidnapping, rape, aggravated child molestation, aggravated sodomy, or aggravated sexual battery and, when so provided by such Act, the board shall not have the authority to* consider such persons for pardon, parole, *or commutation during that portion of the sentence.*

(3)   The General Assembly may by general law approved by two-thirds of the members elected to each branch of the General Assembly in a roll-call vote provide for the imposition of sentences of life without parole for persons convicted of murder and for persons who having been previously convicted of murder, armed robbery, kidnapping, rape, aggravated child molestation, aggravated sodomy, or aggravated sexual battery or having been previously convicted under the laws of any other state or of the United States of a crime which if committed in this state would be one of those offenses and who after such previous conviction subsequently commits and is convicted of one of those offenses and, when so provided by such Act, the board shall not have the authority to consider such persons for pardon, parole, or commutation from any portion of such sentence.

(4)   Any general law previously enacted by the General Assembly providing for life without parole or for mandatory service of sentences without suspension, probation, or parole is hereby ratified and approved but such provisions shall be subject to amendment or repeal by general law. (Source: Sec. St., 1997)

(c)   Notwithstanding the provisions of subparagraph (b) of this Paragraph, the General Assembly, by law, may prohibit the board from granting and may prescribe the terms and conditions for the board's granting a pardon or parole to:

(1)   Any person incarcerated for a second or subsequent time for any offense for which such person could have been sentenced to life imprisonment; and

(2)   Any person who has received consecutive life sentences as the result of offenses occurring during the same series of acts.

(d)   The chairman of the board, or any other member designated by the board, may suspend the execution of a sentence of death until the full board shall have an opportunity to hear the application of the convicted person for any relief within the power of the board.

(e)   Notwithstanding any other provisions of this Paragraph, the State Board of Pardons and Paroles shall have the authority to pardon any person convicted of a crime who is subsequently determined to be *innocent of said crime or to issue a medical reprieve to an entirely incapacitated person suffering a progressively debilitating terminal illness or parole any person who is age 62 or older.* (Source: Sec. St. 1997)

Section III.
State Personnel Board

Paragraph I. State Personnel Board.

(a) There shall be a State Personnel Board which shall consist of five members appointed by the Governor, subject to confirmation by the Senate. The members of the board in office on June 30, 1983, shall serve out the remainder of their respective terms. As each term of office expires, the Governor shall appoint a successor as herein provided. All such terms of members shall be for five years. Members shall serve until their successors are appointed and qualified. A member of the State Personnel Board may not be employed in any other capacity in state government. A chairman shall be selected by the members of the board from its membership.

(b) The board shall provide policy direction for a State Merit System of Personnel Administration and may be vested with such additional powers and duties as provided by law. State personnel shall be selected on the basis of merit as provided by law.

Paragraph II. Veterans preference. Any veteran who has served as a member of the armed forces of the United States during the period of a war or armed conflict in which any branch of the armed forces of the United States engaged, whether under United States command or otherwise, and was honorably discharged therefrom, shall be given such veterans preference in any civil service program established in state government as may be provided by law. Any such law must provide at least ten points to a veteran having at least a 10 percent service connected disability as rated and certified by the Veterans Administration, and all other such veterans shall be entitled to at least five points.

Section IV.
State Transportation Board

Paragraph I. State Transportation Board; commissioner.

(a) There shall be a State Transportation Board composed of as many members as there are congressional districts in the state. The member of the board from each congressional district shall be elected by a majority vote of the members of the House of Representatives and Senate whose respective districts are embraced or partly embraced within such congressional district meeting in caucus. The members of the board in office on June 30, 1983, shall serve out the remainder of their respective terms. The General Assembly shall provide by law the procedure for the election of members and for filling vacancies on the board. Members shall serve for terms of five years and until their successors are elected and qualified.

(b) The State Transportation Board shall select a commissioner of transportation, who shall be the chief executive officer of the Department of Transportation and who shall have such powers and duties as provided by law.

Section V.
Veterans Service Board

Paragraph I. Veterans Service Board; commissioner.
(a) There shall be a State Department of Veterans Service and Veterans Service Board which shall consist of seven members appointed by the Governor, subject to confirmation by the Senate. The members in office on June 30, 1983, shall serve out the remainder of their respective terms. As each term of office expires, the Governor shall appoint a successor as herein provided. All such terms of members shall be for seven years. Members shall serve until their successors are appointed and qualified.
(b) The board shall appoint a commissioner who shall be the executive officer of the department. All members of the board and the commissioner shall be veterans of some war or armed conflict in which the United States has engaged. The board shall have such control, duties, powers, and jurisdiction of the State Department of Veterans Service as shall be provided by law.

Section VI.
Board of Natural Resources

Paragraph I. Board of Natural Resources.
(a) There shall be a Board of Natural Resources which shall consist of one member from each congressional district in the state and five members from the state at large, one of whom must be from one of the following named counties: Chatham, Bryan, Liberty, McIntosh, Glynn, or Camden. All members shall be appointed by the Governor, subject to confirmation by the Senate. The members of the board in office on June 30, 1983, shall serve out the remainder of their respective terms. As each term of office expires, the Governor shall appoint a successor as herein provided. All such terms of members shall be for seven years. Members shall serve until their successors are appointed and qualified. Insofar as it is practicable, the members of the board shall be representative of all areas and functions encompassed within the Department of Natural Resources.

(b) The board shall have such powers and duties as provided by law.

Section VII.
Qualifications, Compensation, Removal from Office, and Powers and Duties of Members of Constitutional Boards and Commissions

Paragraph I. Qualifications, compensation, and removal from office. The qualifications, compensation, and removal from office of members of constitutional boards and commissions provided for in this article shall be as provided by law.

Paragraph II. Powers and duties. The powers and duties of members of constitutional boards and commissions provided for in this article, except the Board of Pardons and Paroles, shall be as provided by law.

Article V.
Executive Branch

Section I.
Election of Governor and Lieutenant Governor

Paragraph I. Governor: term of office; compensation and allowances. There shall be a Governor who shall hold office for a term of four years and until a successor shall be chosen and qualified. Persons holding the office of Governor may succeed themselves for one four-year term of office. Persons who have held the office of Governor and have succeeded themselves as hereinbefore provided shall not again be eligible to be elected to that office until after the expiration of four years from the conclusion of their term as Governor. The compensation and allowances of the Governor shall be as provided by law.

Paragraph II. Election for Governor. An election for Governor shall be held on Tuesday after the first Monday in November of 1986, and the Governor-elect shall be installed in office at the next session of the General Assembly. An election for Governor shall take place quadrennially thereafter on said date unless another date be fixed by the General Assembly. Said election shall be held at the places of holding general elections in the several counties of this state, in the manner prescribed for the election of members of the General Assembly, and the electors shall be the same.

Paragraph III. Lieutenant Governor. There shall be a Lieutenant Governor, who shall be elected at the same time, for the same term, and in the same manner as the Governor. The Lieutenant Governor shall be the President of the Senate and shall have such executive duties as prescribed by the Governor and as may be prescribed by law not inconsistent with the powers of the Governor or other provisions of this Constitution. The compensation and allowances of the Lieutenant Governor shall be as provided by law.

Paragraph IV. Qualifications of Governor and Lieutenant Governor. No person shall be eligible for election to the office of Governor or Lieutenant Governor unless such person shall have been a citizen of the United States 15 years and a legal resident of the state six years immediately preceding the election and shall have attained the age of 30 years by the date of assuming office.

Paragraph V. Succession to executive power.
(a) In case of the temporary disability of the Governor as determined in the manner provided in Section IV of this article, the Lieutenant Governor shall exercise the powers and duties of the Governor and receive the same compensation as the Governor until such time as the temporary disability of the Governor ends.
(b) In case of the death, resignation, or permanent disability of the Governor or the Governor-elect, the Lieutenant Governor or the Lieutenant Governor-elect, upon becoming the Lieutenant Governor, shall become the Governor until a successor shall be elected and qualified as hereinafter provided. A successor to serve for the unexpired term shall be elected at the next general election; but, if such death, resignation, or permanent disability shall occur within 30 days of the next general election or if the term will expire within 90 days after the next general election, the Lieutenant Governor shall become Governor for the unexpired term. No person shall be elected or appointed to the office of Lieutenant Governor for the unexpired term in the event the Lieutenant Governor shall become Governor as herein provided.

(c) In case of the death, resignation, or permanent disability of both the Governor or the Governor-elect and the Lieutenant Governor or the Lieutenant Governor-elect or in case of the death, resignation, or *permanent disability of the Governor and there shall be no* Lieutenant Governor, the Speaker of the House of Representatives shall *exercise the powers and duties of the Governor until the election and qualification of a Governor at a special election, which shall be held within 90 days from the date on which the Speaker of the House of Representatives shall* have assumed the powers and duties of the Governor, and the person elected shall serve out the unexpired term.

Paragraph VI. Oath of office. The Governor and Lieutenant Governor shall, before entering on the duties of office, take such oath or affirmation as prescribed by law.

Section II.
Duties and Powers of Governor

Paragraph I. Executive powers. The chief executive powers shall be vested in the Governor. The other executive officers shall have such powers as may be prescribed by this Constitution and by law.

Paragraph II. Law enforcement. The Governor shall take care that the laws are faithfully executed and shall be the conservator of the peace throughout the state.

Paragraph III. Commander in chief. The Governor shall be the commander in chief of the military forces of this state.

Paragraph IV. Veto power. Except as otherwise provided in this Constitution, before any bill or resolution shall become law, the Governor shall have the right to review such bill or resolution intended to have the effect of law which has been passed by the General Assembly. The Governor may veto, approve, or take no action on any such bill or resolution. In the event the Governor vetoes any such bill or resolution, the General Assembly may, by a two-thirds' vote, override such veto as provided in Article III of this Constitution.

Paragraph V. Writs of election. The Governor shall issue writs of election to fill all vacancies that may occur in the Senate and in the House of Representatives.

Paragraph VI. Information and recommendations to the General Assembly. At the beginning of each regular session and from time to time, the Governor may give the General Assembly information on the state of the state and recommend to its consideration such measures as the Governor may deem necessary or expedient.

Paragraph VII. Special sessions of the General Assembly.
(a) The Governor may convene the General Assembly in special session by proclamation which may be amended by the Governor prior to the convening of the special session or amended by the Governor with the approval of three-fifths of the members of each house after the special session has convened; but no laws shall be enacted at any such special session except those which relate to the purposes stated in the proclamation or in any amendment thereto.

(b) The Governor shall convene the General Assembly in special session for all purposes whenever three-fifths of the members to which each house is entitled certify to the Governor in writing, with a copy to the Secretary of State, that in their opinion an emergency exists in the affairs of the state. The General Assembly may convene itself if, after receiving such certification, the Governor fails to do so within three days, excluding Sundays.

(c) Special sessions of the General Assembly shall be limited to a period of 40 days unless extended by three-fifths' vote of each house and approved by the Governor or unless at the expiration of such period an impeachment trial of some officer of state government is pending, in which event the House shall adjourn and the Senate shall remain in session until such trial is completed.

Paragraph VIII. Filling vacancies.

(a) When any public office shall become vacant by death, resignation, or otherwise, the Governor shall promptly fill such vacancy unless otherwise provided by this Constitution or by law; and persons so appointed shall serve for the unexpired term unless otherwise provided by this Constitution or by law.

(b) In case of the death or withdrawal of a person who received a majority of votes cast in an election for the office of Secretary of State, Attorney General, State School Superintendent, Commissioner of Insurance, Commissioner of Agriculture, or Commissioner of Labor, the Governor elected at the same election, upon becoming Governor, shall have the power to fill such office by appointing, subject to the confirmation of the Senate, an individual to serve until the next general election and until a successor for the balance of the unexpired term shall have been elected and qualified.

Paragraph IX. Appointments by Governor. The Governor shall make such appointments as are authorized by this Constitution or by law. If a person whose confirmation is required by the Senate is once rejected by the Senate, that person shall not be renominated by the Governor for appointment to the same office until the expiration of a period of one year from the date of such rejection.

Paragraph X. Information from officers and employees. The Governor may require information in writing from constitutional officers and all other officers and employees of the executive branch on any subject relating to the duties of their respective offices or employment.

Section III.
Other Elected Executive Officers

Paragraph I. Other executive officers, how elected. The Secretary of State, Attorney General, State School Superintendent, Commissioner of Insurance, Commissioner of Agriculture, and Commissioner of Labor shall be elected in the manner prescribed for the election of members of the General Assembly and the electors shall be the same. Such executive officers shall be elected at the same time and hold their offices for the same term as the Governor.

Paragraph II. Qualifications.

(a) No person shall be eligible to the office of the Secretary of State, Attorney General, State School Superintendent, Commissioner of Insurance, Commissioner of Agriculture, or Commissioner of Labor unless such person shall have been a citizen of the United States for ten years and a legal resident of the state for four years immediately preceding election or appointment and shall have attained the age of 25 years by the date of assuming office. All of said officers shall take such oath and give bond and security, as prescribed by law, for the faithful discharge of their duties.

(b) No person shall be Attorney General unless such person shall have been an active-status member of the State Bar of Georgia for seven years.

Paragraph III. Powers, duties, compensation, and allowances of other executive officers. Except as otherwise provided in this Constitution, the General Assembly shall prescribe the powers, duties, compensation, and allowances of the above executive officers and provide assistance and expenses necessary for the operation of the department of each.

Paragraph IV. Attorney General; duties. The Attorney General shall act as the legal advisor of the executive department, shall represent the state in the Supreme Court in all capital felonies and in all civil and criminal cases in any court when required by the Governor, and shall perform such other duties as shall be required by law.

Section IV.
Disability of Executive Officers

Paragraph I. "Elected constitutional executive officer," how defined. As used in this section, the term "elected constitutional executive officer" means the Governor, the Lieutenant Governor, the Secretary of State, the Attorney General, the State School Superintendent, the Commissioner of Insurance, the Commissioner of Agriculture, and the Commissioner of Labor.

Paragraph II. Procedure for determining disability. Upon a petition of any four of the elected constitutional executive officers to the Supreme Court of Georgia that another elected constitutional executive officer is unable to perform the duties of office because of a physical or mental disability, the Supreme Court shall by appropriate rule provide for a speedy and public hearing on such matter, including notice of the nature and cause of the accusation, process for obtaining witnesses, and the assistance of counsel. Evidence at such hearing shall include testimony from not fewer than three qualified physicians in private practice, one of whom must be a psychiatrist.

Paragraph III. Effect of determination of disability. If, after hearing the evidence on disability, the Supreme Court determines that there is a disability and that such disability is permanent, the office shall be declared vacant and the successor to that office shall be chosen as provided in this Constitution or the laws enacted in pursuance thereof. If it is determined that the disability is not permanent, the Supreme Court shall determine when the disability has ended and when the officer shall resume the exercise of the powers of office. During the period of temporary disability, the powers of such office shall be exercised as provided by law.

Article VI.
Judicial Branch

Section I.
Judicial Power

Paragraph I. Judicial power of the state. *The judicial power of the state shall be vested exclusively in the following classes of courts: magistrate courts, probate courts, juvenile courts, state courts, superior courts, Court of Appeals, and Supreme Court. Magistrate courts, probate courts, juvenile courts, and state courts shall be courts of limited jurisdiction. In addition, the General Assembly may establish or authorize the establishment of municipal courts and may authorize administrative agencies to exercise quasi-judicial powers. Municipal courts shall have jurisdiction over ordinance violations and such other jurisdiction as provided by law. Except as provided in this paragraph and in Section X, municipal courts, county recorder's courts and civil courts in existence on June 30, 1983, and administrative agencies shall not be subject to the provisions of this article. The General Assembly shall have the authority to confer "by law" jurisdiction upon municipal courts to try state offenses.* (Authority OLC, p. 86) NOTE: THE STATE 1983 WEB SITE SEEMS TO HAVE OMITTED ANY JUDICIAL CHAPTER WHEN DOWNLOADED JANUARY, 2011.

Paragraph II. Unified judicial system. All courts of the state shall comprise a unified judicial system.

Paragraph III. Judges; exercise of power outside own court; scope of term "judge." Provided the judge is otherwise qualified, a judge may exercise judicial power in any court upon the request and with the consent of the judges of that court and of the judge's own court under rules prescribed by law. The term "judge," as used in this article, shall include Justices, judges, senior judges, magistrates, and every other such judicial office of whatever name existing or created.

Paragraph IV. Exercise of judicial power. Each court may exercise such powers as necessary in aid of its jurisdiction or to protect or effectuate its judgments; but only the superior and appellate courts shall have the power to issue process in the nature of mandamus, prohibition, specific performance, quo warranto, and injunction. Each superior court, state court, and other courts of record may grant new trials on legal grounds.

Paragraph V. Uniformity of jurisdiction, powers, etc. Except as otherwise provided in this Constitution, the courts of each class shall have uniform jurisdiction, powers, rules of practice and procedure, and selection, qualifications, terms, and discipline of judges. The provisions of this Paragraph shall be effected by law within 24 months of the effective date of this Constitution.

Paragraph VI. Judicial circuits; courts in each county; court sessions. The state shall be divided into judicial circuits, each of which shall consist of not less than one county. Each county shall have at least one superior court, magistrate court, a probate court, and, where needed, a state court and a juvenile court. The General Assembly may provide by law that the judge of the probate court may also serve as the judge of the magistrate court. In the absence of a state court or a juvenile court, the superior court shall exercise that jurisdiction. Superior courts shall hold court at least twice each year in each county.

Paragraph VII. Judicial circuits, courts, and judgeships, law changed. The General Assembly may abolish, create, consolidate, or modify judicial circuits and courts and judgeships; but no circuit shall consist of less than one county.

Paragraph VIII. Transfer of cases. Any court shall transfer to the appropriate court in the state any civil case in which it determines that jurisdiction or venue lies elsewhere.

Paragraph IX. Rules of evidence; law prescribed. All rules of evidence shall be as prescribed by law.

Paragraph X. Authorization for pilot projects. The General Assembly may by general law approved by a two-thirds' majority of the members of each house enact legislation providing for, as pilot programs of limited duration, courts which are not uniform within their classes in jurisdiction, powers, rules of practice and procedure, and selection, qualifications, terms, and discipline of judges for such pilot courts and other matters relative thereto. Such legislation shall name the political subdivision, judicial circuit, and existing courts affected and may, in addition to any other power, grant to such court created as a pilot program the power to issue process in the nature of mandamus, prohibition, specific performance, quo warranto, and injunction. The General Assembly shall provide by general law for a procedure for submitting proposed legislation relating to such pilot programs to the Judicial Council of Georgia or its successor. Legislation enacted pursuant to this Paragraph shall not deny equal protection of the laws to any person in violation of Article I, Section I, Paragraph II of this Constitution. (Source: Sec. St. 1997)

Section II.
Venue

Paragraph I. Divorce cases. Divorce cases shall be tried in the county where the defendant resides, if a resident of this state; if the defendant is not a resident of this state, then in the county in which the plaintiff resides; provided, however, a divorce case may be tried in the county of residence of the plaintiff if the defendant has moved from that same county within six months from the date of the filing of the divorce action and said county was the site of the marital domicile at the time of the separation of the parties, and provided, further, that any person who has been a resident of any United States army post or military reservation within the State of Georgia for one year next preceding the filing of the petition may bring an action for divorce in any county adjacent to said United States army post or military reservation. (Authority OLC, p. 89)

Paragraph II. Land titles. Cases respecting titles to land shall be tried in the county where the land lies, except where a single tract is divided by a county line, in which case the superior court of either county shall have jurisdiction.

Paragraph III. Equity cases. Equity cases shall be tried in the county where a defendant resides against whom substantial relief is prayed.

Paragraph IV. Suits against joint obligors, copartners, etc. Suits against joint obligors, joint tort-feasors, joint promisors, copartners, or joint trespassers residing in different counties may be tried in either county.

Paragraph V. Suits against maker, endorser, etc. Suits against the maker and endorser of promissory notes, or drawer, acceptor, and endorser of foreign or inland bills of exchange, or like instruments, residing in different counties, shall be tried in the county where the maker or acceptor resides.

Paragraph VI. All other cases. All other civil cases, except juvenile court cases as may otherwise be provided by the Juvenile Court Code of Georgia, shall be tried in the county where the defendant resides; venue as to corporations, foreign and domestic, shall be as provided by law; and all criminal cases shall be tried in the county where the crime was committed, except cases in the superior courts where the judge is satisfied that an impartial jury cannot be obtained in such county.

Paragraph VII. Venue in third-party practice. The General Assembly may provide by law that venue is proper in a county other than the county of residence of a person or entity impleaded into a pending civil case by a defending party who contends that such person or entity is or may be liable to said defending party for all or part of the claim against said defending party.

Paragraph VIII. Power to change venue. The power to change the venue in civil and criminal cases shall be vested in the superior courts to be exercised in such manner as has been, or shall be, provided by law.

Section III.
Classes of Courts of Limited Jurisdiction

Paragraph I. Jurisdiction of classes of courts of limited jurisdiction. The magistrate, juvenile, and state courts shall have uniform jurisdiction as provided by law. Probate courts shall have such jurisdiction as now or hereafter provided by law, without regard to uniformity.

Section IV.
Superior Courts

Paragraph I. Jurisdiction of superior courts. The superior courts shall have jurisdiction in all cases, except as otherwise provided in this Constitution. They shall have exclusive jurisdiction over trials in felony cases, except in the case of juvenile offenders as provided by law; in cases respecting title to land; in divorce cases; and in equity cases. The superior courts shall have such appellate jurisdiction, either alone or by circuit or district, as may be provided by law.

Section V.
Court of Appeals

Paragraph I. Composition of Court of Appeals; Chief Judge. The Court of Appeals shall consist of not less than nine Judges who shall elect from among themselves a Chief Judge.

Paragraph II. Panels as prescribed. The Court of Appeals may sit in panels of not less than three Judges as prescribed by law or, if none, by its rules.

Paragraph III. Jurisdiction of Court of Appeals; decisions binding. The Court of Appeals shall be a court of review and shall exercise appellate and certiorari jurisdiction in all cases not reserved to the Supreme Court or conferred on other courts by law. The decisions of the Court of Appeals insofar as not in conflict with those of the Supreme Court shall bind all courts except the Supreme Court as precedents.

Paragraph IV. Certification of question to Supreme Court. The Court of Appeals may certify a question to the Supreme Court for instruction, to which it shall then be bound.

Paragraph V. Equal division of court. In the event of an equal division of the Judges when sitting as a body, the case shall be immediately transmitted to the Supreme Court.

Section VI.
Supreme Court

Paragraph I. Composition of Supreme Court; Chief Justice; Presiding Justice; quorum; substitute judges. The Supreme Court shall consist of not more than nine Justices who shall elect from among themselves a Chief Justice as the chief presiding and administrative officer of the court and a Presiding Justice to serve if the Chief Justice is absent or is disqualified. A majority shall be necessary to hear and determine cases. If a Justice is disqualified in any case, a substitute judge may be designated by the remaining Justices to serve.

Paragraph II. Exclusive appellate jurisdiction of Supreme Court. The Supreme Court shall be a court of review and shall exercise exclusive appellate jurisdiction in the following cases:
(1) All cases involving the construction of a treaty or of the Constitution of the State of Georgia or of the United States and all cases in which the constitutionality of a law, ordinance, or constitutional provision has been drawn in question; and
(2) All cases of election contest.

Paragraph III. General appellate jurisdiction of Supreme Court. Unless otherwise provided by law, the Supreme Court shall have appellate jurisdiction of the following classes of cases:
(1) Cases involving title to land;
(2) All equity cases;
(3) All cases involving wills;
(4) All habeas corpus cases;
(5) All cases involving extraordinary remedies;
(6) All divorce and alimony cases;
(7) All cases certified to it by the Court of Appeals; and
(8) All cases in which a sentence of death was imposed or could be imposed. Review of all cases shall be as provided by law.

Paragraph IV. Jurisdiction over questions of law from state appellate or federal district or appellate courts. The Supreme Court shall have jurisdiction and authority to answer any question of law from any state appellate or federal district or appellate court.

Paragraph V. Review of cases in Court of Appeals. The Supreme Court may review by certiorari cases in the Court of Appeals which are of gravity or great public importance.

Paragraph VI. Decisions of Supreme Court binding. The decisions of the Supreme Court shall bind all other courts as precedents.

Section VII.
Selection, Term, Compensation, and Discipline of Judges

Paragraph I. Election; term of office. All superior court and state court judges shall be elected on a nonpartisan basis for a term of four years. All Justices of the Supreme Court and the Judges of the Court of Appeals shall be elected on a nonpartisan basis for a term of six years. The terms of all judges thus elected shall begin the next January 1 after their election. All other judges shall continue to be selected in the manner and for the term they were selected on June 30, 1983, until otherwise provided by local law.

Paragraph II. Qualifications.

(a) Appellate and superior court judges shall have been admitted to practice law for seven years.

(b) State court judges shall have been admitted to practice law for seven years, provided that this requirement shall be five years in the case of state court judges elected or appointed in the year 2000 or earlier. Juvenile court judges shall have been admitted to practice law for five years.

(c) Probate and magistrate judges shall have such qualifications as provided by law.

(d) All judges shall reside in the geographical area in which they are selected to serve.

(e) The General Assembly may provide by law for additional qualifications, including, but not limited to, minimum residency requirements.

Paragraph III. Vacancies. Vacancies shall be filled by appointment of the Governor except as otherwise provided by law in the magistrate, probate, and juvenile courts.

Paragraph IV. Period of service of appointees. An appointee to an elective office shall serve until a successor is duly selected and qualified and until January 1 of the year following the next general election which is more than six months after such person's appointment.

Paragraph V. Compensation and allowances of judges. All judges shall receive compensation and allowances as provided by law; county supplements are hereby continued and may be granted or changed by the General Assembly. County governing authorities which had the authority on June 30, 1983, to make county supplements shall continue to have such authority under this Constitution. An incumbent's salary, allowance, or supplement shall not be decreased during the incumbent's term of office.

Paragraph VI. Judicial Qualifications Commission; power; composition. The power to discipline, remove, and cause involuntary retirement of judges shall be vested in the Judicial Qualifications Commission. It shall consist of seven members, as follows:

(1) Two judges of any court of record, selected by the Supreme Court;

(2) Three members of the State Bar of Georgia who shall have been active status members of the state bar for at least ten years and who shall be elected by the board of governors of the state bar; and

(3) Two citizens, neither of whom shall be a member of the state bar, who shall be appointed by the Governor.

Paragraph VII. Discipline, removal, and involuntary retirement of judges.
(a) *Any judge may be removed, suspended, or otherwise disciplined for willful misconduct in office, or for willful and persistent failure to perform the duties of office, or*

for habitual intemperance, or for conviction of a crime involving moral turpitude, or for conduct prejudicial to the administration of justice which brings the judicial office into disrepute. Any judge may be retired for disability which constitutes a serious and likely permanent interference with the performance of the duties of office. The Supreme Court shall adopt rules of implementation.

(b) (1) Upon indictment for a felony by a grand jury of this state or by a grand jury of the United States of any judge, the Attorney General or district attorney shall transmit a certified copy of the indictment to the Judicial Qualifications Commission. The commission shall, subject to subparagraph (b)(2) of this Paragraph, review the indictment, and, if it determines that the indictment relates to and adversely affects the administration of the office of the indicted judge and that the rights and interests of the public are adversely affected thereby, the commission shall suspend the judge immediately and without further action pending the final disposition of the case or until the expiration of the judge's term of office, whichever occurs first. During the term of office to which such judge was elected and in which the indictment occurred, if a nolle prosequi is entered, if the public official is acquitted, or if after conviction the conviction is later overturned as a result of any direct appeal or application for a writ of certiorari, the judge shall be immediately reinstated to the office from which he was suspended. While a judge is suspended under this subparagraph and until initial conviction by the trial court, the judge shall continue to receive the compensation from his office. After initial conviction by the trial court, the judge shall not be entitled to receive the compensation from his office. If the judge is reinstated to office, he shall be entitled to receive any compensation withheld under the provisions of this subparagraph. For the duration of any suspension under this subparagraph, the Governor shall appoint a replacement judge. Upon a final conviction with no appeal or review pending, the office shall be declared vacant and a successor to that office shall be chosen as provided in this Constitution or the laws enacted in pursuance thereof.

(2) The commission shall not review the indictment for a period of 14 days from the day the indictment is received. This period of time may be extended by the commission. During this period of time, the indicted judge may, in writing, authorize the commission to suspend him from office. Any such voluntary suspension shall be subject to the same conditions for review, reinstatement, or declaration of vacancy as are provided in this subparagraph for a nonvoluntary suspension.

(3) After any suspension is imposed under this subparagraph, the suspended judge may petition the commission for a review. If the commission determines that the judge should no longer be suspended, he shall immediately be reinstated to office.

(4) The findings and records of the commission and the fact that the public official has or has not been suspended shall not be admissible in evidence in any court for any purpose. The findings and records of the commission shall not be open to the public.

(5) The provisions of this subparagraph shall not apply to any indictment handed down prior to January 1, 1985.

(6) If a judge who is suspended from office under the provisions of this subparagraph is not first tried at the next regular or special term following the indictment, the suspension shall be terminated and the judge shall be reinstated to office. The judge shall not be reinstated under this provision if he is not so tried based on a continuance granted upon a motion made only by the defendant.

(c)   Upon initial conviction of any judge for any felony in a trial court of this state or the United States, regardless of whether the judge has been suspended previously under subparagraph (b) of this Paragraph, such judge shall be immediately and without further action suspended from office. While a judge is suspended from office under this subparagraph, he shall not be entitled to receive the compensation from his office. If the conviction is later overturned as a result of any direct appeal or application for a writ of certiorari, the judge shall be immediately reinstated to the office from which he was suspended and shall be entitled to receive any compensation withheld under the provisions of this subparagraph. For the duration of any suspension under this subparagraph, the Governor shall appoint a replacement judge. Upon a final conviction with no appeal or review pending, the office shall be declared vacant and a successor to that office shall be chosen as provided in this Constitution or the laws enacted in pursuance thereof. The provisions of this subparagraph shall not apply to any conviction rendered prior to January 1, 1987. (Authority OLC, 105–107)*

Paragraph VIII. Due process; review by Supreme Court. No action shall be taken against a judge except after hearing and in accordance with due process of law. No removal or involuntary retirement shall occur except upon order of the Supreme Court after review.

Section VIII.
District Attorneys

Paragraph I. District attorneys; vacancies; qualifications; compensation; duties; immunity.

(a)   There shall be a district attorney for each judicial circuit, who shall be elected circuit-wide for a term of four years. The successors of present and subsequent incumbents shall be elected by the electors of their respective circuits at the general election held immediately preceding the expiration of their respective terms. District attorneys shall serve until their successors are duly elected and qualified. Vacancies shall be filled by appointment of the Governor.

(b)   No person shall be a district attorney unless such person shall have been an active-status member of the State Bar of Georgia for three years immediately preceding such person's election.

(c)   The district attorneys shall receive such compensation and allowances as provided by law and shall be entitled to receive such local supplements to their compensation and allowances as may be provided by law.

(d)   It shall be the duty of the district attorney to represent the state in all criminal cases in the superior court of such district attorney's circuit and in all cases appealed from the superior court and the juvenile courts of that circuit to the Supreme Court and the Court of Appeals and to perform such other duties as shall be required by law.

(e)   District attorneys shall enjoy immunity from private suit for actions arising from the performance of their duties.

Paragraph II. Discipline, removal, and involuntary retirement of district attorneys. Any district attorney may be disciplined, removed or involuntarily retired as provided by general law.

Section IX.
General Provisions

Paragraph I. Administration of the judicial system; uniform court rules; advice and consent of councils. The judicial system shall be administered as provided in this Paragraph. Not more than 24 months after the effective date hereof, and from time to time thereafter by amendment, the Supreme Court shall, with the advice and consent of the council of the affected class or classes of trial courts, by order adopt and publish uniform court rules and record-keeping rules which shall provide for the speedy, efficient, and inexpensive resolution of disputes and prosecutions. Each council shall be comprised of all of the judges of the courts of that class.

Paragraph II. Disposition of cases. The Supreme Court and the Court of Appeals shall dispose of every case at the term for which it is entered on the court's docket for hearing or at the next term.

Section X.
Transition

Paragraph I. Effect of ratification. On the effective date of this article:

(1) Superior courts shall continue as superior courts.

(2) State courts shall continue as state courts.

(3) Probate courts shall continue as probate courts.

(4) Juvenile courts shall continue as juvenile courts.

(5) Municipal courts not otherwise named herein, of whatever name, shall continue as and be denominated municipal courts, except that the City Court of Atlanta shall retain its name. Such municipal courts, county recorder's courts, the Civil Courts of Richmond and Bibb counties, and administrative agencies having quasi-judicial powers shall continue with the same jurisdiction as such courts and agencies have on the effective date of this article until otherwise provided by law.

(6) Justice of the peace courts, small claims courts, and magistrate courts operating on the effective date of this Constitution and the County Court of Echols County shall become and be classified as magistrate courts. The County Court of Baldwin County and the County Court of Putnam County shall become and be classified as state courts, with the same jurisdiction and powers as other state courts.

Paragraph II. Continuation of judges. Each judge holding office on the effective date of this article shall continue in office until the expiration of the term of office, as a judge of the court having the same or similar jurisdiction. Each court not named herein shall cease to exist on such date or at the expiration of the term of the incumbent judge, whichever is later; and its jurisdiction shall automatically pass to the new court of the same or similar jurisdiction, in the absence of which court it shall pass to the superior court.

Article VII.
Taxation and Finance

Section I.
Power of Taxation

Paragraph I. Taxation; limitations on grants of tax powers. The state may not suspend or irrevocably give, grant, limit, or restrain the right of taxation and all laws, grants, contracts, and other acts to effect any of these purposes are null and void. Except as otherwise provided in this Constitution, the right of taxation shall always be under the complete control of the state.

Paragraph II. Taxing power limited.

(a) The annual levy of state ad valorem taxes on tangible property for all purposes, except for defending the state in an emergency, shall not exceed one-fourth mill on each dollar of the assessed value of the property.

(b) So long as the method of taxation in effect on December 31, 1980, for the taxation of shares of stock of banking corporations and other monied capital coming into competition with such banking corporations continues in effect, such shares and other monied capital may be taxed at an annual rate not exceeding five mills on each dollar of the assessed value of the property.

Paragraph III. Uniformity; classification of property; assessment of agricultural land; utilities. *NOTE: THIS SECTION WILL BE RE-WRITTEN TO REFLECT THE AMENDMENT ON THE CONSERVATION OF GEORGIA FORESTS PASSED IN 2008.*

(a) *All taxes shall be levied and collected under general laws and for public purposes only. Except as otherwise provided in subparagraphs (b), (c), (d), and (e), and (f) of this Paragraph, all taxation shall be uniform upon the same class of subjects within the territorial limits of the authority levying the tax.*

(b) *(1) Except as otherwise provided in this subparagraph (b), classes of subjects for taxation of property shall consist of tangible property and one or more classes of intangible personal property including money; provided, however, that any taxation of intangible personal property may be repealed by general law without approval in a referendum effective for all taxable years beginning on or after January 1, 1996.*

(2) Subject to the conditions and limitations specified by law, each of the following types of property may be classified as a separate class of property for ad valorem property tax purposes and different rates, methods, and assessment dates may be provided for such properties:

(A) Trailers.

(B) Mobile homes other than those mobile homes which qualify the owner of the home for a homestead exemption from ad valorem taxation.

(C) Heavy-duty equipment motor vehicles owned by nonresidents and operated in this state.

(3) Motor vehicles may be classified as a separate class of property for ad valorem property tax purposes, and such class may be divided into separate subclasses for ad valorem purposes. The General Assembly may provide by general law for the ad valorem taxation of motor vehicles including, but not limited to, providing for different rates, methods, assessment dates, and taxpayer liability for such class and for each of its subclasses and need not provide for uniformity of taxation with other classes of property or between or within its subclasses. The General Assembly may also determine what portion of any ad valorem tax on motor vehicles shall be retained by the state. As used in this subparagraph, the term "motor vehicles" means all vehicles which are self-propelled.

(c) *Tangible real property, but no more than 2,000 acres of any single property owner, which is devoted to bona fide agricultural purposes shall be assessed for ad valorem taxation purposes at 75 percent of the value which other tangible real property is assessed. No property shall be entitled to receive the preferential assessment provided for in this subparagraph if the property which would otherwise receive such assessment would result in any person who has a beneficial interest in such property, including any interest in the nature of stock ownership, receiving the benefit of such preferential assessment as to more than 2,000 acres. No property shall be entitled to receive the preferential assessment provided for in this subparagraph unless the conditions set out below are met:*

   (1) *The property must be owned by:*

      (A) *(i)* *One or more natural or naturalized citizens;*

         (ii) *An estate of which the devisee or heirs are one or more natural or naturalized citizens; or*

         (iii) *A trust of which the beneficiaries are one or more natural or naturalized citizens; or*

      (B) *A family-owned farm corporation, the controlling interest of which is owned by individuals related to each other within the fourth degree of civil reckoning, or which is owned by an estate of which the devisee or heirs are one or more natural or naturalized citizens, or which is owned by a trust of which the beneficiaries are one or more natural or naturalized citizens, and such corporation derived 80 percent or more of its gross income from bona fide agricultural pursuits within this state within the year immediately preceding the year in which eligibility is sought.*

   (2) *The General Assembly shall provide by law:*

      (A) *For a definition of the term "bona fide agricultural purposes," but such term shall include timber production;*

      (B) *For additional minimum conditions of eligibility which such properties must meet in order to qualify for the preferential assessment provided for herein, including, but not limited to, the requirement that the owner be required to enter into a covenant with the appropriate taxing authorities to maintain the use of the properties in bona fide agricultural purposes for a period of not less than ten years and for appropriate penalties for the breach of any such covenant.*

   (3) *In addition to the specific conditions set forth in this subparagraph (c), the General Assembly may place further restrictions upon, but may not relax, the conditions of eligibility for the preferential assessment provided for herein.*

(d) *(1)* *The General Assembly shall be authorized by general law to establish as a separate class of property for ad valorem tax purposes any tangible real property which is listed in the National Register of Historic Places or in a state historic register authorized by general law. For such purposes, the General Assembly is authorized by general law to establish a program by which certain properties within such class may be assessed for taxes at different rates or valuations in order to encourage the preservation of such historic properties and to assist in the revitalization of historic areas.*

   (2) *The General Assembly shall be authorized by general law to establish as a separate class of property for ad valorem tax purposes any tangible real property on which there have been releases of hazardous waste, constituents, or substances into the environment. For such purposes, the General Assembly is authorized by general law to establish a program by which certain properties within such class may be assessed for taxes at different rates or valuations in order to encourage the cleanup, reuse, and redevelopment of such properties and to assist in the revitalization thereof by encouraging remedial action.*

(e) The General Assembly shall provide by general law:
   (1) For the definition and methods of assessment and taxation, such methods to include a formula based on current use, annual productivity, and real property sales data, of: "bona fide conservation use property" to include bona fide agricultural and timber land not to exceed 2,000 acres of a single owner; and "bona fide residential transitional property," to include private single-family residential owner occupied property located in transitional developing areas not to exceed five acres of any single owner. Such methods of assessment and taxation shall be subject to the following conditions:
      (A) A property owner desiring the benefit of such methods of assessment and taxation shall be required to enter into a covenant to continue the property in bona fide conservation use or bona fide residential transitional use; and
      (B) A breach of such covenant within ten years shall result in a recapture of the tax savings resulting from such methods of assessment and taxation and may result in other appropriate penalties;
   (2) That standing timber shall be assessed only once, and such assessment shall be made following its harvest or sale and on the basis of its fair market value at the time of harvest or sale. Said assessment shall be two and one-half times the assessed percentage of value fixed by law for other real property taxed under the uniformity provisions of subparagraph (a) of this Paragraph but in no event greater than its fair market value; and for a method of temporary supplementation of the property tax digest of any county if the implementation of this method of taxing timber reduces the tax digest by more than 20 percent, such supplemental assessed value to be assigned to the properties otherwise benefiting from such method of taxing timber.

(f) (1) The General Assembly shall provide by general law for the definition and methods of assessment and taxation, such methods to include a formula based on current use, annual productivity, and real property sales data, of "forest land conservation use property" to include only forest land each tract of which exceeds 200 acres of a qualified owner. Such methods of assessment and taxation shall be subject to the following conditions:
      (A) A qualified owner shall consist of any individual or individuals or any entity registered to do business in this state;
      (B) A qualified owner desiring the benefit of such methods of assessment and taxation shall be required to enter into a covenant to continue the property in forest land use;
      (C) All contiguous forest land conservation use property of an owner within a county for which forest land conservation use assessment is sought under this subparagraph shall be in a single covenant;
      (D) A breach of such covenant within 15 years shall result in a recapture of the tax savings resulting from such methods of assessment and taxation and may result in other appropriate penalties; and
      (E) The General Assembly may provide by general law for a limited exception to the 200 acre requirement in the case of a transfer of ownership of all or a part of the forest land conservation use property during a covenant period to another owner qualified to enter into an original forest land conservation use covenant if the original covenant is continued by both such acquiring owner and the transferor for the remainder of the term, in which event no breach of the covenant shall be deemed to have occurred even if the total size of a tract from which the transfer was made is reduced below 200 acres.

(2) No portion of an otherwise eligible tract of forest land conservation use property shall be entitled to receive simultaneously special assessment and taxation under this subparagraph and either subparagraph (c) or (e) of this Paragraph.

(3) (A) The General Assembly shall appropriate an amount for assistance grants to counties, municipalities, and county and independent school districts to offset revenue loss attributable to the implementation of this subparagraph. Such grants shall be made in such manner and shall be subject to such procedures as may be specified by general law.

(B) If the forest land conservation use property is located in a county, municipality, or county or independent school district where forest land conservation use value causes an ad valorem tax revenue reduction of 3 percent or less due to the implementation of this subparagraph, in each taxable year in which such reduction occurs, the assistance grants to the county, each municipality located therein, and the county or independent school districts located therein shall be in an amount equal to 50 percent of the amount of such reduction.

(C) If the forest land conservation use property is located in a county, municipality, or county or independent school district where forest land conservation use value causes an ad valorem tax revenue reduction of more than 3 percent due to the implementation of this subparagraph, in each taxable year in which such reduction occurs, the assistance grants to the county, each municipality located therein, and the county or independent school districts located therein shall be as follows:

(i) For the first 3 percent of such reduction amount, in an amount equal to 50 percent of the amount of such reduction; and

(ii) For the remainder of such reduction amount, in an amount equal to 100 percent of the amount of such remaining reduction amount.

(4) Such revenue reduction shall be calculated by utilizing forest land fair market value. For purposes of this subparagraph, forest land fair market value means the 2008 fair market value of the forest land. Such 2008 valuation may increase from one taxable year to the next by a rate equal to the percentage change in the price index for gross output of state and local government from the prior year to the current year as defined by the National Income and Product Accounts and determined by the United States Bureau of Economic Analysis and indicated by the Price Index for Government Consumption Expenditures and General Government Gross Output (Table 3.10.4). Such revenue reduction shall be determined by subtracting the aggregate forest land conservation use value of qualified properties from the aggregate forest land fair market value of qualified properties for the applicable tax year and the resulting amount shall be multiplied by the millage rate of the county, municipality, or county or independent school district.

(5) For purposes of this subparagraph, the forest land conservation use value shall not include the value of the standing timber located on forest land conservation use property.

(g)   *The General Assembly may provide for a different method and time of returns, assessments, payment, and collection of ad valorem taxes of public utilities, but not on a greater assessed percentage of value or at a higher rate of taxation than other properties, except that property provided for in subparagraph (c), (d), (e), or (f) of this Paragraph* (Authority: OLC pp. 112–115).

Section II.
Exemptions from Ad Valorem Taxation

Paragraph I. Unauthorized tax exemptions void. Except as authorized in or pursuant to this Constitution, all laws exempting property from ad valorem taxation are void.

Paragraph II. Exemptions from taxation of property.
(a)   (1)   Except as otherwise provided in this Constitution, no property shall be exempted from ad valorem taxation unless the exemption is approved by two-thirds of the members elected to each branch of the General Assembly in a roll-call vote and by a majority of the qualified electors of the state voting in a referendum thereon.

   (2)   Homestead exemptions from ad valorem taxation levied by local taxing jurisdictions may be granted by local law conditioned upon approval by a majority of the qualified electors residing within the limits of the local taxing jurisdiction voting in a referendum thereon.

   (3)   Laws subject to the requirement of a referendum as provided in this subparagraph (a) may originate in either the Senate or the House of Representatives.

   (4)   The requirements of this subparagraph
      (a)   shall not apply with respect to a law which codifies or recodifies an exemption previously authorized in the Constitution of 1976 or an exemption authorized pursuant to this Constitution.
      (b)   The grant of any exemption from ad valorem taxation shall be subject to the conditions, limitations, and administrative procedures specified by law.

Paragraph III. Exemptions which may be authorized locally.
(a)   (1)   *The governing authority of any county or municipality, subject to the approval of a majority of the qualified electors of such political subdivision voting in a referendum thereon, may exempt from ad valorem taxation, including all such taxation levied for educational purposes and for state purposes, inventories of goods in the process of manufacture or production, and inventories of finished goods.*

   (2)   *Exemptions granted pursuant to this subparagraph (a) may only be revoked by a referendum election called and conducted as provided by law. The call for such referendum shall not be issued within five years from the date such exemptions were first granted and, if the results of the election are in favor of the revocation of such exemptions, then such revocation shall be effective only at the end of a five-year period from the date of such referendum.*

   (3)   *The implementation, administration, and revocation of the exemptions authorized in this subparagraph (a) shall be provided for by law. Until otherwise provided by law, the grant of the exemption shall be subject to the same conditions, limitations, definitions, and procedures provided for the grant of such exemption in the Constitution of 1976 on June 30, 1983.* (Source: Sec St. 2000)
(b)   Repealed (Ibid).

Paragraph IV. Current property tax exemptions preserved. Those types of exemptions from ad valorem taxation provided for by law on June 30, 1983, are hereby continued in effect as statutory law until otherwise provided for by law. Any law which reduces or repeals any homestead exemption in existence on June 30, 1983, or created thereafter must be approved by two-thirds of the members elected to each branch of the General Assembly in a roll-call vote and by a majority of the qualified electors of the state or the affected local taxing jurisdiction voting in a referendum thereon. Any law which reduces or repeals exemptions granted to religious or burial grounds or institutions of purely public charity must be approved by two-thirds of the members elected to each branch of the General Assembly.

Paragraph V. Disabled veteran's homestead exemption. Except as otherwise provided in this paragraph, the amount of the homestead exemption granted to disabled veterans shall be the greater of $32,500.00 or the maximum amount which may be granted to a disabled veteran under Section 802 of Title 38 of the United States Code as hereafter amended. Such exemption shall be granted to: those persons eligible for such exemption on June 30, 1983; to disabled American veterans of any war or armed conflict who are disabled due to loss or loss of use of one lower extremity together with the loss or loss of use of one upper extremity which so affects the functions of balance or propulsion as to preclude locomotion without the aid of braces, crutches, canes, or a wheelchair; and to disabled veterans hereafter becoming eligible for assistance in acquiring housing under Section 801 of the United States Code as hereafter amended. The General Assembly may by general law provide for a different amount or a different method of determining the amount of or eligibility for the homestead exemption granted to disabled veterans. Any such law shall be enacted by a simple majority of the votes of all the members to which each house is entitled and may become effective without referendum. Such law may provide that the amount of or eligibility for the exemption shall be determined by reference to laws enacted by the United States Congress. (Authority OLC, p. 118)

Section IIA.
Homeowner's Incentive Adjustment

Paragraph I. State grants; adjustment amount. For each taxable year, a homeowner's incentive adjustment may be applied to the return of each taxpayer claiming such state-wide homestead exemption as may be specified by general law. The amount of such adjustment may provide a taxpayer with a benefit equivalent to a homestead exemption of up to $18,000.00 of the assessed value of a taxpayer's homestead or the taxpayer's ad valorem property tax liability on the homestead, whichever is lower. The General Assembly may appropriate such amount each year for grants to local governments and school districts as homeowner tax relief grants. The adjustments and grants authorized by this Paragraph shall be made in such manner and shall be subject to the procedures and conditions as may be specified by general law heretofore or hereafter enacted (TBD).

Section III.
Purposes and Method of State Taxation

Paragraph I. Taxation; purposes for which powers may be exercised.

(a) Except as otherwise provided in this Constitution, the power of taxation over the whole state may be exercised for any purpose authorized by law. *Any purpose for which the powers of taxation over the whole state could have been exercised on June 30, 1983, shall continue to be a purpose for which such powers may be exercised.*

(b)   Subject to conditions and limitations as may be provided by law, the power of taxation may be exercised to make grants for tax relief purposes to persons for sales tax paid and not otherwise reimbursed on prescription drugs. Credits or relief provided hereunder may be limited only to such reasonable classifications of taxpayers as may be specified by law.

Paragraph II. Revenue to be paid into general fund.

(a)   Except as otherwise provided in this Constitution, all revenue collected from taxes, fees, and assessments for state purposes, as authorized by revenue measures enacted by the General Assembly, shall be paid into the general fund of the state treasury.

(b)   (1)   As authorized by law providing for the promotion of any one or more types of agricultural products, fees, assessments, and other charges collected on the sale or processing of agricultural products need not be paid into the general fund of the state treasury. The uniformity requirement of this article shall be satisfied by the application of the agricultural promotion program upon the affected products.

       (2)   As used in this subparagraph, "agricultural products" includes, but is not limited to, registered livestock and livestock products, poultry and poultry products, timber and timber products, fish and seafood, and the products of the farms and forests of this state.

Paragraph III. Grants to counties and municipalities. State funds may be granted to counties and municipalities within the state. The grants authorized by this Paragraph shall be made in such manner and form and subject to the procedures and conditions specified by law. The law providing for any such grant may limit the purposes for which the grant funds may be expended.

Section IV.
State Debt

Paragraph I. Purposes for which debt may be incurred.

The state may incur:

(a)   Public debt without limit to repel invasion, suppress insurrection, and defend the state in time of war.

(b)   Public debt to supply a temporary deficit in the state treasury in any fiscal year created by a delay in collecting the taxes of that year. Such debt shall not exceed, in the aggregate, 5 percent of the total revenue receipts, less refunds, of the state treasury in the fiscal year immediately preceding the year in which such debt is incurred. The debt incurred shall be repaid on or before the last day of the fiscal year in which it is incurred out of taxes levied for that fiscal year. No such debt may be incurred in any fiscal year under the provisions of this subparagraph (b) if there is then outstanding unpaid debt from any previous fiscal year which was incurred to supply a temporary deficit in the state treasury.

(c)   General obligation debt to acquire, construct, develop, extend, enlarge, or improve land, waters, property, highways, buildings, structures, equipment, or facilities of the state, its agencies, departments, institutions, and of those state authorities which were created and activated prior to November 8, 1960.

(d)   General obligation debt to provide educational facilities for county and independent school systems and *to provide public library facilities for county and independent school systems, counties, municipalities, and boards of trustees of public libraries or boards of trustees of public library systems, and, when the construction of such educational or library facilities has been completed, the title to such facilities shall be vested in the respective local boards of education, counties, municipalities, or public library boards of trustees for which such facilities were constructed.*

(e) *General obligation debt in order to make loans to counties, municipal corporations, political subdivisions, local authorities, and other local government entities for water or sewerage facilities or systems or for regional or multijurisdictional solid waste recycling or solid waste facilities or systems. It shall not be necessary for the state or a state authority to hold title to or otherwise be the owner of such facilities or systems. General obligation debt for these purposes may be authorized and incurred for administration and disbursement by a state authority created and activated before, on, or after November 8, 1960.*

(f) Guaranteed revenue debt by guaranteeing the payment of revenue obligations issued by an instrumentality of the state if such revenue obligations are issued to finance:

(1) Toll bridges or toll roads.

(2) Land public transportation facilities or systems.

(3) Water facilities or systems.

(4) Sewage facilities or systems.

(5) Loans to, and loan programs for, citizens of the state for educational purposes.

(6) *Regional or multijurisdictional solid waste recycling or solid waste facilities or systems.* (Source: GA.L. p. 3329)

Paragraph II. State general obligation debt and guaranteed revenue debt; limitations.

(a) As used in this Paragraph and Paragraph III of this section, "annual debt service requirements" means the total principal and interest coming due in any state fiscal year. With regard to any issue of debt incurred wholly or in part on a term basis, "annual debt service requirements" means an amount equal to the total principal and interest payments required to retire such issue in full divided by the number of years from its issue date to its maturity date.

(b) No debt may be incurred under subparagraphs (c), (d), and (e) of Paragraph I of this section or Paragraph V of this section at any time when the highest aggregate annual debt service requirements for the then current year or any subsequent year for outstanding general obligation debt and guaranteed revenue debt, including the proposed debt, and the highest aggregate annual payments for the then current year or any subsequent fiscal year of the state under all contracts then in force to which the provisions of the second paragraph of Article IX, Section VI, Paragraph I(a) of the Constitution of 1976 are applicable, exceed 10 percent of the total revenue receipts, less refunds of the state treasury in the fiscal year immediately preceding the year in which any such debt is to be incurred.

(c) No debt may be incurred under subparagraphs (c) and (d) of Paragraph I of this section at any time when the term of the debt is in excess of 25 years.

(d) No guaranteed revenue debt may be incurred to finance water or sewage treatment facilities or systems when the highest aggregate annual debt service requirements for the then current year or any subsequent fiscal year of the state for outstanding or proposed guaranteed revenue debt for water facilities or systems or sewage facilities or systems exceed 1 percent of the total revenue receipts less refunds, of the state treasury in the fiscal year immediately preceding the year in which any such debt is to be incurred.

(e)   The aggregate amount of guaranteed revenue debt incurred to make loans for educational purposes that may be outstanding at any time shall not exceed $18 million, and the aggregate amount of guaranteed revenue debt incurred to purchase, or to lend or deposit against the security of, loans for educational purposes that may be outstanding at any time shall not exceed $72 million.

Paragraph III. State general obligation debt and guaranteed revenue conditions upon issuance; sinking funds and reserve funds.

(a)   (1)   General obligation debt may not be incurred until legislation is enacted stating the purposes, in general or specific terms, for which such issue of debt is to be incurred, specifying the maximum principal amount of such issue and appropriating an amount at least sufficient to pay the highest annual debt service requirements for such issue. All such appropriations for debt service purposes shall not lapse for any reason and shall continue in effect until the debt for which such appropriation was authorized shall have been incurred, but the General Assembly may repeal any such appropriation at any time prior to the incurring of such debt. The General Assembly shall raise by taxation and appropriate each fiscal year, in addition to the sum necessary to make all payments required under contracts entitled to the protection of the second paragraph of Paragraph I(a), Section VI, Article IX of the Constitution of 1976, such amounts as are necessary to pay debt service requirements in such fiscal year on all general obligation debt.

(2)   (A)   The General Assembly shall appropriate to a special trust fund to be designated "State of Georgia General Obligation Debt Sinking Fund" such amounts as are necessary to pay annual debt service requirements on all general obligation debt. The sinking fund shall be used solely for the retirement of general obligation debt payable from the fund. If for any reason the monies in the sinking fund are insufficient to make, when due, all payments required with respect to such general obligation debt, the first revenues thereafter received in the general fund of the state shall be set aside by the appropriate state fiscal officer to the extent necessary to cure the deficiency and shall be deposited by the fiscal officer into the sinking fund. The appropriate state fiscal officer may be required to set aside and apply such revenues at the suit of any holder of any general obligation debt incurred under this section.

(B)   The obligation to make sinking fund deposits as provided in subparagraph (2)(A) shall be subordinate to the obligation imposed upon the fiscal officers of the state pursuant to the provisions of the second paragraph of Paragraph I(a) of Section VI of Article IX of the Constitution of 1976.

(b)   (1)   Guaranteed revenue debt may not be incurred until legislation has been enacted authorizing the guarantee of the specific issue of revenue obligations then proposed, reciting that the General Assembly has determined such obligations will be self-liquidating over the life of the issue (which determination shall be conclusive), specifying the maximum principal amount of such issue and appropriating an amount at least equal to the highest annual debt service requirements for such issue.

(2)   (A)   Each appropriation made for the purposes of subparagraph (b)(1) shall be paid upon the issuance of said obligations into a special trust fund to be designated "State of Georgia Guaranteed Revenue Debt Common Reserve Fund" to be held together with all other

sums similarly appropriated as a common reserve for any payments which may be required by virtue of any guarantee entered into in connection with any issue of guaranteed revenue obligations. No appropriations for the benefit of guaranteed revenue debt shall lapse unless repealed prior to the payment of the appropriation into the common reserve fund.

(B) If any payments are required to be made from the common reserve fund to meet debt service requirements on guaranteed revenue obligations by virtue of an insufficiency of revenues, the amount necessary to cure the deficiency shall be paid from the common reserve fund by the appropriate state fiscal officer. Upon any such payment, the common reserve fund shall be reimbursed from the general funds of the state within ten days following the commencement of any fiscal year of the state for any amounts so paid; provided, however, the obligation to make any such reimbursements shall be subordinate to the obligation imposed upon the fiscal officers of the state pursuant to the second paragraph of Paragraph I(a) of Section VI, Article IX of the Constitution of 1976 and shall also be subordinate to the obligation to make sinking fund deposits for the benefit of general obligation debt. The appropriate state fiscal officer may be required to apply such funds as provided in this subparagraph (b)(2)(B) at the suit of any holder of any such guaranteed revenue obligations.

(C) The amount to the credit of the common reserve fund shall at all times be at least equal to the aggregate highest annual debt service requirements on all outstanding guaranteed revenue obligations entitled to the benefit of the fund. If at the end of any fiscal year of the state the fund is in excess of the required amount, the appropriate state fiscal officer, as designated by law, shall transfer the excess amount to the general funds of the state free of said trust.

(c) The funds in the general obligation debt sinking fund and the guaranteed revenue debt common reserve fund shall be as fully invested as is practicable, consistent with the requirements to make current principal and interest payments. Any such investments shall be restricted to obligations constituting direct and general obligations of the United States government or obligations unconditionally guaranteed as to the payment of principal and interest by the United States government, maturing no longer than 12 months from date of purchase.

Paragraph IV. Certain contracts prohibited. The state, and all state institutions, departments and agencies of the state are prohibited from entering into any contract, except contracts pertaining to guaranteed revenue debt, with any public agency, public corporation, authority, or similar entity if such contract is intended to constitute security for bonds or other obligations issued by any such public agency, public corporation, or authority and, in the event any contract between the state, or any state institution, department or agency of the state and any public agency, public corporation, authority or similar entity, or any revenues from any such contract, is pledged or assigned as security for the repayment of bonds or other obligations, then and in either such event, the appropriation or expenditure of any funds of the state for the payment of obligations under any such contract shall likewise be prohibited.

Paragraph V. Refunding of debt. The state may incur general obligation debt or guaranteed revenue debt to fund or refund any such debt or to fund or refund any obligations issued upon the security of contracts to which the provisions of the second paragraph of Paragraph I(a), Section VI, Article IX of the Constitution of 1976 are applicable. The issuance of any such debt for the purposes of said funding or refunding shall be subject to the 10 percent limitation in Paragraph II(b) of this section to the same extent as debt incurred under Paragraph I of this section; provided, however, in making such computation the annual debt service requirements and annual contract payments remaining on the debt or obligations being funded or refunded shall not be taken into account. The issuance of such debt may be accomplished by resolution of the Georgia State Financing and Investment Commission without any action on the part of the General Assembly and any appropriation made or required to be made with respect to the debt or obligation being funded or refunded shall immediately attach and inure to the benefit of the obligations to be issued in connection with such funding or refunding. Debt incurred in connection with any such funding or refunding shall be the same as that originally authorized by the General Assembly, except that general obligation debt may be incurred to fund or refund obligations issued upon the security of contracts to which the provisions of the second paragraph of Paragraph I(a), Section VI, Article IX of the Constitution of 1976 are applicable and the continuing appropriations required to be made under this Constitution shall immediately attach and inure to the benefit of the obligation to be issued in connection with such funding or refunding with the same force and effect as though said obligations so funded or refunded had originally been issued as a general obligation debt authorized hereunder. The term of a funding or refunding issue pursuant to this Paragraph shall not extend beyond the term of the original debt or obligation and the total interest on the funding or refunding issue shall not exceed the total interest to be paid on such original debt or obligation. The principal amount of any debt issued in connection with such funding or refunding may exceed the principal amount being funded or refunded to the extent necessary to provide for the payment of any premium thereby incurred.

Paragraph VI. Faith and credit of state pledged debt may be validated. The full faith, credit, and taxing power of the state are hereby pledged to the payment of all public debt incurred under this article and all such debt and the interest on the debt shall be exempt from taxation. Such debt may be validated by judicial proceedings in the manner provided by law. Such validation shall be incontestable and conclusive.

Paragraph VII. Georgia State Financing and Investment Commission; duties.
(a) There shall be a Georgia State Financing and Investment Commission. The commission shall consist of the Governor, the President of the Senate, the Speaker of the House of Representatives, the State Auditor, the Attorney General, the director, Fiscal Division, Department of Administrative Services, or such other officer as may be designated by law, and the Commissioner of Agriculture. The commission shall be responsible for the issuance of all public debt and for the proper application, as provided by law, of the proceeds of such debt to the purposes for which it is incurred; provided, however, the proceeds from guaranteed revenue obligations shall be paid to the issuer thereof and such proceeds and the application thereof shall be the responsibility of such issuer. Debt to be incurred at the same time for more than one purpose may be combined in one issue without stating the purpose separately but the proceeds thereof must be allocated, disbursed and used solely in accordance with the original purpose and without exceeding the principal amount authorized for each purpose set forth in the authorization of the General Assembly and to the extent not so used shall be used to purchase and retire public debt. The commission shall be responsible for the investment of all proceeds to be administered by it and, as provided by law, the income earned on any such investments may be used to pay operating expenses of the commission or placed in a common debt retirement fund

and used to purchase and retire any public debt, or any bonds or obligations issued by any public agency, public corporation or authority which are secured by a contract to which the provisions of the second paragraph of Paragraph I(a) of Section VI, Article IX of the Constitution of 1976 are applicable. The commission shall have such additional responsibilities, powers, and duties as are provided by law.

(b) *Notwithstanding subparagraph (a) of this Paragraph, proceeds from general obligation debt issued for making loans to local government entities for water or sewerage facilities or systems or for regional or multijurisdictional solid waste recycling or solid waste facilities or systems as provided in Paragraph I(e) of this section shall be paid or transferred to and administered and invested by the unit of state government or state authority made responsible by law for such activities, and the proceeds and investment earnings thereof shall be applied and disbursed by such unit or authority.* (Source: GA.L., 1962 p. 3329)

Paragraph VIII. State aid forbidden. Except as provided in this Constitution, the credit of the state shall not be pledged or loaned to any individual, company, corporation, or association. The state shall not become a joint owner or stockholder in or with any individual, company, association, or corporation.

Paragraph IX. Construction. Paragraphs I through VIII of this section are for the purpose of providing an effective method of financing the state's needs and their provisions and any law now or hereafter enacted by the General Assembly in furtherance of their provisions shall be liberally construed to effect such purpose. Insofar as any such provisions or any such law may be inconsistent with any other provisions of this Constitution or of any other law, the provisions of such Paragraphs and laws enacted in furtherance of such Paragraphs shall be controlling; provided, however, the provisions of such Paragraphs shall not be so broadly construed as to cause the same to be unconstitutional and in connection with any such construction such Paragraphs shall be deemed to contain such implied limitations as shall be required to accomplish the foregoing.

Paragraph X. Assumption of debts forbidden; exceptions. The state shall not assume the debt, or any part thereof, of any county, municipality, or other political subdivision of the state, unless such debt be contracted to enable the state to repel invasion, suppress civil disorders or insurrection, or defend itself in time of war.

Paragraph XI. Section not to unlawfully impair contracts or revive obligations previously voided. The provisions of this section shall not be construed so as to:
(a) Unlawfully impair the obligation of any contract in effect on June 30, 1983.
(b) Revive or permit the revival of the obligation of any bond or security declared to be void by the Constitution of 1976 or any previous Constitution of this state.

Paragraph XI. NOTE: THERE WILL BE A NEW PARAGRAPH XII INSERTED HERE, WRITTEN TO REFLECT THE AMENDMENT ON THE ALLOWANCE OF MULTI-YEAR CONTRACTS FOR ENERGY CONSERVATION AS PASSED IN 2010.

Article VIII.
Education

Section I.
Public Education

Paragraph I. Public education; free public education prior to college or post-secondary level; support by taxation. The provision of an adequate public education for the citizens shall be a primary obligation of the State of Georgia. Public education for the citizens prior to the college or postsecondary level shall be free and shall be provided for by taxation. The expense of other public education shall be provided for in such manner and in such amount as may be provided by law.

Section II.
State Board of Education

Paragraph I. State Board of Education.
(a) There shall be a State Board of Education which shall consist of one member from each congressional district in the state appointed by the Governor and confirmed by the Senate. The Governor shall not be a member of said board. The ten members in office on June 30, 1983, shall serve out the remainder of their respective terms. As each term of office expires, the Governor shall appoint a successor as herein provided. The terms of office of all members appointed after the effective date of this Constitution shall be for seven years. Members shall serve until their successors are appointed and qualified. In the event of a vacancy on the board by death, resignation, removal, or any reason other than expiration of a member's term, the Governor shall fill such vacancy; and the person so appointed shall serve until confirmed by the Senate and, upon confirmation, shall serve for the unexpired term of office.
(b) The State Board of Education shall have such powers and duties as provided by law.
(c) The State Board of Education may accept bequests, donations, grants, and transfers of land, buildings, and other property for the use of the state educational system.
(d) The qualifications, compensation, and removal from office of the members of the board of education shall be as provided by law.

Section III.
State School Superintendent

Paragraph I. State School Superintendent. There shall be a State School Superintendent, who shall be the executive officer of the State Board of Education, elected at the same time and in the same manner and for the same term as that of the Governor. The State School Superintendent shall have such qualifications and shall be paid such compensation as may be fixed by law. No member of the State Board of Education shall be eligible for election as State School Superintendent during the time for which such member shall have been appointed.

Section IV.
Board of Regents

Paragraph I. University System of Georgia; Board of Regents.

(a) There shall be a Board of Regents of the University System of Georgia which shall consist of one member from each congressional district in the state and five additional members from the state at large, appointed by the Governor and confirmed by the Senate. The Governor shall not be a member of said board. The members in office on June 30, 1983, shall serve out the remainder of their respective terms. As each term of office expires, the Governor shall appoint a successor as herein provided. All such terms of members shall be for seven years. Members shall serve until their successors are appointed and qualified. In the event of a vacancy on the board by death, resignation, removal, or any reason other than the expiration of a member's term, the Governor shall fill such vacancy; and the person so appointed shall serve until confirmed by the Senate and, upon confirmation, shall serve for the unexpired term of office.

(b) The Board of Regents shall have the exclusive authority to create new public colleges, junior colleges, and universities in the State of Georgia, subject to approval by majority vote in the House of Representatives and the Senate. Such vote shall not be required to change the status of a college, institution or university existing on the effective date of this Constitution. The government, control, and management of the University System of Georgia and all of the institutions in said system shall be vested in the Board of Regents of the University System of Georgia.

(c) All appropriations made for the use of any or all institutions in the university system shall be paid to the board of regents in a lump sum, with the power and authority in said board to allocate and distribute the same among the institutions under its control in such way and manner and in such amounts as will further an efficient and economical administration of the university system.

(d) The Board of Regents may hold, purchase, lease, sell, convey, or otherwise dispose of public property, execute conveyances thereon, and utilize the proceeds arising therefrom; may exercise the power of eminent domain in the manner provided by law; and shall have such other powers and duties as provided by law.

(e) The Board of Regents may accept bequests, donations, grants, and transfers of land, buildings, and other property for the use of the University System of Georgia.

(f) The qualifications, compensation, and removal from office of the members of the Board of Regents shall be as provided by law.

Section V.
Local School Systems

Paragraph I. School systems continued; consolidation of school systems authorized; new independent school systems prohibited. Authority is granted to county and area boards of education to establish and maintain public schools within their limits. Existing county and independent school systems shall be continued, except that the General Assembly may provide by law for the consolidation of two or more county school systems, independent school systems, portions thereof, or any combination thereof into a single county or area school system under the control and management of a county or area board of education, under such terms and conditions as the General Assembly may prescribe; but no such consolidation shall become effective until approved by a majority of the qualified voters voting thereon in each separate school system proposed to be consolidated. No independent school system shall hereafter be established.

Paragraph II. Boards of education. Each school system shall be under the management and control of a board of education, the members of which shall be elected as provided by law. School board members shall reside within the territory embraced by the school system and shall have such compensation and additional qualifications as may be provided by law. *Any board of education to which the members are appointed as of December 31, 1992, shall continue as an appointed board of education through December 31, 1993, and the appointed members of such board of education who are in office on December 31, 1992, shall continue in office as members of such appointed board until December 31, 1993, on which date the terms of office of all appointed members shall end.* (Source: GA.L. 1991, p. 3032)

Paragraph III. School superintendents. There shall be a school superintendent of each system appointed by the board of education who shall be the executive officer of the board of education and shall have such qualifications, powers, and duties as provided by general law. *Any elected school superintendent in office on January 1, 1993, shall continue to serve out the remainder of his or her respective term of office and shall be replaced by an appointee of the board of education at the expiration of such term.* (Source: GA.L. 1991, p. 3032)

Paragraph IV. Note: Old wording repealed and section is Reserved. (Ibid).

Paragraph V. Power of boards to contract with each other.
(a) Any two or more boards of education may contract with each other for the care, education, and transportation of pupils and for such other activities as they may be authorized by law to perform.
(b) The General Assembly may provide by law for the sharing of facilities or services by and between local boards of education under such joint administrative authority as may be authorized.

Paragraph VI. Power of boards to accept bequests, donations, grants, and transfers. The board of education of each school system may accept bequests, donations, grants, and transfers of land, buildings, and other property for the use of such system.

Paragraph VII. Special schools.
(a) The General Assembly may provide by law for the creation of special schools in such areas as may require them and may provide for the participation of local boards of education in the establishment of such schools under such terms and conditions as it may provide; but no bonded indebtedness may be incurred nor a school tax levied for the support of special schools without the approval of a majority of the qualified voters voting thereon in each of the systems affected. Any special schools shall be operated in conformity with regulations of the State Board of Education pursuant to provisions of law. The state is authorized to expend funds for the support and maintenance of special schools in such amount and manner as may be provided by law.
(b) Nothing contained herein shall be construed to affect the authority of local boards of education or of the state to support and maintain special schools created prior to June 30, 1983.

Section VI.
Local Taxation for Education

Paragraph I. Local taxation for education.

(a) The board of education of each school system shall annually certify to its fiscal authority or authorities a school tax not greater than 20 mills per dollar for the support and maintenance of education. Said fiscal authority or authorities shall annually levy said tax upon the assessed value of all taxable property within the territory served by said school system, provided that the levy made by an area board of education, which levy shall not be greater than 20 mills per dollar, shall be in such amount and within such limits as may be prescribed by local law applicable thereto.

(b) School tax funds shall be expended only for the support and maintenance of public schools, public vocational-technical schools, public education, and activities necessary or incidental thereto, including school lunch purposes.

(c) The 20 mill limitation provided for in subparagraph (a) of this Paragraph shall not apply to those school systems which are authorized on June 30, 1983, to levy a school tax in excess thereof.

(d) The method of certification and levy of the school tax provided for in subparagraph(a) of this Paragraph shall not apply to those systems that are authorized on June 30, 1983, to utilize a different method of certification and levy of such tax; but the General Assembly may by law require that such systems be brought into conformity with the method of certification and levy herein provided.

Paragraph II. Increasing or removing tax rate. The mill limitation in effect on June 30, 1983, for any school system may be increased or removed by action of the respective boards of education, but only after such action has been approved by a majority of the qualified voters voting thereon in the particular school system to be affected in the manner provided by law.

Paragraph III. School tax collection reimbursement. The General Assembly may by general law require local boards of education to reimburse the appropriate governing authority for the collection of school taxes, provided that any rate established may be reduced by local act.

Paragraph IV. Sales tax for educational purposes.

(a) *The board of education of each school district in a county in which no independent school district is located may by resolution and the board of education of each county school district and the board of education of each independent school district located within such county may by concurrent resolutions impose, levy, and collect a sales and use tax for educational purposes of such school districts conditioned upon approval by a majority of the qualified voters residing within the limits of the local taxing jurisdiction voting in a referendum thereon. This tax shall be at the rate of 1 percent and shall be imposed for a period of time not to exceed five years, but in all other respects, except as otherwise provided in this Paragraph, shall correspond to and be levied in the same manner as the tax provided for by Article 3 of Chapter 8 of Title 48 of the Official Code of Georgia Annotated, relating to the special county 1 percent sales and use tax, as now or hereafter amended. Proceedings for the reimposition of such tax shall be in the same manner as proceedings for the initial imposition of the tax, but the newly authorized tax shall not be imposed until the expiration of the tax then in effect.*

(b) *The purpose or purposes for which the proceeds of the tax are to be used and may be expended include:*

(1) *Capital outlay projects for educational purposes;*

(2) *The retirement of previously incurred general obligation debt with respect only to capital outlay projects of the school system; provided, however, that the tax authorized under this Paragraph shall only be expended for the purpose authorized under this subparagraph (b)(2) if all ad valorem property taxes levied or scheduled to be levied prior to the maturity of any such then outstanding general obligation debt to be retired by the proceeds of the tax imposed under this Paragraph shall be reduced by a total amount equal to the total amount of proceeds of the tax imposed under this Paragraph to be applied to retire such bonded indebtedness. In the event of failure to comply with the requirements of this subparagraph (b)(2), as certified by the Department of Revenue, no further funds shall be expended under this subparagraph (b)(2) by such county or independent board of education and all such funds shall be maintained in a separate, restricted account and held solely for the expenditure for future capital outlay projects for educational purposes; or*

(3) *A combination of the foregoing.*

(c) *The resolution calling for the imposition of the tax and the ballot question shall each describe:*

(1) *The specific capital outlay projects to be funded, or the specific debt to be retired, or both, if applicable;*

(2) *The maximum cost of such project or projects and, if applicable, the maximum amount of debt to be retired, which cost and amount of debt shall also be the maximum amount of net proceeds to be raised by the tax; and*

(3) *The maximum period of time, to be stated in calendar years or calendar quarters and not to exceed five years.*

(d) *Nothing in this Paragraph shall prohibit a county and those municipalities located in such county from imposing as additional taxes local sales and use taxes authorized by general law.*

(e) *The tax imposed pursuant to this Paragraph shall not be subject to and shall not count with respect to any general law limitation regarding the maximum amount of local sales and use taxes which may be levied in any jurisdiction in this state.*

(f) *The tax imposed pursuant to this Paragraph shall not be subject to any sales and use tax exemption with respect to the sale or use of food and beverages which is imposed by law.*

(g) *The net proceeds of the tax shall be distributed between the county school district and the independent school districts, or portion thereof, located in such county according to the ratio the student enrollment in each school district, or portion thereof, bears to the total student enrollment of all school districts in the county or upon such other formula for distribution as may be authorized by local law. For purposes of this subparagraph, student enrollment shall be based on the latest FTE count prior to the referendum on imposing the tax.*

(h) *Excess proceeds of the tax which remain following expenditure of proceeds for authorized projects or purposes for education shall be used solely for the purpose of reducing any indebtedness of the school system. In the event there is no indebtedness, such excess proceeds shall be used by such school system for the purpose of reducing its millage rate in an amount equivalent to the amount of such excess proceeds.*

(i) *The tax authorized by this Paragraph may be imposed, levied, and collected as provided in this Paragraph without further action by the General Assembly, but the General Assembly shall be authorized by general law to further define and implement its provisions including, but not limited to, the authority to specify the percentage of net proceeds to be allocated among the projects and purposes for which the tax was levied.*

(j) (1) *Notwithstanding any provision of any constitutional amendment continued in force and effect pursuant to Article XI, Section I, Paragraph IV(a) and except as otherwise provided in subparagraph (j)(2) of this Paragraph, any political subdivision whose ad valorem taxing powers are restricted pursuant to such a constitutional amendment may receive the proceeds of the tax authorized under this Paragraph or of any local sales and use tax authorized by general law, or any combination of such taxes, without any corresponding limitation of its ad valorem taxing powers which would otherwise be required under such constitutional amendment.*

(2) *The restriction on and limitation of ad valorem taxing powers described in subparagraph (j)(1) of this Paragraph shall remain applicable with respect to proceeds received from the levy of a local sales and use tax specifically authorized by a constitutional amendment in force and effect pursuant to Article XI, Section I, Paragraph IV(a), as opposed to a local sales and use tax authorized by this Paragraph or by general law.* (Source: Sec. St. 1997)

Section VII.
Educational Assistance

Paragraph I. Educational assistance programs authorized.

(a) Pursuant to laws now or hereafter enacted by the General Assembly, public funds may be expended for any of the following purposes:

(1) To provide grants, scholarships, loans, or other assistance to students and to parents of students for educational purposes.

(2) To provide for a program of guaranteed loans to students and to parents of students for educational purposes and to pay interest, interest subsidies, and fees to lenders on such loans. The General Assembly is authorized to provide such tax exemptions to lenders as shall be deemed advisable in connection with such program.

(3) To match funds now or hereafter available for student assistance pursuant to any federal law.

(4) To provide grants, scholarships, loans, or other assistance to public employees for educational purposes.

(5) To provide for the purchase of loans made to students for educational purposes who have completed a program of study in a field in which critical shortages exist and for cancellation of repayment of such loans, interest, and charges thereon.

(b) Contributions made in support of any educational assistance program now or hereafter established under provisions of this section may be deductible for state income tax purposes as now or hereafter provided by law.

(c) *The General Assembly shall be authorized by general law to provide for an education trust fund to assist students and parents of students in financing postsecondary education and to provide for contracts between the fund and purchasers for the advance payment of tuition by each purchaser for a qualified beneficiary to attend a state institution of higher education. Such general law shall provide for such terms, conditions, and limitations as the General Assembly shall deem necessary for the implementation of this subparagraph. Notwithstanding any provision of this Constitution to the contrary, the General Assembly shall be authorized to provide for the guarantee of such contracts with state revenues.* (Authority OLC, pp. 128–129)

Paragraph II. Guaranteed revenue debt. Guaranteed revenue debt may be incurred to provide funds to make loans to students and to parents of students for educational purposes, to purchase loans made to students and to parents of students for educational purposes, or to lend or make deposits of such funds with lenders which shall be secured by loans made to students and to parents of students for educational purposes. Any such debt shall be incurred in accordance with the procedures and requirements of Article VII, Section IV of this Constitution.

Paragraph III. Public authorities. Public authorities or public corporations heretofore or hereafter created for such purposes shall be authorized to administer educational assistance programs and, in connection therewith, may exercise such powers as may now or hereafter be provided by law.

Paragraph IV. Waiver of tuition. The Board of Regents of the University System of Georgia shall be authorized to establish programs allowing attendance at units of the University System of Georgia without payment of tuition or other fees, but the General Assembly may provide by law for the establishment of any such program for the benefit of elderly citizens of the state.

Article IX.
Counties and Municipal Corporations

Section I.
Counties

Paragraph I. Counties a body corporate and politic. Each county shall be a body corporate and politic with such governing authority and with such powers and limitations as are provided in this Constitution and as provided by law. The governing authorities of the several counties shall remain as prescribed by law on June 30, 1983, until otherwise provided by law.

Paragraph II. Number of counties limited; county boundaries and county sites; county consolidation.
(a) There shall not be more than 159 counties in this state.
(b) The metes and bounds of the several counties and the county sites shall remain as prescribed by law on June 30, 1983, unless changed under the operation of a general law.
(c) The General Assembly may provide by law for the consolidation of two or more counties into one or the division of a county and the merger of portions thereof into other counties under such terms and conditions as it may prescribe; but no such consolidation, division, or merger shall become effective unless approved by a majority of the qualified voters voting thereon in each of the counties proposed to be consolidated, divided, or merged.

Paragraph III. County officers; election; term; compensation.
(a) The clerk of the superior court, judge of the probate court, sheriff, tax receiver, tax collector, and tax commissioner, where such office has replaced the tax receiver and tax collector, shall be elected by the qualified voters of their respective counties for terms of four years and shall have such qualifications, powers, and duties as provided by general law.
(b) County officers listed in subparagraph (a) of this Paragraph may be on a fee basis, salary basis, or fee basis supplemented by salary, in such manner as may be directed by law. Minimum compensation for said county officers may be established by the General Assembly by general law. Such minimum compensation may be supplemented by local law or, if such authority is delegated by local law, by action of the county governing authority.
(c) The General Assembly may consolidate the offices of tax receiver and tax collector into the office of tax commissioner.

Paragraph IV. Civil service systems. The General Assembly may by general law authorize the establishment by county governing authorities of civil service systems covering county employees or covering county employees and employees of the elected county officers.

Section II.
Home Rule for Counties and Municipalities

Paragraph I. Home rule for counties.
(a) The governing authority of each county shall have legislative power to adopt clearly reasonable ordinances, resolutions, or regulations relating to its property, affairs, and local government for which no provision has been made by

general law and which is not inconsistent with this Constitution or any local law applicable thereto. Any such local law shall remain in force and effect until amended or repealed as provided in subparagraph (b). This, however, shall not restrict the authority of the General Assembly by general law to further define this power or to broaden, limit, or otherwise regulate the exercise thereof. The General Assembly shall not pass any local law to repeal, modify, or supersede any action taken by a county governing authority under this section except as authorized under subparagraph (c) hereof.

(b) Except as provided in subparagraph (c), a county may, as an incident of its home rule power, amend or repeal the local acts applicable to its governing authority by following either of the procedures hereinafter set forth:

   (1) Such local acts may be amended or repealed by a resolution or ordinance duly adopted at two regular consecutive meetings of the county governing authority not less than seven nor more than 60 days apart. A notice containing a synopsis of the proposed amendment or repeal shall be published in the official county organ once a week for three weeks within a period of 60 days immediately preceding its final adoption. Such notice shall state that a copy of the proposed amendment or repeal is on file in the office of the clerk of the superior court of the county for the purpose of examination and inspection by the public. The clerk of the superior court shall furnish anyone, upon written request, a copy of the proposed amendment or repeal. No amendment or repeal hereunder shall be valid to change or repeal an amendment adopted pursuant to a referendum as provided in (2) of this subparagraph or to change or repeal a local act of the General Assembly ratified in a referendum by the electors of such county unless at least 12 months have elapsed after such referendum. No amendment hereunder shall be valid if inconsistent with any provision of this Constitution or if provision has been made therefor by general law.

   (2) Amendments to or repeals of such local acts or ordinances, resolutions, or regulations adopted pursuant to subparagraph (a) hereof may be initiated by a petition filed with the judge of the probate court of the county containing, in cases of counties with a population of 5,000 or less, the signatures of at least 25 percent of the electors registered to vote in the last general election; in cases of counties with a population of more than 5,000 but not more than 50,000, at least 20 percent of the electors registered to vote in the last general election; and, in cases of a county with a population of more than 50,000, at least 10 percent of the electors registered to vote in the last general election, which petition shall specifically set forth the exact language of the proposed amendment or repeal. The judge of the probate court shall determine the validity of such petition within 60 days of its being filed with the judge of the probate court. In the event the judge of the probate court determines that such petition is valid, it shall be his duty to issue the call for an election for the purpose of submitting such amendment or repeal to the registered electors of the county for their approval or rejection. Such call shall be issued not less than ten nor more than 60 days after the date of the filing of the petition. He shall set the date of such election for a day not less than 60 nor more than 90 days after the date of such filing. The judge of the probate court shall cause a notice of the date of said election to be published in the official organ of the county once a week for three weeks immediately preceding such date. Said notice shall also contain a synopsis of the proposed amendment or repeal and shall

state that a copy thereof is on file in the office of the judge of the probate court of the county for the purpose of examination and inspection by the public. The judge of the probate court shall furnish anyone, upon written request, a copy of the proposed amendment or repeal. If more than one-half of the votes cast on such question are for approval of the amendment or repeal, it shall become of full force and effect; otherwise, it shall be void and of no force and effect. The expense of such election shall be borne by the county, and it shall be the duty of the judge of the probate court to hold and conduct such election. Such election shall be held under the same laws and rules and regulations as govern special elections, except as otherwise provided herein. It shall be the duty of the judge of the probate court to canvass the returns and declare and certify the result of the election. It shall be his further duty to certify the result thereof to the Secretary of State in accordance with the provisions of subparagraph (g) of this Paragraph. A referendum on any such amendment or repeal shall not be held more often than once each year. No amendment hereunder shall be valid if inconsistent with any provision of this Constitution or if provision has been made therefor by general law. In the event that the judge of the probate court determines that such petition was not valid, he shall cause to be published in explicit detail the reasons why such petition is not valid; provided, however, that, in any proceeding in which the validity of the petition is at issue, the tribunal considering such issue shall not be limited by the reasons assigned. Such publication shall be in the official organ of the county in the week immediately following the date on which such petition is declared to be not valid.

(c) The power granted to counties in subparagraphs (a) and (b) above shall not be construed to extend to the following matters or any other matters which the General Assembly by general law has preempted or may hereafter preempt, but such matters shall be the subject of general law or the subject of local acts of the General Assembly to the extent that the enactment of such local acts is otherwise permitted under this Constitution:

(1) Action affecting any elective county office, the salaries thereof, or the personnel thereof, except the personnel subject to the jurisdiction of the county governing authority.

(2) Action affecting the composition, form, procedure for election or appointment, compensation, and expenses and allowances in the nature of compensation of the county governing authority.

(3) Action defining any criminal offense or providing for criminal punishment.

(4) Action adopting any form of taxation beyond that authorized by law or by this Constitution.

(5) Action extending the power of regulation over any business activity regulated by the Georgia Public Service Commission beyond that authorized by local or general law or by this Constitution.

(6) Action affecting the exercise of the power of eminent domain.

(7) Action affecting any court or the personnel thereof.

(8) Action affecting any public school system.

(d) The power granted in subparagraphs (a) and (b) of this Paragraph shall not include the power to take any action affecting the private or civil law governing private or civil relationships, except as is incident to the exercise of an independent governmental power.

(e) Nothing in subparagraphs (a), (b), (c), or (d) shall affect the provisions of subparagraph (f) of this Paragraph.

(f) The governing authority of each county is authorized to fix the salary, compensation, and expenses of those employed by such governing authority and to establish and maintain retirement or pension systems, insurance, workers' compensation, and hospitalization benefits for said employees.

(g) No amendment or revision of any local act made pursuant to subparagraph (b) of this section shall become effective until a copy of such amendment or revision, a copy of the required notice of publication, and an affidavit of a duly authorized representative of the newspaper in which such notice was published to the effect that said notice has been published as provided in said subparagraph has been filed with the Secretary of State. The Secretary of State shall provide for the publication and distribution of all such amendments and revisions at least annually.

Paragraph II. Home rule for municipalities. The General Assembly may provide by law for the self-government of municipalities and to that end is expressly given the authority to delegate its power so that matters pertaining to municipalities may be dealt with without the necessity of action by the General Assembly.

Paragraph III. Supplementary powers.

(a) In addition to and supplementary of all powers possessed by or conferred upon any county, municipality, or any combination thereof, any county, municipality, or any combination thereof may exercise the following powers and provide the following services:

(1) Police and fire protection.

(2) Garbage and solid waste collection and disposal.

(3) Public health facilities and services, including hospitals, ambulance and emergency rescue services, and animal control.

(4) Street and road construction and maintenance, including curbs, sidewalks, street lights, and devices to control the flow of traffic on streets and roads constructed by counties and municipalities or any combination thereof.

(5) Parks, recreational areas, programs, and facilities.

(6) Storm water and sewage collection and disposal systems.

(7) Development, storage, treatment, purification, and distribution of water.

(8) Public housing.

(9) Public transportation.

(10) Libraries, archives, and arts and sciences programs and facilities.

(11) Terminal and dock facilities and parking facilities.

(12) Codes, including building, housing, plumbing, and electrical codes.

(13) Air quality control.

(14) The power to maintain and modify heretofore existing retirement or pension systems, including such systems heretofore created by general laws of local application by population classification, and to continue in effect or modify other benefits heretofore provided as a part of or in addition to such retirement or pension systems and the power to create and maintain retirement or pension systems for any elected or appointed public officers and employees whose compensation is paid in whole or in part from county or municipal funds and for the beneficiaries of such officers and employees.

(b) Unless otherwise provided by law,

(1) No county may exercise any of the powers listed in subparagraph (a) of this Paragraph or provide any service listed therein inside the boundaries of any municipality or any other county except by contract with the municipality or county affected; and

(2) No municipality may exercise any of the powers listed in subparagraph (a) of this Paragraph or provide any service listed therein outside its own boundaries except by contract with the county or municipality affected.

(c) Nothing contained within this Paragraph shall operate to prohibit the General Assembly from enacting general laws relative to the subject matters listed in subparagraph (a) of this Paragraph or to prohibit the General Assembly by general law from regulating, restricting, or limiting the exercise of the powers listed therein; but it may not withdraw any such powers.

(d) Except as otherwise provided in subparagraph (b) of this Paragraph, the General Assembly shall act upon the subject matters listed in subparagraph (a) of this Paragraph only by general law.

Paragraph IV. Planning and zoning. The governing authority of each county and of each municipality may adopt plans and may exercise the power of zoning. This authorization shall not prohibit the General Assembly from enacting general laws establishing procedures for the exercise of such power.

Paragraph V. Eminent domain. The governing authority of each county and of each municipality may exercise the power of eminent domain for *any public purpose subject to any limitations on the exercise of such power as may be provided by general law. Notwithstanding the provisions of any local amendment to the Constitution continued in effect pursuant to Article XI, Section I, Paragraph IV or any existing general law , each exercise of eminent domain by a nonelected housing or development authority shall be first approved by the elected governing authority of the county or municipality within which the property is located.*

Paragraph VI. Special districts. As hereinafter provided in this Paragraph, special districts may be created for the provision of local government services within such districts; and fees, assessments, and taxes may be levied and collected within such districts to pay, wholly or partially, the cost of providing such services therein and to construct and maintain facilities therefor. Such special districts may be created and fees, assessments, or taxes may be levied and collected therein by any one or more of the following methods:

(a) By general law which directly creates the districts.

(b) By general law which requires the creation of districts under conditions specified by such general law.

(c) By municipal or county ordinance or resolution, except that no such ordinance or resolution may supersede a law enacted by the General Assembly pursuant to subparagraphs (a) or (b) of this Paragraph.

Paragraph VII. Community redevelopment.

(a) Each condemnation of privately held property for redevelopment purposes must be approved by vote of the elected governing authority of the city within which the property is located, if any, or otherwise by the governing authority of the county within which the property is located. The power of eminent domain shall not be used for redevelopment purposes by any entity, except for public use, as defined by general law (Source: Kemp, 2006). *NOTE: THIS PARAGRAPH WILL BE REWRITTEN AGAIN TO REFLECT THE PASSAGE OF AN ADDITIONAL AMENDMENT IN 2008 TO ALLOW THE SCHOOL DISTRICTS TO USE TAX FUNDS FOR COMMUNITY REDEVELOPMENT PURPOSES.*

(1) The General Assembly may authorize any county, municipality, or housing authority to undertake and carry out community redevelopment (Source: Kemp Election results, 2006). *NOTE: THIS SECTION WAS CHANGED IN 2006 TO DELETE THE PHRASE: "which may include*

the sale or other disposition of property acquired by eminent domain to private enterprise for private uses." THIS WAS DUE TO POPULAR HOSTILITY TO THE U.S. SUPREME COURT DECISION IN KELO v. CITY OF NEW LONDON [545 U.S. 469 2005].

(b) The General Assembly is also authorized to grant to counties or municipalities for redevelopment purposes and in connection with redevelopment programs, as such purposes and programs are defined by general law, the power to issue tax allocation bonds, as defined by such law, and the power to incur other obligations, without either such bonds or obligations constituting debt within the meaning of Section V of this article, and the power to enter into contracts for any period not exceeding 30 years with private persons, firms, corporations, and business entities. *Such general law may authorize the use of county, municipal, and school tax funds, or any combination thereof, to fund such redevelopment purposes and programs, including the payment of debt service on tax allocation bonds, notwithstanding Section VI of Article VIII or any other provision of this Constitution and regardless of whether any county, municipality, or local board of education approved the use of such tax funds for such purposes and programs before January 1, 2009. No county, municipal, or school tax funds may be used for such purposes and programs without the approval by resolution of the applicable governing body of the county, municipality, or local board of education. No school tax funds may be used for such purposes and programs except as authorized by general law after January 1, 2009; provided, however, that any school tax funds pledged for the repayment of tax allocation bonds which have been judicially validated pursuant to general law shall continue to be used for such purposes and programs.* Notwithstanding the grant of these powers pursuant to general law, no county or municipality may exercise these powers unless so authorized by local law and unless such powers are exercised in conformity with those terms and conditions for such exercise as established by that local law. The provisions of any such local law shall conform to those requirements established by general law regarding such powers. No such local law, or any amendment thereto, shall become effective unless approved in a referendum by a majority of the qualified voters voting thereon in the county or municipality directly affected by that local law.

(c) *The General Assembly is authorized to provide by general law for the creation of enterprise zones by counties or municipalities, or both. Such law may provide for exemptions, credits, or reductions of any tax or taxes levied within such zones by the state, a county, a municipality, or any combination thereof. Such exemptions shall be available only to such persons, firms, or corporations which create job opportunities within the enterprise zone for unemployed, low, and moderate income persons in accordance with the standards set forth in such general law. Such general law shall further define enterprise zones so as to limit such tax exemptions, credits, or reductions to persons and geographic areas which are determined to be underdeveloped as evidenced by the unemployment rate and the average personal income in the area when compared to the remainder of the state. The General Assembly may by general law further define areas qualified for creation of enterprise zones and may provide for all matters relative to the creation, approval, and termination of such zones.*

(d) *The existence in a community of real property which is maintained in a blighted condition increases the burdens of state and local government by increasing the need for governmental services, including but not limited to social services, public safety services, and code enforcement services. Rehabilitation of blighted property decreases the need for such governmental services. In recognition of such service needs and in order to encourage community redevelopment, the counties and municipalities of* this state are authorized to establish community redevelopment tax incentive programs as authorized in this subparagraph. A community redevelopment tax incentive program shall be established by ordinance of the county or municipality. Any such program and ordinance shall include the following elements:

(1) The ordinance shall specify ascertainable standards which shall be applied in determining whether property is maintained in a blighted condition. The ordinance shall provide that property shall not be subject to official identification as maintained in a blighted condition and shall not be subject to increased taxation if the property is a dwelling house which is being used as the primary residence of one or more persons; and

(2) The ordinance shall establish a procedure for the official identification of real property in the county or municipality which is maintained in a blighted condition. Such procedure shall include notice to the property owner and the opportunity for a hearing with respect to such determination.

(3) The ordinance shall specify an increased rate of ad valorem taxation to be applied to property which has been officially identified as maintained in a blighted condition. Such increase in the rate of taxation shall be accomplished through application of a factor to the millage rate applied to the property, so that such property shall be taxed at a higher millage rate than the millage rate generally applied in the county or municipality, or otherwise as may be provided by general law.

(4) The ordinance may, but shall not be required to, segregate revenues arising from any increased rate of ad valorem taxation and provide for use of such revenues only for community redevelopment purposes;

(5) The ordinance shall specify ascertainable standards for rehabilitation through remedial actions or redevelopment with which the owner of property may comply in order to have the property removed from identification as maintained in a blighted condition. As used herein, the term "blighted condition" shall include, at a minimum, property that constitutes endangerment to public health or safety;

(6) The ordinance shall specify a decreased rate of ad valorem taxation to be applied for a specified period of time after the county or municipality has accepted a plan submitted by the owner for remedial action or redevelopment of the blighted property and the owner is in compliance with the terms of the plan. Such decrease in the rate of taxation shall be accomplished through application of a factor to the millage rate applied to the property, so that such property shall be taxed at a lower millage rate than the millage rate generally applied in the county or municipality, or otherwise as may be provided by general law.

(7) The ordinance may contain such other matters as are consistent with the intent and provisions of this subparagraph and general law. Variations in rate of taxation as authorized under this subparagraph shall be a permissible variation in the uniformity of taxation otherwise required. The increase or decrease in rate of taxation accomplished through a change in the otherwise applicable millage rate shall affect only the general millage rate for county or municipal maintenance and operations. A county and one or more municipalities in the county may, but shall not be required to, establish a joint community redevelopment tax incentive program through the adoption of concurrent ordinances. No Act of the General Assembly shall be required for counties and municipalities to establish community redevelopment tax incentive programs. However, the General Assembly may by general law regulate, restrict, or limit the powers granted to counties and municipalities under this subparagraph.

Paragraph VIII. Limitation on the taxing power and contributions of counties, municipalities, and political subdivisions. The General Assembly shall not authorize any county, municipality, or other political subdivision of this state, through taxation, contribution, or otherwise, to appropriate money for or to lend its credit to any person or to any nonpublic corporation or association except for purely charitable purposes.

Paragraph IX. Immunity of counties, municipalities, and school districts. The General Assembly may waive the immunity of counties, municipalities, and school districts by law.

Section III.
Intergovernmental Relations

Paragraph I. Intergovernmental contracts.

(a)   The state, or any institution, department, or other agency thereof, and any county, municipality, school district, or other political subdivision of the state may contract for any period not exceeding 50 years with each other or with any other public agency, public corporation, or public authority for joint services, for the provision of services, or for the joint or separate use of facilities or equipment; but such contracts must deal with activities, services, or facilities which the contracting parties are authorized by law to undertake or provide. *By way of specific instance and not limitation, a mutual undertaking by a local government entity to borrow and an undertaking by the state or a state authority to lend funds from and to one another for water or sewerage facilities or systems or for regional or multijurisdictional solid waste recycling or solid waste facilities or systems pursuant to law shall be a provision for services and an activity within the meaning of this Paragraph.*

(b)   *Subject to such limitations as may be provided by general law, any county, municipality, or political subdivision thereof may, in connection with any contracts authorized in this Paragraph, convey any existing facilities or equipment to the state or to any public agency, public corporation, or public authority.*

(c)   *Any county, municipality, or any combination thereof, may contract with any public agency, public corporation, or public authority for the care, maintenance, and hospitalization of its indigent sick and may as a part of such contract agree to pay for the cost of acquisition, construction, modernization, or repairs of necessary land, buildings, and facilities by such public agency, public corporation, or public authority and provide for the payment of such services and the cost to such public agency, public corporation, or public authority of acquisition, construction, modernization, or repair of land, buildings, and facilities from revenues realized by such county, municipality, or any combination thereof from any taxes authorized by this Constitution or revenues derived from any other source.* (Source: Authority OLC, p. 141)

Paragraph II. Local government reorganization.

(a)   The General Assembly may provide by law for any matters necessary or convenient to authorize the consolidation of the governmental and corporate powers and functions vested in municipalities with the governmental and corporate powers and functions vested in a county or counties in which such municipalities are located; provided, however, that no such consolidation shall become effective unless separately approved by a majority of the qualified voters of the county or each of the counties and of the municipality or each of the municipalities located within such county or counties containing at least 10 percent of the population of the county in which located voting thereon in such manner as may be prescribed in such law. Such law may provide procedures and requirements for the establishment of charter commissions to draft proposed charters for the consolidated government, and the General Assembly is expressly authorized to delegate its powers to such charter commissions for such purposes so that the governmental consolidation proposed by a charter commission may become effective without the necessity of further action by the General Assembly; or such law may require that the recommendation of any such charter commission be implemented by a subsequent local law.

(b) The General Assembly may provide by general law for alternatives other than governmental consolidation as authorized in subparagraph (a) above for the reorganization of county and municipal governments, including, but not limited to, procedures to establish a single governing body as the governing authority of a county and a municipality or municipalities located within such county or for the redistribution of powers between a county and a municipality or municipalities located within the county. Such law may require the form of governmental reorganization authorized by such law to be approved by the qualified voters directly affected thereby voting in such manner as may be required in such law.

(c) Nothing in this Paragraph shall be construed to limit the authority of the General Assembly to repeal municipal charters without a referendum.

Section IV.
Taxation Power of County and Municipal Governments

Paragraph I. Power of taxation.

a) Except as otherwise provided in this Paragraph, the governing authority of any county, municipality, or combination thereof may exercise the power of taxation as authorized by this Constitution or by general law.

(b) In the absence of a general law:

(1) County governing authorities may be authorized by local law to levy and collect business and occupational license taxes and license fees only in the unincorporated areas of the counties. The General Assembly may provide that the revenues raised by such tax or fee be spent for the provision of services only in the unincorporated areas of the county.

(2) Municipal governing authorities may be authorized by local law to levy and collect taxes and fees in the corporate limits of the municipalities.

(c) The General Assembly may provide by law for the taxation of insurance companies on the basis of gross direct premiums received from insurance policies within the unincorporated areas of counties. The tax authorized herein may be imposed by the state or by counties or by the state for county purposes as may be provided by law. The General Assembly may further provide by law for the reduction, only upon taxable property within the unincorporated areas of counties, of the ad valorem tax millage rate for county or county school district purposes or for the reduction of such ad valorem tax millage rate for both such purposes in connection with imposing or authorizing the imposition of the tax authorized herein or in connection with providing for the distribution of the proceeds derived from the tax authorized herein.

Paragraph II. Power of expenditure. The governing authority of any county, municipality, or combination thereof may expend public funds to perform any public service or public function as authorized by this Constitution or by law or to perform any other service or function *as authorized by this Constitution or by general law.*

Paragraph III. Purposes of taxation; allocation of taxes. No levy need state the particular purposes for which the same was made nor shall any taxes collected be allocated for any particular purpose, unless *otherwise provided by this Constitution or by law.*

Paragraph IV. Tax allocation; regional facilities. *As used in this Paragraph, the term "regional facilities" means industrial parks, business parks, conference centers, convention centers, airports, athletic facilities, recreation facilities, jails or correctional facilities, or other similar or related economic development parks, centers, or facilities or any combination thereof. Notwithstanding any other provision of this Constitution, a county or municipality is authorized to enter into contracts with:*

(1)   *any county which is contiguous to such county or the county in which such municipality is located;*

(2)   *any municipality located in such a contiguous county or the same county; or*

(3)   *any combination thereof. Any such contract may be for the purpose of allocating the proceeds of ad valorem taxes assessed and collected on real property located in such county or municipality with such other counties or municipalities with which the assessing county or municipality has entered into agreements for the development of one or more regional facilities and the allocation of other revenues generated from such regional facilities. Any such regional facility may be publicly or privately initiated. The allocation of such tax proceeds and other revenues shall be determined by contract between the affected local governments. Such contract shall provide for the manner of development, operation, and management of the regional facility and the sharing of expenses among the contracting local governments and shall specify the percentage of ad valorem taxes and other revenues to be allocated and the method of allocation to each contracting local government. Unless otherwise provided by law, such a regional facility will qualify for the greatest dollar amount of income tax credits which may be provided for by general law for any of the counties or municipalities which have entered into an agreement for the development of the regional facility, regardless of the county or municipality in which the business is physically located. The authority granted to counties and municipalities under this Paragraph shall be subject to any conditions, limitations, and restrictions which may be imposed by general law.* (Source: Sec. St. 1997)

Section V.
Limitation on Local Debt

Paragraph I. Debt limitations of counties, municipalities, and other political subdivisions.

(a)   The debt incurred by any county, municipality, or other political subdivision of this state, including debt incurred on behalf of any special district, shall never exceed 10 percent of the assessed value of all taxable property within such county, municipality, or political subdivision; and no such county, municipality, or other political subdivision shall incur any new debt without the assent of a majority of the qualified voters of such county, municipality, or political subdivision voting in an election held for that purpose as provided by law.

(b)   Notwithstanding subparagraph (a) of this Paragraph, all local school systems which are authorized by law on June 30, 1983, to incur debt in excess of 10 percent of the assessed value of all taxable property therein shall continue to be authorized to incur such debt.

Paragraph II. Special district debt. Any county, municipality, or political subdivision of this state may incur debt on behalf of any special district created pursuant to Paragraph VI of Section II of this article. Such debt may be incurred on behalf of such special district where the county, municipality, or other political subdivision shall have, at or before the time of incurring such debt, provided for the assessment and collection of an annual tax within the special district sufficient in amount to pay the principal of and interest on such debt within 30 years from the incurrence thereof; and no such county, municipality, or other political subdivision shall incur any debt on behalf of such special district without the assent of a majority of the qualified voters of such special district voting in an election held for that purpose as provided by law. No such county, municipality, or other political subdivision shall incur any debt on behalf of such special district in an amount which, when taken together with all other debt outstanding incurred by such county, municipality, or political subdivision and on behalf of any such special district, exceeds 10 percent of the assessed value of all taxable property within such county, municipality, or political subdivision. The proceeds of the tax collected as provided herein shall be placed in a sinking fund to be held on behalf of such special district and used exclusively to pay off the principal of and interest on such debt thereafter maturing. Such moneys shall be held and kept separate and apart from all other revenues collected and may be invested and reinvested as provided by law.

Paragraph III. [R]efunding of outstanding indebtedness. *The governing authority of any county, municipality, or other political subdivision of this state may provide for the refunding of outstanding bonded* indebtedness without the necessity of a referendum being held therefor, provided that neither the term of the original debt is extended nor the interest rate of the original debt is increased. The principal amount of any debt issued in connection with such refunding may exceed the principal amount being refunded in order to reduce the total principal and interest payment requirements over the remaining term of the original issue. The proceeds of the refunding issue shall be used solely to retire the original debt. The original debt refunded shall not constitute debt within the meaning of Paragraph I of this section; but the refunding issue shall constitute a debt such as will count against the limitation on debt measured by 10 percent of assessed value of taxable property as expressed in Paragraph I of this section.

Paragraph IV. Exceptions to debt limitations. Notwithstanding the debt limitations provided in Paragraph I of this section and without the necessity for a referendum being held therefor, the governing authority of any county, municipality, or other political subdivision of this state may, subject to the conditions and limitations as may be provided by general law:

(1) Accept and use funds granted by and obtain loans from the federal government or any agency thereof pursuant to conditions imposed by federal law.

(2) Incur debt, by way of borrowing from any person, corporation, or association as well as from the state, to pay in whole or in part the cost of property valuation and equalization programs for ad valorem tax purposes.

Paragraph V. Temporary loans authorized. The governing authority of any county, municipality, or other political subdivision of this state may incur debt by obtaining temporary loans in each year to pay expenses. The aggregate amount of all such loans shall not exceed 75 percent of the total gross income from taxes collected in the last preceding year. Such loans shall be payable on or before December 31 of the calendar year in which such loan is made. No such loan may be obtained when there is a loan then unpaid obtained in any prior year. No such county, municipality, or other political subdivision of this state shall incur in any one calendar year an aggregate of such temporary loans or other contracts, notes, warrants, or obligations for current expenses in excess of the total anticipated revenue for such calendar year.

Paragraph VI. **Levy of taxes to pay bonds; sinking fund required.** Any county, municipality, or other political subdivision of this state shall at or before the time of incurring bonded indebtedness provide for the assessment and collection of an annual tax sufficient in amount to pay the principal and interest of said debt within 30 years from the incurring of such bonded indebtedness. The proceeds of this tax, together with any other moneys collected for this purpose, shall be placed in a sinking fund to be used exclusively for paying the principal of and interest on such bonded debt. Such moneys shall be held and kept separate and apart from all other revenues collected and may be invested and reinvested as provided by law.

Paragraph VII. **Validity of prior bond issues.** Any and all bond issues validated and issued prior to June 30, 1983, shall continue to be valid.

Section VI.
Revenue Bonds

Paragraph I. **Revenue bonds; general limitations.** Any county, municipality, or other political subdivision of this state may issue revenue bonds as provided by general law. The obligation represented by revenue bonds shall be repayable only out of the revenue derived from the project and shall not be deemed to be a debt of the issuing political subdivision. No such issuing political subdivision shall exercise the power of taxation for the purpose of paying any part of the principal or interest of any such revenue bonds.

Paragraph II. **Revenue bonds; special limitations.** Where revenue bonds are issued by any county, municipality, or other political subdivision of this state in order to buy, construct, extend, operate, or maintain gas or electric generating or distribution systems and necessary appurtenances thereof and the gas or electric generating or distribution system extends beyond the limits of the county in which the municipality or other political subdivision is located, then its services rendered and property located outside said county shall be subject to taxation and regulation in the same manner as are privately owned and operated utilities.

Paragraph III. **Development authorities.** The development of trade, commerce, industry, and employment opportunities being a public purpose vital to the welfare of the people of this state, the General Assembly may create development authorities to promote and further such purposes or may authorize the creation of such an authority by any county or municipality or combination thereof under such uniform terms and conditions as it may deem necessary. The General Assembly may exempt from taxation development authority obligations, properties, activities, or income and may authorize the issuance of revenue bonds by such authorities which shall not constitute an indebtedness of the state within the meaning of Section V of this article.

Paragraph IV. **Validation.** The General Assembly shall provide for the validation of any revenue bonds authorized and shall provide that such validation shall thereafter be incontestable and conclusive.

Paragraph V. **Validity of prior revenue bond issues.** All revenue bonds issued and validated prior to June 30, 1983, shall continue to be valid.

Section VII.
Community Improvement Districts

Paragraph I. Creation. The General Assembly may by local law create one or more community improvement districts for any county or municipality or provide for the creation of one or more community improvement districts by any county or municipality.

Paragraph II. Purposes. The purpose of a community improvement district shall be the provision of any one or more of the following governmental services and facilities:

(1) Street and road construction and maintenance, including curbs, sidewalks, street lights, and devices to control the flow of traffic on streets and roads.

(2) Parks and recreational areas and facilities.

(3) Storm water and sewage collection and disposal systems.

(4) Development, storage, treatment, purification, and distribution of water.

(5) Public transportation.

(6) Terminal and dock facilities and parking facilities.

(7) Such other services and facilities as may be provided for by general law.

Paragraph III. Administration.

(a) Any law creating or providing for the creation of a community improvement district shall designate the governing authority of the municipality or county for which the community improvement district is created as the administrative body or otherwise shall provide for the establishment and membership of an administrative body for the community improvement district. Any such law creating or providing for the creation of an administrative body for the community improvement district other than the municipal or county governing authority shall provide for representation of the governing authority of each county and municipality within which the community improvement district is wholly or partially located on the administrative body of the community improvement district.

(b) Any law creating or providing for the creation of a community improvement district shall provide that the creation of the community improvement district shall be conditioned upon:

(1) The adoption of a resolution consenting to the creation of the community improvement district by:

(A) The governing authority of the county if the community improvement district is located wholly within the unincorporated area of a county;

(B) The governing authority of the municipality if the community improvement district is located wholly within the incorporated area of a municipality; or

(C) The governing authorities of the county and the municipality if the community improvement district is located partially within the unincorporated area of a county and partially within the incorporated area of a municipality; and

(2) Written consent to the creation of the community improvement district by:

(A) A majority of the owners of real property within the community improvement district which will be subject to taxes, fees, and assessments levied by the administrative body of the community improvement district; and

(B) The owners of real property within the community improvement district which constitutes at least 75 percent by value of all real property within the community improvement district which will be subject to taxes, fees, and assessments levied by the administrative body of the community improvement district; and for this purpose value shall be determined by the most recent approved county ad valorem tax digest.

(c)   The administrative body of each community improvement district may be authorized
to levy taxes, fees, and assessments within the community improvement district only
on real property used nonresidentially, specifically excluding all property used for residential, agricultural, or forestry purposes and specifically excluding tangible personal property and intangible property. Any tax, fee, or assessment so levied shall not
exceed 2 1/2 percent of the assessed value of the real property or such lower limit as
may be established by law. The law creating or providing for the creation of a community improvement district shall provide that taxes, fees, and assessments levied by
the administrative body of the community improvement district shall be equitably
apportioned among the properties subject to such taxes, fees, and assessments according to the need for governmental services and facilities created by the degree of density of development of each such property. The law creating or providing for the
creation of a community improvement district shall provide that the proceeds of
taxes, fees, and assessments levied by the administrative body of the community
improvement district shall be used only for the purpose of providing governmental
services and facilities which are specially required by the degree of density of development within the community improvement district and not for the purpose of providing those governmental services and facilities provided to the county or
municipality as a whole. Any tax, fee, or assessment so levied shall be collected by
the county or municipality for which the community improvement district is created
in the same manner as taxes, fees, and assessments levied by such county or municipality. The proceeds of taxes, fees, and assessments so levied, less such fee to cover
the costs of collection as may be specified by law, shall be transmitted by the collecting county or municipality to the administrative body of the community improvement district and shall be expended by the administrative body of the community
improvement district only for the purposes authorized by this Section.

Paragraph IV. Debt. The administrative body of a community improvement district may
incur debt, as authorized by law, without regard to the requirements of Section V of this Article,
which debt shall be backed by the full faith, credit, and taxing power of the community improvement district but shall not be an obligation of the State of Georgia or any other unit of government of the State of Georgia other than the community improvement district.

Paragraph V. Cooperation with local governments. The services and facilities provided
pursuant to this Section shall be provided for in a cooperation agreement executed jointly by the
administrative body and the governing authority of the county or municipality for which the
community improvement district is created. The provisions of this section shall in no way limit
the authority of any county or municipality to provide services or facilities within any community improvement district; and any county or municipality shall retain full and complete authority and control over any of its facilities located within a community improvement district. Said
control shall include but not be limited to the modification of, access to, and degree and type of
services provided through or by facilities of the municipality or county. Nothing contained in
this Section shall be construed to limit or preempt the application of any governmental laws,
ordinances, resolutions, or regulations to any community improvement district or the services or
facilities provided therein.

Paragraph VI. Regulation by general law. The General Assembly by general law may
regulate, restrict, and limit the creation of community improvement districts and the exercise of
the powers of administrative bodies of community improvement districts (Source: Authority
OLC, pp. 147–150).

Article X.
Amendments to the Constitution

Section I.
Constitution, How Amended

Paragraph I. Proposals to amend the Constitution; new Constitution. Amendments to this Constitution or a new Constitution may be proposed by the General Assembly or by a constitutional convention, as provided in this article. Only amendments which are of general and uniform applicability throughout the state shall be proposed, passed, or submitted to the people.

Paragraph II. Proposals by the General Assembly; submission to the people. A proposal by the General Assembly to amend this Constitution or to provide for a new Constitution shall originate as a resolution in either the Senate or the House of Representatives and, if approved by two-thirds of the members to which each house is entitled in a roll-call vote entered on their respective journals, shall be submitted to the electors of the entire state at the next general election which is held in the even-numbered years. A summary of such proposal shall be prepared by the Attorney General, the Legislative Counsel, and the Secretary of State and shall be published in the official organ of each county and, if deemed advisable by the "Constitutional Amendments Publication Board," in not more than 20 other newspapers in the state designated by such board which meet the qualifications for being selected as the official organ of a county. Said board shall be composed of the Governor, the Lieutenant Governor, and the Speaker of the House of Representatives. Such summary shall be published once each week for three consecutive weeks immediately preceding the day of the general election at which such proposal is to be submitted. The language to be used in submitting a proposed amendment or a new Constitution shall be in such words as the General Assembly may provide in the resolution or, in the absence thereof, in such language as the Governor may prescribe. A copy of the entire proposed amendment or of a new Constitution shall be filed in the office of the judge of the probate court of each county and shall be available for public inspection; and the summary of the proposal shall so indicate. The General Assembly is hereby authorized to provide by law for additional matters relative to the publication and distribution of proposed amendments and summaries not in conflict with the provisions of this Paragraph. If such proposal is ratified by a majority of the electors qualified to vote for members of the General Assembly voting thereon in such general election, such proposal shall become a part of this Constitution or shall become a new Constitution, as the case may be. Any proposal so approved shall take effect as provided in Paragraph VI of this article. When more than one amendment is submitted at the same time, they shall be so submitted as to enable the electors to vote on each amendment separately, provided that one or more new articles or related changes in one or more articles may be submitted as a single amendment.

Paragraph III. Repeal or amendment of proposal. Any proposal by the General Assembly to amend this Constitution or for a new Constitution may be amended or repealed by the same General Assembly which adopted such proposal by the affirmative vote of two-thirds of the members to which each house is entitled in a roll-call vote entered on their respective journals, if such action is taken at least two months prior to the date of the election at which such proposal is to be submitted to the people.

Paragraph IV. Constitutional convention; how called. No convention of the people shall be called by the General Assembly to amend this Constitution or to propose a new Constitution, unless by the concurrence of two-thirds of the members to which each house of the General Assembly is entitled. The representation in said convention shall be based on population as near as practicable. A proposal by the convention to amend this Constitution or for a new Constitution shall be advertised, submitted to, and ratified by the people in the same manner provided for advertisement, submission, and ratification of proposals to amend the Constitution by the General Assembly. The General Assembly is hereby authorized to provide the procedure by which a convention is to be called and under which such convention shall operate and for other matters relative to such constitutional convention.

Paragraph V. Veto not permitted. The Governor shall not have the right to veto any proposal by the General Assembly or by a convention to amend this Constitution or to provide a new Constitution.

Paragraph VI. Effective date of amendments or of a new Constitution. Unless the amendment or the new Constitution itself or the resolution proposing the amendment or the new Constitution shall provide otherwise, an amendment to this Constitution or a new Constitution shall become effective on the first day of January following its ratification.

Article XI.
Miscellaneous Provisions

Section I.
Miscellaneous Provisions

Paragraph I. Continuation of officers, boards, commissions, and authorities.

(a) Except as otherwise provided in this Constitution, the officers of the state and all political subdivisions thereof in office on June 30, 1983, shall continue in the exercise of their functions and duties, subject to the provisions of laws applicable thereto and subject to the provisions of this Constitution.

(b) All boards, commissions, and authorities specifically named in the Constitution of 1976 which are not specifically named in this Constitution shall remain as statutory boards, commissions, and authorities; and all constitutional and statutory provisions relating thereto in force and effect on June 30, 1983, shall remain in force and effect as statutory law unless and until changed by the General Assembly.

Paragraph II. Preservation of existing laws; judicial review. All laws in force and effect on June 30, 1983, not inconsistent with this Constitution shall remain in force and effect; but such laws may be amended or repealed and shall be subject to judicial decision as to their validity when passed and to any limitations imposed by their own terms.

Paragraph III. Proceedings of courts and administrative tribunals confirmed. All judgments, decrees, orders, and other proceedings of the several courts and administrative tribunals of this state, heretofore made within the limits of their several jurisdictions, are hereby ratified and affirmed, subject only to reversal or modification in the manner provided by law.

Paragraph IV. Continuation of certain constitutional amendments for a period of four years.

(a) The following amendments to the Constitutions of 1877, 1945, and 1976 shall continue in force and effect as part of this Constitution until July 1, 1987, at which time said amendments shall be repealed and shall be deleted as a part of this Constitution unless any such amendment shall be specifically continued in force and effect without amendment either by a local law enacted prior to July 1, 1987, with or without a referendum as provided by law, or by an ordinance or resolution duly adopted prior to July 1, 1987, by the local governing authority in the manner provided for the adoption of home rule amendments to its charter or local act:

    (1) amendments to the Constitution of 1877 and the Constitution of 1945 which were continued in force and effect as a part of the Constitution of 1976 pursuant to the provisions of Article XIII, Section I, Paragraph II of the Constitution of 1976 which are in force and effect on the effective date of this Constitution;

    (2) amendments to the Constitution of 1976 which were ratified as general amendments but which by their terms applied principally to a particular political subdivision or subdivisions which are in force and effect on the effective date of this Constitution;

    (3) amendments to the Constitution of 1976 which were ratified not as general amendments which are in force and effect on the effective date of this Constitution; and

(4) amendments to the Constitution of 1976 of the type provided for in the immediately preceding two subparagraphs (2) and (3) of this Paragraph which were ratified at the same time this Constitution was ratified.

(b) Any amendment which is continued in force and effect after July 1, 1987, pursuant to the provisions of subparagraph (a) of this Paragraph shall be continued in force and effect as a part of this Constitution, except that such amendment may thereafter be repealed but may not be amended. The repeal of any such amendment shall be accomplished by local Act of the General Assembly, the effectiveness of which shall be conditioned on its approval by a majority of the qualified voters voting thereon in each of the particular political subdivisions affected by the amendment.

(c) All laws enacted pursuant to those amendments to the Constitution which are not continued in force and effect pursuant to subparagraph (a) of this Paragraph shall be repealed on July 1, 1987. All laws validly enacted on, before, or after July 1, 1987, and pursuant to the specific authorization of an amendment continued in force and effect pursuant to the provisions of subparagraph (a) of this Paragraph shall be legal, valid, and constitutional under this Constitution. Nothing in this subparagraph (c) shall be construed to revive any law not in force and effect on June 30, 1987.

(d) Notwithstanding the provisions of subparagraphs (a) and (b), the following amendments to the Constitutions of 1877 and 1945 shall be continued in force as a part of this Constitution: amendments to the Constitution of 1877 and the Constitution of 1945 which created or authorized the creation of metropolitan rapid transit authorities, port authorities, and industrial areas and which were continued in force as a part of the Constitution of 1976 pursuant to the provisions of Article XIII, Section I, Paragraph II of the Constitution of 1976 and which are in force on the effective date of this Constitution.

(e) *Any person owning property in an industrial area described in subparagraph (d) may voluntarily remove the property from the industrial area by filing a certificate to that effect with the clerk of the superior court for the county in which the property is located, but only if the property is located on an island. Once the certificate is filed, the property described in the certificate, together with all public streets and public rights of way within the property, abutting the property, or connecting the property to property outside the industrial area will no longer be in the industrial area and may be annexed by an adjacent city. The filing of a certificate will be irrevocable and will bind the owners, their heirs, and their assigns. The term "owner" includes anyone with a legal or equitable ownership in property but does not include a beneficiary of any trust or a partner in any partnership owning an interest in the property or anyone owning an easement right in the property. NOTE: THIS PARAGRAPH WILL BE REWRITTEN TO REFLECT THE PASSAGE OF AN AMENDMENT IN 2010 TO ALLOW GENERAL REMOVAL OF THE PROPERTY.*

Paragraph V. Special commission created. Amendments to the Constitution of 1976 which were determined to be general and which were submitted to and ratified by the people of the entire state at the same time this Constitution was ratified shall be incorporated and made a part of this Constitution as provided in this Paragraph. There is hereby created a commission to be composed of the Governor, the President of the Senate, the Speaker of the House of Representatives, the Attorney General, and the Legislative Counsel, which is hereby authorized and directed to incorporate such amendments into this Constitution at the places deemed most appropriate to the commission. The commission shall make only such changes in the language of this Constitution and of such amendments as are necessary to incorporate properly such amendments into this Constitution and shall complete its duties prior to July 1, 1983. The commission shall deliver to the Secretary of State this Constitution with those amendments incorporated therein, and such document shall be the Constitution of the State of Georgia. In order that the commission may perform its duties, this Paragraph shall become effective as soon as it has been officially determined that this Constitution has been ratified. The commission shall stand abolished upon the completion of its duties.

   Paragraph VI. Effective date. Except as provided in Paragraph V of this section, this Constitution shall become effective on July 1, 1983; and, except as otherwise provided in this Constitution, all previous Constitutions and all amendments thereto shall thereupon stand repealed.

Bibliography

Books and Publications

ACCG, *1995 Survey of County Governments.*

Ammons, David N. and Campbell, Richard W. (1993). "County Government Structures" in Weeks, J. Devereaux and Hardy, Paul T., eds. *Handbook for Georgia County Commissioners.* Athens: Carl Vinson Institute of Government, University of Georgia.

Argyle, Nolan J. (1991). *New Federalism and Public Mass Transit: The Case of SCAT.* Discussion Paper 91-6. Atlanta GA: Institute of Public Administration, Georgia State University.

Allen, Lee M. (1989). "Civil Service Reform Act of 1978" in Vol. 11 *Encyclopedia USA.* Gulf Breeze, FL: Academic International Press.

Banks, Carolyn L. *"Councilmembers marched to the Capitol in protest of unfunded mandates"* in *Council Contact* (In-house publication of the Atlanta City Council), Winter, 1994.

Barber, James D. (1965). *The Lawmakers.* New Haven: Yale University Press.

Barber, James David. (1972) *The Presidential Character: Predicting Performance in the White House.* Englewood Cliffs, NJ: Prentice Hall.

Barber, James David. (1973) *The Lawmakers: Recruitment and Adaptation to Legislative Life.* Clinton, MA: The Colonial Press, Inc.

Black, Earl and Merle. (2002) *The Rise of Southern Republicans.* Cambridge, Mass: Harvard University Press.

Bullock, Charles S. III. (1991). *The Georgia Political Almanac: The General Assembly.* Decatur, GA: Cornerstone Publications.

———. (1993). *The Partisan, Racial and Gender Makeup of Georgia County Offices,* Public Policy Research Series, (Carl Vinson Institute of Government: The University of Georgia).

Burke, Edmund. (1967) "Address to the Electorate at Bristol" in *The Works of Edmund Burke.* New York: Harper.

Busbee, George D. (1981). *Proposed Constitution of the State of Georgia.* Atlanta, GA: Select Committee on Constitutional Revision, Georgia General Assembly.

Christianberry, George A. Jr. (1991). "The Facts: The Department of Administration" in *Georgia State Telephone Directory*. Atlanta, GA: Office of the Secretary of State, January.

Cooper, Philip J. (1988). *Public Law and Public Administration*. Englewood Cliffs, NJ: Prentice Hall.

Crutchfield, James A. (1990). *The Georgia Almanac and Book of Facts 1989–1990*. Nashville, TN: Rutledge Hill Press.

Current, Richard N.; Williams, T.H.; Fredal, Frank and Brinkley, Alan. (1983). *A Survey of American History*. 6th ed. New York: Alfred A. Knopf.

Dahl, Robert. (1967). *Pluralist Democracy in the United States*. Chicago, IL: Rand McNally.

Dye, Thomas R. (1997). *Politics in States and Communities*. 9th ed. Englewood Cliffs, NJ: Prentice-Hall.

Elza, Jane L. (1991). "Teaching Research Skills in Administrative Law" in the *Preceedings of the 14th National Teaching Public Administration Conference*. Knoxville, TN: American Society of Public Administration.

Elazar, Daniel J. (1984). *American Federalism: A View from the States*. 5th ed. New York: Thomas Y. Crowell Company.

——— and Grodzin, Morton. (1966). *The American System*. Chicago, IL: Rand-McNally Press.

Eldersveld, Samuel J. (1964). *Political Parties: A Behavioral Analysis*. Chicago, IL: Rand-McNally.

Fleischmann, Arnold and Pierannunzi, Carol. (1997). *Politics in Georgia*. Athens: UGA Press.

Gifis, Steven H. (2003). Dictionary, 5th Edition, New York, Hauppauge: Barrons Educational Series Inc.

Gray, Virginia and Jacob, Herbert. (1996). *Politics in the American States: A Comparative Analysis*. 6th ed. Washington, D.C.: CQ Press.

Gray, Virginia and Eisinger, Peter. (1997). *American States and Cities*. New York: Longman.

Grodzin, Morton and Elazar, Daniel J. (1966). *The American System*. Chicago, IL: Rand-McNally Press.

Friedman, Barry. (1991). *Regulations in the Reagan Era: New Procedures, New Results*. Unpublished Ph.D. Dissertation at the University of Connecticut.

Hanson, Larry H. (2003). *City of Valdosta Georgia Annual Budget. FY 2003*. Valdosta, GA: Office of the City Manager.

Hardy (see Weeks and Hardy, Handbook for Georgia Mayors and Council members, 1993).

———. (1982). *The Georgia History Book*. Athens, GA: Carl Vinson Institute of Government, University of Georgia.

Henry, Nicholas. (1987). "Report on Evaluation of the 50 State Legislatures" in *Governing at the Grass Roots.* 3rd ed. Englewood Cliffs, NJ: Prentice-Hall.

Hepburn, Lawrence R. (1987). "Politics and Government" in *Contemporary Georgia.* Athens, GA: Carl Vinson Institute of Government, University of Georgia.

Holder v. Hall (No. 91202, 1994).

Hy, Ronn and Saeger, Richard T. (1976). "The Nature and Role of Political Parties" in *Mississippi Government and Politics in Transition,* edited by David M. Landry and Joseph B. Parker. Dubuque, IA: Kendall/ Hunt Publishing Company.

Jackson, Edwin L. and Stakes, Mary E. (1988). *Handbook of Georgia State Agencies.* Athens, GA: Carl Vinson Institute of Government, University of Georgia.

Joiner, Oscar H. (1979) gen. ed., *A History of Public Education in Georgia, 1734–1976.* Columbia, S.C.: R. B. Bryan Co.

Katz, Robert N. "The History of the Georgia Bill of Rights," *Georgia State University Law Review* 3 (fall–winter 1986).

LWV. (1991). League of Women Voters of Georgia, Inc. *The Georgia Government.* Atlanta, GA: The League of Women Voters of Georgia, Inc.

Lasswell, Harold. (1936). *Who Gets What, When and How?* New York: McGraw-Hill.

Lehan, Edward A. (1984). *Budgetmaking: A Workbook of Public Budgeting Theory and Practice.* New York: St. Martin's Press.

Lauth, Thomas P. and Reese, Catherine C. (1993). *"The Line-Item Veto in Georgia: Incidence and Fiscal Effects. "* A scholarly paper presented at the Annual Meeting of the Georgia Political Science Association, Savannah, GA, February 25–27, 1993.

Lewis, Eugene. (1977) *American Politics in a Bureaucratic Age: Citizens, Constituents, Clients and Victims.* Cambridge, Mass.: Winthrop Publishing Inc.

Locke, John. Two Treatises of Government, any edition.

Love, Margaret Colgate. *Relief from the Collateral Consequences of a Criminal Conviction,* March 7, 2007.

Machiavelli, Niccolo. (1952). *The Prince.* Translated by Luigi Ricci, Introduction by Christian Gauss. New York: Mentor Books.

Madison, James; Hamilton, Alexander and Jay, John. (1961). *The Federalist Papers.* (New York: New American Library).

Maitland, F. W. (1962). *The Forms of Action at Common Law.* Cambridge University Press.

Nachmias, David and Rosenbloom, David H. (1980). *Bureaucratic Government USA.* New York: St. Martin's Press.

Nice, David C. (1987). *Federalism—The Politics of Intergovernmental Relations.* NY: St. Martin's Press.

OLC. (1991). Office of the Legislative Council, *Official Code of Georgia, Annotated.* Charlottesville, Va.: The Michie Company.
————. (1991). *The Pocket Part.* The Michie Company.
Parenti, Michael. (1988). *Democracy for the Few,* 5th ed. Boston: St. Martin's Press.
Pound, Merritt B. and Saye, Albert B. (1971). *Handbook on the Constitutions of the United States and Georgia.* 9th ed. Athens, Ga.: Department of Political Science, University of Georgia.
Rousseau, Jean J. Du Contrat Social, St. Martin's Press, 1978.
Saeger, Richard T. and Hy, Ronn. (1976). "The Nature and Role of Political Parties" in *Mississippi Government and Politics in Transition,* edited by D.M. Landry and J.B. Parker. Dubuque, IA: Kendall/Hunt Publishing Company.
Smith, Edward C. (1979). *Constitution of the United States, with Case Summaries.* New York: Harper and Row, Publishers.
Thomas, William R. and Prather, James E. (1993). *"Race, Politics and redistricting in Georgia: Analysis of the 1992 Congressional Election"* a scholarly paper presented at the Annual Meeting of the Georgia Political Science Association, Savannah, Georgia, February 25–27, 1993.
Tocqueville, Alexis de. *Democracy in America.* New York: Knopf.
Tucker, Stephen G. N. (2001). *Beyond Atlanta: The Struggle for Racial Equality in Georgia, 1940–1980.* Athens: University of Georgia Press.
Weber, Max. (1958). *From Max Weber: Essays in Political Sociology,* edited by H.H. Gerth, and C. Wright Mills. New York: Oxford University Press.
————. (1961). *Basic Concepts in Sociology.* New York: Citadel, 1913, or see Amitai etzioni, ed. *Complex Organizations.* New York: Holt, 1961 at pp. 4–14.
Weeks, J. Devereaux and Hardy, Paul T., eds. (1993). *Handbook for Georgia Mayors and Council members.* Athens: Carl Vinson Institute of Government, UGA.
Wilson, James Q. (1992). *American Government: Institutions and Policies.* Lexington, Mass.: D.C. Heath & Company.
Wilson, James Q., Editor. (1980). *The Politics of Regulation.* New York: Basic Books, Inc.
Winder, David W. *"Governor Miller Drops Proposal to Change the Georgia State Flag for 1993"* in *Comparative State Politics* Vol. 14, (June 1993).
————. (1991). *"The Powers of the Attorneys General: A Quantitative Assessment"* in Vol. 19, *Southeastern Political Review.*
Wolfe, W.H. (1991). *Decatur County, Georgia: Past and Present.* Roswell, GA: Historical Publications.

Journals and Newspapers

AJC, 2/13/11. *http://www.ajc.com/news/content/metro/stories/2009/02/02/perdue_st*

AJC, 2/13/11. *http://www.ajc.com/news/nation-world/georgia-says-stimulus-funds*

AJ/AC. (02–21–1992). Editorial. "Miller's Roads to Glory" in the *Atlanta Journal/Atlanta Constitution*. (February 21, 1992) at A12.

———. Jan. 13, (1994). "*A Greener Year for State Spending*" in the *Atlanta Journal/Atlanta Constitution*, at p. E4.

Associated Press. (03–29–1992). "300-pound Woman Sues in Bus Arrest" in the *Florida Times-Union, Georgia Section*. (Atlanta, GA: AP, March 29, 1992) at B8.

———. (04–29–1992). "Busted Bingo Players Pledge to Change Law" in the *Florida Times-Union, Georgia Section*. (Lavonia, Georgia: AP, April 29, 1992) at A1.

———. (01–01–1992) "Who Should Draw State's Districts?" *Valdosta Daily Times*. (Valdosta, GA: January 1, 1992) at 5-A.

———. (02–23–1992). Paulding Ponders County Manager. *Florida Times-Union, Georgia Section*. (Dallas, Georgia: AP, February 23, 1992) at B4.

Associated Press. (1993). "*Bowers: Murphy threatened child protection funding*" in the *Tifton Gazette*, October 5, 1993.

Associated Press. (1993). "*Atlanta's archbishop urges support for voucher law*" in the *Florida Times-Union*, October 10–19–93.

Associated Press. (1993). "*State would need big-time bucks to take over Georgia education costs*" in the *Tifton Gazette*, 11–15–93.

Associated Press. (1994). "*Gov. gives lawmakers new agenda as he prepares for re-election bid*" in the *Tifton Gazette*, January 1, 1994.

Associated Press. (1994). "*Weeping Murphy growls over guide dog coverage*" in the *Tifton Gazette*, February 23, 1994.

Associated Press. (1994). "*How will Georgia House be ruled after Speaker Murphy*" in the *Tifton Gazette*, March 28, 1994.

The Atlanta Journal Constitution (AJC Jan 12 2011-02-17) "Deal warns of cuts, promises progress in first State of the State" Jan. 12, 2011.

Beasley, Dorothy T. "The Georgia Bill of Rights: Dead or Alive?" *Emory Law Journal* 34, Spring, 1985.

Beer, Samuel H. (1978). "Federalism, Nationalism and Democracy in America" in *American Political Science Review*. (March, 1978).

Bergstrom. Retrieved September 29, 2010 from: *ttp://lake.typepad.com/on-the-lake-front/2010/09/brad-bergstrom-unsubstantiated-assertions-are-not-facts.html*.

Blackmon, Douglas A. (1993). *"Council avoids risk, supports stadium"* in the *Atlanta Journal/Atlanta Constitution,* March 2, 1993.

Bratcher, Stewart D. (2005). *Georgia Bill of Rights,* The New Georgia Encyclopedia, *Georgia Humanities Council, http://www. georgiaencyclopedia.org/nge/Article.jsp?id=h-3015* (accessed January 31, 2011).

Census. 2011 Statistical Abstract of the United States, *http://www.census.goc/compendia/statab*

Cook, Rhonda. (04–02–1992). "Feds Play 'Partisan Politics' with Redistricting, Miller says" in the *Atlanta Journal/Atlanta Constitution* (April 2, 1992) at D3.

———. (10–14–1991). "Backlog of State Inmates Is Growing" in the *Atlanta Journal/Atlanta Constitution* (October 14, 1991), at D1.

Cook, Rhonda and Hendricks, Gary. (01–22–1992). "Black vote was 'minimalized,' so redistricting starts again today." *The Atlanta Journal/The Atlanta Constitution* (Wednesday, January 22, 1992) at A1, A8.

Debt Clock, Georgia. 02/17/11, 9:57pm EST. *http://www.usdebtclock.org*

Deeptha Thattai A. History of Public Education in the United States. Retrieved from: *www.servintfree.net/~aidmn-ejournal/publications/2001-11/PublicEducationInTheUnited*

Delk, Glenn. (1993). *"School choice law is common sense"* in the *Atlanta Journal/Atlanta Constitution,* September 26, 1993.

Digby, Michael F. 2004. Capitol Budgeting and State Debt. New Georgia Encyclopedia. A project of the Georgia Humanities Council, in partnership with the University of Georgia Press, the University System of Georgia/GALILEO, and the Office of the Governor. Retrieved from: *http://dlg.galileo.usg.edu.*

Fayette FrontPage *http://gaeducation.blogspot.com/2008/08/2008-sat-results-released-georgia-ranks.html.*

Flags that have Flown Over Georgia. *http://www.sos.ga.gov/museum/html/georgia_flag_history.html*

Froman, Lewis L. (1985). "Some Effects of Interest Group Strength in State Politics" in *American Journal of Political Science* Vol. 29, (February).

Galloway, Jim. 07-06-2010. *http://blogs.AJC.com/political-insider-jim-galloway/2010/07/06/kathy-cox*

The Georgia Department of Education, "Georgia Wins Race to the Top." Retrieved August 24, 2010 from: *http://www.doe.k12.ga.us/pea_communications.aspx?ViewMode=1&obj=1969).*

Georgia State Office of Planning and Budget. 2009. Budget in Brief, Amended FY 2008 and FY 2009, p. 14.

Georgia Peace Officer Standards and Training Council v. Mullis, 281 S.E.2d 569 (Ga. 1981). *Official Code of Georgia Annotated.*

Gibson, James L. (1985). "Whither the Local Parties?" *American Journal of Political Science* Vol. 29 (February).

Gold, Steven D. (1990). "Demystifying Those Scary Statistics" in *State Legislatures* (May/June).

Grillo, Jerry (2009), "How Low Can They Go?" Retrieved December 2009 from: *http://www.georgiatrend.com/cover-story/12_09_education.shtml*.

Haines, Errin. Originally reported in the Athens Banner-Herald. Retrieved January 25, 2011 from: *http://onlineathens.com/stories/012511/new_ 775802352.shtml*

Harvey, Steve. (04–01–1992). "$8.2 Billion Budget OK'ed on Eve of Adjournment" in *The Atlanta Journal/The Atlanta Constitution*, April 1, 1992), at A1 and A8.

Hinton, Kendra. (2011). Placement of Amendments within Constitution.

Kirchner, Joan. (AP 2–12–1998). "Few Select Groups in the Running for Georgia Sales Tax Exemptions" in the Valdosta Daily Times. Valdosta, GA: February 12, 1998, at 3-A.

LoMonte, Frank. (04–02–1992). "Miller Proclaims Session a Success" in the Georgia Section of the *Florida Times-Union* (April 2, 1992) Georgia Section.

———. (04–02–1992). "Zell Miller to Sign New Ethics Bill Monday" in the Georgia Section of the *Florida Times-Union*, (April 2, 1992) Georgia Section.

Maitland F. W. (1962). The Forms of Action at Common Law. Cambridge University Press. *Perdue v. Baker*. 2003. SO3A1154 Supreme Court of Georgia.

Mewborn, Denise S. (2009). Public Education (PreK–12, New Georgia Encyclopedia, Georgia Humanities Council. Retrieved from: *http://www.georgiaencyclopedia.org/nge/Article.jsp?id=h-2619*

Miller, Zell. Feb. 24, (1994). "*House Embraces Tax Cut*" in the *Atlanta Journal/ Atlanta Constitution*, at p. A1.

Morris v. Hartsfield, 197 S.E. 251 (Ga. 1938).

The Office of the Attorney General of the State of Georgia, *http://www.georgia.gov/02/ago/home/0,2705,87670814,00.html* (accessed February 1, 2011).

Office of Communications, Office of the Governor of the State of Georgia, "Governor Perdue Signs $17.9 Billion Fiscal Year 2011 Budget." Retrieved June 8, 2010 from: *http://www.georgia.gov/ 00/press/detail/0,2668,78006749_160096907_160266268,00.html*

Orr, Dorothy. (1950). A *History of Education in Georgia*, Chapel Hill: University of North Carolina Press.

Orwell, George. *1984*. Any edition.

Osinski, Bill. (1994). "*Law has towns fighting Oblivion*" in *The Atlanta Journal/ Atlanta Constitution*, 03–28–94, p. B6.

Parker, Jennifer F. (1993). *"Business owners worry about bus disruption"* in *Atlanta Journal/Atlanta Constitution*, August 29, 1993.

Paulk, Harold. 2002. Melvin Thompson (1903–1980). New Georgia Encyclopedia. A project of the Georgia Humanities Council, in partnership with the University of Georgia Press, the University System of Georgia/GALILEO, and the Office of the Governor. Retrieved from: *http://dlg.galileo.usg.edu.*

Perdue, Sonny. Press Release, Governor Perdue, Chief Justice Sears Resolve DA Funding Crisis. Retrieved June 7, 2007 from: *http://www.georgia.gov/ 00press/detail/0,2668,78006749*

Pettys, Dick. (06-26-1990). *"Lobbying a Thriving Business in Georgia, Even IF IT Is Illegal"* in the *Brunswick News* (June 26, 1990).

Rankin, Bill. (1993). *"Top judges say they need a pay increase"* in the *Atlanta Journal/Atlanta Constitution*, December 07, 1993.

Salter, Sallye. (1993). *"Nearby merchants excited about project"* in *Atlanta Journal/Atlanta Constitution*, August 29, 1993.

Salzer, James. (1994). *"State Flag Supporters Fire Angry Volley"* in *Savannah Morning News*, 2–25–94, Morris News Service.

Seabrook, Charles. *"State Lawmakers debate impact of reprimand"* in *Atlanta Journal/Atlanta Constitution*, Jan. 14, 1993.

Sherman, Mark. (01-22-1992). *"Primary change boosts Ga.'s profile"* in *The Atlanta Journal/The Atlanta Constitution* (Wednesday, January 22, 1992) page A1.

Staff Report. (04-01-1992). *"Status of Major Bills in Legislature"* in *The Atlanta Journal/The Atlanta Constitution* (Wednesday, April 1, 1992) at A1 and A8.

The World Almanac and Book of Facts 2002. Mahwah, NJ: World Almanac Books.

Vickers, Robert J. (1994). *"Friends and contributors all"* in the *Atlanta Journal/ Atlanta Constitution*, January 2, 1994.

WALB News. 03-06-11. *http://www.walb.com/Global/story.asp?S=14075512*

Walston, Charles and Cook, Rhonda. (01–22–1992). *"Blame the Legislature, not Justice, Brooks says"* in *The Atlanta Journal/The Atlanta Constitution* (January 22, 1992) at A-8.

Watson, Tom. (1993). *"Gay fight unfolds in Georgia"* in *USA Today*, August 23, 1993.

Whitt, Richard. (1994). *"Study commissions: Where bills go to die"* in the *Atlanta Journal/Atlanta Constitution*, January 10, 1994.

Wooten, Jim. (1993). *"I give up in the war on lottery"* in the *Atlanta Journal/Atlanta Constitution*, September 26, 1993.

World Almanac and Book of Facts. 2010. Sarah Johnson (Ed.) Infobase Publishing.

Yarbrough, Dick, *"Bad Weather Doesn't Alter Political Landscape,"* January 22, 2011. *Valdosta Daily Times*, p. 6A.

Yarbrough, Dick. "Ralston Could Have Gone to Power Springs," *The Valdosta Daily Times*, p. 6A, February 19, 2011.

Zanardi, David. (1994). *"Experts say mega-school is unwise"* in the *Tifton Gazette*, (September 17, 1993).

http://www.publiceye.org/magazine/v19n3/carter_wallace.html. The voter ID bill has both pros and cons. On the one hand preventing voter fraud is a worthy goal; on the other hand every single step necessary to comply with such requirements can discourage disadvantaged citizens. For more on this issue see: *http://www.nationalreview.com/corner/ 261537/georgia-voter-id-law*.

Index